WITNESS TO HISTORY

WITNESS TO HISTORY

The Life of
John Wheeler-Bennett

Victoria Schofield

YALE UNIVERSITY PRESS
NEW HAVEN AND LONDON

For information about this and other Yale University Press publications, please contact:

U.S. office: sales.press@yale.edu   www.yalebooks.com
Europe Office: sales@yaleup.co.uk   www.yalebooks.co.uk

Set in China by Toppan Best-set Premedia Limited

Printed in Great Britain by TJ International Ltd, Padstow, Cornwall

Library of Congress Cataloging-in-publication Data

Schofield, Victoria.
  Witness to history : the life of John Wheeler-Bennett / Victoria Schofield.
    p. cm.
  Includes bibliographical references and index.
  ISBN 978-0-300-17901-9 (cl : alk. paper)
1. Wheeler-Bennett, John Wheeler, Sir, 1902-1975.   2. Historians–Great Britain–Biography.   I. Title.
  D15.W45S36   2012
  941.082072'02–dc23
  [B]

                                                          2012006661

A catalogue record for this book is available from the British Library.

10 9 8 7 6 5 4 3 2 1

Contents

List of Illustrations and Maps vii

Acknowledgements ix

1 The Undertow of History 1
2 Youthful Illusions 14
3 International Traveller 23
4 The Tragedy of Weimar 60
5 Twilight 89
6 The Perils of War 117
7 Political Warfare in America 143
8 The Horrors of Peace 170
9 High Honour 197
10 The Sixties 217
11 Memories 252

Notes 285
Select Bibliography 326
Index 330

Illustrations and Maps

Illustrations

1 John Wheeler-Bennett, 1950s (by kind permission of Mr and Mrs David Heaton).

2 John and Clement with their father John Wheeler-Bennett (by kind permission of the Estate of the Very Reverend Hon. Oliver Twisleton-Wykeham-Fiennes).

3 Christina Wheeler-Bennett (by kind permission of Mr and Mrs David Heaton).

4 Ravensbourne, Keston, Kent (by kind permission of the Estate of the Very Reverend Hon. Oliver Twisleton-Wykeham-Fiennes).

5 John Wheeler-Bennett, 1920s (by kind permission of the Hon. Mrs Richard Wheeler-Bennett).

6 Signed photograph of Benito Mussolini given to John Wheeler-Bennett, 25 February 1935 (from John Wheeler-Bennett, *Knaves, Fools and Heroes: Europe between the Wars* (1974)).

7 Marriage of John Wheeler-Bennett to Ruth Risher, University of Virginia Chapel, Charlottesville, USA, 26 March 1945 (by kind permission of the Hon. Mrs Richard Wheeler-Bennett).

8 Pacific Relations Conference, Virginia Beach, November 1939 (from Giles MacDonogh, *A Good German: Adam von Trott zu Solz* (1989)).

9 Garsington Manor, Oxfordshire (by kind permission of Mr and Mrs David Heaton).

10 John and Ruth Wheeler-Bennett at Garsington, 1960s (by kind permission of the Hon. Mrs Richard Wheeler-Bennett).

11   John Wheeler Bennett with Lewis Charles-Edwards and Harold
     Macmillan, Malvern College Centenary, July 1965 (by kind permis-
     sion of Malvern College, Worcs).
12   The Queen Mother, John Wheeler-Bennett and Donald Lindsey,
     Malvern College Centenary, July 1965 (by kind permission of
     Malvern College, Worcs).
13   Portrait of Sir John Wheeler-Bennett (1972) by Juliet Pannett (by
     kind permission of the artist and of Mr and Mrs David Heaton).

Maps

Europe Between the Wars   xi
The Far East, pre–World War II   xii

Acknowledgements

I should like to acknowledge the permission of Her Majesty Queen Elizabeth II for use of material from the Royal Archives, as well as permission to cite Her Majesty the Queen Mother's letter to Sir John Wheeler-Bennett in 1974 and to acknowledge the permission granted by her late Majesty the Queen Mother to quote her message at the time of Wheeler-Bennett's death in 1975. I should also like to thank the Countess of Avon and the Cadbury Research Library – Special Collections, University of Birmingham (hereafter referred to as Special Collections, University of Birmingham) for permission to publish excerpts from the correspondence between the Earl of Avon and Sir John Wheeler-Bennett; the Warden and Fellows of St Antony's College for permission to quote extracts from Sir John Wheeler-Bennett's unpublished memoirs held in the Library at St Antony's College, Oxford; the Royal Institute of International Affairs (Chatham House) for permission to publish extracts from Sir John Wheeler-Bennett's personal files of correspondence; and Mark Logue for permission to quote from correspondence between his grandfather Lionel Logue and Wheeler-Bennett. Information from the Harold Nicolson diaries (1927–29) is by kind permission of the Master and Fellows of Balliol College, Oxford. Crown Copyright material is reproduced with the permission of the controller of Her Majesty's Stationery Office.

I am grateful to the Warden and Fellows of St Antony's College for the award of the Visiting Alistair Horne Fellowship at St Antony's College, 2004–05 and to Sir Alistair Horne personally for his encouragement to write the life of Sir John Wheeler-Bennett. I should like to thank, in particular, Mrs Joan Wheeler-Bennett, who not only deposited invaluable archives at St Antony's College, without which the narrative would not be as rich as it is, but who also assisted me by providing further contacts and making many useful comments on the manuscript. I should like to acknowledge the kindness and hospitality of the late Sir Marrack Goulding, KCMG, Warden of St Antony's, 1997–2006, and of Dr Rashmi Shankar, a personal friend for many years, during my numerous research visits to Oxford. I am grateful to Ms Rosamund Campbell, Librarian at St Antony's, who was unfailingly helpful, as was her assistant, Mrs Hilary Maddicott. As always, I am thankful to the London Library for its liberal lending policy and to the staff at the National Archives for their assistance.

I should also like to thank all those who gave me valuable time to discuss their recollections of Sir John Wheeler-Bennett, as listed in the bibliography, especially, in addition to Mrs Joan Wheeler-Bennett, other family members, the late Richard Clement Wheeler-Bennett, David and Joan Heaton, Mrs Mary Sandford, the late Very Reverend the Hon. Oliver and the late Juliet Twisleton-Wykeham-Fiennes, as well as Sir John Wheeler-Bennett's literary collaborator, Anthony Nicholls, who also made many useful comments on the manuscript. Finally, I should like to thank Robert Baldock of Yale University Press and his colleague Candida Brazil for seeing the manuscript through to publication. As always, the support of my agent, Sara Menguc, has been invaluable, as has that of my friends and family, my husband, Stephen Willis, and our three children, Alexandra, Anthony and Olivia.

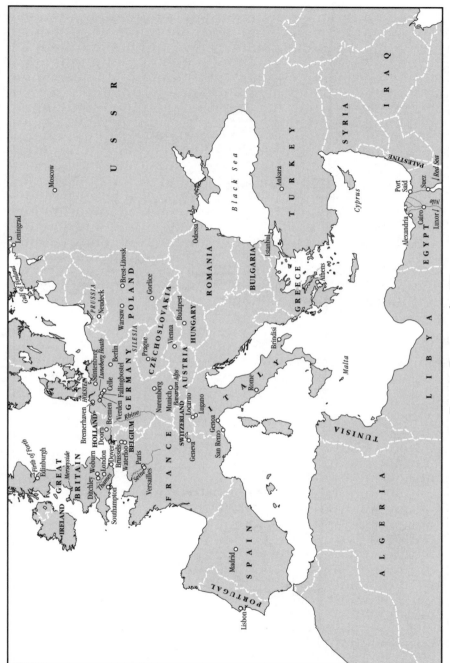

Europe Between the Wars

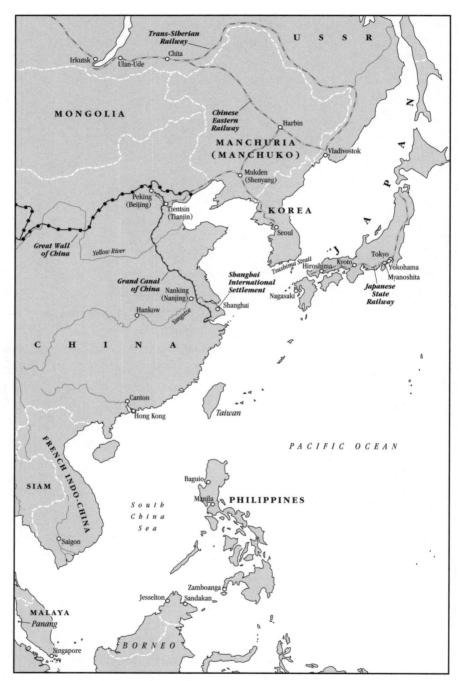

The Far East, pre-World War II

1

The Undertow of History

I spent my childhood in the age of security.[1]

John Wheeler Wheeler-Bennett was born just after the dawn of a new century and of a new reign. When Queen Victoria died in 1901, her son, Edward VII – the Peacemaker – ascended the throne. Acute appendicitis meant that the new king's coronation was postponed until June 1902 – the year of John's birth. As a future royal biographer, he would have liked the rough coincidence of a coronation with his own arrival in the world, on 13 October. John's father, John Wheeler-Bennett, was over sixty; the son of John Bennett of Portsmouth and Mary Wheeler, in 1889 he had added Wheeler to create, by Deed Poll, his hyphenated surname.[2] When the young John was christened, he too was given his grandmother's name which explains how he became John Wheeler Wheeler-Bennett; to his family and friends he was always 'Jack'. His mother, Christina, the daughter of Alexander and Ruby McNutt, was half-Canadian, since her father came from Nova Scotia, and half-American, because her mother was from Virginia. Jack's eldest brother, Jamie, had died from typhoid fever aged nine in 1894. His other brother, Clement, was born in 1887.[3] His sister, Constance Irene, was born in 1895. 'When Jack was born I was very jealous,' Irene later recollected. 'I had been almost an "only" for seven years, and I distinctly remember climbing on to my father's knee and saying, "You will love me best, won't you, Daddy?"' Irene soon got over her jealousy and remained 'devoted' to her younger brother all his life.[4]

The Wheeler-Bennetts' home was near the village of Keston, near Bromley in Kent. They lived in a grand Victorian house, surrounded by acres of land, gardens and a lake where the Ravensbourne river had been dammed and from which the house took its name. Wheeler-Bennett senior was a wealthy businessman with an interest in the firm of Canada Packers, one of the pioneering meat packaging concerns in Canada. His partner was the Canadian Joseph Flavelle.[5] With Wheeler-Bennett's worldwide business interests, which included ownership of Hay's Wharf in the docks of London, there was easily enough money in the family to have servants, gardeners and a chauffeur. In his leisure time, John Wheeler-Bennett senior enjoyed shooting and was an early golf enthusiast. In 1912, he sent the first private economic mission into Siberia in collaboration with the Russian administrator Prince Paul Dolgorouki, a progressive aristocrat who was interested in developing the resources of this part of the tsarist empire. On this occasion, the venture got no further than generating a report.[6] Also among Wheeler-Bennett's commercial contacts were Chinese traders; some lines of verse, current at the time of the Sino-Japanese War in the late nineteenth century, had pervaded the young Jack's nursery – sung to him by his nursemaid ('it had to be my nursemaid, my nurse was far too dignified and stately to countenance anything so vulgar as doggerel!'):[7]

Chinee soljee man
He wavee piecee fan,
He shoutee hipollay for Empelor
He winkee-blinkee eye
Say mally bye-and-bye
When Chinee soljee marchee home from war.

Although, as the young Wheeler-Bennett later wrote, by the time 'this piece of pro-Chinese propaganda' had reached his night nursery – 'somewhere about 1905' – it was wonderfully out of date, it engendered in his mind a fascination with the Orient. Jack also had an early career in acting: at the age of five he performed in a play called *The Season*, written by a young (and later celebrated) writer, Margaret Kennedy, who lived near by. As his sister recalled, 'Jack, with his red hair and alabaster complexion, was Autumn, and looked lovely in flame-coloured trousers and little green tunic.'[8] Jack was not athletic but he enjoyed riding, and Irene remembered how they used to be sent together to an old-fashioned hotel at St Leonards-on-Sea: 'We loved this and used to ride from the local riding stable.'[9] By contrast, their elder brother, Clement, was a remote figure; by the time Jack emerged from the nursery, he had finished at Rugby and was studying medicine at Christ Church, Oxford.

Jack's father was old enough to be his grandfather, and he describes being transfixed by 'the undertow of history' while listening to his description of the Battle of Waterloo. 'He was a brilliant and vivid raconteur, and, so animated and realistic were his descriptions of the carnage of the Sunken Road and the desperate courage of the last charge of the Old Guard, that I was both terrified and fascinated and spent many a sleepless night in consequence.'[10] Contemporary events were also making a lasting impression: in 1910, Edward VII died and the Wheeler-Bennetts occupied a stand in the Edgware Road along which the funeral cortege would process to Paddington station and onwards to Windsor for the late king's burial at Frogmore. Together with the new king, George V, marched his cousin the German emperor, Wilhelm II, and the old duke of Connaught, Queen Victoria's last surviving son. 'Although what impressed me most deeply at the time was the sight of Caesar, the late King's wire-headed terrier, being led by a royal groom behind the charger with boots reversed in the stirrups, I do remember these three figures in scarlet with plumed helmets and thinking that the one with the upturned moustaches [Kaiser Wilhelm] was the most regal-looking of all.'[11] The following year, the coronation of King George V 'was the occasion for a big house-party' at Ravensbourne. 'Every room was filled with visitors from all parts of the Empire and from the United States.' One of his mother's friends who had come from the United States presented her with a copy of *The Long Roll*, a novel on the American Civil War by Mary Johnston.

My mother was not particularly interested in it but she read parts of it aloud to me, and far-reaching effects upon my life began. At nine years old I had barely heard of the great American struggle, but I became immediately fired with its magnificent gallantry and its poignant tragedy

[. . . From this early experience derived not only my lifetime avocation
but in due course my deep affection and admiration for the United
States and for its fundamental greatness and virtue.[12]

As a young boy, Wheeler-Bennett also became aware of certain
domestic political issues that made his father's blood pressure rise: the
Parliament Act of 1911 and the Home Rule Bill of 1913, as well as
growing unemployment. 'My father,' he later recalled, 'would become
choleric, speaking of His Majesty's Government of the day as "a pack of
confounded radicals" and of Mr Lloyd George as "a howling yahoo".'
At such times, his mother found it prudent to keep the newspapers
hidden until after lunch.[13] When, following the formation of the Balkan
League in 1912, war was declared on Turkey, first by Montenegro, then
jointly by Greece, Serbia and Bulgaria, the young Wheeler-Bennett
followed the events of the 'Balkan wars' with 'keen interest in the newspapers and on war maps, on which I moved parti-coloured flags as the
fronts ebbed and flowed in the tide of battle'.[14] Nursing 'delicate' health,
he had 'plenty of time for reading',[15] developing what he called 'a kind
of schizophrenic romance between the actual happenings in Europe and
the lure of the past glories of the Orient'. He 'devoured all Chinese
history', following avidly the chronicles of Marco Polo, determining one
day to see for himself 'the palms and temples of the East'.[16]

Jack Wheeler-Bennett's preparatory school was Wellington House,
Westgate-on-Sea, near Margate, on the Isle of Thanet at the extreme
eastern tip of Kent. In the Easter holidays of 1914, with Irene at finishing
school in Paris, the Wheeler-Bennetts took a European tour. 'It was a
memorable experience for a boy of [nearly] twelve and, though I have
subsequently travelled throughout the world, the romance of that first
contact with Europe is still with me,' he recalled. But, much as he
enjoyed the experience, in later years he thought that he had inherited
some of his father's xenophobia, which made him prefer Americans to
continental Europeans. On their itinerary were the cathedral cities of
Belgium and, at the young Wheeler-Bennett's insistence, they visited
the battleground of Waterloo. To his disappointment, the guide
lacked his father's narrative skills. In Berlin, he saw again his moustached
hero, Emperor Kaiser Wilhelm II, reviewing the Prussian Guard at

Tempelhof, outside Berlin. The Wheeler-Bennetts then travelled onwards to Austria. A visit to the opera in Vienna provided a glimpse of the ageing Emperor Franz Joseph I seated in his imperial box. 'When I next returned to Europe, Belgium was in ruins, and the German and Austro-Hungarian empires had ceased to exist.'[17] The year 1914 brought another excitement. Irene turned eighteen and her younger brother was allowed out of school to attend her 'coming-out' ball in July. 'To my young eyes it was the loveliest thing I had ever seen. A ballroom under a marquee was built out over the lawn . . . thousands of fairy-lights illuminated the grounds . . . it was a warm moonlit night . . . there were fireworks and lovely things to eat and I was allowed to stay up till midnight.' Describing the experience as a 'dream of delight', only later did he recognise that 'we were even then dancing on the brink of a volcano'.[18]

In distant Bosnia, Emperor Franz Joseph's nephew and heir, Archduke Ferdinand, inspector general of the army, was overseeing manoeuvres.[19] The Serbian nationalists, however, were displeased by his presence. In their opinion, Bosnia, formerly part of the Ottoman Empire, occupied by Austria in 1878 and annexed thirty years later, was still under 'foreign' rule. Impervious to warnings that his life might be in danger, on Sunday, 28 June the archduke and his wife, Sophie, Duchess of Hohenberg, processed openly through the streets of Sarajevo. An assassination attempt failed. Instead, an officer travelling in the next carriage was wounded by a Serbian assailant. Later the same day, when the archduke and the duchess went to visit the wounded officer in hospital, another assassin – Gavrilo Princip – got close enough to the royal cavalcade to draw his revolver and fire two fatal shots. The duchess took the first bullet; the second bullet hit the archduke. Instead of exacting retribution within the confines of the empire, the Austrian government did not wish to move against the Serbs without German support. Unlike many of his colleagues, Wheeler-Bennett senior foresaw the danger of a widening conflict: during the weeks after the assassination, he reorganised his finances, divesting himself of his European interests and reinvesting the capital in Australian and Canadian securities, as well as transferring holdings in the United States to Canada. 'It was,' Wheeler-Bennett later recollected, 'a singularly wise decision.'[20]

Over the next few weeks, diplomatic exchanges took place. Russia announced that it would defend the Serbians – its Slavic brothers – and vacillated between partial and full mobilisation. A month after the assassination, Austria declared war on Serbia. When the Austro-Hungarians mobilised their army, the Germans followed suit. On 1 August, Russia and Germany declared war on each other. France, an ally of Russia, came out in support of Russia. Within days, Britain, which had signed an 'Entente Cordiale' with France in 1904, was drawn into the conflagration. In the preceding years, influenced both by improving relations with France and Russia and fears of German naval expansion, which seemed to threaten the British Empire, an expectation had already arisen that Britain would support the French if they were attacked by Germany. Furthermore, an 1839 treaty pledged Britain and other signatories (including Prussia) to defend Belgium's neutrality. Thus, when German troops advanced across the Belgian border, the British government felt compelled to honour its obligations and, on 4 August, war was declared on Germany.[21] Italy remained neutral, but Austro-Hungary and Germany acquired a new ally in Turkey, whose diplomatic approaches to Britain and France had been rejected. Although Turkey did not undertake offensive action until the end of October, that country's allegiance to Germany was evident in the presence of the German warships *Goeben* and *Breslau* in the Dardanelles.

For the young Jack Wheeler-Bennett, the late summer of 1914 'was the most exciting I had ever spent'. Clement, who had gone from Christ Church to St Thomas's Hospital to become a doctor, joined the Royal Navy as a surgeon lieutenant. Irene was working with one of the Voluntary Aid Detachments – known as VADs – which had been formed to provide medical assistance to the wounded, and was busy cleaning the rooms of buildings which had been requisitioned as hospitals. Within no time, as the toll of the fighting grew, the beds were filled with wounded Belgian and British soldiers. Although the Belgians were initially received warmly, Wheeler-Bennett senior refused to let them stay at Ravensbourne, instead encouraging his wife to rent a separate house for them. In later life, Wheeler-Bennett appreciated his father's decision as the Wheeler-Bennetts were thus distanced from the commotion when rows broke out among the refugees. On the other hand, the British soldiers 'were heroes whom I could comprehend, and my greatest delight was to visit them, bringing with me cigarettes and sweets, and listening to their stories'. When Irene was transferred to the Third London General Hospital in Wandsworth, her younger brother was allowed to attend the concerts given there at weekends. 'I recall the exhilaration of sitting among that vast audience in their hospital "blues" and joining in the choruses of every popular music-hall song, ancient and modern.' 'It's a Long Way to Tipperary', 'The Broken Doll' and 'Roses of Picardy' were among his favourites.[22]

Jack Wheeler-Bennett found that the war had an impact at school too. Most of the young teachers had volunteered. The headmaster at Westgate became 'the personification of a British jingo', exhorting the boys to accept that there were some things they were going to have to go without and giving them daily renditions of the despatches in the news-papers. 'He read very well, and his rendering of the account of the landings at Gallipoli, for example, moved me greatly.' Wheeler-Bennett's first personal experience of the war came when he was lying on the lawn at school watching 'with feverish excitement' a dogfight between a British and a German airman.[23]

Adjustments also had to be made at home. Petrol rationing and difficulties in getting servants meant that the Wheeler-Bennetts closed Ravensbourne during the winter. They took up residence in the fashion-able Alexandra Hotel just off Hyde Park Corner in London.[24] Wheeler-Bennett senior was working for the Red Cross and was also one of the original members of Major Rothschild's Military Advisory Committee, as well as being chairman of the finance department of the Kent County hospitals, for which service he was made a Companion of the British Empire (CBE). Family lore related that – together with his business associate, Joseph Flavelle – Wheeler-Bennett was responsible for importing much needed bacon from Canada. He refused the peerage he was offered because his North American wife, Christina, did not 'fancy it'.[25] Flavelle, on the other hand, was happy to accept a baronetcy for reor-ganising the munitions industry during the war as chairman of the Muni-tions Board.

By the summer of 1915, the fear of a large-scale invasion of the south coast of England meant that extra precautions had to be taken, which, for the boys at Westgate, involved preparing to evacuate the school at a few hours' notice. Jack Wheeler-Bennett, still only twelve, had been made 'head of the school, and thus occupied the unenviable position of a sort of quasi-adjutant to the Headmaster'.[26] Even so, he enjoyed the secrecy – lest the younger boys get frightened – of the preparations which involved planning to cross the Stour river, which separated the Isle of Thanet from the rest of Kent. Each boy was to carry a knapsack containing a change of underwear and some toiletry articles. Jack's particular duty was to organise the boys in groups under his fellow monitors. 'Fortunately – for the thought now of shepherding some sixty small boys on a trek in the grey dawn fills me with horror' – they were never required to put the plan into action.

Increasing air raids on the naval depot at Sheerness to the west posed a significant threat, however, and rudimentary air-raid shelters with bunks for the younger boys and benches for the older ones were set up in the school's cellars. Early one morning in April 1916, an attack was made by a single German plane on the Royal Flying Corps base at Manston. Driven away by anti-aircraft flak, the German pilot jettisoned his bombs as he made for the coast. Jack awoke to the noise of them dropping. As the sound drew closer, he and the other boys made for the cellars. Suddenly a bomb fell in the school yard 'with a tremendous detonation which pitched me down the stairs and into oblivion'. Jack was the only boy to suffer repercussions from the explosion. He was shell-shocked and he became afflicted with a bad stammer which turned him from a boy who enjoyed reading the school lesson to one who was 'virtually inarticulate'.[27] He also developed a facial tic which was 'disfiguring' and he began to suffer from nervous disorders. His parents' plans for him to follow in his brother's footsteps at Rugby or to go to Charterhouse were shelved. In the summer term of 1917, he was sent to Malvern College in Worcestershire, where a neighbour of the family's in Kent, Arthur Boosey, founder of the music publishers Boosey & Hawkes, was also educating his boys.

There were ten houses at Malvern and Wheeler-Bennett, as he was now called, in keeping with the public-school tradition of using surnames, was put in House 5, a four-storey Tudor-style redbrick building. The housemaster there was F.U. Mugliston, whom the boys called 'Mugs'.[28]

Shortly before the outbreak of war, the headmaster, F.S. Preston, a classical scholar and Cambridge graduate, had taken over the running of the school, putting into practice his belief that public schools should provide leadership, balancing a respect for games with the pursuit of more academic studies.[29] Wheeler-Bennett never excelled at games, and it was at Malvern that his ambition to become a historian 'took shape and meaning'. With his poor health and the knowledge that his dream of becoming a soldier was 'unrealisable', he became even more determined 'to find out why and how things had happened in the past and might well be repeated in future'. Rather than focusing on dates and reigns of kings, his teachers 'taught me the broad scope of history'. The novels of Alexandre Dumas, George Henty and Nicholas Breton further contributed to his 'itch to become a historian'.[30] He also developed an early interest in social gossip: he later recollected that, in the style of Edward Gibbon's *Decline and Fall*, William Coxe's *Memoirs of the House of Austria* consisted of ten to twenty lines of text with the remainder printed as footnotes 'recounting the more scandalous doings of the Habsburgs'.[31]

But, despite providing him with a 'well-balanced grounding' in the study of history, he believed that the school as a whole was not at its peak. The reason was, he said, 'the tragedy of the times'.[32] By 1917, the war was in its third year, with no obvious end in sight. Britain's supplies were at their lowest, and rationing at its most severe, meaning that the boys lived mainly on a diet of potatoes mixed with margarine.[33] Although a brave face was put on the shortages, even the headmaster noticed that 'the cheek-bones of the adolescent boys were unpleasantly prominent'.[34] 'National morale,' Wheeler-Bennett recollected in later life, 'had touched its nadir.'[35] Inevitably, this state of mind affected the school. Since teachers of serviceable age and appropriate fitness had joined up, their places had been taken by 'the physically unfit or the over-aged, or worse still, by inexperienced enthusiasts who had always believed that they had a flair for teaching and grasped eagerly at an opportunity to prove the fact — it usually proved to be an illusion'.[36]

The war had a more depressing impact on the schoolboys. Since the life expectancy of a subaltern on the Western Front was rated in weeks rather than months, Wheeler-Bennett and his friends became accustomed to hearing the name of a boy read out in the weekly roll of honour in chapel whom they might perhaps have known as a school prefect the previous term.[37] Inevitably there was a corollary: if the teachers' discipline was lax, 'discipline of a kind was at its strongest and most tyrannical among the elder boys, who, faced with this imminent gamble with fate, were not in their last years at school overly gifted with a sense of responsibility'.[38] The prefects' minute book during the war years was concerned less with the usual misdemeanours of smoking than with 'general indiscipline, and an unhealthy moral atmosphere'.[39] Wheeler-Bennett found that the older boys had acquired a fatalistic attitude towards life and 'there was much bullying'.[40]

Like the other boys, Wheeler-Bennett was a member of the Officers Training Corps, which, because of the war, now drilled twice a week. Occasionally there were night operations. Inevitably, their marching songs had an anti-Kaiser Wilhelm innuendo:

Tramp, tramp, tramp, along the road to Ber-lin,
Singing, cheering, seeking all the way
A wild cat whose moustaches want uncurling,
A man-eating tiger brought at last to bay.

In the autumn term of 1917, Mr Brown, organising secretary of the YMCA, visited Malvern to give a talk in the school gymnasium about the soldiers' lives in France. His suggestion was that, somewhere in France or even in Mesopotamia, a Malvern College Hut should be established. A Hut Fund was therefore launched with a target of raising £600 to establish a small hut, but with the goal of bringing this up to £1,000 for 'one more likely to prove of permanent value'. Within a short period of time the requisite money had been raised among the boys, their parents and Old Malvernians, and the hut was erected at Leulinghem near St Omer, between Calais and Amiens. The boys were encouraged to send out books, magazines and newspapers to the soldiers.[41] There was already a Debating Society at Malvern whose meetings focused on certain moral aspects of the war ('Is a nation entitled to advance its own interests at the expense of every other nation? Are reprisals justifiable?'). In 1917, one of the masters, H.B. Davies, started a Discussion Society, which met once a fortnight to discuss similar topics.

Meanwhile Wheeler-Bennett was continuing to pursue his own interests. Having realised that he had 'not the smallest or most elementary ability to absorb arithmetic, algebra or geometry' – a subject which he gave up altogether in his last year – he had discovered the English poets and 'became drunk on a solid orgy of verse', which began with Keats, Shelley and Byron, and continued with Tennyson and Browning, leading on to Rudyard Kipling, James Elroy Flecker and Rupert Brooke. 'In the peace of the school library, on Sunday evenings in the summer before Chapel, I would climb into a window-sill and sit entranced, now with the treasures of my current poet, now with the beauty of the view before me, stretching with lengthening shadows over the Vale of Evesham across the wooded slopes of Bredon and The Rhydd – as lovely an expanse as anywhere in England.'[42]

Wheeler-Bennett was still at school when the guns of war fell silent on 11 November 1918. Even so, he was keenly following events, identifying especially with the beliefs of one man, the president of the United States, Woodrow Wilson, who visited Britain in December. 'I remember vividly being taken by my father to the Guildhall to see the President receive the Freedom of the City of London, a rare honour to be bestowed on foreigners.' Recording the occasion in later life, Wheeler-Bennett recognised that for the peoples of Europe, 'war-weary and longing for peace', Wilson's presence was 'little short of the Second Coming. Here was the new saviour of mankind who came "with healing in his wings" to make real the promises of "a war to end war" and of a "world safe for democracy".'[43] As a sixteen-year-old schoolboy, this experience made a lasting impression. Although he did not realise it at the time, the Paris Peace Conference at Versailles and the formation of Woodrow Wilson's brainchild, the League of Nations, marked the starting point of Wheeler-Bennett's own career as a historian. The first journal to which he contributed was the Discussion Society's literary magazine, *The Beacon*, of which he became the editor.[44]

While at Malvern, Wheeler-Bennett made several lifelong friends. One such was a senior boy, Rajendra Sinhji, one of four brothers who were great cricketers. Rajendra later went to Sandhurst, rising to become commander-in-chief of the Indian army in 1953.[45] Wheeler-Bennett's friends among his immediate contemporaries included George Courtauld,

later director of the family textile manufacturing business, Courtaulds
Ltd. 'For some years we used to meet for lunch together and re-live
the common memories of our old school. They were very enjoyable
luncheons!'[46] Another friend, Errol Holmes, arrived at Malvern with a
reputation for excelling in athletics and was selected to be Wheeler-
Bennett's 'fag'. 'This feudal relationship was of the briefest duration for
Holmes was awarded his House Colours at cricket in his first term and
was thus rendered free of these subservient duties.' A friendship, however,
which 'gladdened' Wheeler-Bennett's remaining time at school had
begun. 'Errol always seemed to me to epitomise the perfect type of public
school product. His success in athletics was phenomenal.' As a senior, he
became head of school, head of his house and captain of cricket and
played in the football XI, but was 'never conceited'.[47] Looking back,
Wheeler-Bennett did not consider that his school days were among the
'most golden' of his life. Although a house prefect, he was not made a
college prefect. Indeed, describing himself as 'very unhappy' at school,
the eighteen-year-old Wheeler-Bennett left Malvern in the autumn of
1920 'a critic, a sceptic and a rebel, determined not to return there under
any circumstances'.[48]

    Throughout his school days, Wheeler-Bennett's poor health 'without
any specific cause' was difficult for his father to understand. The latter
believed that 'either a person was well or he was ill', and when neighbours professed concern at Wheeler-Bennett's physical condition,
Wheeler-Bennett senior would pull himself up a little taller and respond:
'As far as I know, the boy is perfectly well.' However, when Wheeler-
Bennett became unwell again after leaving school, it was not thought
wise for him to take up a place at Christ Church, where Clement had
studied. In later life, Wheeler-Bennett expressed his 'bitter disappointment'. [49] Instead he began to travel. He was issued with his first passport
in April 1921 – a large folding sheet of paper, which noted his 'medium'
forehead, 'blue' eyes, 'large' nose, 'square' chin, 'thick lower lip', 'pale'
complexion, 'long' face and 'auburn' hair, and described his profession as
that of a 'student'.[50] Departing from England in May, his first stops were
Portugal, Madeira and the Canary Islands. According to his sister Irene's
recollections, he was to travel around the world 'with a companion
whose credentials had been carefully investigated, but as it happened, not

carefully enough'. By the time the two young men reached Australia, Wheeler-Bennett's father had become suspicious of the amount of money his son was requesting. Further investigation disclosed that the companion was living 'entirely off Jack'. When confronted, the young man duly disappeared in possession of Wheeler-Bennett senior's Zeiss field glasses. Wheeler-Bennett returned home, sharing a cabin with a man who suffered from delirium. As Irene recollected, 'this was rough stuff for a delicate eighteen year old, but Jack stood up to it very well, and was doubtless richer for these experiences.'[51]

2

Youthful Illusions

I attained my manhood at a time when we still believed in the possibility
of building a world safe for democracy.[1]

Unable to attend university, Jack Wheeler-Bennett shunned following in his father's footsteps and going into business. Instead he secured a voluntary job working for the League of Nations Union, formed in 1918 to promote international justice and peace, whose ethos was based on the ideals of the League of Nations. Imbued with a strong belief in the value of the League and having attended one of their summer conferences in Bruges, he wrote a short account of their work that was published in his old school Discussion Society's magazine, *The Beacon*. Assuring his readers confidently that 'Ignorance is the predominant characteristic of the opponents of the League of Nations', he went on to express his enthusiasm for the organisation. 'Although it is not apparently a well-known fact,' he opined, 'the League has successfully averted two wars: One between Persia and Soviet Russia over the occupation of various Persian coast towns; the second between Sweden and Finland over the ownership of the Aaland Islands. As history has shown, small wars have often developed into struggles in which continents have become embroiled.'[2] For a young man who was only just nineteen, the strength of his convictions, or 'youthful illusions' as he was later to call his early beliefs, meant that, like many of his generation, he believed that universal peace was attainable.[3]

Before long, Wheeler-Bennett had graduated to become assistant secretary to the publicity director, William Ewart Gladstone Murray, 'that redoubtable, lovable, erratic and now almost forgotten pioneer in British Broadcasting'.[4] Bill, as he was known, had been a Canadian Rhodes Scholar at Oxford in 1913; he had also had a distinguished war career with the Canadian Flying Corps. When Wheeler-Bennett met him in the early 1920s, Murray was dividing his time between pursuing 'a very genuine devotion' to the cause of the League of Nations and following 'a passionate interest' in the development of broadcasting as publicity manager of Radio Communications Co. Ltd, later becoming director of public relations for the BBC. Since he spent more time on broadcasting than at the League of Nations offices, the publicity department was left in Wheeler-Bennett's 'amateurish and neophytic hands'. In later life, he recognised his debt of gratitude to Bill Murray: 'he taught me the rudiments and fundamentals of running an information and publicity department'.[5] As was already becoming a pattern in Wheeler-Bennett's life, one friendship led to another: through Murray, he met Vernon Bartlett, a journalist for the *Daily Chronicle*, later famous as one of the original British radio commentators on international affairs. In 1938, Bartlett became an independent MP, making a name for himself 'for his courageous and forthright speeches' in opposition to Neville Chamberlain's policy of appeasement.[6]

Wheeler-Bennett's parents continued to live at Ravensbourne. His father, now retired after his exertions during the Great War, was watching his younger son's career with some concern. Clement, meanwhile, was working in general practice as a doctor and in 1919 had married Enid, a daughter of their Kent neighbours the Booseys. In December 1920, Irene married Dr Trevor Braby Heaton, a don at Christ Church.[7] Their first child, Mary, was born the following year; two years later they had a son, David. Clement and Enid likewise had a son, John, and soon afterwards a daughter, Gillian. As a young man, Wheeler-Bennett had no desire to settle down and was just beginning to get established in the realm of a new discipline which fascinated him, that of 'international relations'. To further his interest, he wanted to join a newly founded organisation, the British Institute of International Affairs (BIIA). With premises in Horseferry Road, Westminster, and then in Malet Street

behind the British Museum, it was the brainchild of the lawyer Lionel
Curtis, a keen advocate of imperial unity. Having seen the benefit of
information being exchanged among 'diplomats and experts' at the Paris
Peace Conference, he had wanted to continue 'this method of analysis
of international problems' with the establishment of an institution 'for
the study of International Questions'.[8] The BIIA was inaugurated in July
1920.[9] The following October, Wheeler-Bennett's membership was
proposed by the Reverend H.W. Fox and Captain Lothian Small, who
described him as 'a traveller and a serious student of foreign affairs who
would have valuable contributions to make to the discussions of the
Institute'.[10] Once inside its doors, Wheeler-Bennett was to further his
contacts immeasurably. Among those he met was a retired major general,
Sir Neill Malcolm, one of the original members of the BIIA and currently
head of the British Military Mission in Berlin. So began a long friendship
– one of four which in later life Wheeler-Bennett acknowledged as
having had the most profound impact on his life.[11]

Part of Wheeler-Bennett's duties working for the League of Nations
Union was travel to Australia and New Zealand. Bill Murray was instru-
mental in organising such trips provided the journey was made at
Wheeler-Bennett's own expense. In the autumn of 1922 he set off, with
the intention of visiting the various affiliated League of Nations societies.
But he did not find Australia and New Zealand 'particularly attractive or
enjoyable . . . for in those days these great Pacific countries were amaz-
ingly parochial in their approach to international affairs and were inclined,
not unnaturally, to view them in the perspective of possible Japanese
aggression'. Attempting to engender popular interest in the work of the
League of Nations, he wrote newspaper articles, gave interviews and
made addresses at various luncheons. Of greater interest for the future of
Dominion relations with Britain, he observed at first hand 'the newly
awakening nationalism and independence of outlook' in both Australia
and New Zealand, which had been stimulated in September 1922 by the
'Chanak affair', when Prime Minister Lloyd George had requested assistance from the Dominion governments against a potential attack by
Turkey on British troops guarding the neutral zone of the Dardanelles.
As Wheeler-Bennett noted, the British government had received 'dusty
answers' in return.[12]

From Australia, he travelled across the Pacific via Hawaii to North America. As noted on his passport, the purpose of his stay was 'pleasure'. First he travelled to Canada and then 'wandered down the Eastern seaboard' of the United States from Maine to Charleston, South Carolina, 'the cradle of secession'.[13] Describing himself as 'part-traveller, part-sightseer', he enjoyed 'strange yet familiar differences'. What he really wanted to do was to meet Woodrow Wilson, who, after suffering a severe stroke in 1919, was living in retirement in Washington, D.C. Having secured an introduction through some Americans he had met in Geneva during the sessions of the League Assembly, he went to see Wilson at his home in S Street – the 'Embassy row' section of Washington. The hero who had so inspired him as a schoolboy in December 1918 and who had been awarded the Nobel Peace Prize, was now a sick man. Paralysed on his left side and blind in one eye, he was, however, still able to describe to Wheeler-Bennett the circumstances under which the League of Nations had been created at Versailles. Wheeler-Bennett found it a 'heart-rending experience', especially since Wilson died soon afterwards, in February 1924.[14]

Wheeler-Bennett's next significant encounter was more cheerful. He had long wanted to meet Mary Johnston, the author of the popular romantic historical novel *The Long Roll* (1911), which had caught his imagination a decade previously. A daughter of the Confederate commander General Joseph E. Johnston, Mary lived with her sisters in Warm Springs, Virginia, on the lower slopes of the Alleghenies 'in an aura of the past, quite incomprehensible' to some of the 'Northerners' who came to stay as lodgers, 'but perfectly understandable to me who had made a study of the social conditions in the post-bellum south'. Wheeler-Bennett found her an 'enchanting person'. On this first visit she inscribed his copy of *The Long Roll*, which had fired his interest in the American Civil War; she also added a verse of 'Dixie' on the flyleaf.[15] Until her death in 1936, Wheeler-Bennett made a point of returning regularly to visit her.

While in the United States, he also met his 'first and greatest friend' in New York, Hamilton Fish Armstrong, managing editor of *Foreign Affairs*, the official quarterly of the recently formed Council on Foreign Relations, of which he was also executive director.[16] Like the BIIA, the

Council had arisen out of the information meetings between experts of the British and American delegations at Versailles and, through his association with the BIIA, Wheeler-Bennett had received an introduction to 'Ham', who lived in Greenwich Village. 'He was one of those rare relics of the old, aristocratic New York way of life before the First World War, an anomaly of elegance and wit and humour . . . He was the most lovable of men, a true friend, an honest enemy and a man capable of righteous wrath to a superb degree.' His first act of kindness was to introduce Wheeler-Bennett to the Chatham Hotel on the corner of East 48th Street and Park Avenue, where the latter remained a regular client until the site was redeveloped after World War II.

Armstrong's second favour was to present Wheeler-Bennett with a ticket for the 1924 National Democratic Convention at Old Madison Square Garden. Describing himself as 'a political animal', Wheeler-Bennett was fascinated by the whole process of a presidential election, 'just as a small child is held in delight by a great circus . . . the smell of the grease-paint, the roar of the crowds, the brass bands playing the campaign-songs'. Lasting for two weeks in the heat of a New York summer, the convention 'beat all conventions'. There, 'the embattled forces' of the governor of New York, Alfred E. Smith, and William McAdoo, Woodrow Wilson's son-in-law, 'stubbornly locked horns in a desperate battle'. After a record 103 ballots, with neither candidate conceding, a compromise candidate emerged in John W. Davis, who went on to be beaten in a landslide victory by the Republican presidential candidate, Calvin Coolidge.[17] On this and subsequent visits to New York, Wheeler-Bennett revelled in the 'charm and excitement' of the city:

> apart from the pleasure of seeing one's friends . . . there were so many nice things to see and do. Youth and beauty still gathered at the Plaza, and one could ride in a hansom cab – long after they had disappeared from the streets of London – round the winding avenues of Central Park and stop to listen to a band-concert on the Mall . . . There were splendid book-shops, both modern and second-hand . . . One danced on the St Regis Roof Garden and always had the address of a reliable bootlegger and a respectable speakeasy.[18]

Meanwhile, with enough money not to have to earn his living, Wheeler-Bennett was trying to construct an occupation for himself in London. Possibly inspired by the Council on Foreign Relations, he decided to set up an Information Service on International Affairs 'where information . . . might be obtained free from any taint of propaganda or political bias'.[19] With offices in Sentinel House, Southampton Row, WC1 and 'with a capital sum of £500', he officially called the organisation the Association for International Understanding. His aim was to provide a fortnightly *Bulletin of International News*.[20] The first of these, 'a multigraphed sheet with a free circulation of twenty-five copies', was issued in February 1925. In the months after its inception, he would sign himself as the 'Editor, John Wheeler Wheeler-Bennett, Jnr'. Later he expanded the organisation to include a proper executive committee, whose chairman was Lieutenant General Sir George Macdonogh, former director of military intelligence in London.[21] Wheeler-Bennett assumed the position of vice-chairman and the Hon. Oliver Brett (later Viscount Esher), became the treasurer.[22] Arnold Toynbee, who, after lecturing at Balliol College, had worked in intelligence during the Great War and attended the Paris Peace Conference, also joined the committee.[23]

Another member was Blanche – known as Baffy – Dugdale, Arthur Balfour's niece, whom Wheeler-Bennett had met through the League of Nations Union, and who had worked in British naval intelligence.[24] She later introduced Wheeler-Bennett to Lewis Namier, who became his 'mentor in the art of writing history' and was another of the men whose influence Wheeler-Bennett would later appreciatively acknowledge. Like Toynbee, Namier had worked in intelligence during the war; a lecturer in modern history at Balliol in the early 1920s, he was working on his classic study *The Structure of Politics at the Accession of George III* when Wheeler-Bennett met him. The two men obviously discussed finances because when Namier published his book in 1929 he acknowledged a loan from Wheeler-Bennett of £500, which had enabled him to complete his book.[25] In the 1920s, Wheeler-Bennett was also influenced by the views of a rising Member of Parliament, Anthony Eden, who had entered the House of Commons in 1924, later becoming political private secretary to Austen Chamberlain, the foreign secretary. 'My generation looked upon him as typifying the generation who had survived the war to become the champion and defender of our pathetic beliefs in what proved to be those ephemeral Wilsonian shibboleths of making the world safe for democracy.[26] Initially, his father was sceptical about his son's prospects and refused to give him any funds beyond his allowance. 'I found myself therefore in somewhat straitened financial circumstances, having to pay out of my own income office rental, staff salaries and general expenses.' But such was the early success of Wheeler-Bennett's enterprise that members of his father's clubs – the Royal Automobile and the City Carlton – began to ask him whether he was related to John Wheeler-Bennett, Jnr; as a result, his father made a 'generous contribution' to the Information Service.[27]

When Wheeler-Bennett made a brief visit in 'the middle twenties' to the new 'German Reich', established at Weimar after Kaiser Wilhelm's forced abdication in November 1918, he considered that the new republic 'had traversed its early stages of uncertainty': the 'agony' of the Versailles Peace Treaty, the Kapp Putsch, when right-wing elements attempted its overthrow, the collapse of the Reichsmark, the deadlock over reparations and the occupation of the Ruhr by the French.[28] Field Marshal Paul von Beneckendorff und von Hindenburg – the hero of the Germans' victory at Tannenberg – was 'in the model era' of his first term as president, Gustav Stresemann was foreign minister, 'and it seemed as if a new Germany, enlightened in outlook and democratic in its political institutions, had been readmitted to the polity of Europe. She had even been elected to the League of Nations.'[29] Edgar Vincent, 1st Viscount D'Abernon, the 'pioneer of appeasement', was the British ambassador.[30] The 'spirit of Locarno' – engendered by the Locarno Treaties, due to be signed on 1 December 1925 by the seven Western Allied countries and the new states of Central and Eastern Europe – was creating a spirit of rapprochement.[31]

Wheeler-Bennett now began to fulfil his ambition to write books. In time – with a literary career spanning fifty years – he was to have his name on the title page of over thirty publications. His first book, *Information on the Permanent Court of International Justice*, was 'privately printed' in 1924 by the Association for International Understanding. A twenty-seven-page pamphlet, *The World Court in 1925*, giving an outline of the work of the Permanent Court of International Justice, was published in

1926, along with a short list of books and articles dealing with the same subject that had appeared during the year. He also began to write a number of books in an 'Information Series', published by George Allen & Unwin, which examined how the world was to be ordered in the aftermath of war. The first titles were: *Information on the Problem of Security* and *Information on the Reduction of Armaments*. For both, Wheeler-Bennett had asked Major General Sir Neill Malcolm to write an introduction, which he willingly did, describing the latter title as 'extremely valuable in that it enables us to form some opinion as to the achievement of the past six years, the position as it is today and the prospects for the future'.[32] The book was dedicated 'by permission' to the Right Hon. Viscount Cecil of Chelwood, KC, President of the League of Nations and a founder president of the BIIA. Perhaps without realising it, Wheeler-Bennett was establishing a new school of history writing, that of 'international relations'. Historian Alan Bullock, who later became a close friend, suggested that the fact that the books were reprinted in the United States fifty years later was 'a striking testimony to the quality of the original workmanship in a field where the discard rate is naturally high'.[33]

As the reputation of Wheeler-Bennett's Information Service grew, so did its relative influence, and he prided himself on his professional nickname of 'The Vulture' for his ability to predict the next trouble spot.[34] As his friends later acknowledged, despite the handicap of his embarrassing stammer, which still dogged him, he had an unusual ability 'to cajole older people, and especially those who were socially or politically influential, into subscribing to his service and providing him with information and introductions'.[35]

In 1926, Neill Malcolm became chairman of the BIIA, which had moved to premises in Chatham House, St James's Square. In the same year, by Royal Grant, the organisation changed its name to the 'Royal Institute of International Affairs' before becoming known as Chatham House, and adopting 'the Chatham House rule' of confidentiality in 1927 which originated with the aim of providing anonymity to speakers in order to encourage openness and sharing of information.[36] The organisation's aims closely matched those of Wheeler-Bennett's Association for International Understanding and the *Bulletin of International News*.

Although reports of the institute's meetings were circulated in a journal, which had begun publication in 1922, it had no comparable 'information' department. Macdonogh therefore wrote to the outgoing chairman, Lord Meston, to enquire whether it 'would be willing to assist the Association in the carrying on of its work in return for services which the Association may be able to render to the Institute and its members'.[37] What he had in mind was assistance in the production of the bulletin and, if possible, the provision of office space. This was agreed and the staff of the Association duly shifted out of Sentinel House. Over the next two years, negotiations for a formal merger continued.

Throughout the 1920s, Wheeler-Bennett lived at A14, Albany, Piccadilly, a short distance from Chatham House. Formerly the town house of Lord Melbourne and then of the duke of York, Albany had been converted into accommodation, known as 'chambers', for those 'nobles and gentry' who did not have a permanent home in London. As a young man, Wheeler-Bennett considered it to be the 'most comfortable and desirable bachelor's quarters in London'. It was also where 'the strangest variety of persons forgathered', and he began the practice of bringing together interesting people from all walks of life – European cabinet ministers, Jesuit fathers, foreign journalists, propagandists from every corner of the Earth, English friends who 'liked meeting foreigners' and ambassadors.[38] In time, 'no one was better informed about the best restaurants in half-a-dozen capitals or a member of more clubs'.[39] Wheeler-Bennett continued to enjoy reading fiction: a favourite author was the prolific writer John Buchan, who had worked as correspondent for *The Times* on the Western Front.[40] The novels of Anthony Hope, especially the popular *Prisoner of Zenda* and *Rupert of Hentzau*, and those of Baroness Orczy remained on his bookshelves.[41] But, as was to become a recurring pattern in Wheeler-Bennett's life, the workload he had assumed for himself meant that he had become 'tired physically and nervously exhausted'; his doctors recommended 'some kind of recuperation, preferably abroad'. Wheeler-Bennett's father had died in June 1926, leaving a 'large fortune' with a gross value of £684,188, and his mother was anxious to travel. Once Wheeler-Bennett had recovered from pneumonia, mother and son decided that they would go 'East to the Orient'.[42]

3

International Traveller

I have always enjoyed long journeys by land and by sea, the longer the better. The powerful lift and thrust of an ocean going liner, the rhythmic throb of a continental express have been ever among that category of Rupert Brooke's 'Things I have loved.'[1]

The journey that Wheeler-Bennett and his mother undertook to the 'gorgeous East' enabled them to see a relatively unknown part of the world which was then immersed in violent change. In 1911, the revolutionary leader Sun Yat-sen had toppled the Manchu dynasty and established the Republic of China. Although he had been unable to consolidate the new order, by the early 1920s revolutionary fervour had once more erupted in Canton. Among the revolutionaries were two young Communist leaders, Mao Tse-tung and Chou En-lai. In the aftermath of Sun Yat-sen's death, an unknown colonel, Chiang Kai-shek, succeeded in proclaiming a 'Nationalist' – Kuomintang – revolution. From Canton, he began a 'northern expedition' to unify the country. By the autumn of 1926 – as the Wheeler-Bennetts were about to embark on their Oriental tour – Chiang Kai-shek had conquered several important towns along the Yangzte river including Hankow.[2] For Wheeler-Bennett, just twenty-four years old and running his own Information Service, what he saw proved another milestone in furthering his understanding of international affairs.

Their journey began in early December 1926, when mother and son departed from Paris on the famous *Train Bleu* for the Italian Riviera. The

Hotel Royal at San Remo, he noted, 'still retained something of the
pre-war atmosphere and much of the comfort of that period'. As Wheeler-
Bennett added, Grand Duke Nicholas Nicholaivitch, the tsar's uncle,
who had incurred the tsarina's jealousy, leading to his removal as supreme
commander of the Russian army in the Great War, was buried in San
Remo and his grave had become 'a shrine for pilgrimage by numerous
white Russians', with 'former displaced royalties' haunting the hotel.
Another frequent visitor was Princess Beatrice, Queen Victoria's youngest
daughter; the widow of Prince Henry of Battenberg, she was a 'charming
dignified old lady', nearly seventy years old, who maintained 'rigid obser-
vance of protocol'.[3] San Remo was also the centre of international tennis
and attracted many enthusiasts, including King Gustav V of Sweden.
While the Wheeler-Bennetts were visiting, the elderly monarch part-
nered the celebrated French champion Suzanne Lenglen, who had
recently retired after inadvertently keeping Queen Mary waiting at a
preliminary match at Wimbledon. At the ball that evening, Wheeler-
Bennett recalled dancing with twenty-seven-year-old Mademoiselle
Lenglen, who informed him that during her tennis match with King
Gustav 'she had several times had to enjoin her royal partner to keep
further to the left of the court, to which he had replied "You sound just
like my Prime Minister." '[4]

A month of Riviera sunshine restored Wheeler-Bennett's 'flagging
energies', and in mid-January he and his mother continued their journey,
setting off for Genoa en route for Egypt. 'We crossed to Alexandria in
what was then alleged to be the finest ship of the Lloyd Trestino line.'
But, 'far from being queen of the seas', the ship 'rolled like a porpoise'
until eventually it arrived at Alexandria. Travelling onwards to Cairo, the
Wheeler-Bennetts stayed at 'that famous caravanserai', Shepheard's Hotel.
'One could not sit for half an hour on its terrace without meeting at
least half a dozen friends and acquaintances, especially in winter.' It was,
Wheeler-Bennett recollected, 'a wondrous place and represented that
golden age when British paramountcy in Egypt went unchallenged'.
Mother and son followed the usual tourist itinerary: they went to the
Pyramids, saw the Sphinx by moonlight, as well as visiting the mosques
and the university – the oldest in the world; they spent hours in the
museum where, following the discovery of Tutankhamun's tomb by the

archaeologist Howard Carter in 1922, the 'fabulous treasures' were being displayed for the first time. Wheeler-Bennett's most vivid memory 'was the legendary hoof print on the battlement of the Citadel' of which it was said that, in 1811 in an attempt to escape massacre by Mehmet Ali, the governor of Egypt, the last of the Mameluke chieftains 'set his horse at the hideous jump into the abyss below, where both were dashed to pieces'.[5]

Wheeler-Bennett continued to collect friends in influential positions. Having first met Sir George Lloyd when he was governor of Bombay in 1922, when Wheeler-Bennett himself had been en route for Australia, he now renewed his acquaintance with him, Lloyd, having since been created 1st baron and appointed high commissioner in Cairo.[6] At the Residency they discussed Egyptian politics and Wheeler-Bennett appreciated the kindness of the older man, who talked 'at length to a young man whom he had only met fleetingly'. During this visit Lloyd arranged for Wheeler-Bennett to meet King Fuad, who, having succeeded his brother Hussein as sultan of Egypt in 1917, had become the first king of an independent Egypt in 1922.[7] 'The king was gracious but not over-whelmingly impressive,' said Wheeler-Bennett, added to which, before speaking, he barked like a dog. The young Englishman found this off-putting until he had the reason explained to him: 'after an attempt on his life, the assassin's bullet had wounded him in the throat with the result that his vocal cords, before beginning to function properly, cleared themselves by this strange process'.

After Cairo, they embarked on a Thomas Cook river steamer and made their way up the Nile to Luxor. One travelling companion was Lady Alexandra Metcalfe, Lord Curzon's daughter, and her husband, Captain Edward 'Fruity' Metcalfe, equerry and loyal friend of Edward, prince of Wales.[8] Like the Hotel Royal at San Remo, the Winter Palace Hotel at Luxor was 'filled with celebrities past and present'. One of these was 'foxy Ferdinand', the former tsar of Bulgaria – 'a portly person, pointed beard and well-trimmed moustache'. He had a cluster of ribbons and decorations in his buttonhole and wore white kid gloves, on the outside of which were a number of jewelled rings, as well as a gold and sapphire bracelet. Noting his 'bizarre appearance', Wheeler-Bennett acknowledged that he was an ornithologist of some repute and was assiduously studying desert bird life in Egypt.[9] Wheeler-Bennett and his mother also met two great Egyptologists – Professor James Henry Breasted, professor of Egyptology and Oriental history at the University of Chicago, who had directed the first expedition to Egypt and western Asia in 1919–20, and Sir Alan Gardiner, Britain's premier expert on ancient Egypt. 'With them and under their direction we explored the Valleys of the Kings and the Queens and the temples at Luxor and at Karnak. Like all great men who really know their subjects they were able to explain in simple language the fascinating wonders and mysteries of the Pharaohs with an ease and knowledge which made it all seem as if it happened yesterday.' Howard Carter, famed for discovering the tomb of Tutankhamun, was found by Wheeler-Bennett to be 'more formidable'.[10]

From Egypt, they travelled onwards to Ceylon (Sri Lanka), which they reached in March 1927. There they hired a car, which John, a young Tamil of 'agreeable disposition and considerable efficiency', drove in addition to looking after them. 'For the first of these jobs he wore brown cotton gloves, for the second white. He also slept outside the door at night.' Travelling south to Galle with its distinctive Dutch colonial architecture and natural harbour, and north to Adam's Peak, the mountain plateau sacred to Buddhists because of their belief that the Lord Buddha stepped across the Palk Straits, separating Ceylon from the Indian subcontinent, leaving his footprint there, they made Kandy their headquarters. From there, they visited the ruined city of Anuradhapura, Ceylon's capital in the fifth century BC and, in its heyday, comparable with Nineveh and Babylon in splendour and beauty; they also travelled to the hill station and health resort of Nurawa Eliya below the 8,000-foot Mt Pidurutalagala. Wheeler-Bennett found the altitude too high and felt ill. It was cold, wet and 'too much like England', so they did not prolong their stay.

After Ceylon, they took passage in the French ship the *D'Artagnan* and headed for Saigon in French Indo-China: 'Travelling French is very different from travelling British . . . especially at sea.' Much to the delight of the unathletic Wheeler-Bennett, there was 'no nonsense about organised deck sports and no attempt to invade one's privacy in any way'. It even took time before they spoke to their fellow passengers, but eventually they formed 'an affable relationship' with Henri Cosme, who was on his way to take up the post of counsellor in the French Embassy in

Peking (Beijing). An admirer of the former president and now prime minister of France, Raymond Poincairé, Cosme had a 'scorn and distrust for the League of Nations [that] was bitter in the extreme'. Since Wheeler-Bennett was still under the influence of the euphoria generated by the Locarno Treaties, he was not 'entirely in accordance' with Cosme's views.[11] The Wheeler-Bennetts found Indo-China pleasant but not very Oriental. The colonial system was prosperous and administered with 'seeming efficiency from Saigon; . . . there were quasi independent emperors in Cambodia and Annam and other subject princes who seemed to spend a considerable amount of time in Paris'. The Nationalist Communist movement was not taken seriously and French imperial influence seemed as secure and enduring as that of the British in other parts of the world. 'The French quarter of Saigon mirrored that of an unindustrialised French provincial city: there was a Grande Place, with Opera house, an excellent hotel, a cabaret, several pavement cafes and a cathedral; shops were smart and well stocked and dressmakers, though out of date in fashion, were sufficiently chic to please.' Thanks to Henri Cosme, they enjoyed some excellent cuisine. In the evenings 'smartly uniformed officers embellished the hotel and the cafes in company with their own or other people's wives'.

As they bade farewell to Cosme, he advised them not to stay long in China since the situation there was precarious. On 1 January 1927, Chiang Kai-shek had formally established his capital in Hankow and the English concession had been taken over by the Chinese. In Shanghai, an uneasy peace prevailed between the Chinese and the Shanghai International Settlement, which harboured the combined American and British concessions. The signatories (the United States, Britain, France, Italy and Japan) to the 1922 Washington Naval Treaty, which had been designed to relieve growing tensions in East Asia, had ordered their armed forces to Shanghai to defend their nationals.[12] As a result of Cosme's bleak portrait, Christina Wheeler-Bennett decided to go straight to Japan to benefit from the thermal baths at Miyanoshita, leaving her son to travel to China alone.

Arriving in Hong Kong, leased to Britain by the Chinese in 1898 for ninety-nine years, Wheeler-Bennett contacted the Chamber of Commerce, the South China Publicity Bureau and various military authorities to assess the prevailing atmosphere around Shanghai, where Chiang Kai-shek was engaged in a brutal campaign against his Communist opponents. On arrival in Shanghai, he found that the International Settlement had 'all the appearance of an armed fortress in a state of siege. Troops of some half dozen nationalities were to be seen in the streets and warships of as many navies lay at anchor on the broad bosom of the Yangtze river or moored along the Bund.'[13] It was, he said, this state of affairs that had prompted Cosme to advise his mother to go directly to Japan, 'and it was for similar reasons that I felt a thrill of excitement'. Undaunted by the visible proof of the Kuomintang's recent purge, which included seeing 'a decomposed communist head on every lamp post on the main thoroughfare', Wheeler-Bennett settled into the Astor House Hotel. His first priority was to get a really good 'boy'. The servant he found – Ah Foo – was one of the 'best' he had ever known, 'with the ageless good manners and courtesy of the Chinese of the older school . . . he could valet and launder and drive a car and wait at table all to perfection. . . He shopped for me and when we travelled he was efficient in making arrangements yet self effacing; on various occasions, when I was ill he looked after me with the tenderness of a mother and the efficiency of a nanny. He was a jewel.' The only drawback appeared to be Ah Foo's inability to pronounce his *r*s, which were substituted by *l*s; 'an invitation for fresh lice rather than rice . . . caused guests to recoil'.

Socially, there was 'immense gaiety coupled with prevalent uncertainty. As against the reassurance of troops and warships in the river, there was the silently hostile nationalist soldiery just beyond the boundaries of the International Settlement.' Trading and commerce were slack but there were 'parties galore'. One party Wheeler-Bennett recollected as being

out of this world . . . all deliciously foolishly romantic . . . British and American flagships were moored side by side with gangways connecting them. Both ships were decked with lights and flags and bunting and the quarter decks of both were cleaned and polished with French chalk until they could compete with any ballroom floor in the world. The two Admirals greeted their guests as we came on board from the Bund and handed us over to a mixed staff of ADCs resplendent in aiguillettes.

It was 'a fabulous spectacle with girls in ball dresses and jewels and men in naval and military mess uniform or civilians in white monkey jackets, with dancing and supper on each ship . . . The beams of the full moon and the stars were reflected in the deep flowing waters of the Yangtze river.'

Since the US navy was dry, the only 'official' drinking permitted was on board the British ship. Thinking back, Wheeler-Bennett realised that the gaiety, while being most enjoyable, only emphasised the curious sense of suspended activity. 'We seemed to be enclosed in a vacuum.' Everything appeared to depend upon Chiang Kai-shek's next move 'and yet no one seemed to be trying to find out what that move would be'. To gain some rudimentary understanding of the situation, Wheeler-Bennett visited the British and American Chambers of Commerce; he also met the American journalist Rodney Gilbert, editor of the *North China Morning News and Herald*, as well as James Powell, editor and founder of the pro-Nationalist *China Weekly Review*.[14] An exception to the average newspaperman, Powell, who had been in China for many years, was unashamedly pro-Chinese, warning Wheeler-Bennett that if he wanted to get around socially, 'don't let it be known that you've seen me or even that you know anything about me . . . I'm considered poison by all the old "China hands"'. As Wheeler-Bennett would recollect, it all sounded 'intriguingly melodramatic' but it was true: 'Powell had been virtually ostracised by many of the foreign community for his outspoken espousal of the nationalist cause.'

Characteristically, Wheeler-Bennett was more interested in learning about China than worrying about his compatriots' reaction and was happy to spend time with Powell. 'Thereupon he undertook my education and in a couple of meetings he opened to me the treasure house of his own rich experience.' On one occasion, Powell asked Wheeler-Bennett if he would like to go for a drive; no questions were to be asked. After proceeding for a while in silence, Powell turned to Wheeler-Bennett and informed him that they were leaving the International Settlement to see Chiang Kai-shek. 'I was beyond comment . . . a mile or two's drive over an almost non-existent road brought us to a small town and we stopped before the main building, a singularly unimpressive headquarters.' After a brief wait in a sparsely furnished anteroom, they were summoned into a larger room. 'Chairs were brought and we sat down in the presence of the future Generalissimo of China who was to negotiate on a basis of equality with Churchill and Roosevelt at the Cairo Conference of 1943 for the future of the Orient.'

Wheeler-Bennett considered that there was something 'Cromwellian' about Chiang Kai-shek and the New Model Army. 'He was imbued with the desire to destroy communism on the one hand and the chicanery of the archaic rule of the warlords on the other. There was much of the puritan about him and it was only later that he became an outstanding example of absolute power corrupting absolutely. When I met him on this summer morning he was a small, lean man with an enigmatic smile and a rather staccato way of speaking.' Wheeler-Bennett listened passively, leaving Powell to interview the Chinese leader. Each used an interpreter and spoke his own language. In answer to a question about the future of the International Settlement, Chiang maintained that the Nationalists had no designs upon either it or the French concession. He was, he said, fully occupied in consolidating the territory that he already held and in dealing with Communist opposition. Eventually, after ceremonial drinking of tea, the Westerners departed.

Back in the International Settlement, Wheeler-Bennett asked Powell what he proposed to do with the knowledge he had acquired. The latter replied that he would print it in his weekly paper and that it would be both 'disbelieved and ignored'. Wheeler-Bennett then asked whether Powell would mind 'if I wrote a report for our Consul General? "Not at all," he answered, "if I wished to waste my time."' As Wheeler-Bennett later noted, Powell was right about the report. 'The only result was a sharp rebuke for having committed an indiscretion in that by going to see Chiang I might have jeopardised the neutral status of the Settlement . . . whether my report had any further destination than the consular waste paper basket I do not know.' By the end of his time in China, Wheeler-Bennett had concluded that 'if only Chiang Kai-shek can shake off Bolshevism and curb the anti-foreign tendencies of his party, he would be by far the best man for China'.[15]

Accompanied by Ah Foo, Wheeler-Bennett next travelled to the city of Tientsin (Tianjin) at the northern end of the Grand Canal of China, connecting the Yellow and Yangtze rivers. The first part of their journey was by water, enlivened by an attack by the northern armies on the

Cantonese batteries and forts guarding the mouth of the Yangzte. 'The engagement lasted for three hours during which three direct hits were registered on the forts and none on the cruisers.'[16] Wheeler-Bennett would like to have caught 'a glimpse of the last of the Manchu emperors who, as Mr Pu Yi, was living in the Japanese concession, awaiting the call of destiny to become the puppet Emperor of Manchukuo'. But he was now anxious to reach Peking, where he stayed at the Grand Hotel de Peking, 'an admirable hostelry outside the Legation Quarter but within a short rickshaw ride of it. The rooms were large with private baths and immaculate linen.' In Peking he enjoyed the 'seemingly inexhaustible store of beauty, whether it was a pool of hyacinths and lotus flowers or a garden of chrysanthemums or a pillared temple or the elegance of a palace . . . I have found nothing else in the world to surpass the sublime peace of the Temple of Heaven or many treasured mysteries of the Forbidden City.' The British minister at the time was the distinguished diplomat Sir Miles Lampson. He and his wife, Rachel, 'were kindness itself'.[17] The United States minister, John McMurray, was 'a wise and experienced China Hand with a sense of humour and also humility'. Wheeler-Bennett also met John Marquand, 'who had rented a temple from a Chinese friend and was busily engaged in turning out his Mr Moto novels which predated James Bond by quarter of a century'.[18]

As Wheeler-Bennett discovered, diplomatic Peking presented a contrast with the smug self-sufficiency of Shanghai. Here, although there was concern at Chiang Kai-shek's nationalism, his hostility towards the Communists went in his favour. Wheeler-Bennett also found a much greater appreciation of the potential menace from Japanese aggression. 'There was no nonsense about treating the Japanese as "honorary Europeans".' He realised that the Japanese 'are very seriously concerned for the position of Japan's trade and political interests in China and feel that above all things they must support the winning side. They are terribly perplexed as to which this is to be.'[19] While in Peking, Wheeler-Bennett updated the 'Chronology of events in China from the Revolution of 1911 to the present time' which the Information Service had compiled before his departure. 'This I now had reprinted in Peking and distributed among the foreign community and legations.' His report for

the committee of management of the Association for International Understanding described how a 'curious fatalism' pervaded the atmosphere and
how it was generally accepted that the southern armies would eventually
reach Peking, 'the only question is how soon'. 'The British legation
shrewdly says "this year", the Americans think "this summer", the Japanese "next month", while the French say quite frankly that they don't
know.'[20]

Wheeler-Bennett did not neglect his sightseeing. Ah Foo was able to
procure one of the few available motor cars, in which they drove out
to the Ming Tombs.

> This group of temples and shrines, approached by their avenue of
> guardian beasts, is a thing of infinite elegance and loveliness, and has a
> store house of treasures far more beautiful to me than those discovered
> in the Egyptian burial grounds. There is a majesty about them . . . they
> are the greatest artistic monument to dynastic China and it is significant
> that when Sun Yat-sen was buried outside Nanking his tomb was built
> on the pattern of that of a Ming emperor.

What Wheeler-Bennett really wanted to see was the Great Wall, but
even Ah Foo's ingenuity was not up to the task of organising transporta-
tion, so Wheeler-Bennett had to persuade one of his Chinese friends to
'wangle' them permission to travel on an armoured troop train – 'an
initiative not viewed entirely favourably by the British legation'. Armed
with a portable gramophone and a case of records, with which Ah Foo
was burdened, as well as several cartons of cigarettes, Wheeler-Bennett
travelled in an open truck with 'other ranks' and had 'a wonderful time.
The troops gladly accepted the cigarettes and were delighted with the
waltz-tunes of the 20s . . . when we were eventually put down at the
station by the Wall we departed in a blizzard of good will.' Recollecting
his experiences later, Wheeler-Bennett considered the Great Wall of
China 'a masterpiece of engineering' – 20 feet high and 13 feet wide, it
was 'unequalled in grandeur and nobility'. Built in the third century BC
by Shih Huang-ti, the first emperor of the Ch'in dynasty, it represented
the 'splendid isolation of China and is one of the wonders of the
world . . . Fortified by watch towers every hundred yards or so, it winds

its way like a great snake over mountains and valleys and rivers for 1,400
miles.' Wheeler-Bennett went for a walk and eventually sat down 'spell-
bound amid the silence and the shadows of past centuries'. After an
excellent lunch, washed down by Kirin beer imported from Japan, they
departed on another armoured train, 'when we repeated our musical
turns with equal success'.

As Wheeler-Bennett realised, he had seen China at an unprecedented
moment in its history. Overall his opinion after three weeks in the
country was a positive one, despite his sensing a strong anti-foreign
feeling among the locals. 'I am convinced that it is not an inherent trait
in the Chinaman and is only the result of external foreign influence and
propaganda.'[21] Soon afterwards, he left Peking to rejoin his mother in
Japan, bidding an almost tearful farewell to Ah Foo, who was returning
to Shanghai. 'I promised that I would let him know if I ever returned
to China.' The journey from Tientsin to Mukden (Shenyang) was
'uneventful, uninteresting and uncomfortable'. The latter city was
'remarkable only for its tombs of early Manchu rulers and for massive
munitions works which were maintained there'. From Mukden, Wheeler-
Bennett travelled onwards on the South Manchurian Railway, by means
of which the Japanese would occupy Manchuria in 1931.

Before reaching Japan, he made a brief stop in Seoul, taking 'an instant
liking to Korean people'. With their curious top hats and flowing
garments, they seemed 'a pleasant and pastoral folk', apart from their
'consuming hatred of the Japanese who had dethroned their emperor and
annexed their country in 1910'. Although Wheeler-Bennett detected
there the air of an 'uneasy colony', there was nothing to suggest 'the
savage conflict which was to devastate the country 25 years later'. Travelling by night across the Tsushima Strait, where the last of the imperial
Russian navy was destroyed by the Japanese in 1904, he went immediately to Miyanoshita to rejoin his mother.

Wheeler-Bennett did not warm to Japan. 'For me it was a mistake to
go to Japan after rather than before I had been to China. Had I travelled
in reverse order I might have acquired a more pleasant memory.' As it
was, he was sadly disappointed. 'All that I had grown to love in China
was the negation of what I found in Japan. The great stretches of the
countryside, the softer, more intimate lines of architecture in China

contrasted disappointingly for me with the tidiness and greater severity
of Japan.' But he was pleased to find that his mother's physical complaints
had been eased by the healing springs of Myanoshita. It was now
late spring and the country was a blaze of azaleas and they enjoyed
the gardens of Kyoto. In Tokyo they saw Frank Lloyd Wright's innova-
tive creation, the Imperial Hotel, which had survived a devastating
earthquake in 1923. Wheeler-Bennett noted that politically Japan was
still under the influence of the liberal leadership which had led the
country out of feudalism. However, the postwar depression had been
accentuated not only by the 1923 earthquake but by the passage of
the 1924 American immigration law that excluded Asiatics from the
United States. Japanese honour been 'acutely affronted' and important
avenues of employment had been closed. There was, he recollected,
a tide of reaction rising against the liberals, marking 'the close of
that period during which Japan might have been described as a non-
aggressor state'.

Leaving Japan, the Wheeler-Bennetts sailed east from Yokohama; their
only port of call as they voyaged across the Pacific was Hawaii, where
'idyllic peace prevailed' and they spent the month of August. 'Here one
swam and lazed and surfed in a world apart, the old traditions predominating because there seemed to be no new ones to challenge them.'
There was no dancing, 'one simply sat and listened to the beach boys
singing to the accompaniment of ukuleles till the moon rose like a great
orb, casting a pathway of shimmering light across the calm waters of the
Pacific'. Wheeler-Bennett also recalled the romance of driving by moonlight up to the Pali Pass on the crest of the mountain, where legend told
how a Hawaiian king of ancient times had jumped to his death with the
remnant of his army rather than be captured by invaders. Their stay in
Hawaii coincided with the first non-stop air race from California to
Honolulu. In May 1927 Charles Lindbergh, the pioneering aviator,
had made a solo non-stop flight from New York to Paris, following
which James Dole, the Hawaiian pineapple magnate, had offered 'a
substantial purse' for the winner of a race from California to Hawaii. 'I
remember spending a somewhat uncomfortable night sitting in the base-
ball park which constituted the winning post waiting for the arrival of
the first plane . . . as dawn was breaking, a fragile little aircraft appeared

in the eastern sky and landed. The weary pilot was welcomed with rapturous applause and handed a handsome cheque from Mr Dole.'[22]

In Honolulu, Wheeler-Bennett had 'ample opportunity' to observe the operations of the Secretariat of the Institute of Pacific Relations, whose work he considered to be 'of very great value, second only perhaps to that of the League of Nations'. Arriving next in California, he divided his time between Los Angeles and San Francisco, where he met the veteran journalist and political reformer Chester Rowell at a luncheon hosted by the English-Speaking Union.[23] Included in the interesting information that Rowell shared with Wheeler-Bennett was a report of his conversation with the Soviet commissar for foreign affairs, Georgy Chicherin, relating to conditions the USSR would be prepared to nego-tiate to reinstate recognition by the USA following the severance of relations by Woodrow Wilson after the October 1917 Revolution.[24] Crossing the continent, mother and son stayed in Kansas City, Missouri, with a distant cousin, Dr Ross Hill, a trustee of the Carnegie Institute, whose wife was treasurer of the National Union of American University Women, 'a somewhat powerful organisation'; as Wheeler-Bennett proudly reported, the couple agreed to become members of the Association for International Understanding.

Travelling east to Chicago, Wheeler-Bennett met Salmon Oliver Levinson, the lawyer, now in his early sixties, who had originated the 'outlawry of war' movement in the United States.[25] Wheeler-Bennett was still clinging to the authority of the League of Nations and found it difficult to believe that Levinson's 'scheme for an international panacea, which provides for compulsory arbitration only after international law has been definitely codified and in which the only provision for sanctions is that each country shall punish its own "war breeders", can ever be an effective substitute'. Progressing onwards, the Wheeler-Bennetts crossed into eastern Canada. There they stayed with Sir Joseph Flavelle, Wheeler-Bennett's father's business partner and, as Wheeler-Bennett proudly asserted to Macdonogh, chairman of the Association for International Understanding (AIU)'s committee of management, the 'first life member of the A.I.U.' 'He very generously offered to make a further contribution to the funds of the Association, the amount to be settled between ourselves later.'[26] Travelling on to Ottawa and Montreal, in all his meetings

Wheeler-Bennett was propagating the concept of international understanding which was to become the hallmark of his future interests.

In Boston, most of his time was spent with the World Peace
Foundation. He also had 'several long conversations' with Professor
Manley O. Hudson of the Harvard Law School and visited the Boston
offices of the Foreign Policy Association and of the League of Nations
Non-Partisan Association. In Washington, D.C., his principal interview
was with the Republican senator William E. Borah, chairman of the Senate
Foreign Relations Committee and well known for his pro-Soviet views,
who maintained that 'he did not fear the result of Communist propaganda
on the hard-headed American farmer and artisan'.[27] After numerous discussions in New York, as well as a visit to the British Library of Information,
a small branch of the Foreign Office News Department, Wheeler-Bennett's
considered view was that 'opinion would seem to differ as to the real state
of mind with regard to the League and the International Court of Justice
in America. The League of Nations Non-Partisan Association assured me
that politically speaking both were dead issues and that neither party would
mention either on its election platform . . . They said however that at no
time since the Armistice was there so keen a public interest in international
affairs generally and in the League in particular.' Finally he concluded that,
throughout his tour of Canada and the United States, he had encountered
'sustained enthusiasm and encouragement in the work of the Association'.[28] Mother and son were back in England by late November 1927,
having been away for nearly a year.

By the time he returned, the third volume in the Information Series,
Information on the Problem of Security 1917–1926, written by Wheeler-
Bennett and F.E. Langermann, the Association's 'Intelligence Secretary',
had been published; this time the Rt Hon. H.A.L. Fisher, warden of New
College and a former president of the Board of Education, supplied the
introduction. Yet again the national press praised it as a 'model of the
manner in which such a book should be written'. 'As a work of reference
this book is invaluable. No one interested in the problem of disarmament
should be without it,' proffered *The Nation* newspaper.[29]

In May 1928, Wheeler-Bennett saw what was to become his future
home, Garsington Manor, an Elizabethan stone manor house in the
village of Garsington, near Oxford. Its former owners, who had bought

the house in 1913, were Philip and Lady Ottoline Morrell, notorious for their open marriage and extra-marital affairs, and parodied in D.H. Lawrence's *Women in Love*. Restoring the house from a near-dilapidated state, they had laid out the gardens in formal Italian style, with statues and peacocks, making Garsington one of the 'prettiest, pleasantest and least spoilt small manor houses in England'.[30] Pacifists during the Great War, their home had served as a refuge for like-minded individuals, including Lytton Strachey and Siegfried Sassoon. Then financial difficulties in the 1920s meant they had to put the house up for sale. Wheeler-Bennett's sister, Irene, and her husband Trevor now had three children – their third, another daughter, Juliet, was born in December 1927 – and they had outgrown their Christ Church accommodation in St Giles. One afternoon, therefore, Wheeler-Bennett accompanied his sister and her husband to Garsington to view the property. 'The sun was shining and the beauty of it was breathtaking,' Irene recalled, although Wheeler-Bennett complained that the décor of the Red Room, with pillarbox-red panels, curtains of canary yellow, lilac and yellow rugs and furniture of red lacquer, was 'obscene'.[31] Once the necessary alterations had been completed, Irene and her family moved in at the end of 1928.

In late August 1928, Wheeler-Bennett embarked on a seven-week tour of Europe in pursuit of new information. His final destination was Prague, where he was to represent the Association for International Understanding as well as the RIIA as a delegate from 'the British group of Interested Persons'. His first stop was Paris – his favourite city after London and New York – to attend the signing of the General Treaty for the Renunciation of War, drafted by Aristide Briand, France's foreign minister, and the American secretary of state, Frank Kellogg. Having taken an interest in Kellogg's statement of policy when addressing the Council of Foreign Relations in New York earlier in the year, Wheeler-Bennett had written a letter to *The Times*.

> Sir, The American concession to the French reservations is embodied in the third paragraph of the revised Preamble to the Draft Treaty for the Renunciation of War, in the following words:–
>
> Convinced that all changes in their relations with one another should be sought only by pacific means, and be the result of a peaceful and

orderly process, and that any signatory power which shall hereafter seek
to promote its national interests by resort to war should be denied the
benefits furnished by this Treaty.

Mr Kellogg in the course of a speech before the Council on Foreign
Relations in New York on March 15, 1928, committed himself to the
definite statement that 'a Preamble is not a binding part of a treaty.' I
believe this point to be of the greatest importance in connexion with
the relation of the proposed Treaty for the renunciation of war to the
Covenant of the League of Nations and the Locarno Agreement.[32]

Convinced that 'legal luminaries' at the Foreign Office in London or in
Paris might also have picked up on Kellogg's comments, Wheeler-
Bennett was delighted to receive a personal letter of thanks from Briand
and an invitation to attend the signing ceremony, held in the Salle de
l'Horloge of the Quai d'Orsay, where, a decade previously, the Covenant
of the League of Nations had been adopted.[33] Writing in later life,
Wheeler-Bennett was hard put to find in history a 'greater monument
of cynical futility' than the Kellogg–Briand Pact. 'Kellogg was probably
alone among his fellow signatories in believing heart and soul in the
potential power of the Pact of Paris to bring about a war-less world.'[34]

As became his habit, 'being a political animal and ever hot upon the
trail of information', he made friends with journalists and civil servants
while in Paris.[35] One of the latter was Ralph Wigram, the first secretary
at the British Embassy, one of the first civil servants to warn about
German rearmament.[36] Of the newspaper correspondents, Wheeler-
Bennett particularly recollected the French philosopher and economist,
Bertrand de Jouvenel, who later became private secretary to the
Czechoslovakian prime minister Edvard Beneš. He also remembered
Geneviève Tabouis, 'petite, attractive, gallant and indefatigable. She never
seemed to rest and she seemed to be everywhere at once . . . wherever
there was a story to be had.'[37] Perhaps because she had been present at
the signing of the Locarno treaties, and repeatedly warned about the rise
of Hitler and German rearmament, Wheeler-Bennett felt he had a special
affinity with her. After Paris, Wheeler-Bennett spent a week in Geneva,
where he was present at six plenary sessions of the League of Nations'
Assembly and several meetings of commissions. 'As a result of the

courtesy of the League officials, I was provided with a seat in the diplomatic Gallery and also with a press pass which enabled me to secure the necessary League documents which were issued.'

On 12 September, he was joined by his colleague Stephen Heald, who accompanied him on the rest of the tour. In Vienna, a common topic of debate was the possibility of an 'Anschluss' with Germany. After listening to a wide range of views, Wheeler-Bennett declared that nearly every Austrian

> believes in his heart that the Anschluss is inevitable . . . The Austrian policy, therefore, is twofold, first to create by means of propaganda in Europe a state of mind sympathetic towards the idea of an Austro-German Union and secondly, by so standardising the laws, tariffs, customs etc of the two countries, that the Anschluss will exist in fact if not in name. This latter they claim will have been achieved in roughly ten years time after which, they say, they can afford to wait until the effect of their propaganda campaign shall have produced the required result. They claim that in Austria 99 per cent and in Germany 80 per cent are in favour of the Anschluss, but I greatly doubt the accuracy of this estimation. I would say that not more than 75% of Austrians desire union with Germany but that nearly all regard it as an inevitability.

As Wheeler-Bennett wrote in his report for the committee of management of the Association for International Understanding, there was a feeling of depression in Vienna, which was only 'thinly veiled under a superficial gaiety', as if the national spirit had been broken. Those who favoured the Anschluss regarded Czechoslovakia as the main obstacle, 'but are assured that if Great Britain can influence France in favour of the union, this would automatically bring about the consent of Czechoslovakia. They set great store by the attitude of Great Britain towards the problem and are anxious to keep the British Public informed on this point.'[38]

In later life, what Wheeler-Bennett remembered most about Vienna were the 'four great ladies' who had survived the 'deluge' of the Great War and the break-up of the Austro-Hungarian Empire 'to resume their lives adaptably under the new regime'. First among these was Princess

Stéphanie Lónyay, widow of the crown prince, Archduke Rudolf, and
daughter of King Leopold II of the Belgians, who had gone on to marry
Count Elmér Lónyay. The second was Archduchess Elisabeth Marie,
(known as 'Erzsi'), Stéphanie's daughter by Rudolf. Since she was a card-
carrying member of the Austrian Socialist Party, Wheeler-Bennett was
intrigued by her domestic surroundings, 'where relics of her past jostled
with evidence of her present life. Revolutionary literature and an imperial snuff-box occupied adjoining shelves.'[39] The third was the actress
Katharina Schratt, selected by Empress Elisabeth as a companion for her
husband, Emperor Franz Joseph I, 'while she indulged in what virtually
amounted to a mania for almost constant travel and sojourn abroad'.[40]
What impressed Wheeler-Bennett about Schratt, now in her seventies,
was her 'chic of conduct'. Although representatives of newspaper propri-
etors, including William Randolph Hearst, 'grovelled before her for an
interview . . . never a word' about her relationship with the emperor
escaped her lips. The fourth of Wheeler-Bennett's great ladies was Frau
Sacher, one of the world's great *hotelières*. 'The whole ambience of
"Sacher's" was something to be savoured, cherished and remembered.'
While he would relate the various bits of scandal recollected from his
early reading of Coxe's *House of Austria* at Malvern, Frau Sacher would
tell her English guest stories about the Austrian aristocracy 'with great
freedom though never with positive malice or indiscretion'.[41]

After Vienna, Wheeler-Bennett went on to Budapest, where he found
that the main topic of conversation was whether the Treaty of Trianon,
concluding peace between the Allies and Austria-Hungary in 1918,
should be revised. According to what he heard, there were three schools
of thought: the first, represented by the large landowners, the nobility
and conservatives, was the so-called 'Integrity School which calls for the
complete restitution of the Old Hungary as a geographical whole' and
which would return to Hungary the two-thirds of its territory that it had
lost; the second school, of which the principal exponent was the former
justice minister, Emil Nagy, 'is endeavouring to secure the revision of
the frontiers, to recreate Hungary as an ethnographical entity. Midway
between these two is a third and, I understand, less important group,
which, while supporting the ethnographical school, calls also for at least
the local autonomy of the large group of Hungarians in Transylvania and

the creation of a corridor connecting this group with the central Hungarian bloc.' To Wheeler-Bennett, the most plausible was the second option. From Budapest, Wheeler-Bennett travelled to Prague. 'Through the kindness of the British delegation I was allowed to attend the two sessions of the Council of the International Federation of League of Nations Societies.' He also attended the International Economic Conference convened by the International Federation of League of Nations Societies to consider progress made by various countries in carrying out the recommendations of the 1927 World Economic Conference held in Geneva.

In Germany, Wheeler-Bennett met Harold Nicolson, who had arrived at the British Embassy in Berlin in October 1927 as chargé d'affaires, later becoming counsellor. Nicolson had already published a biography of the French poet Paul Verlaine, as well as of Tennyson and Byron, and the two men became friends.[42] According to Wheeler-Bennett's memoirs, when asked by Nicolson, either on this visit or the following year, whom he would most like to see, Wheeler-Bennett did not hesitate to suggest General Hans von Seeckt, former commander-in-chief of the German army, the Reichswehr.[43] He believed that Seeckt and General Max Hoffmann were 'the two ablest soldiers whom Germany had produced during the war'. Hoffmann, he thought, deserved the 'strategic laurels' for the Russian defeat at Tannenberg, since he was the senior staff officer, rather than Ludendorff or Hindenburg.[44]

Wheeler-Bennett did not relate exactly how Nicolson convinced General von Seeckt to grant an interview to the young and relatively unknown British gentleman, but he 'was as good as his word'. He duly received a message that the German general would see him at eleven o'clock the following day. As Wheeler-Bennett recalled, his admiration for Seeckt was based on 'the fact that he had shown brilliant leadership in both victory and defeat. His highly successful use of the "breakthrough" tactics at Gorlice on the Eastern Front had broken the deadlock of trench warfare.' It was therefore 'with some trepidation' that he rang the doorbell of Seeckt's flat on the Lichtensteinallee. Ushered into a room 'decorated with bronzes of horses and naked warriors and elk-horns', Wheeler-Bennett waited until General von Seeckt, in civilian clothes, made his 'dramatic' entry. 'At first glance he seemed like a typical Prussian officer, with his thin, red turkey-neck, his inscrutable face and its inevitable monocle.' Once Wheeler-Bennett had introduced himself as a historian and 'an observer of men and events', Seeckt revealed his skills as a raconteur. Mention of the word 'Gorlice' proved the 'open sesame' to 'a cavern of precious jewels'. Not only did Seeckt give a first-hand account of the German victory over the Russians there during the Great War but 'an acrid and abrasive estimate of Hindenburg and Luden-dorff as military strategists . . . he spoke vividly, with precision and without hyperbole'. After over two hours, including lunch with the general and his wife (rather than the ten minutes he had anticipated), Wheeler-Bennett took his leave; this was the beginning of a surprisingly friendly relationship. Wheeler-Bennett's admiration was for Seeckt and not for his wife. In his opinion, it was the politically ambitious Frau von Seeckt, who wanted her husband to succeed Hindenburg as chancellor and who was later responsible for propelling him into the 'Nazi orbit'.[45]

During his Berlin visit in 1928, Wheeler-Bennett also met a number of diplomats from the German Foreign Office and Ministry of the Interior. One such was the general secretary of the Deutsche Kolonialgesell-schaft (German Colonial Society), who explained that the society's aims were to encourage interest in Germany in colonial affairs, to explain the economic necessity of the possession of colonies by Germany and to gain support among the German people as well as fostering 'Germanism' in ex-German colonies, especially in South-West Africa (i.e. Namibia) and East Africa. Wheeler-Bennett diligently wrote up his report for the committee of management so that it would be ready in time for the committee meeting and praised the 'excellent services' that he had consistently received from Stephen Heald. 'His knowledge of the German language and the able assistance which he has rendered me on every occasion has contributed very materially to the amount of information which I have been able to obtain.'[46]

Back in Paris, Wheeler-Bennett went to see Florence Wilson of the European Centre of the Carnegie Endowment, 'with the view to their placing an order for a large number of the Information Service's publication *Information on the Renunciation of War 1927–1928*, which was to be the fourth book in the Information Series'.[47] Published in November 1928, by which time Wheeler-Bennett was in London, the book was well received. 'Here is the Paris Pact complete, speeches and documents, with a minimum of commentary, and Mr Wheeler-Bennett deserves our heartfelt thanks,' opined *The Spectator*. An eminent historian, Philip Kerr|| *Lothian* (later Lord Lothian), wrote the introduction.[48] An additional project was editing the first volume of *Documents on International Affairs*, a publication which fell under the auspices of Chatham House.[49]

In January 1929, Wheeler-Bennett had the opportunity to travel once more to the Orient. This time he was acting as the personal assistant of Sir Neill Malcolm, who, while remaining chairman of Chatham House, had taken up an appointment as president of the Court of Directors of the British North Borneo Chartered Company, 'one of the last of those great mercantile concerns which, operating under Royal Charter, played so important a role in the expansion of empire'. In view of the respect and friendship that Wheeler-Bennett already had for the older man, he was 'flattered' to be invited. An added incentive was that they would be visiting Borneo and the Philippines, which represented 'new territory' for Wheeler-Bennett. Furthermore, Malcolm was proposing to return to Europe via the Trans-Siberian Railway, 'brainchild of Tsar Nicholas II's great minister, Count Witte'.[50] Wheeler-Bennett appreciated Malcolm's kindness:

> He was wonderfully considerate and patient with a somewhat preco-
> cious young man who always wanted to ask something but stammered
> badly – for I was still in the grip of that hideous affliction which I had
> acquired during the First World War. He was never impatient or irri-
> table in the face of my disability nor was he aggressively helpful in
> supplying a blocked word. He just waited for me to get it out. If for
> nothing else but this my gratitude was overflowing.

Departing by ship from Marseille, both had well-filled book boxes, the contents of which they shared with one another. For the first time Wheeler-Bennett was introduced to the nineteenth-century diarists Thomas Creevy, John Wilson Croker and Charles Greville. The latter had written an account of the 1866 Austro-Prussian War and was recog-nised as an authority on the American Civil War. 'Since the confederacy and army of Northern Virginia was my special hobby it may be imagined //

what profit and pleasure I derived from our long talks by sea and rail.'[51] Since it had only been two years since his last visit to China, he was confident of again being able to call upon the services of Ah Foo. 'I had written to him and sent his passage money from Shanghai and there he was on the dock at Singapore to greet us.' On this occasion, Wheeler-Bennett saw the island fortress, where guns had recently been installed for its protection, from a different perspective. No longer an 'inmate' of Raffles Hotel, where he had stayed with his mother, he got to know the 'inner workings' of Government House and also enjoyed 'a greater intimacy with the powerful Chinese magnates' who ran at least two-thirds of the great business concerns in Malaya and whom Malcolm knew from his time as General Officer Commanding the Troops in the Straits settlements in Singapore in the early 1920s. 'I lived in the most magnificent official residence in the world, was treated with great courtesy and consideration by the then Governor, Sir Hugh Clifford.'[52]

There was, however, an incident at dinner one day when the atmosphere suddenly turned decidedly cool. 'When the men were left at table, I confess somewhat to my perturbation, Sir Hugh beckoned Neill Malcolm to sit on his right and me on his left. Cigars and brandy were passed and no one had told me that a special box and a special bottle were reserved for His Excellency's special use only and whose contents were better quality than those offered to his guests.' Wheeler-Bennett then made his 'first bêtise' by indicating his preference for the better brand of cognac. 'I thought I detected a certain hissing intake of breath from the ADC at the end of the table but I saw no reason why I shouldn't have the best brandy since no one had told me that I shouldn't. I also selected one of the best cigars. His Excellency had been talking to Neill Malcolm when the first of these transgressions occurred, but he turned to me just as I had got my cigar well and truly drawing.' As Wheeler-Bennett recollected, there was 'a shocked silence'.

'Young man,' said His Excellency, 'let me tell you that you are smoking one of my cigars.' Since it would appear that all the cigars belonged to him, it seemed to me that this was an almost unanswerable remark; however, I thanked him with all due courtesy. 'And I suppose you took some of my brandy too?' he thundered. By this time the storm warnings from each end of the table were beginning to register and I noted a slightly sardonic smile on Neill Malcolm's face, as he wondered how I should get out of my dilemma. Shaken but having no means of escape, I determined to brazen it out. 'Yes, Sir,' I said, 'and it's a very fine brandy [Napoleon 1868].' 'Indeed it is', said this terrifying pro-consul. 'Are you man enough to enjoy a cigar and brandy of that calibre.' 'Oh yes, I think so, Sir' I answered, 'Sir Neill has really trained me very well.' The tension eased instantly. HE [His Excellency] let out a whoop of laughter and was appeased. Sir Neill was delighted and the ADCs resumed their normal breathing, for they had forgotten to warn me in advance of this discrimination on the part of their Master and would have suffered accordingly. What is more, I made free of Hugh Clifford's cigar box and brandy bottle for the rest of my stay.

Proceeding onwards some six hundred miles 'in an absurdly small and rather evil-smelling ship of Chinese ownership', their arrival at Jesselton, the main western port of Borneo, was 'spectacular'. The governor came on board to be greeted by Malcolm:

in all the glory of the full tropical uniform of a Major-General. With the star and cross of a Knight of the Bath, several rows of medal ribbons and decorations beginning with the DSO and the Legion of Honour, with sword and sword belt and crowned by a topee surmounted by a plume of red and white cock's feathers, he looked very impressive, as he stepped ashore to be greeted by a double row of local dignitaries, headed by the Colonial Secretary and the Officer Commanding the local garrison.

Amid such finery, Wheeler-Bennett felt 'a little anti-climactic in my simple suit of white drill'. Acting as Malcolm's PA, one of his first responsibilities was to oversee the safe disembarkation of the official motor car. It was the first car ever to be seen in Borneo. 'I confess that I had expected something of a scene, a vision of awe-struck and terrified natives bowing down before this snorting juggernaut or running into the jungle to escape the evident manifestation of evil spirits.' But the villagers were less interested than he had anticipated.

Wheeler-Bennett's time in Borneo was 'sheer delight'. His duties were not 'over burdensome'. They consisted of looking after Malcolm's official correspondence, drafting replies to letters, preparing memoranda for ultimate transmission to London and the outlines of speeches at official functions, as well as watching 'endless' football and cricket matches. He also accompanied Malcolm on trips to various commercial enterprises. The 'highpoint' was a week's journey on horseback across country from Jesselton to Sandakan. Malcolm had said he had always wanted to do this and feared that, already aged sixty, by his next visit he would be too lame to ride. 'I can remember few experiences which gave me greater pleasure,' recalled Wheeler-Bennett. 'The trails were beautiful and varied with tree orchids growing beside the track and flame of forest trees blazing above us. A colony of monkeys would swing from tree to tree, a flight of vividly tinted parrots would sweep in a rainbow of colour across our path and at each ford at which we halted there would be a shimmering cloud of large butterflies of flashing blues and reds and yellows.' In this 'paradise unspoiled by man', considerable comfort was provided by the camp followers, including Ah Foo. 'Tents, beds, tables and chairs miraculously appeared or we might spend a night as guests of a local district officer.' Starting very early in the morning, they rode until noon, with a break in mid morning 'for refreshment from green cocoa nuts providing a refreshing drink'.

One episode caused embarrassment.

It was a blazing hot day and we halted at noon beside a stream which seemed to gush out of the very heart of the mountain. The one thing I most wanted at that moment was a swim before lunch and in a trice I had stripped and plunged in. I sank like a stone; the water, mountain pure, was also ice cold. The shock caused my heart to stop beating and it was with difficulty that I was pulled onto the bank and given artificial respiration. When I came round it was to find brandy being poured down my throat and Ah Foo clucking over me like an old hen.

For some time afterwards, Malcolm asserted that Wheeler-Bennett's first coherent remark was: 'That's not the Napoleon brandy, I hope, I can't do justice to it, I'm afraid.'

The routine in Sandakan was much the same as in Jesselton, with the exception of one 'mildly exciting' interlude. Goods and drugs were being smuggled down the river and some action was required. 'The chief of Police asked me if I would like to go out with a police patrol launch in an attempt to intercept the miscreants. Of course I was delighted; even at the age of 26, I was school boy enough to be caught by the excitement of chasing smugglers and I spent three days in one of their motor craft, cruising by night on a broad stream where mangrove swamps came down to the river's edge.' The police were armed with rifles and Wheeler-Bennett carried an automatic, 'with which, had I been called upon to use it, I should doubtless have been far more of a danger to myself or my friends than to the smugglers'. On the third night, to Wheeler-Bennett's disappointment, the cornered miscreants surrendered without a fight.

Soon afterwards, Neill Malcolm gave Wheeler-Bennett an assignment in the Philippines concerning a horse-breeding deal between the North Borneo and Philippine governments, which had got bogged down in 'a sea of obscurities'. Sailing some three hundred miles in the governor's yacht – a two-masted schooner – from Sandakan to Zamboanga, he should have completed the journey in about three days, but the yacht's propeller fell off. 'We were becalmed in windless waveless sea like nothing so much as a painted ship upon a painted ocean.' Once the wind picked up, they had to return to Borneo for another propeller, before resuming the journey to the Philippines. After resolving the horse-breeding problem in Zamboanga ('somebody somewhere along the line was not getting his requisite "squeeze"'), Wheeler-Bennett was able to explore, spending five days in Baguio, the summer capital of the islands, and the remaining two weeks in and around Manila. 'At the time I was there the country was emerging from one stage of autonomy towards another. Behind it lay a period of military government established by the United States after acquiring the islands from Spain in 1898 at the end of the war for the sum of $20,000,000. – It was no mean deal when one remembers that Puerto Rico and Guam were thrown in for good measure.'

In 1929, the governor-general of the Philippines was Dwight Davis, secretary of war in President Coolidge's cabinet, who became internationally known as the founder of the International Lawn Tennis

Challenge, later renamed the Davis Cup in his honour. While Wheeler-
Bennett was there, he met Manuel Quezon, destined to be the first
president of the Commonwealth of the Philippines – currently president
of the Philippines Senate – and his future vice-president, Sergio Osmena,
who also later became president.[53] Even more memorable was meeting
the 'legendary figure' of Philippine history, Emilio Aguinaldo, regarded
by Filipinos as their first and youngest president, although his government
had failed to gain international recognition. As a young man, Aguinaldo
had raised the standard of independence after the American victory over
the Spanish, fighting a fierce guerrilla war against US forces until he was
captured in 1901. Since then he had lived in 'dignified' retirement and
was reluctant to see foreigners. But he was 'kind enough' to receive
Wheeler-Bennett and 'for an hour or more this remarkable figure from
the past regaled me with stories of his struggle against the US cavalry
and inveighed against the perfidy of the American government, who he
said had first promised his country independence in return for revolt
against Spain and had then reneged on its promise'.[54]

When Wheeler-Bennett came to write his report for the committee
of management, he was sanguine about the Philippines' future prospects.
'As regards the independence issue, the feeling may be fairly divided into
three categories: a majority who want immediate, complete and absolute
independence; a large minority who, while desirous of ultimate independence, realise that they are not yet suited for it; a smaller minority who
desire permanent annexation by the USA . . . While accepting the general
desire of the Philippine people for independence, there remains the question of the intention of the United States to grant it.' Wheeler-Bennett,
however, was wrong in his remarks about Japan: 'With regard to the
Japanese menace, I do not believe that Japan would attempt to create a
political domination or to annex the islands. The Japanese are not good
colonisers and do not thrive in tropical countries.'[55]

Their next stop was Hong Kong. 'To be back in China, even the
peripheral atmosphere of Hong Kong was a joy to me. We did not stay
long but there was certain business of the Chartered Company to be
transacted', which resulted in a lunch invitation from Sir Robert Ho-tung,
who had begun his career as a 'comprado' or manager in the powerful
British trading company Jardine, Matheson & Co., and was now among

the most respected and richest men in Hong Kong.[56] As they discovered, the political situation was static. Chiang Kai-shek and the Nationalists had consolidated the territory south of the Yangtze and established the Kuomintang government in Nanking (Nanjing). From Hong Kong, Wheeler-Bennett accompanied Malcolm to Shanghai, where he found that the international defence force had now been withdrawn and 'no obstacles or concerns seemed to trammel the even tenor of the settlement'. But an hour's conversation with James Powell was sufficient to deflate any optimism. As Powell said, it was only a matter of time before the Japanese moved into Manchuria and Peking. 'He was as usual correct.'[57] In Shanghai, Wheeler-Bennett met the 'notorious' Colonel Max Bauer, who had been General Erich Ludendorff's chief of operations during the Great War. In 1920, he had been involved in the Kapp Putsch to overthrow the new German Republic. When the coup failed, he had escaped to China, officially becoming Chiang's economic and military adviser and assisting with training and intelligence. Not long after their meeting, in May 1929, Bauer died of smallpox, the infection suspected to have been the handiwork of Chiang's enemies. He was buried in China with full military honours.[58]

Their next destination was Nanking, where Malcolm was to discuss 'affairs of state' with the Nationalist government. As a result, they received VIP treatment, which meant being flown to their destination in a Chinese aircraft. 'Flying even in 1929 was not too advanced and our plane was far from the most comfortable, nor did it seem to me the most secure. Malcolm was fatalistic – I expected the plane to fall to pieces at any moment. The pilot would take both hands off the controls and with pretty good English turn round and discourse with Malcolm on some obscure aspect of philosophy.' The experience left Wheeler-Bennett wishing that he had gone by train with Ah Foo and the baggage. 'It was a very pallid personal assistant who followed his chief out of the aircraft on our arrival.' Wheeler-Bennett found that Nanking was 'practically untouched by modern progress . . . its one concession to modernity was a hotel. The streets were packed with shouting rickshaw coolies, snorting water-buffaloes, shrieking women and children and yelling men. Through this mob our driver ploughed his way by the simple method of keeping his hand clamped to the horn.' Much to their surprise, in the middle of

Nanking, capital of Nationalist China, they were confronted by a large granite building, executed in Scottish baronial style, complete with pepper-pot turrets. 'I had to shut my eyes and look again to make sure it was true and I was relieved to see that even Neill Malcolm was a little startled.' This was their hotel, owned by a Briton who had been running it for a number of years and had survived 'all manner of adventures, good and bad, including, he told us, being raped by Chinese soldiery when Nanking was occupied by the victorious Nationalist army'.

Chiang Kai-shek was not in Nanking during their visit, but Malcolm's business was with the 'very astute and sophisticated' foreign minister, C.T. Wang (Wang Cheng-T'ing).[59] Both excellent players, Malcolm and Wang spent their evenings playing bridge with partners drawn from Wang's staff; as a result, Wheeler-Bennett noted a 'good amity' between them. Meanwhile, he enjoyed some leave. Furnished with a motor car and a soldier driver 'armed to the teeth with rifle and bayonet and what looked like several hand grenades', he set off with Ah Foo in front, 'me in solitary state behind'. Wheeler-Bennett wanted to visit the tomb of Sun Yat-sen just outside Nanking. It was an 'impressive and beautiful mausoleum with just the hint of a Ming tomb about it, and within lay the body of the revered father of the revolution in a glass coffin similar to that of Lenin in Red Square'. According to a prevailing rumour, on Sun Yat-sen's death in 1925, the Soviet government had offered a glass coffin in the style of Lenin's as a tribute to a great fellow revolutionary. The gift was accepted and the casket arrived; however, when relations soured, the gift was followed by a bill.

From Nanking the two men resumed their journey by train to Peking, where Wheeler-Bennett spent time among the treasures of the Forbidden City. At last, as they headed for Japan, it was time to bid farewell to Ah Foo at Tientsin – for, as it would prove, the last time: 'He will ever remain in my heart as the most complete example of a devoted and efficient servant.'

Wheeler-Bennett's second visit to Japan was conditioned by business that Malcolm had to transact on behalf of the Chartered Company with the ministers of foreign affairs and commerce, which left Wheeler-Bennett free to see some of the 'liberal' friends he had met two years previously. 'I found them just that degree more depressed and anxious as to where the pursuit of the new policy of overseas expansion was going to lead them.' As he later realised, 'some were already under the shadow of assassination'. The following year there was an attempt on the life of the prime minister, Osachi Hamaguchi; although he survived, he was physically weakened and resigned in 1931, dying soon afterwards.[60] As a result of Malcolm's successful negotiations, they were granted the honour of an imperial audience. Neither Malcolm nor Wheeler-Bennett was sartorially prepared, but the local Moss Bros. came to their aid 'and turned us out in two well fitting morning dress suits'. The audience was 'formality distilled and personified'. Emperor Hirohito – only a year older than Wheeler-Bennett – received his guests standing: 'a longish speech was read on his behalf by a court official in Japanese and English. Another courtier read a reply on behalf of Neill Malcolm in both languages. Bows were exchanged. We then bowed again and the thing was over.'[61]

The two men next embarked on the longest railway journey Wheeler-Bennett ever made – a distance of some seven thousand miles – from Tokyo to London via Siberia, which he described as 'no mean jaunt', involving several changes, two different gauges and a brief sea voyage across the North Sea. The first stage, via the Japanese State Railway and South Manchurian Railway, was 'old hat', since Wheeler-Bennett had taken the same route in 1927, but beyond Mukden it was 'terra incognita'. In Mukden, Wheeler-Bennett managed to buy a magnificent sculpture of a horse dating from the T'ang dynasty, when the Chinese spent their lives in the saddle, fighting the barbarians.[62]

Their next stop was Harbin, 'a wild mad city' populated more by White Russians than Chinese, and where the culture of imperial Russia still survived, though perhaps 'a little ragged and tawdry: a sort of poor man's Petersburg in an oriental setting. There were night clubs galore and handsome girls performing in them; there was an officers' club where full protocol and precedence of rank and seniority was scrupulously observed; there were restaurants where caviar and blinis and most varied sekuska were washed down with copious drafts of vodka and champagne.' Although he found that the shops were filled with relics of past glories – ikons, samovars and jewels, books in all languages – he, alas, realised that such treasures were not for those who were planning to continue their journey across the Soviet Union.

At Harbin, they changed from the South Manchurian Railway to the Chinese Eastern Railway. As both men had been warned, the latter 'could be depended upon to feed one adequately, but no such hopes could be entertained' once they changed trains to take the Trans-Siberian. Before continuing their journey, therefore, they filled two enormous hampers with 'game pies and cold chickens and quantities of tinned foods, gallons of vodka and pounds of caviar'. When Malcolm saw that Wheeler-Bennett had a copy of Leon Trotsky's *The History of the Russian Revolution*, he firmly advised leaving it behind.[63] From Harbin, they continued their journey to the frontier. 'The arrival of our train coincided with that of the Trans-Siberian Express and utter pandemonium at once broke loose. There were those who wished to leave Manchuria and those who wished to enter it as well as those who were evidently "wanted" by the police on either side. Those whose activities were suspect to the customs and passport control authorities of both countries and there were just plain travellers like ourselves.'

Treatment varied depending upon the class of one's ticket. 'One young Chinese who was travelling "hard" [i.e. rough] was stripped naked on the platform and, after being searched, was led away in handcuffs still in his under clad condition.' Most passengers were herded into a series of very small, very dirty customs sheds and their baggage was subjected to a thorough examination. 'Neill Malcolm and I fared a good deal better, our visas being of the highest priority, but even we were not exempt from a pretty ruthless search of our baggage, which at least took place in the station master's office.' Not surprisingly, their book boxes were the subject of particular interest and/or suspicion and Wheeler-Bennett

blessed Neill Malcolm's wisdom in telling me to get rid of Trotsky's history. I was greatly amused that our Soviet inspector examined each book page by page but was holding them upside down most of the time and even had he got them the right way up, it was pretty clear that he understood no word of any language save his own. I decided that what he was really searching for was currency or letters which we might have been smuggling into the Soviet Union.

Finally, they boarded the train to take them to Moscow. 'In the great and spacious days of Tsarist Russia, the regular paraphernalia of the Trans-Siberian Railway included a Greek Orthodox chapel, a sumptuous bath-room and high-grade dining car.' But after the Revolution, although the trains were 'scrupulously' clean, none of these luxuries existed any longer. Ensconced in their cabin, the two men settled down 'to a very pleasant quiet regime of reading and talking and sleeping and eating when we felt like it, as the train journeyed at a leisurely pace along what was for the most part then a single track with various allotted points at which trains going in opposite directions might pass'. The countryside was beautiful, 'very like the Maritime provinces of Canada with groves of silver birches, like clusters of enchanted fairy princesses, spreading along the banks of clear flowing streams and calm, deserted lakes'. Their journey was not without adventure. Between the towns of Ulan-Ude and Irkutsk the train suddenly halted: the engine had run off the tracks and gently ploughed its way into sandy soil without overturning. Helped by men from a nearby village, who arrived with great baulks of timber, 'which had every appearance of being the door-posts and lintels of their cottages', they levered the engine back onto the tracks. It was all done 'in great good humour and primitive efficiency'.

As they journeyed onwards, Wheeler-Bennett found that the 'enforced propinquity extending for over a week' with Malcolm meant their friendship developed 'a greater intimacy and understanding . . . I cannot recall a single abrasive moment. We both read for a good deal but at certain moments, as if by some telepathic instinct, we would put down our books and talk for an hour or so.' Malcolm was a good talker, Wheeler-Bennett recollected, 'a historian manqué'. As well as discussing the American Civil War 'in both speculative and positive terms, the Napoleonic wars and the relative qualities of the Emperor and the Duke of Wellington as strategists and tacticians', they discussed the Great War. 'I listened to first hand accounts of the tragedies of the early battles in France and Flanders, at Gallipoli and during the near disaster of the disintegration of the Fifth Army in March 1918.' He also heard about Malcolm's postwar experiences in Germany, where he had watched 'the natal pangs and the first faltering steps of the Weimar Republic'. Recollecting these conversations forty years later,

Wheeler-Bennett described them as 'titillating' his appetite for what followed. 'For it was then that he spoke of the future and of its relation to me. What I relate now was not delivered in one session; it extended over many hours of talk, but, when added up, it came to this: the Germans were the only remaining vital force in Europe. The French had little fire left in their bellies and were relying too greatly on the illusion of being able to keep Germany in a permanent state of subjection.' Although, Malcolm said, the British might be able to fight another war, 'we were always late starters' and the Germans had greater resilience and so might possibly win. 'If the policy of rapprochement engendered at Locarno failed, and there were clear signs that it might, the issue of peace and war would lie with Germany. If it came to war the decision of victory or defeat would lie, not in the hands of Britain and France but in those of Russia and the United States. In which case there would be a need for experts.'

Malcolm continued:

the books you have written so far have been excellent and almost clinically objective, but what you ought to do now is to make yourself a specialist so that, when the time comes, people will turn to you for solid, practical advice and if, as we hope, there is no war, you will be a recognised authority. There's no good trying to be a Russian scholar, it would take you too long to learn the language and there are too many imponderables. You already know a good deal about the United States and have good contacts; you must keep these up and extend them. But what I urge you to do is study Germany and the German people from within. Don't just be satisfied with knowing the 'nobs', the upper military and political and social echelons; they have their place and their importance but there are even more important factors. Get down underground and study the grass-roots, learn what the people are thinking and saying, especially in the country districts, where consular and embassy people don't, as a rule, penetrate. Earn the confidence of 'good' Germans if you can find them, and be able to assess the villainy of the 'bad' Germans too. In fact like John Buchan's character Peter Pienaar, think yourself into being a German, but don't neglect or ignore the Americans.

As Wheeler-Bennett readily admitted, 'the wisdom and far-sightedness of his counsel were of the most vital importance to me, for they set the pattern of my life'. Although he may not have recognised it at the time, he was at a crossroads in his career and Malcolm was providing him with the direction he needed. As he later observed, it was also possible that the general's advice may not have been 'professionally entirely disinterested' because it would enable his protégé to become 'an unofficial channel of communication' between leading German politicians and London.[64]

The two men reached Moscow on a sunny morning in the spring of 1929. Following the rupture in relations between Britain and the Soviet Union, and the closure of the British Embassy, British travellers in the Soviet Union were looked after by the Norwegians, who provided the two visitors with a car and an interpreter. They were also given tickets for the Bolshoi Ballet, where Wheeler-Bennett observed the now familiar figure of the general secretary of the Communist Party's Central Committee, Joseph Stalin, returning to his box as the lights dimmed and leaving before they went up again at the end of the performance. 'He was ever after to me that man of shadows, sealed in the crepuscules.'[65]

They visited the rooms in the Kremlin that were open to the public, galleries and cathedrals including the famous ikon shop in Red Square. They went to the Central Museum of the Revolution, housed in the former English Club, haunt of the pre-Revolutionary elite, whose haphazard memorabilia included a number of stones which had been thrown at policemen during the 1905 Revolution. Wheeler-Bennett was interested to note that Trotsky, sidelined by Stalin after Lenin's death in 1924 and recently exiled to Alma-Ata in the Central Asian republics, was still accorded 'a place of honour' in the room allocated to the 1917–18 Brest-Litovsk peace negotiations between the Soviet Union and Germany.[66] In Red Square, they watched the long winding queue, as visitors waited to pass by Lenin's tomb, 'the man who had left his personal imprint on the 20th century more deeply than any other individual'. Wheeler-Bennett made a pilgrimage to the tablet in the Kremlin Wall Necropolis, where the American journalist and Communist activist John Reed was buried, 'because I felt that I owed him a gesture of personal gratitude for the inspiration which reading his account of the Bolshevik revolution, *Ten Days that Shook the World*, had given me'.[67]

As he later recollected, it was largely this book that had aroused his interest in the Russian Revolution, inspiring him to write his book on the Treaty of Brest-Litovsk.

During their stay, the two men encountered a number of the journalists posted to Moscow. Yet again, Wheeler-Bennett was building up contacts: one of these was the German journalist Paul Scheffer, correspondent of the *Berliner Tageblatt* and one of the 'first professional Kremlinologists', who was later expelled from the Soviet Union for writing about collectivisation. At the other end of the political spectrum there was Walter Duranty, British journalist and correspondent of the *New York Times*, who had been in the Soviet Union since 1921 and who was already gaining a reputation as Stalin's apologist.[68] Travelling on to Leningrad (St Petersburg), they visited the Hermitage. As well as marvelling at its treasures, they enjoyed seeing 'the northern sunlight reflected on those splendid facades of Leningrad' and 'the Neva flowing grandly to the Gulf of Finland'.

Leaving the Soviet Union, the companions travelled through Poland to Germany, arriving in Berlin 'on a fine May morning'. In the comfort of the Belle Vue Hotel, Wheeler-Bennett luxuriated in his first hot bath since leaving Harbin some ten days earlier. They lunched at the British Embassy with the ambassador, Sir Horace Rumbold, who had been in Berlin since 1928 and who had already established himself as 'the best informed and most perceptive member of the diplomatic corps'.[69] A conversation with Richard von Kühlmann, the German foreign secretary at the time of the Treaty of Brest-Litovsk, 'confirmed that unless a miracle occurred, we were witnessing the beginning of the end of the Weimar system'.[70] They also met 'the most powerful civil servant of the time', Otto Meissner, who had known Malcolm in post-Great War Berlin. Wheeler-Bennett remembered him radiating 'confidence and optimism', stating that the newly founded Nationalist Socialist German Workers' Party – the Nazis – led by the Austrian-born corporal Adolf Hitler, was not really a menace, 'only an ephemeral manifestation of nationalist braggadocio'.[71]

After five months away, they returned to London on a perfect early summer's day. As a result of his interviews in the Philippines with Aguinaldo, Quezon and Osmena, Wheeler-Bennett wrote an article entitled

'Thirty Years of American-Filipino Relations, 1899–1929', which was published in the RIIA Journal.[72] Despite expressing a fascination for the Orient, Wheeler-Bennett never returned to China, and made only one further visit to Hong Kong, Japan and Taiwan, in 1969.[73] 'The charm and lure of the East remained but the old life is gone, the tempo has changed, the elegance of antiquity modified by the benefits of progress. I have never ceased to be thankful that I knew it as it was.'

In London, Wheeler-Bennett enjoyed staying at Albany, while his mother lived at Ravensbourne. He was collecting a group of intellectual friends with a mutual interest in international affairs and a concern for the future: one of these was Robert Bruce Lockhart. Although neither man could remember when they first met, Lockhart recalled a lunch together at Albany on 27 August 1929 at which Lewis Namier and Egon Erwin Kisch, the Czechoslovak writer and roving reporter, were also present.[74] Lockhart, known as Bruce rather than Robert because so many other members of his family had the name Robert, and fifteen years older than Wheeler-Bennett, had already had a varied career – working on a rubber plantation, as a diplomat in Moscow, and as an author and banker. His *Memoirs of a British Agent*, describing his experiences and arrest in Moscow during the 1917 Revolution, had already become a best-seller. When Wheeler-Bennett met him, he was working as a journalist for Lord Beaverbrook on the London *Evening Standard*. The two men became firm friends, with Lockhart frequently applauding Wheeler-Bennett's writing and general sociability.[75] Meanwhile, the fifth book in the Information Series, *Information on the World Court*, was published in 1929. For this, Wheeler-Bennett's collaborator was Maurice Fanshawe, director of inquiries and reports at the League of Nations and recent author of *The World Court in 1926*. Yet again the reviews were favourable. 'There is nothing better, or as good, existing in the same compass,' said the *Spectator*.

Wheeler-Bennett had also finally secured a permanent future for the Information Service as part of the RIIA, of which Neill Malcolm was still chairman. On 1 July 1930, the formal fusion with the Information Department of Chatham House was effected. The original function of the Information Department – the answering of enquiries and the supply of information to members – was to be maintained and developed. To this was now added the issuance of the *Bulletin of International News*, the maintenance of the 'Wheeler-Bennett collection of documents on International Affairs', the writing of memoranda and the compilation of the annual volume of *Documents on International Affairs*, which Wheeler-Bennett had undertaken to edit, 'which activities formerly pertaining to the "Information Service on International Affairs"' were, as a result of the fusion, to be continued under 'the direct auspices of Chatham House'.[76] By the terms of the agreement, Wheeler-Bennett agreed to contribute on a diminishing scale towards the cost of the Information Department.[77] In view of the funds he had already donated, according to the Institute's bye-laws, in 1930 he became a founder member of the RIIA.[78] Subsequently, when reviewing the organisation of the Information Department, Wheeler-Bennett suggested splitting the honorary secretary's position by appointing an information secretary. What he had in mind was that he should become honorary director of the Information Department as an 'advisory official . . . free from departmental work' whereas the information secretary – Stephen Heald – would be responsible for enquiries and answering correspondence addressed to the department. 'Rightly or wrongly I have always believed that one of the most useful contributions which I can make to the work of the Department is to keep in touch personally with people in different countries, to visit organisations and make contacts abroad, and to study international situations as they actually exist. It would, I submit, be a mistake for me to curtail my activities in this direction in order to give more time to office work,' he wrote.

While praising the staff, Wheeler-Bennett soon had a complaint about their offices.

When the staff of the department were originally housed in 18 Ormond Yard in July 1929 the conditions were very different. The mews were quiet and comparatively unfrequented. Since that time a garage has been opened exactly opposite the offices of the department and the results have been devastating. The continual passing in and out of cars; the racing and 'trying out' of engines, the daily dumping of petrol cans and the vituperative arguments which inevitably ensue between chauffeurs, not forgetting the fact that the yard becomes a children's

play-ground after school-hours, combine to create an atmosphere very
unconducive to the serious study of international affairs . . . it is no
exaggeration to say that on a number of occasions it has been impossible to carry on a telephone conversation without first shutting all
windows.[79]

In time, the department moved to Chatham House and the issues
Wheeler-Bennett raised were resolved. In later life, he considered that
he had driven 'a good bargain' for his Information Service. As a result
of the merger, he was invited to join the Council of the Institute, 'a
factor which opened many doors to me in Europe'.[80]

The Tragedy of Weimar

I watched the fragile structure of German democracy first crack, then crumble and finally disintegrate.[1]

By focusing on Germany, Wheeler-Bennett was beginning to shape his career as an expert on German affairs. He was to spend over four years staying intermittently in Germany, observing the inner workings of the German Reich. He continued to travel, making contacts and increasing his wide circle of friends. While in Berlin, he rented rooms at the Kaiserhof Hotel, venue of the 1878 Congress of Berlin, conveniently located close to the Chancellery in Wilhelmstrasse. Much to Wheeler-Bennett's amusement, the coincidence of his physical resemblance to some members of the German Royal House of Hohenzollern, especially Kaiser Wilhelm's youngest son, Prince August-Wilhelm, and the fact that 'mini-royalty' often stayed at the Kaiserhof, started a rumour that he 'was in some degree not entirely legitimately connected with the Hohenzollerns'. So persistent was the rumour that when it later reached Winston Churchill's ears, he deputed 'a somewhat embarrassed Foreign Office official' to find out whether 'there was anything in it'. As Wheeler-Bennett avowed, there was none. 'My dear mother had never even met a Hohenzollern in her life!'[2]

Initially, Wheeler-Bennett enjoyed his time in Germany. There was as yet no sign of the effects of the Great Depression, which hit the United States in 1929. Germany's factories and mines were producing at high

levels and new department stores were opening in the major cities, a
welcome indication of the revival of commerce and consumption.[3]
Wheeler-Bennett was later to describe this period as 'halcyon days', with
the Locarno spirit still in being, 'albeit as an hallucination'. There was
'good music and opera, an indifferent theatre and a night life which had
become notorious throughout Europe'. A Grand Coalition, composed of
the Social Democrat Party, the Catholic Centre Party and the German
National People's Party, was in power, led by the Social Democrat chancellor, Hermann Müller. Now in his eighties, Hindenburg was still
president. However, as Wheeler-Bennett noted, intrigue was 'seething in
all quarters. Already the great divisive factors which were to ruin Germany
and destroy Europe were becoming manifest.'[4] Right-wing extremists
and Communists were rallying support while 'the parties of "respecta-
bility" raged furiously together'.[5] The chancellor, Müller, together with
the foreign minister, Gustav Stresemann, and the finance minister,
Hermann Dietrich, were often away from Berlin attending the Reparation Conferences in The Hague. In their absence, a small cabinet ran the
government, presided over by the defence minister, General Wilhelm
Gröner, the man who, in November 1918, had had the unenviable task
of telling Kaiser Wilhelm that he no longer commanded the loyalty of
the German army.[6]

As advised by Neill Malcolm, in order to penetrate both the German
ruling elite and the ordinary people, as well as learning the language
proficiently, Wheeler-Bennett had decided to 'black' himself out (i.e.,
integrate himself among the German people). Having a love of horses
and being a 'passable' rider, he believed the best 'ploy' was to indulge
in horse-breeding and racing ('too costly a pastime in England'). He
therefore rented a small stud on the Lüneburg Heath near Fallingbostel
between Bremen and Berlin, which he judged to be a good strategic
position, close to Verden, the heart of the horse-breeding region and
training headquarters for the German army Olympic team, and Celle,
home to one of the two German national studs, the other being in East
Prussia. Within a short time, his strategy had begun to pay off and he
was meeting a number of Germans who were to become influential in
the political hierarchy. One of these was Franz von Papen, a former
champion 'gentleman-rider' who had entered politics after the Great War

by joining the Catholic Centre Party and whom Wheeler-Bennett considered to have 'considerable charisma'. Another was General Kurt von Schleicher, a former student of Gröner and now his chief of staff. Although Wheeler-Bennett recognised that Schleicher was an amiable companion, writing in later life, he considered that, where politics were concerned, 'there was no vestige of loyalty or innate decency in him . . . friendship with von Schleicher was the Kiss of Death'.[7] Another acquaintance was General Walter von Reichenau, chairman of the German Olympic Committee, and later the chief liaison officer between the Nazi Party and the German army.[8] Among his new friends, the two Wheeler-Bennett liked best were Lieutenant Count Hans-Viktor von Salviati, whose sister had made a morganatic marriage to the Kaiser's son, Prince Friedrich-Wilhelm. The other was Lieutenant Hans von Brandt – 'a superb horseman' – who was to play a fatal part in the attempt in July 1944 to assassinate Hitler.

Wheeler-Bennett considered himself 'exceedingly happy' in his surroundings. He owned three horses and a Great Dane, called Argon von Huntermayer, whom, as an experiment, he raised as a vegetarian 'and I have never seen a fitter dog'. Every Sunday he attended race meetings in the nearby villages. After numerous falls, he judged that he had become a 'competent' horseman. One challenge he mastered was keeping his monocle in his eye without a rim or cord while jumping a fence. Besides improving his 'equestrian proficiency', he met many people who were 'of great service' in Berlin.[9] Franz von Papen put Wheeler-Bennett up for the Gentleman Riders' Club (akin to the Turf Club in London), and the German financier Hjalmar Schacht, president of the Reichsbank since 1923, proposed him for the Union Club, 'a curious amalgam' of the Athenaeum and Brooks's.[10] In addition to his conservative friends, Wheeler-Bennett had some left-wing acquaintances, among whom were the chancellor, Hermann Müller, the Communist Ernst Torgler and Carl von Ossietzky, winner of the 1935 Nobel Peace Prize and editor of the *Weltbühne*, a left-wing political weekly.[11] The man with whom he developed the greatest affinity was a forty-five-year-old German from Westphalia, Heinrich Brüning, who had entered the Reichstag as a deputy of the Catholic Centre Party in 1924. Apart from their common love of horses, Wheeler-Bennett found that he was exceptionally frank

THE TRAGEDY OF WEIMAR

in discussing the German political situation. 'He understood earlier than most men the vital connection between the economic dangers in respect of reparation payments and disarmament.'[12] Following the sudden death of the foreign minister, Stresemann, from a stroke in October 1929, and the resignation of Müller in March 1930, Brüning became chancellor. Since he had already gained his confidence as a friend, 'there now began an even closer relationship between the new Chancellor and myself'.[13]

Wheeler-Bennett also befriended a number of foreign journalists 'with a galaxy of genius' – *The Times*'s correspondent in Berlin was Norman Ebbutt, 'a benign, roly-poly, figure with a brilliant mind and a fine sense of journalistic morality';[14] then there was D'Arcy Gillie, who wrote for the *Manchester Guardian*, as did another 'regular', Frederick Voigt, who had been in Germany since 1920. Later Hugh Carleton Greene came to Germany to report for the *Daily Telegraph*.[15] Wheeler-Bennett's 'special buddy', though, was Hubert Knickerbocker, known as 'Knick', 'a gangling red-haired, raw-boned Texan' who had come to Germany in the early 1920s to study psychiatry but who had switched careers to become a journalist. Having been awarded a Pullitzer Prize in 1931 for his article on the practical operation of the five year plan in the Soviet Union, he was currently working as the chief Berlin correspondent for the *New York Evening Post* and the *Philadelphia Public Ledger*.[16] Also in Berlin were Edgar Mowrer of the *Chicago Daily News*, whose manuscript 'Germany Turns the Clock Back' Wheeler-Bennett later tried unsuccessfully to place with a publisher in London, and Frederick Birchall of the *New York Times*, as well as the 'gallant' Elizabeth Wiskemann, who wrote for a number of periodicals including the *New Statesman*.[17] 'Night after night we met to eat and drink – or just to drink – in the smoke-laden crepuscule of the Taverne.' Wheeler-Bennett attributed his acceptance by this group of 'working journalists' to the fact that he had access to sources 'which were denied to them. Although I never abused a confidence which had been made to me by a German, I was able, on occasion, to confirm some-body's story or to indicate when I thought somebody else had been given what in American slang is known as a "bum steer".'[18]

Wheeler-Bennett's stated goal to his friends was to write a book on Germany during the period between the Great War and the German Reich. His contacts, especially his friendship with Neill Malcolm, had given him back-channel access to Britain's Foreign Ministry. The permanent under-secretary at the Foreign Office was Sir Robert Vansittart – another of the four men whom Wheeler-Bennett later considered as having influenced his career as a historian. While in Germany Wheeler-Bennett was happy to share his assessments of the situation with both Malcolm and Vansittart. 'I was neither a professional diplomat nor in any sense a "secret agent". I was paid neither salary nor expenses.'[19] At this stage, by far the most useful information that he could impart came through his friendship with Brüning, whom Wheeler-Bennett was later to describe as 'the hero (or non-hero) of the last period of the history of the Weimar Republic'.[20] While the chancellor attempted to extract Germany from the quagmire into which it was sinking as the effects of the Depression began to be felt, Wheeler-Bennett observed events from a 'ringside seat'. What he witnessed was depressing. To revitalise the German economy, reforms were necessary. To make these more palatable to the German people, increasingly burdened by debt and inflation, Brüning hoped to gain some diplomatic success in relation to the onerous demand for the payment of reparations. The Young Plan schedule of loans and repayments agreed by Müller at The Hague in 1929 – and about which Wheeler-Bennett had written in the sixth book in the Information Series, *Information on the Reparation Settlement* – had imposed a sixty-year timetable.[21] Brüning's objective was to create the conditions so that reparations would be abolished.[22] He also wanted to reassess the restrictions placed on German rearmament as a prelude to disarmament by all the Great Powers, due to be negotiated at the General Disarmament Conference in Geneva in 1932.[23]

Unable to agree a budget to deal with the impact of the Depression, in March 1930 the Grand Coalition collapsed and President Hindenburg invoked Article 48 of the Weimar Constitution, enabling the chancellor to govern by decree. When elections were held in September, the beneficiaries were not the centre parties but the National Socialists led by Adolf Hitler. In the previous elections, the Nazis had only won twelve seats; after September 1930, they emerged as the second largest party after the Social Democrats, with 107 seats. 'From that moment,' Wheeler-Bennett recalled, 'Brüning realized that he was engaged in a race against time in which he knew that he was competing against the Nazis, making it the

more imperative to obtain concessions from the Great Powers, who, if
they did not make them to him, would be called upon to conciliate a
far more dangerous successor. Of these facts Brüning spoke frankly to
me in our not infrequent talks.'[24] At the time, however, the danger was
not generally perceived as being so grave and there was a feeling that
Hindenburg would never allow the Nazis to take power.

When the Nazi delegates in the Reichstag embarked on a series of
obstructionist tactics, calling for a no-confidence motion and then walking
out when they failed to win it, Wheeler-Bennett was lulled into a false
sense of security. 'All danger of a Nazi putsch is I believe over,' he wrote
in February 1931, while holidaying in Egypt at the Luxor Winter Palace.[25]
'And there is no immediate reason why the present government should
not remain in power until next autumn. With their failure to achieve
anything dramatic, except a withdrawal from the Reichstag, the Nazis
would seem to have lost a certain amount of their prestige. The first
wave of Nazism may be said to have passed over.' But he readily recognised the rising bitterness and resentment of the German people. Unless
Germany received 'some measure of satisfaction at the Disarmament
Conference', he believed that not only would there be 'a strong campaign
for her withdrawal from the League [of Nations] but also a great increase
in Nazism. The danger of the Nazis lies, I feel, not so much in present
politics as in the outcome of the great events of next year.' Presidential
elections were due in 1932 and it was assumed that Hitler would want
to contest them. The only person who could defeat him was Hindenburg. 'If von Hindenburg will stand again he would meet with no
opposition except perhaps from the Communists. But he is an old man
and very naturally longs for retirement and rest. His health is at the
moment good but his great age (eighty-four) makes political speculation
uncertain.'[26]

After visiting Bremen, Wheeler-Bennett wrote to Neill Malcolm at
the end of April 1931. 'I find a deep sense of depression everywhere and
a general feeling as regards the disarmament conference that it might as
well not take place at all . . . I was told that Nazism had lost much of its
support in North Germany and that the youth of the party had shown
a distinct inclination to drift to the Left,' which Wheeler-Bennett also
considered a potential danger. 'I hope you will not be bored with these

reflections but I have been rather deeply exercised in my mind on this subject, and we seem to have reached an impasse from which it is very hard to see a way out.'[27] Unsurprisingly, the attempt that Brüning had made to create a Customs Union with Austria was being thwarted by France, fearful of the resurgence of a 'Greater' Germany. In May 1931, in the first of a series of bank closures, the Austrian Kredit Anstalt went bankrupt. With a reparations payment pending, political violence in Germany was increasing. 'Sunday after Sunday, throughout the Reich, was marked and marred by clashes between the Nazi SA [Sturmabteilung, or Stromtroopers, led by Ernst Röhm, one of Hitler's early supporters] and the Communist Red Front Fighters, resulting in dead and wounded on both sides.'[28] In June, Brüning carried his message personally to his European counterparts. But Brüning's meeting with the British prime minister, Ramsay MacDonald, at Chequers brought no reprieve. Later Brüning met Wheeler-Bennett, who was back in England, at dinner at the German Embassy and asked him to return with him on board the *Europa* to Bremerhaven. When the two men were alone, Brüning shared the dismal outcome of the talks with him. There was to be no moratorium on the repayment of reparations. Brüning also learnt from the American ambassador to Germany, Frederic Sackett, also returning to Germany on the *Europa*, that there was to be no change of US policy either. As Wheeler-Bennett noted, 'the effect of returning empty-handed from Chequers was a grave blow to the Chancellor's political stature'.[29]

Back in Berlin, Wheeler-Bennett was continuing to gather information. One of his informants was the former chancellor Hans Luther, now president of the Reichsbank, following Schacht's resignation in 1930.[30] At a lunch in June, Luther informed the young British writer: 'This is a historic day in German banking. For the first time in our history we have not enough gold to cover our paper.' As Wheeler-Bennett came to note, 'in that more conventional period' this remark was of staggering importance. Writing over forty years later, he attempted to recapture the climate of despair in Germany in June 1931. 'It was like being suspended in a vacuum, isolated from reality, waiting for some cataclysm to occur which should break the spell which held everyone in thrall.' On Sunday, 21 June, it happened. Wheeler-Bennett was out riding in Berlin's Tiergarten when he saw crowds streaming out of the churches to be greeted by newsboys selling special *Extrablätter* – an extra edition of the news-papers. The US president, Herbert Hoover, had proposed a 'War-debt holiday' – a year's moratorium on payments of reparation and inter-Allied debts from 1 July. 'The effect was amazing. A grey blanket of depression seemed to have been lifted from the German souls.'[31] But a precondition of the proposal was the agreement of the other Allies, and the recently elected French prime minister, Pierre Laval, was demanding confirmation that reparation payments would be resumed the following year under the schedule set out by the Young Plan. While the Franco-American discus-sions continued, the positive psychological impact of the reprieve on Germany was lost.[32]

The Geneva Disarmament Conference, which opened on 2 February 1932, heralded the publication of the seventh book in the Information Series, *Disarmament and Security since Locarno 1925–31: Being the Political and Technical Background of the General Disarmament Conference 1932*, a sequel to the second book in the series (*Information on the Reduction of Armaments and Information on the Problem of Security*). As usual, in writing it, Wheeler-Bennett had drawn from articles he and his colleagues had already written for the *Bulletin*. On an earlier visit to the US in 1927, through Willmott ('Bill') Lewis, *The Times* correspondent in Washington, Wheeler-Bennett had secured a meeting with President Coolidge. 'Mr Coolidge has gone down to history as the most silent of presidents and I cannot say that I charmed him into verbosity,' he later noted. But as a result of their conversation, Wheeler-Bennett had understood the issues relating to the recent failure of the Geneva Naval Disarmament Confer-ence – which formed part of his survey – 'in a greater perspective than I had, perhaps, previously'.[33] Before publication, various friends had read and commented on the manuscript, including Arnold Toynbee and Hubert Knickerbocker. Neill Malcolm wrote the Introduction, offering a gloomy prognosis for the future: 'Civilisation, as you and I have known it, is at stake.'[34] Malcolm was echoing Wheeler-Bennett's findings: 'The spirit of confidence, lacking so much in every sphere of modern life, whether political, financial or economic, must be restored. This way alone lies economic reconstruction, this way alone lies European security. The alternative is chaos, and chaos more complete and devastating than ever existed during the Great War . . . Upon the issue of the Conference of 1932 hangs more than the solution of the technical and political problem of disarmament, but also the ultimate future of modern civilisation.'[35]

Wheeler-Bennett did not stay long in Berlin. At the end of January 1932 he had embarked on another long-distance trip which began in Malta, where he was joined by Neill Malcolm. Together the two men travelled east, stopping at the usual ports of call: Port Said, Aden, Colombo and Singapore. Malcolm went on to Borneo while Wheeler-Bennett returned to Malta via Penang and Bombay. In early April, he was in Rome, where, although not a Roman Catholic, he had a papal audience. His concerns ever wide-ranging, he had become involved in talks regarding the teaching of Italian in Malta. 'I concentrated on discussing the language problem so far as Italy was concerned. I saw the British Ambassador and discussed the language question both with him and with officials of the British Embassy, and also with officials of the Palazzo Chigi – the Italian foreign office.'[36]

Returning to England in mid-April, Wheeler-Bennett slotted back into his London routine, which still involved attendance at Chatham House, where he now had his own office. 'Do let me say how much I appreciate and enjoy the privacy and situation of my room,' he wrote to the secretary, Ivison Macadam, in April 1932. 'It is indeed a very great pleasure to have at last a "haven of rest" after being either exiled to my own Flat or buried in the depths of the beyond. Its ground floor position is particularly felicitous, for at the moment, though I am much better in health, I am advised not to go up and down stairs more than is absolutely necessary, and I am immensely grateful to you for arranging it.'[37] Wheeler-Bennett had also recently joined the governing council of Sir Evelyn Wrench's All Peoples' Association, set up in 1930 to promote 'international friendship and understanding'.[38] He kept in touch with the German Embassy, making a particular friend of Count Albrecht von Bernstorff, who had been in London since 1923 and was already mistrustful of the rising power of the National Socialists.[39] In Germany, where Wheeler-Bennett returned at the end of April 1932, the political situation was going from bad to worse. Over six million Germans were unemployed, an estimated third of the labour force.[40] 'Hitler's star was in the ascendant,' he recalled; 'the country in sheer desperation was responding more and more to Nazi propaganda.'[41] With Brüning managing Hindenburg's presidential election campaign, Wheeler-Bennett took up his spectator's role once more. 'I attended a number of his meetings in Berlin and in Silesia where he spoke to vast audiences, compelling their attention with magnetism and personal charm . . . I was impressed beyond measure with the masterly and gallant way in which he dealt with the truly vitriolic tactics of his Nazi opponents, who employed every vulgarity and ballyhoo of the circus parade.'[42] Although, after two rounds of voting in March and April, Hindenburg was re-elected president, Brüning's days were numbered. After the elections, he made a last-ditch effort to gain popularity against the rising tide of Nazism. When he went to Geneva to attempt to adjust the restrictions relating to German armaments, Wheeler-Bennett 'tagged along'. During Brüning's informal meetings with Ramsay MacDonald, the American secretary of state, Henry Stimson, and the Italian foreign minister, Dino Grandi, some progress was made. However, André Tardieu, prime minister of France since February, had been obliged to return home to take part in his own election campaign.[43] In his absence, agreement in principle on Brüning's proposed formula for German equality in armaments was reached, only needing confirmation from France. According to Wheeler-Bennett, the chancellor was outmanoeuvred by von Schleicher, who had informed Tardieu that Brüning was 'on the way out' and so the French prime minister did not formalise the agreement. Without his assent, Brüning once more had to return empty-handed to Germany.[44] Wheeler-Bennett was seeing the chancellor nightly, making 'copious' notes on events as they unfolded.

On 30 May 1932, Brüning was told by Hindenburg that he was to remain chancellor *ad interim*, until a successor could be appointed. This turned out to be none other than Wheeler-Bennett's 'old racing acquaintance', Franz von Papen. He was the first chancellor of the German Republic to be appointed without reference to the Reichstag. Soon after he had taken office, Wheeler-Bennett went to see him. 'He reminded me of nothing so much as a cocky little house sparrow.'[45] For his part in elevating him to the chancellorship, Schleicher was appointed minister of defence. Well placed as Wheeler-Bennett remained, he deeply regretted Brüning's departure. 'Poor Brüning,' he wrote at the end of May to

Hubert Knickerbocker: 'I am very sorry he has gone. I don't think anybody has put up a more excellent fight than he during the past year. There was every reason to expect his resignation after his return from Chequers last June, and he has hung on by the skin of his teeth for almost twelve months. However, even this adhesive substance wears out in time, and we can only await the future with certain querulousness.' Thanks to his contacts, Wheeler-Bennett was pleased to note that he had warned the Foreign Office of Brüning's departure 'some hours' before it appeared in the press.[46] Writing in later life, Wheeler-Bennett echoed his earlier views: 'For me it is an article of faith that the tragedy of Brüning is the tragedy of Weimar. He wished to do so much, he was allowed to accomplish so little. He was fated to be the undertaker rather than the physician.'[47]

In June, Wheeler-Bennett was again in London, giving substance to his views in an address at Chatham House. 'In order to understand the present situation, we need to understand the circumstances which have led up to it.' In his opinion, Brüning had assumed office with a '*damnosa hereditas* in the shape of the Young Plan' which had been negotiated by his predecessors, and in the 'complete absence of any budget.' He went on to explain how, since the members of the Reichstag had failed to take the financial situation seriously, Brüning had been obliged to advise Hindenburg to prorogue the Reichstag and govern by a series of emergency decrees, which inevitably undermined Germany's fragile democratic institutions. In conclusion, he suggested that the world had lived for the past year under the impression that if Dr Brüning resigned some appalling calamity would ensue. 'We cannot do such and such, we have said, because if we do Brüning will fall. For once in our lives events have forced us to call fate's bluff. Dr Brüning has fallen, the world still moves. We do not know what is in front of us.'[48] However, with Nazi students 'swarming around shouting "Wir scheissen auf die Freiheit" [We shit on freedom]', as Wheeler-Bennett realised, the situation might well get worse.[49]

During his frequent visits to Germany, Wheeler-Bennett had been assiduously gathering research material for his book on that country. Not long after Brüning's dismissal, he changed his mind about the subject matter. One evening, while dining with friends, 'the conversation turned

to the most important news item of the day – Hindenburg's announcement of elections'. During the conversation, a different view from the
idolizing one that Wheeler-Bennett had of the ageing president emerged.
Wheeler-Bennett decided to make his book a biography of Hindenburg,
sifting through 'with the greatest care all possible evidence for and against'
the censorious views he had heard around the dinner table.[50] At the same
time, he intended to keep up his contemporary analysis of the situation,
maintaining access to the corridors of power through his friendship with
Dr Erwin Planck, Papen's secretary. He also continued to observe the
rising popularity of the National Socialists. Writing to Macadam at
Chatham House from Bavaria in July 1932, he noted how detached the
region was 'from the bad goings on in the rest of this poor distracted
Germany'. Here we are Nazi to a man and are convinced that Hitler
alone can save us from our ills and from France and her rapacity. I am
having a perfect fortnight's vacation with my horses in the midst of this
beautiful riding country and it is doing me a lot of good. I go to Berlin
on the 28th for the last few days of the election campaign and for the
polling day (July 31.) . . . Auf Wiedersehn!'[51] The result of the elections
would see the Nazi Party further strengthening its hand, returning to the
Reichstag as the largest party.

Shortly before his thirtieth birthday, having been back in England
during the summer, Wheeler-Bennett returned to Germany in October
1932, immediately asking Planck to arrange an interview with Papen.[52]
By now there was martial law in Berlin and all visitors had to get a police
pass. Wheeler-Bennett had already liquidated his assets in Germany. 'I was
now convinced that unless something miraculous occurred, Hitler would be
in power within a year,' he later wrote.[53] He had ended his lease at Fallingbostel, sold his horses and his dog, and paid off his stable hands. His visits
to Germany became less frequent. 'I find it more than difficult to keep away
from Berlin but am particularly restrained from one of my periodic dashes,'
he wrote to Knickerbocker in December 1932, 'by the uncommendable
(from my point of view) downward course of the £stg, which, though
admirable for the commercial prestige of the British Raj, is detrimental to
the comfort and welfare of his individual subjects travelling abroad!'[54]

Gloomy as things were in Germany, Wheeler-Bennett was always
able to find respite at home, where he could relax into his role of

raconteur. On one occasion he entertained Bruce Lockhart to lunch at
Albany with the diplomat Victor Mallett and his wife, Christiana,[55] and
Neill Malcolm and his daughter, Angela. Wheeler-Bennett told a 'good
story' of Hindenburg, related Lockhart: 'Hindenburg has a dream;
thinks he is at gates of Heaven. St Peter asks: "Who are you?" "Paul
Hindenburg." "What did you do on earth?" "I did my duty." "Are you
sure you did your duty or did you only keep your oath to the constitution?" Before Hindenburg can think of the answer he wakes up.'[56]

Wheeler-Bennett had also been keeping up his commitments at
Chatham House. In addition to editing the *Documents*, he wrote the
eighth and last book in the Information Series aptly called *The Wreck of
Reparations: Being the Political Background of the Lausanne Agreement 1932*,
published in 1933, as representatives of Britain, France and Germany
were meeting in Lausanne to discuss suspension of the reparations. The
editor of *The Economist*, Sir Walter Layton, wrote the introduction.[57]
Wheeler-Bennett had also recently joined the Anglo-German Association, which had been formed in 1929 'to promote general friendly
relations between Great Britain and Germany and to secure a better
understanding between the two countries'. Its president was the former
viceroy of India, jurist and politician, the marquess of Reading.[58] Among
its members were a number of Members of Parliament, as well as various
friends and acquaintances, including Philip Kerr, now the 11th marquess
of Lothian, Viscount Chelwood, Harold Nicolson and Sir Evelyn
Wrench.[59]

Meanwhile, Wheeler-Bennett continued his research on Hindenburg.
Brüning was now living in a flat in Berlin and, when visiting Germany,
Wheeler-Bennett used to bring him 'Rhine wine, cigars and gossip'.
Having told Brüning that he wanted to write the life of Hindenburg, he
found that the former chancellor was prepared to share his knowledge,
including describing the events surrounding his own dismissal. 'He told
me all, or as much as he decently could, including the fact that, to add
insult to injury von Papen had offered him the post of Ambassador to
London, an offer which he had peremptorily refused.' Brüning advised
Wheeler-Bennett to see the former defence minister Wilhelm Gröner.[60]
In time, Wheeler-Bennett sent Brüning the proofs for approval of 'that
part of the book which concerned his chancellorship. This he gave

unhesitatingly and asked me to make only one alteration. He thought I had been too unkind to Kurt von Schleicher! I replied that to me this was impossible and in the interests of history I could not modify what I had written – and I didn't.'[61]

Papen was 'taking his fences in domestic politics at a perilous pace'.[62] As a result of the July 1932 elections to the Reichstag, the Nazi Party now had 230 seats, whereas Papen's government no longer even had the support of the Centre Party, on whose ticket Papen had been elected as a deputy.[63] Despite Wheeler-Bennett's lack of confidence in the current administration, he believed that 'a government as invincibly lunatic' as Papen's was better than 'an ideological dictatorship' led by Hitler. Through his journalist contacts, he attempted to strengthen Papen's position in relation to the disarmament negotiations which 'had degenerated into an exchange of polemics and insinuations between Herr von Papen and [French prime minister] M. Herriot on the subject of Germany's claim to equality'.[64] Having discussed the issue with Norman Ebbutt of *The Times*, Wheeler-Bennett talked to Papen, Konstantin von Neurath, now foreign minister, and state secretary Bernhard von Bülow. 'I pointed out that Germany's attitude at the Disarmament Conference had so far been purely negative.' What Wheeler-Bennett was suggesting was that the German government should lay all its cards on the table and restate the terms that Brüning had given earlier in the year and which had been accepted by all the Western Powers including, belatedly, France (although the latter's assent had come too late to save Brüning). Having written to Papen informing him of his attempt to highlight Germany's position, he went to see Vansittart in London, bringing with him a proposal on behalf of the German government. 'My part in this was of course unofficial and unauthorised, but it had the advantage in that the whole thing could thus be disavowed by the German Government if nothing came of it.'[65]

After consulting Vansittart and being assured that it would take time for the Foreign Office to digest, as well as discussing the formula with Anthony Eden, under-secretary for foreign affairs, Wheeler-Bennett somewhat precipitately, but knowing that time was of the essence, published his suggestion in a letter to *The Times*. 'It is, I think, of great importance to emphasize the fact that the question of Germany's right to equality still remains unsettled, and that while this is so, no advance can be made in the process of disarmament. May I, therefore, ask your assistance in putting forward the following formula as a means of solution of the problem of equality, and one which I have the best possible reason to believe would be acceptable to the German government?' Wheeler-Bennett proceeded to outline eight points which he considered essential. Knowing what was in Papen's mind, he stressed the need for fairness, if not equality; for example, Germany was 'to be given the means of maintaining and supplying the Reichswehr and Reichsmarine on a more economic scale than that provided under the Treaty of Versailles, and under the same terms as other Powers'. In return, Germany would renounce immediately 'those aggressive weapons which the other nations agree to give up within a limited period of years'. Finally, Wheeler-Bennett noted that what he was suggesting did not go any further than the suggestions put forward by Brüning to MacDonald and Stimson in Geneva the previous April.[66]

On the day of publication he wrote to Brüning: 'I am enclosing herewith a letter which appeared in *The Times* this morning, the gist of which will, I know, have already been made known to you. I think that it may interest you, in that I have insisted on the fact that the true formula of equality is yours and dates from your conversations with British and American statesmen last April. I am following political events in Germany with the greatest interest and attention.'[67] Wheeler-Bennett's friends at the Foreign Office were not pleased at the 'intervention of a non-professional on their preserves' and as a result he got 'an imperial wigging at the highest level'.[68] Even so, he considered that his efforts were not entirely in vain. The letter was reprinted in full in the German press. From Ebbutt, Wheeler-Bennett heard that Brüning was delighted. Although Ramsay MacDonald was at first 'so furious that he meditated breaking his rule and writing to *The Times*', after Wheeler-Bennett had supplied him with a detailed synopsis of the train of events which had caused him to write the letter, the Prime Minister's attitude was 'substantially moderated'. When the foreign secretary, Sir John Simon, subsequently made a policy statement at the Disarmament Conference at Geneva, Wheeler-Bennett considered that greater consideration had been given to German concerns than previously.[69]

Schleicher, however, had again been intriguing. This time it was against Papen. After another general election in November 1932, in which the Nazis again emerged as the strongest parliamentary group (although with fewer deputies), Schleicher stepped into the chancellor's shoes in December. As Hubert Knickerbocker was to describe to Wheeler-Bennett in early 1933, 'much stabbing in the back is going on now in the Wilhelmstrasse . . . it is too bad you are not around when the daggers begin to drip old friends' blood. I know your appetite.'[70] Schleicher's chancellorship was short-lived. In a counter-coup, Papen engineered his dismissal on 28 January 1933. The new chancellor was to be Adolf Hitler at the head of a coalition government, in which Papen would be vice-chancellor and prime minister of Prussia. Only two other Nazis held portfolios: Hermann Goering and Wilhelm Frick.[71] With Hindenburg still president, a veneer of 'moral assurance' remained. Wheeler-Bennett was reserved in his judgement, admitting that many friends, 'decent people of good family and upbringing', were ready to support the new government. For a people who had suffered a 'terrifying national bankruptcy' since 1918, Hitler had 'something for everyone in his bag of promises, and above all he offered an attractive – almost a romantic – prospect for youth'. Adolf Hitler, forty-three years old, took office on 30 January 1933. In celebration, a great torchlight procession 'wound its way through the city of Berlin'.[72]

Relations between the Nazis and Communists remained explosive. Wheeler-Bennett was recuperating from a minor operation in England, which meant that he had to miss watching 'the pot boil on this crackling German fire', as Knickerbocker described the situation to him in mid-February.[73] He was back in Berlin at the end of February, in time to see the smouldering Reichstag, which had been set on fire on the 27th.[74] The incident was immediately used to allege that the Communists were hatching a plot against the German government and led to the arrest of over four thousand Communists. Hitler also persuaded Hindenburg to pass the Reichstag Fire Decree, which suspended most civil liberties in Germany. 'All the Articles of the Constitution guaranteeing personal liberty, the rights of free expression of opinion, the freedom of the press, and security against house searching were suspended.'[75] Foreign correspondents were threatened with expulsion depending on the manner in which they described the events they witnessed.

When elections were held on 5 March, the Nazi Party had already effectively silenced its leftist rivals. As Wheeler-Bennett later recalled, the election campaign – the eighth election to the Reichstag since 1920 – was 'the most bitter and brutal' that he had ever witnessed. When he accompanied Brüning to an election rally, the former chancellor's speech was disrupted by the sound of rifle fire from fighting in the street outside. Opposition party meetings were broken up by the SA. When the election results were announced, the Nazis had won an unprecedented 288 seats out of 642, leaving the Centre Party with just 74 seats. Although the Communists had been permitted to field candidates and had secured 81 seats, the delegates were then arrested, which effectively meant that the only opposition was provided by the Social Democrat Party, which had won 120 seats. According to Wheeler-Bennett, when he met Papen, the new vice-chancellor did not see the danger in the situation, giving Wheeler-Bennett the 'immortal' reply: 'Nothing to worry about, my dear fellow; we can always outvote them in cabinet.' But within a few weeks Papen had been replaced by Goering as prime minister of Prussia leaving him only with the authority of vice-chancellor. Three more Nazis entered the cabinet: Joseph Goebbels, Rudolf Hess and Hitler's old friend Ernst Röhm.[76] According to Wheeler-Bennett, the only potential check on the power of the Nazis was the army, but it had 'neither the desire nor the courage to take action'. As General Walter von Reichenau said to him: 'We shall tolerate this regime just as long as it suits our interests to do so.'[77]

Next on Hitler's agenda was the passage of the Enabling Act, which would further strengthen his position. Although the Nazi Party had not gained the necessary two-thirds majority to pass the act without support from the other parties, Hitler played on national-security concerns as well as using intimidation to obtain their backing, including that of the Centre Party. Only the Social Democrats voted against.[78] Wheeler-Bennett described the passage of the act as 'nightmarish'. 'What we saw was a grim set-faced Führer; a man bent on power, ruthless and cruel.'[79] On 27 March, the Enabling Act came into effect. Henceforward, Hitler and his cabinet were 'enabled' to pass legislation without consulting the

Reichstag. The only check on the Führer's power now was the promise
he had given the president that he would discuss matters with him before
acting. As Hindenburg was pleased to confirm, 'the Chancellor has given
me his assurance that, even without being formally obliged by the
Constitution, he will not use the power conferred on him by the
Enabling Act without having first consulted me. In this connection I shall
always endeavour to secure our intimate co-operation and to fulfil my
oath "to do justice to all men." '[80] When writing his biography of
Hindenburg (eventually published in 1936), Wheeler-Bennett was sceptical about the value of such a pledge: 'Here then was the one remaining
check upon Hitler's power, a gentleman's agreement to consult the
President, and it may be asked why did Hindenburg not more energeti-
cally defend his oath. The answer is obvious. A weary Old Gentleman
of eighty-six, of rigid mind and slow reasoning, anxious to avoid responsibility and surrounded by a pack of watch dogs, is no match for a virile
young politician of forty-four.'[81]

Before the act became law, Wheeler-Bennett was back in England,
where he took up an invitation to speak at Chatham House on the
'new regime' in Germany. Neill Malcolm was in the chair. For all his
concerns, Wheeler-Bennett's speech put the rise of Hitler in context of
the dismal failure of previous governments during the Weimar
Republic:

> The events which took place at the end of January brought into being
> a new regime in Germany and a fresh factor in European affairs. For
> Germany it means the end of the system which began in November
> 1918. But this step, revolutionary as it may seem, is really only the
> culmination of a period of evolution which began in 1930. Democracy
> during the last three years has gradually broken down in Germany,
> and the first person, unexpected as it may seem, to strike a blow at
> democratic institutions in Germany was Dr Brüning. Parliamentary
> government received its death-blow, not from Herr von Papen or Herr
> Hitler, but from Dr Brüning when in 1930 he prorogued the Reichstag,
> and with the President, ruled by decree . . . it is important to remember
> that the Nazis had to come to power; it was inevitable . . . sooner or
> later.

[Germany] has to set her own house in order in her own way, and what we are principally concerned with is her foreign policy . . . I think to a certain extent we have been apt to place too great an emphasis on the internal policy of Germany. We must allow her, I think, to make her own bed. The problem is, what is her foreign policy? Is it to be a policy of peace or is she going to make the mistake that Germany made in 1914 in taking on both France and Russia at the same time? Is it to be a war on both fronts, or only on one? Is it to be a war on any front?

At the time of giving his talk, Wheeler-Bennett had met Hitler only once when Brüning, as chancellor, had been trying to negotiate with the National Socialists to create a centre-right coalition, and he confessed to being 'impressed by his [Hitler's] qualities as a political negotiator which were tough and unyielding'. At this stage, he was convinced that Hitler, whom he regarded as 'a man of sense with an appreciation of the realities', did not want a war and was the 'most moderate member of his party'. Although Wheeler-Bennett conceded his audience might have a different opinion, his view was that they had to accept that 'whether we like it or not the Nazi regime has come to stay. We cannot assume an attitude of complete detachment. The real reason for the Nazi movement is desperation, the longing of German youth to get out of the system that was created around it – I will not put it stronger than that – at Versailles, and Hitler is more than anything else the child of Poincaré and Clemenceau.' Wheeler-Bennett also proffered the opinion that the Nazis would probably remain in power for four years. Although he had to admit that he had not read Hitler's *Mein Kampf*, he suggested that the twenty-five points of the Nazi programme were so contradictory that nobody could carry them out; furthermore, he said, it was not unusual for a political party to attain power and then disregard its election manifesto.[82] Later, he said that he had been 'severely criticised' in relation to his remarks that 'it behoved the Continent to look to its armaments and defences' so that, when the need arose, the 'Versailles Powers' could meet any challenge with a united front.[83]

In the early days of Nazi rule, Wheeler-Bennett continued to scrutinise the key political players in Germany. Although he described himself as never being 'intimate' with the Nazi hierarchy in the same way that he

had made friends with the Weimar politicians, nor falling victim to
Hitler's 'almost mesmeric magnetism', as a historian he felt the need to
maintain his 'ringside' seat. His insights were helped by Hitler's regular
visits to sit at an 'elite' tea table at the Kaiserhof Hotel, where Wheeler-
Bennett continued to stay when in Berlin. 'What struck one was Hitler's
utter lack of humanity or humour. He gave the impression of a self-
invented self-inspired robot.' After his first personal encounter with
Hitler, before he became chancellor, Wheeler-Bennett met him again at
the Chancellery, when the Führer was in one of his 'exalted moods,
coming at times near to hysteria'.[84] On several occasions Wheeler-
Bennett went to observe the immense rallies of Nazi supporters at the
Sportspalast. 'That terrifying repetition of "Sieg Heil" and "Ein Volk,
ein Reich, ein Führer" still haunts me and the idolisation reflected in
the faces of the listeners, especially the young men and girls, was both
poignant and frightening. There is no doubt that for twelve years Hitler
held the souls of the majority of the German people under an evil and
shameful spell.'[85]

Wheeler-Bennett remained in touch with those he had met in the
pre-Nazi era. One of these was the former ambassador to Britain,
Konstantin von Neurath, who had been appointed foreign minister under
Papen and had retained the position under Hitler. In April 1933, he was
writing to Neurath, who had requested to be kept informed of how
Germany was perceived in England. 'The attitude is only too easy to
define,' Wheeler-Bennett responded from London. 'It would seem that
all the struggles to promote friendship during the last 13 or 14 years have
gone to nothing.' Hitler's policy towards the Jews, he continued, 'has
had the most unfortunate repercussions in this country, and has in many
respects resulted in people losing both their sense of proportion and their
sense of perspective. It is difficult to convince people here of the great
and powerful spirit of regeneration and liberation which animates the
present revolutionary movement in Germany, or to persuade them that
to a very great extent responsibility lies in the Treaty of Versailles.'
Wheeler-Bennett went on to warn Neurath that his friends were
considering making either a public or an official protest to Germany, 'but
I have urged them not to do this, as so far as I can understand, it would
inevitably have quite the contrary effect to that which they desire'.

Instead, he said that he was endeavouring to persuade them 'that the present situation calls for the greatest patience and forbearance on all sides and that the position is so critical that any rash or impolitic action might have the most unfortunate effect. Please believe that my most cordial good wishes and sympathy are with you in your most difficult task, and I can only hope that the situation throughout the world will soon improve.'[86]

Later, again from England, he wrote to Knickerbocker, asking if he could suggest someone who might write a chapter on Nazi educational policy for the *Year Book of Education*, which his friend Lord Eustace Percy was editing. 'The Year Book has a very good international reputation and would present an admirable opportunity for explaining to the world the Nazi educational ideals.'[87]

Throughout this period, Wheeler-Bennett was still working on his biography of Hindenburg, for which Brüning remained an important source. After the Centre Party's support for the Enabling Act (with which Brüning had reluctantly complied on the grounds that it would maintain party discipline), the former chancellor had withdrawn completely from public life. As the Nazis grew in strength they began to harass his residence. One evening, when Wheeler-Bennett was visiting Brüning, some Nazis turned up in the street singing the Nazi anthem, 'Raise High the Flag' more popularly known by the name of its author as the 'Horst Wessel Song'.[88] Lest they make a scene outside his window, Brüning calmly put out the lights and waited until they had passed, before resuming his conversation 'at the exact point where he had broken it off'.[89]

As Wheeler-Bennett realised, violence against political dissenters was increasing. Thousands of young Nazis were enlisted as special constables and permitted to take arbitrary action against anyone branded as a Communist or Social Democrat, the latter being smeared as supporters of 'Jewish Bolshevism'. When he questioned Papen on the outrages being committed, the vice-chancellor apparently shrugged, giving the 'despicable answer': 'You can't make an omelette without breaking eggs.'[90] Worse was to come. The 'Brown Terror' – domestic espionage – was at first rather amateurish, but, as the system for monitoring conversations improved, Wheeler-Bennett found himself becoming more discreet in what he said. As he later wrote, the fear of being spied upon never really left him. 'I am still, even after forty years, very careful on the telephone; I have a phobia against talking in a room with a door open; and a marked preference for sitting with my back to the wall in a restaurant.'[91] So oppressive was he finding the atmosphere in totalitarian Germany that he shortened his visits. 'I felt myself to be in a kind of waking nightmare from which one only became free on crossing the frontier back into the Western world, where one literally and physically took great gulps of free air.'[92]

In June 1933, Wheeler-Bennett attended the World Economic Conference in England, organised by the industrial nations to discuss a collective response to the Great Depression. Having listened to Engelbert Dollfuss, the Austrian chancellor, make an impassioned speech warning of the danger from Germany, Wheeler-Bennett was pleased to meet him at the Austrian legation in Belgrave Square. 'Dollfuss's charm lay in his wit and his smile, his grace of mien and his undoubted sincerity.'[93] Still living at Albany in London, Wheeler-Bennett continued to enjoy hosting close friends: Neill Malcolm, Vernon Bartlett and the economist Harry Hodson, soon to become editor of *The Round Table, The Commonwealth Journal of International Affairs*.[94] Another friend was the journalist Claud Cockburn, correspondent for *The Times*, whom Wheeler-Bennett had met in Washington. Cockburn's style of journalism, especially his radical views and his opposition to appeasement, resulted in his departure from *The Times* in 1932. The following year, he founded what Wheeler-Bennett described as a 'fearsome' periodical, *The Week*. Forerunner of *Private Eye*, 'it employed the same shock tactics . . . it was vitriolic and even venomous'.[ ] For the conservative-minded Wheeler-Bennett, Cockburn sometimes went too far in his pronouncements, but he still valued his friendship, based as it was 'on a common sense of humour, perhaps the soundest foundation of all . . . I enjoyed his basic sense of irreverent disregard for many of the things which I held in respect.'[95]

As was becoming his custom, Wheeler-Bennett spent the autumn in the United States, undertaking a rigorous programme of travelling. He went first to Toronto to attend the British Commonwealth Relations Conference in September 1933, where he was a member of the British delegation, led by Viscount Chelwood. At the beginning of October, he was in Chicago, then Boston, Montreal, New York, West Point, Philadelphia, and back in Boston at the end of October, before returning again to New York, where, as always, he could expect a warm welcome from Ham Armstrong. When in Boston, 'if one was lucky one was invited to lunch at the Somerset Club, that impeccable palladium of tradition and convention, the very epitome of Bostonian Brahmanism'.[96]

While in the US, Wheeler-Bennett had become interested in the National Recovery Administration (NRA), one of the agencies created by the new president, Franklin D. Roosevelt as part of his promised New Deal for the American people. To promote economic recovery, the NRA gave the president the authority to propose codes of fair competition for US industries. For his own reasons, Wheeler-Bennett wanted to understand 'this new political phenomenon', which brought him into contact with one of its leading lights, Mary Romsey, and her brother Averell Harriman, later to become Roosevelt's special envoy during World War II.[97] They in turn introduced him to General Hugh Johnson, the director of the NRA and the man responsible for directing the draft during the Great War. Of interest, during their brief meeting, was Johnson's boast that he would 'break up' Henry Ford's automobile industry for openly defying the NRA. 'In this he actually failed.'[98]

Wheeler-Bennett reached Southampton at the beginning of November 1933, dining with his mother on the evening of his arrival. At the end of the month he was travelling in Europe again, but stopped for only a few days in Berlin. His principal destination was Hungary, where he had been invited by Emil Nagy to lecture to the Foreign Affairs Committee of the Hungarian parliament in Budapest.[99] The topic was 'The American Revolution', which Wheeler-Bennett considered within his capabilities, 'primed' as he was with the work of the NRA. In case some of his audience failed to understand English, he had his forty-five-minute lecture translated into German and Magyar. After Hungary, he went to Vienna, where Dollfuss was governing by emergency decree. What most remained in Wheeler-Bennett's mind afterwards was seeing the room in the Austrian Chancellery, the Ballhausplatz, where the Congress of Vienna had met in 1814–15. Six months after his visit, in July 1934, Dollfuss was assassinated by Austrian Nazi sympathisers.[100]

In December 1933 Wheeler-Bennett went to Prague. Through an American cousin on his mother's side, he had received an introduction to the president of Czechoslovakia, Dr Thomas Masaryk.[101] According to Wheeler-Bennett's recollections, he was invited to the presidential country seat of Lany and told to bring his riding kit. Although Masaryk was a keen horseman, his doctors had forbidden the eighty-three-year-old head of state to ride on the slippery forest roads in winter and so Wheeler-Bennett rode accompanied only by a mounted forester. 'I had a wonderful two days, with a choice of magnificent mounts and, in the evenings, alone with one of the wisest statesmen in the world at that time. I listened to him with fascination as he talked on a wide variety of subjects – . . . of his early battles as a deputy in the Austrian parliament, of his first-hand experiences of the Russian Revolution and of his memories of the Paris Peace Conference.' As Wheeler-Bennett recalled, at Versailles, Masaryk had offered to reconstitute the traditional frontiers of Bohemia in order to cede to Germany those areas of the Sudetenland which had a population constituted mainly of Germans. 'Had his wise and far-seeing proposal been accepted, the whole Munich tragedy might have been avoided.'[102]

On a lighter note, Masaryk asked him what the appropriate footwear was for a horse in winter. 'At length I found that the Royal Canadian Mounted Police used a type of rubber galosh, which fitted over each hoof and which rendered them exceedingly secure.' Back in England Wheeler-Bennett duly obtained a set and sent them to President Masaryk. He was later amused to see a statement in the London press announcing the flotation of a Czechoslovak company engaged in the manufacture of equestrian rubber overshoes. He also received a letter of thanks from the president's office: 'Mr President has been deeply pleased by your kindness you proved in forwording [sic] the special rubber horse shoes, and by your sympathy as to Mr. President's riding in winter season, when the riding on the slippering [sic] roads, if using iron shoes, is dangerous.'[103] Wheeler-Bennett had developed a close friendship with the president's son, Jan, who had been in London since 1925 as a minister for Czechoslovakia. 'He was often at A14 Albany, and I at his little flat in Marsham Court, where he would cook succulent Czech peasant dishes and play with tremendous verve splendid barbaric yet haunting Slav melodies,

which tore at the heart-strings and gave one an inkling of the impenetra-
bility of the Slav mind to Western understanding.'[104]

Although his visits to Germany had become less frequent, Wheeler-
Bennett was still in touch with like-minded people, eager to understand
the developing situation in the country. In late 1933, he joined yet
another organisation that aimed at creating a better understanding of Nazi
Germany known as the Anglo-German Group and chaired by Lord Allen
of Hurtwood. Other members included his friends Neill Malcolm,
Vernon Bartlett and Sir Walter Layton. The group had a strong pacifist
element and most of its members stood to the centre or left of the
political spectrum. Later it became known as the D'Abernon Club,
named after the former British ambassador at the time of Wheeler-
Bennett's first visit to Germany, who was also a vice-president of the
Anglo-German Association.

That Christmas was spent at Garsington with Irene and her family
before a return to London.[105] In the new year, Wheeler-Bennett was in
Paris. France was going through difficult days and Wheeler-Bennett
lingered long enough in the capital to take in the consequences of the
February riots of 'Les Ligues', the combined group of royalists, Fascists
and ex-servicemen who succeeded in forcing the resignation of prime
minister Edouard Daladier after only ten days in office. Anti-government
protests had come to a head against the previous government of the
Radical Socialist politician Camille Chautemps with the publicity
surrounding the financial dealings of the embezzler Serge Alexandre
Stavisky. In early January, when Stavisky was found dead, it was widely
believed that he had been murdered to hide his connections with senior
government ministers. When Daladier, also a member of the Radical
Socialist Party, took over from Chautemps, he immediately moved against
right-wing sympathisers who were suspected of being responsible for anti-
government demonstrations. His actions led directly to the riots of 6
February and his resignation.[106]

According to Wheeler-Bennett, who arrived in Paris shortly afterwards, the rioters 'were in an ugly mood, exemplified by the use of
hat-pins with which the mob stabbed the horses of the mounted police,
and of marbles thrown on the streets to make the horses lose their
footing'.[107] The protesters' intention was to march across the bridge to

gain entry to the Palais Bourbon, the seat of the Assembleé Nationale. After the police fired on them, leading to at least fourteen deaths, the situation had become ugly. Writing in hindsight, Wheeler-Bennett believed that the road to Munich and Vichy began with that 'bleak and bloody February day'. Daladier was succeeded as prime minister by Gaston Doumergue, who presided over a conservative national unity government. 'In the salons and clubs and restaurants one noticed the difference. The desirability of an accommodation with Hitler now became openly canvassed whereas before it had been only whispered.'[108] However, at the time neither the French government nor Wheeler-Bennett believed that Hitler wanted war 'just for the hell of it'.[109] Until his assassination in October 1934, the French foreign minister and former prime minister, Louis Barthou worked assiduously against German expansionism.[110]

Back in Germany for brief visits in March and April, Wheeler-Bennett was finding the atmosphere exceedingly uncomfortable. Hindenburg was obviously dying, and a power struggle was taking place between the supporters of the elite Nazi defence corps, the Schutzstaffel (SS), dominated by Heinrich Himmler and backed by Hitler, and those of Ernst Röhm's Stormtroopers the SA.[111] As Wheeler-Bennett noted, lists of those to be 'liquidated' were being drawn up. Both Brüning and Schleicher had already received warnings that their names were on them. Since the previous autumn, Brüning had felt compelled to move from place to place, staying with friends. According to the Jesuit priest Friedrich Muckermann, the once-courageous Brüning now resembled 'a hunted animal, constantly startled and already exhausted, just waiting for the final bullet'.[112] Whereas Schleicher decided to weather the storm by temporarily absenting himself from Berlin, Brüning took the situation more seriously and allowed himself to be driven across the border to the Netherlands by Muckermann's brother, Hermann. His departure on 21 May — ostensibly for health reasons — was organised by 'a group of Englishmen', of whom Wheeler-Bennett admitted to being one, keeping secret to the last the details of Brüning's escape.[113]

Of his journalist friends, Knickerbocker had already been expelled from Germany in 1933 and had been writing a book, *Will War Come in Europe?*, published in 1934. His narrative recorded the fruits of an investigation undertaken on behalf of the International News Service, posing the question contained in the title of his book to numerous leaders and ordinary people throughout Europe. He had asked Wheeler-Bennett to write the introduction. Praising Knickerbocker as 'the European star of the International News Service', Wheeler-Bennett said that 'all Europe is his oyster, and in the pages which follow he has given lavishly of the pearls that he has extracted therefrom'. He proceeded to give his own analysis of the current situation. 'The internal and external policies of Nazi Germany have resulted in Europe becoming once more an armed camp. Old differences have been sunk in the face of the greater and common danger. Italy and France, France and the Soviet Union, have reached rapprochements in order to leave their hands free to deal with this new menace to their interests.'

Wheeler-Bennett also wanted to highlight two events that had occurred since Knickerbocker had finished his text and which, in his opinion, went a considerable way to answering the question posed by the title of the book.

Germany by the publication of her military budget, showing an increase of some £17,800,000 (gold) on the army, navy and air estimates over those of the previous year, clearly indicated that she intended, come what might, to re-arm. This was the signal for the French government to break off all diplomatic conversations which had been in progress since October 1933, and to demand a return to the Disarmament Conference and the position prior to Germany's withdrawal from Geneva. In other words, the chances of disarmament have dwindled to a point almost negligible.

Second, Wheeler-Bennett had been watching events on the other side of the world that further complicated the situation.

With the attention of Europe concentrated upon Germany, and America fully occupied with measures for her own internal recovery, Japan has taken the opportunity to declare 'unofficially' a Monroe Doctrine for Asia in the nature of a warning to the Powers that she would oppose any measures of assistance given by them to China, such as the provision of military instruction and the granting of political loans. It is too soon to judge the full import of this declaration, but its implications are sufficiently great to cause grave anxiety.[114]

Meanwhile, in Germany, as Wheeler-Bennett realised, cracks were appearing not only within the Nazi hierarchy, between the SA and the SS, but also between their allies in the coalition. While Wheeler-Bennett was in England, Papen, still vice-chancellor, had been asked to give an address in the Auditorium Maximum of the old University of Marburg on Sunday, 17 June. He had decided to 'make a public issue' out of some of the excesses being committed by the Nazis against their political opponents. All seats were filled.

> I am so convinced of the need for the regeneration of our public life that I would fail in my duty both as a private citizen and a statesman if I did not give expression at this point in the German revolution to what it is now necessary to say . . . No nation can live in a continuous state of revolution, if it wishes to justify itself before history . . . Germany cannot live in a continuous state of unrest to which no one sees an end.[115]

His plea was that Hitler should be urged to abandon the arbitrary tactics of the leftist Nazis, as well as permitting freedom of the press. At the end of this speech, the applause drowned out any murmurs of protest. As Wheeler-Bennett later wrote, the speech was 'courageous and digni-fied in tone, it conveyed both a warning of the danger of a second radical wave of revolution and a very thinly disguised attack upon Goebbels personally'.[116] Goebbels was furious and all copies of the Marburg speech were ordered to be destroyed. But reports of what he said had already reached the British press and Wheeler-Bennett went immediately to Berlin, meeting Papen and lunching with former foreign secretary Richard von Kühlmann on 21 June.[117]

A few days later, Wheeler-Bennett was dining with two of Papen's adjutants on the terrace of the Kaiserhof. The summer heat, he recalled, was almost unbearable. In the middle of dinner, he was called to the telephone. Neill Malcolm was on the line from London, informing Wheeler-Bennett that Angela, Malcolm's daughter, was ill in Switzerland

and requesting that Wheeler-Bennett visit her. Wheeler-Bennett promised he would depart the following day.

'Thus it was in the safety of Switzerland that I read of the horrors of
the Night of the Long Knives, the massacre of 30 June 1934, when Hitler
chose to destroy his enemies' – among whom were Röhm and George
Strasser, the leader of the left wing of the Nazi Party. The 'evil genius'
Kurt von Schleicher and his wife were shot in their drawing room.
Papen's friend and associate Edgar Jung, who had written the Marburg
speech, was also killed. 'Only Edgar Jung sensed the coming danger;'
Wheeler-Bennett wrote soon afterwards, 'but, though he went into
hiding, he tried too late to fly the country. I met him in a secluded part
of one of the many wooded districts surrounding Berlin one afternoon
in that momentous week, and he was then convinced that nothing could
save him. He was entirely calm and fatalistic, but he spoke with the
freedom of a man who has nothing before him and therefore nothing to
lose.'[118] Several hundred other people were killed, including Wheeler-
Bennett's two dinner companions at the Kaiserhof.[119] To make matters
worse, the ageing president, Hindenburg, appeared to have accepted at
face value Hitler's justification for the purge. 'From the reports placed
before me I learn that you, by your determined action and your brave
personal intervention, have nipped treason in the bud,' Hindenburg
wrote in a telegram of thanks to Hitler. 'You have saved the German
nation from serious danger. For this I express to you my most profound
thanks and sincere appreciation.'[120] As Wheeler-Bennett was to write in
his biography of Hindenburg: 'The world, already nauseated by the
events of June 30, was shocked to hear that the President of the Republic
had warmly congratulated Hitler upon his exploits.'[121] For the German
people, the Night of the Long Knives revealed Hitler as the supreme
ruler of Germany, with the power to be both judge and jury.

5

Twilight

When we are dead,
We do not need to ask
To be forgotten. Our dynamic past
Disperses with its self-appointed task,
Ends as all ardour must.

Robert Vansittart.[1]

As far as Wheeler-Bennett was concerned, the timely telephone call from
Neill Malcolm had saved his life. Had he remained in Berlin, he believed
he too would have been killed.[2] From Switzerland, Wheeler-Bennett
returned to London. The next few months were spent engaged in
historical research and keeping up with his commitments at Chatham
House. In September 1934, he left for a tour of the United States and
Canada, where he undertook a number of speaking engagements including
at the Toronto, Ottawa and Montreal branches of the Canadian Institute
of International Affairs. He also visited his favourite haunts in the US:
Charleston and Charlottesville, as well as Washington, D.C., Annapolis
and Richmond.

Christmas was spent back in England, at Garsington. To Irene's three
children, Wheeler-Bennett was a 'favourite' uncle. 'We regarded him as
an exotic bird of paradise, flying in to visit an ordinary family of linnets
or chaffinches, but very warm and approachable at the same time,'
recalled his niece Mary, Irene's elder daughter. 'He used to come for the

weekend bringing a mound of luggage with him. In winter he arrived in a great coat with an astrakhan collar. Life went up several notches when he was around. We were allowed to stay up for dinner during the years just before the war, and although some of his stories of pre-war Germany had one gripping the edge of one's chair, my chief impression remains of laughter, cigar smoke and the aroma of liqueur brandy.' A 'wonderful raconteur', he 'roared with laughter at his own jokes. He knew and often used to recite the verses of every witty musical in London.'[3] Of his nephews and nieces, he developed a special bond with Irene's younger daughter, Juliet, who, like Wheeler-Bennett, was asthmatic. 'He used to come and sit by my bed when I was wheezing away and read me Kipling's poetry.'[4]

At the end of January 1935, Wheeler-Bennett left London, arriving in Luxor on 1 February. The following day, ensconced once more in the Grand Hotel, he noted in his diary: 'Began Hindenburg.' To date, the books he had written had been information reports, which, as the historian Alan Bullock later observed, 'gave no indication of the historian's power of handling narrative, analysis, and characterization'. In the decade since he had first visited Germany, Wheeler-Bennett had gleaned enough knowledge of both the man and his times to demonstrate 'the author's gift of historical interpretation and political judgement'.[5] In the middle of his Luxor stay, he went to Rome, securing another audience with Pope Pius XI on 23 February, later recollecting that the pope was known for speaking a great many languages badly. When he knelt at the altar rail with several others, the pope said a few words to him, which he failed to understand. When His Holiness was out of earshot, Wheeler-Bennett asked an aide what language the pope was speaking. 'English, Sir,' came the reply.[6]

Two days later Wheeler-Bennett met Italy's Fascist leader, Benito Mussolini. The focus of his interview was the deteriorating situation between Italy and Ethiopia: following a border clash at Walwal, the Ethiopian government had protested to the League of Nations about Italian aggression. Undoubtedly unknown to Wheeler-Bennett, Mussolini had already dispatched troops for a full-scale invasion. When he came to record his conversation with 'Il Duce' in his memoirs, Wheeler-Bennett simply related that he 'talked at length and told me some interesting things'. Mussolini presented Wheeler-Bennett with a signed photograph of himself sitting on his horse.[7] Reflecting in later life, Wheeler-Bennett did not believe the Italian leader had Hitler's 'black heart', or, if he did, 'it was of a lighter shade of black . . . he was a human being with all the failings and a few of the virtues thereof'.[8] After another fortnight in Luxor, he returned to England via Athens, Brindisi, Lugano and Paris.

While working on his book on Hindenburg, Wheeler-Bennett already had another project in mind based on the Treaty of Brest-Litovsk, signed between Russia and Germany in 1918. In his opinion, this treaty 'was the high-water mark of stupidity on the part of German military-political diplomacy in disclosing the predatory nature of the terms of peace which they envisaged in the event of victory and thereby ensuring the whole-hearted support of America for the Allied cause'. He also believed that the treaty ensured the success of the Bolshevik Revolution. In addition to preventing the March 1918 German offensive from being successful, 'it set the ultimate pattern for Stalin's foreign policy and it greatly influenced the Ostpolitik of Adolf Hitler'. Of the numerous books he was to author, he would come to describe *Brest-Litovsk: The Forgotten Peace* as the most enjoyable to write.[9]

He had already managed to carry out some of his early research on previous visits to Germany, making use of the contacts he had made to probe and question 'the chief actors on both sides'. Max Hoffman he regarded as 'an unlikeable figure', whom he held responsible for making known the new East European boundaries to which Germany hoped Russia would agree.[10] Wheeler-Bennett had also discussed Brest-Litovsk with the foreign minister at the time, Richard von Kühlmann, whom he had met with Malcolm in 1929 and saw periodically in London. 'I always knew when he [Kühlmann] thought he might have temporarily antagonised the Nazi bosses because I would receive a telegram asking if I could arrange for him to give a lecture at Chatham House. For old times' sake, I was usually able to do so.'[11] The favour worked both ways: during their conversations, Wheeler-Bennett learnt how, during Kühlmann's brief appointment as foreign minister in 1918, he had been appalled to find that external and domestic policy had been 'usurped' by Hindenburg and Ludendorff. 'Every person and every institution, from the Kaiser to the Chancellor and the party leaders in the Reichstag, from the tycoons of capital to the bosses of the trade unions, had surrendered the ultimate authority to these representatives of the military elite with the claret-coloured stripe of the General Staff on their field-grey breeches.'[12]

Having spoken briefly to Hindenburg about Brest-Litovsk, he considered that the president was much clearer in his mind about the current problems than he had been about those of the past. Ludendorff, Hindenburg said, had been 'utterly unreasonable' and his monologue 'consisted of a diatribe against a great international conspiracy in which the unlikely alliance of the Roman Catholic Church, World Jewry and the Grand Orient were combining to destroy civilisation'.[13] Bruce Lockhart had also let Wheeler-Bennett read the diaries he had written in Moscow, when he was employed by the Foreign Office as head of a special mission to establish unofficial relations with the Bolsheviks in early 1918.[14] On an earlier visit to New York, Wheeler-Bennett had also met the late Count Ottokar Czernin, minister for foreign affairs of the Austro-Hungarian Empire and Austria's representative during the peace negotiations with Russia. 'He spoke with emotion and sadness, nostalgia battled with courage. It was most moving. As I left him I felt that I had seen the last of an ancient regime which was as dead as Thebes or Carthage.'[15]

The people Wheeler-Bennett most wanted to see were the Bolsheviks. In the summer of 1935, he set off for the Soviet Union – his first visit since returning from the Orient with Neill Malcolm on the Trans-Siberian Express in 1929. Later, he considered that he had made this journey just in time because the 'grim shadows' of Stalin's purges were already hanging over Moscow: 'within a very short space of time most of the men I had talked with were either dead or in labour camps'.[16] On the way he decided to revisit Waterloo, mindful of his father's graphic descriptions of the battle. He then spent a week in Vienna, where two friends greeted him: Sir Walford Selby, the British envoy extraordinary and minister plenipotentiary, whom Wheeler-Bennett had known when Selby was at the Foreign Office; the other was George Messersmith, American consul-general in Berlin in the early 1930s.[17] There was also Franz von Papen, who, having been spared assassination during the Night of the Long Knives, had been posted as German ambassador to

Vienna. Wheeler-Bennett made a point of not calling on him, 'considering it unwise to stray even on to the diplomatic territory of a German legation', but the two men did meet socially. From both Selby and Messersmith, he learnt that Papen 'was busily engaged in clandestine operations directed towards the infiltration of the Federal Cabinet by the introduction of Ministers who, if they were not openly declared Nazis, were certainly well disposed toward an Anschluss between Germany and Austria on a common basis of National Socialism'.[18] Wheeler-Bennett was surprised to find that the House of Habsburg was regaining prominence. Having already met Otto von Habsburg ('charming, good-looking, witty and highly intelligent') and his mother, the empress Zita, through some Belgian friends a few years previously, Wheeler-Bennett was introduced into what was known as the Iron Ring, the close monarchist circle, headed by the sons of the assassinated Archduke Ferdinand and Sophie, Duchess of Hohenberg. 'Here I found a state of euphoria which I felt to be wholly inconsistent with reality, but these fanatical royalists seemed convinced that "when the crunch came", rather than a Nazi takeover, the monarchy would be restored.'[19]

Travelling on to Warsaw, where he spent a further week, Wheeler-Bennett reached Moscow on 21 June, to be joined by Neill Malcolm a few days later. There, as usual, he made use of his contacts: William Bullitt, the United States' first ambassador to the Soviet Union, who organised a translator for him, and Maxim Litvinov, the Soviet commissar for foreign affairs. Wheeler-Bennett had first met Litvinov, who had been responsible for facilitating the USSR's acceptance into the League of Nations, in Geneva during the sessions of the Preparatory Disarmament Commission. 'He had a rather benign appearance suggestive of a large teddy-bear that had lost most of its cuddlesomeness.'[20] As a result of these contacts, Wheeler-Bennett saw some important documents in the Marx-Engels Institute, originals buried deep in the vaults, preserved in silk and rice paper. Pleased to have met several 'Old' Bolsheviks, Wheeler-Bennett believed the 'star turn' was meeting the Bolshevik and international Communist leader Karl Radek in his dacha outside Moscow. 'We walked for hours among the pinewoods, accompanied by his little dog Tchortik.'[21] Not only was Radek involved in the secret negotiations with the German General Staff during the Great War regarding funding of the

Radek.
D [ ]unding!

Bolsheviks, but he had spent the immediate postwar years in Germany organising the German Communist movement. In return for his interview, Wheeler-Bennett sent Radek an English pipe from Dunhill's: 'whether it ever reached him or whether, if it did, it contributed to the cumulative suspicion directed against him, I shall never know for I received no acknowledgement.' In 1936, Radek was arrested and charged with 'Trotskyist deviation'. Spared the death sentence, he was sent to a labour camp, where he was reported to have died in a prison fight.[22]

In July, Wheeler-Bennett stayed for a few days in Berlin, where he made sure to dine at the Taverne with his journalist friends. He also had a meeting with William Dodd, the American ambassador, and breakfasted with Paul Scheffer, whom he had first met in Moscow in 1929 as the correspondent for the *Berliner Tageblatt*, of which Scheffer was now editor.[23]

In England in early August, he was invited by Lockhart to lunch with Jan Masaryk; also present was Bernstorff, who, after a decade in London at the embassy, had been forcibly retired from the foreign service in 1933 because of his opposition to the Nazi regime. By late September 1935, Wheeler-Bennett was on the move again, retracing his steps to Vienna via Berlin and Prague. Leaving Southampton, he arrived at Bremen, travelling directly to stay with Bernstorff at his home the Schloss Stintenburg in Holstein for the weekend of 28–29 September. Other house guests included a British journalist, Shiela Grant Duff, whose father, killed at the Battle of Aisne in September 1914, had been a friend of Neill Malcolm.[24] She was accompanied by a young German, Adam von Trott zu Solz, who was working for the Deutsche Levante Line, which operated between Hamburg and west Mediterranean ports. Trott and Grant Duff had met while she was an undergraduate at Lady Margaret Hall, Oxford, and he was a Rhodes Scholar at Balliol College. Also present was Basil Newton, minister at the British Embassy in Berlin. As Grant Duff noted, both Bernstorff and Wheeler-Bennett were 'eager to find out from him what was afoot in Anglo-German circles'. These developments were of special interest because, with the Nuremberg Laws, Hitler had recently taken the first 'lethal' steps against the Jews, depriving them of German citizenship and forbidding marriage between Germans and Jews. However, Newton 'divulged little' and their after-dinner conversation related to the ancient pedigrees, as evidenced by their tombstones, of the Trotts and Bernstorffs.[25] Over the weekend, Wheeler-Bennett obviously made an impression on Adam von Trott since the latter wrote to his father that he had met 'an especially interesting English writer who was writing a book about Hindenburg'.[26]

Travelling on to Berlin, Wheeler-Bennett saw Dodd again and had dinner with Paul Scheffer. During a meeting with Eric Phipps, the British ambassador, he described how, in his biography of Hindenburg, he was going to reveal the 'dubious parts' played by Dr Otto Meissner and the president's son, Colonel Oskar von Hindenburg, especially in relation to the Night of the Long Knives, officially known as the 'Röhm purge'. What Wheeler-Bennett intended to expose was that, with the conniv-ance of both Meissner and Colonel Oskar, the president had been delib-erately kept in the dark over the extent of the 'butchery'. Instead, Hindenburg had been encouraged to sign his telegram on 2 July, thanking Hitler for crushing the seeds of revolt. The only person who might have protested, Papen, had been arrested and kept isolated until the contents were published. As Phipps reported back to King George V, Wheeler-Bennett's book was likely to be 'interesting'. However, in view of the revelations he was going to make, at the conclusion of their meeting Phipps had suggested to Wheeler-Bennett 'that this would presumably be the last time I should have the pleasure of seeing him in Berlin. He smilingly agreed.'[27]

During this period, Wheeler-Bennett remained in regular correspon-dence with Heinrich Brüning. After leaving Germany in 1934, the former chancellor had come to London, making it his mission to enlighten the public on the liberal aspects of Germany as distinct from the Nazi regime. In the autumn of 1935, he secured a teaching position at the Immaculate Conception Seminary on Long Island, New York. Hence-forward, like Wheeler-Bennett, he divided his time between Europe and the United States. Having met Wheeler-Bennett with Neill Malcolm in August and ascertained that the British government had 'absolutely no policy' towards Germany, he was writing again to Wheeler-Bennett in October, urging him to speak with Vansittart 'and others to tell them how essential it was that British policy adopt a definite direction, before it is too late'.[28] No record exists of what Wheeler-Bennett reported to Vansittart but, at this stage, he was sympathetic to Brüning's concerns.

Less than a year after he began writing, despite all his travelling, Wheeler-Bennett noted in his diary on 4 December: 'finished Hindenburg.' As he was anxious to highlight in his narrative, towards the end of his life Hindenburg had spent more and more of his time 'in the seclusion of Neudeck', his country estate in Prussia, shielded from reality. As a result, the president was undoubtedly unaware of the extent of the Röhm purge at the end of June 1934. 'How much news of the ghastly week-end penetrated to Neudeck?' Wheeler-Bennett asked his readers. 'Very little, it is to be believed, and that in a suitably prepared form. It is certain that the murder of Schleicher and the arrest of Papen were kept from Hindenburg, and it is probable that only the story of the S.A. conspiracy was told to him.' Wheeler-Bennett even questioned Hindenburg's authorship of the telegram to Hitler. 'Did Hindenburg authorise the telegraph or was it merely sent in his name by some of those zealous officials who "protected" him so effectively? Let us believe that the latter was the case, as it may well have been, for it is a fearful thing to find Hindenburg, in the last weeks of his life, openly condoning murder even in the name of justice.'[29]

Wheeler-Bennett's final appraisal was that Hindenburg's life was both pitiful and tragic, 'for no figures in history are more tragic than those who have outlived the faith in their greatness'.[30] That he chose as the book's subtitle the phrase 'The Wooden Titan' was evidence enough of Wheeler-Bennett's controversial opinion that, as impressive as Hindenburg may have appeared, he was less of a giant than his protagonists maintained. In later life, at a critical juncture in Germany's political evolution, those close to him, most evidently Hitler, were able to take advantage of Hindenburg's mental decline. Wheeler-Bennett dedicated the book, 'With gratitude and affection', to the newly elected Conservative MP Gerald Palmer and his mother who had frequently entertained him at their Berkshire home, Prior's Court. First among the others Wheeler-Bennett acknowledged was Lewis Namier, 'whose searching criticism, inexhaustible patience, and warm encouragement have meant so much both to me and to the book'.[31] Namier later told Lockhart that *Hindenburg* was 'the best book written for a long time – brilliantly done and very valuable'.[32] Namier was also responsible for introducing Wheeler-

Bennett to Harold Macmillan, MP, who, over the next forty years, would be Wheeler-Bennett's friend and publisher.[33] With the publication of *Hindenburg: The Wooden Titan*, Wheeler-Bennett's reputation as a historian was assured. George Messersmith, the American minister in Vienna, later commented that he had done 'a great service' in covering 'certain phases' of Hindenburg's life.[34] As the British ambassador Eric Phipps had intimated would be the case, Wheeler-Bennett made no attempt to visit Germany after the book's publication.

New Year's Eve 1935 was spent in Paris. Wheeler-Bennett then went to Rome again to see the 'Holy Father', as he noted in his diary, before returning directly to London. The mood in Britain was one of change and royal confusion. King George V had died on 20 January; his funeral took place a week later. It was assumed that his eldest son would ascend the throne as Edward VIII. His desire to marry Wallis Simpson, the American divorcee, however, meant that during protracted discussions no date for the coronation could be fixed. Although a staunch royalist, no contemporary record exists of what Wheeler-Bennett thought of the constitutional crisis, perhaps because he spent most of the year in the United States. His health was still unstable, and he had written to Ivison Macadam at Chatham House requesting further leave of absence from his duties. 'I have unfortunately been pretty unwell since I left England and am only now beginning to get back anything like my old form,' he wrote from Augusta, Georgia, describing his 'distressing attacks of fainting and sleeplessness'. As a result, he had been advised by his doctors to remain in the US for the summer, 'unless of course the crisis in Europe becomes more acute and it is necessary for all of us to return from wherever we are'.[35] The situation on the other side of the Atlantic did indeed look ominous. Already Italy, under Mussolini, had been censured for its aggression against Ethiopia. On 7 March 1936, Hitler defiantly repudiated Locarno by sending troops into the demilitarised Rhineland.

In April, Wheeler-Bennett's mother, Christina, sailed from England to join her son, and the next few months were spent based in Charlottesville, which, with its attractive buildings, designed by the third US president, Thomas Jefferson, Wheeler-Bennett was beginning to consider a second home.[36] From these safe surroundings, he continued to reconstruct the story of the Treaty of Brest-Litovsk. Basing himself at the

Farmington Country Club, which offered views of the Blue Ridge Mountains, he had taken up riding again, having acquired a 'splendid' horse called Red Match. One May morning, while sitting on the terrace of the club, he observed a group of faculty members, accompanied by their 'belles', one of whom was 'petite, blue-eyed, golden haired'. As Wheeler-Bennett later recollected, his heart turned a somersault. 'That is the girl I am going to marry,' he informed his mother, to which she replied that he could do a lot worse. Her name was Ruth Risher and she worked in the registrar's office of the university: like Wheeler-Bennett, she was in her mid-thirties and unmarried.[37]

Christina Wheeler-Bennett returned to England in October. Meanwhile her son remained in the US, enjoying his riding and working on Brest-Litovsk. As in England, he was also gathering around him an eclectic group of friends, professors and students, lawyers, architects and doctors. Since his early visits to New York, he had established a link with Harvard. Among those he met there were Manley O. Hudson of the Law School and Bruce Hopper in the School of Government. 'At first I sat at the feet of these pundits. I attended their lectures and was hospitably entertained by them in their houses, or at the Faculty Club, of which I was usually made a temporary member.' Later, as Wheeler-Bennett's reputation grew, he was asked to address some of their classes and seminar sessions, 'and of this I was, not unnaturally, extremely proud'. One of the high points was representing the Royal Institute for International Affairs at Harvard's three-hundredth-anniversary celebrations in 1936, in the company of Ham Armstrong, who was representing his journal, *Foreign Affairs*, and at which President Roosevelt gave an address.[38]

At the same time, Wheeler-Bennett continued to make excursions to Washington, D.C. and New York; in September, he was in Quebec and in November he went to Toronto, where he addressed the Canadian Institute of International Affairs and dined with Flavelle.[39] He did not return to England until the first week of December. During his absence the attention of the British public had been focused on the tortuous decision of Edward VIII to abdicate, which he did formally on 10 December, shortly after Wheeler-Bennett's return home. The new king was Edward's younger brother, Albert, known by his family as Bertie, who took the name George VI. On the day he ascended the throne, Wheeler-Bennett was having lunch at the Ritz with Baffy Dugdale, who noted in her diary that he 'talked about Germany. He is convinced Ribbentrop used Mrs Simpson [to push for Anglo-German rapprochement] but proofs are hard to come by.' Wheeler-Bennett also repeated to her what he had heard Edward VII's mistress, Mrs George Keppel, say about Edward VIII's abdication. 'The King has shown neither decency, nor wisdom, nor regard for tradition!'[40] Christmas was spent with Irene and Trevor and their children at Garsington.

As always, although continuing to write books, Wheeler-Bennett was pursuing other interests with his friends. One of these concerned Vernon Bartlett, who had started a monthly magazine, *The World Review*. Wheeler-Bennett considered it to be an excellent publication but it was suffering financially. At the same time, the more famous *The Review of Reviews*, in which the British journalist W.T. Stead had conducted his campaigns for social reform and world peace at the beginning of the century, came on the market at a low price.[41] As 'a romantic idealist, fervent believer in world peace, I hated to see this monthly, which in its hey day exercised considerable influence, sink without trace. I bought it and proposed to Vernon that we should pool our assets and talents in a combined publication called *World Review of Reviews*. We launched it with Vernon as editor, that wise and experienced counsellor Ian Parsons of Chatto and Windus as publisher and myself chairman of the editorial board.' This was in early 1937. According to Wheeler-Bennett's recollections, they 'blasted' away against the policy of appeasement currently being pursued by prime minister Neville Chamberlain, giving their support to Winston Churchill, who was beginning to take centre stage as the leader of a breakaway faction of Conservatives opposing Chamberlain. 'The paper continued to be highly successful until on the brink of hostilities we sold it at a good profit. It then became a war casualty.' After the war, Wheeler-Bennett was 'flattered' to discover that both Vernon and he had been included on the Nazi 'Black List' of those who were to be 'arrested and liquidated in the event of a successful invasion of Britain. In this document I figured as "Bennet (sic) of the Royal Institute of International Affairs".'[42] Meanwhile, Wheeler-Bennett was having a literary spring-clean and in January had written to a Miss Cleeve at Chatham House, asking her if the Institute would like some of the books he could do without, which were primarily those on the Chinese revolution and the Philippines, since these subjects were now outside his sphere of specialised interest.[43]

Back in the United States, where his doctors had once more recommended he spend the spring and summer, Wheeler-Bennett continued to work on Brest-Litovsk. Basing himself in Charlottesville, where he furthered his relationship with the young woman, Ruth Risher, he had glimpsed with his mother, he made trips to New York and Boston. At a dinner at the Century in New York, he met Theodore Roosevelt, Jnr, the eldest son of the late president Theodore Roosevelt. Not long afterwards, Wheeler-Bennett was invited to spend a weekend at their rambling house on the waterfront at Oyster Bay. As he realised, Ted junior, who had served as governor-general of the Philippines, was 'a man of many interests', yet living under his father's shadow. A favourite pastime shared by the two men was swapping and capping quotations from their favourite poets: Kipling, Macaulay, Browning, Tennyson, Longfellow and Rupert Brooke.[44] When Wheeler-Bennett first met Ted Roosevelt, the former First Lady was still alive and the two men frequently called on this 'formidable *grande dame*'. The other person with whom Wheeler-Bennett established a lasting friendship was Ted's half-sister, Alice Longworth, who, since her childhood, had had a reputation for being a headstrong, unconventional woman. She was in her late forties when they met, and Wheeler-Bennett confessed to being 'in love' with her for nearly half a century thereafter. 'I revel in her wit and humour and mischievous gossip.'[45]

While working on the Brest-Litovsk book, Wheeler-Bennett realised there was a gap in his research that could 'only be filled after a talk with Leon Trotsky'.[46] As usual he was able to pull an introduction out of the hat. On this occasion Max Eastman, an old friend who had become a Trotskyist and translated many of Trotsky's writings into English, provided a letter of introduction. Following his expulsion from the Soviet Union and Central Asia, Trotsky had lived first in Turkey and then in a villa in Coyoyacan, a suburb of Mexico City. Security was extremely tight and on arrival in September 1937 Wheeler-Bennett was subjected to 'as thorough a "frisking" as I think is possible. No article of my clothing, no part of my body was left unexamined.' When he finally came face to face with Stalin's arch–enemy, he found him 'almost friendly'. Now in his late fifties, Trotsky admitted that he had not thought about the Treaty of Brest-Litovsk for some time.

> Would I refresh his memory? I began to recount the story of the negotiations and it was like watching a machine gradually come to life. He came from behind his table and began to pace the floor; he plunged his hands into his abundant hair as if in search of inspiration, as if cudgelling his brain to remembrance, and then it happened. In the middle of a sentence of mine, the penny dropped in his mind and out came a torrent of reminiscence, justification, accusation and recrimination. He spoke in English, French, German, Russian and even Yiddish (the last two of which were incomprehensible to me) and it seemed as if I were submerged in a flood which had been dammed up for years awaiting release.

Stalin, he told Wheeler-Bennett, was 'a terrible man. He has stolen my thunder. He has said that it is he, Stalin, who has created the Red Army. I tell you it was I, Trotsky, who created the Red Army.' As a parting gift, Trotsky gave Wheeler-Bennett a signed copy of his book *The Stalin School of Falsification* and his autobiography, *My Life: The Rise and Fall of a Dictator*. Looking back, Wheeler-Bennett recognised that he had been fortunate to meet the Bolshevik leader. 'I had talked with one of the single most destructive forces in the twentieth century and had learned a lot.'[47] In 1940, Trotsky was assassinated with an ice pick by a young man who, acting on Stalin's orders, had successfully penetrated his security.

Wheeler-Bennett then returned to Charlottesville. While continuing to write *Brest-Litovsk*, he was watching the current European situation. Throughout this period, he had remained in touch with Brüning, who was still seeking to demonstrate to his British and American friends that there was an anti-Fascist movement in Germany. In the autumn of 1936, Harvard University had offered Brüning the opportunity to teach international relations, and he had taken the opportunity to visit Wheeler-Bennett in Charlottesville. In September 1937, at Brüning's request, Wheeler-Bennett had entertained Carl Goerdeler, former mayor of Leipzig and a member of the German National People's Party, who had been price commissioner under Brüning.[48] Through Wheeler-Bennett's friendship with Vansittart, Brüning wanted Goerdeler to keep in touch with the British establishment, and he urged Wheeler-Bennett to commend him to Vansittart.[49] According to Wheeler-Bennett, Goerdeler, who had become increasingly disillusioned with Nazi rule, 'was now an acknowledged leader in the German Resistance movement'. When the two men met in Charlottesville, Wheeler-Bennett described how they 'sat late talking and he told me *inter alia* of his hopes that the overthrow of Hitler would result in the restoration of the monarchy, at any rate in Prussia, and possibly the reconstitution of the German Empire on a more liberal, constitutional basis.' But the visit was marred by an unfortunate occurrence. 'He nearly scared the wits out of me, however, by having a heart attack during the night. Though it proved to be only a minor one, I had visions of his dying on my hands.'[50]

Another visitor was Paul Scheffer, who had resigned as editor of the *Berliner Tageblatt* in 1936 and come to New York, 'whence,' as Wheeler-Bennett related, 'he did not hesitate to report the rising tide of American opinion against National Socialist Germany'. Like Brüning, he was anxious to highlight that not all Germans supported Hitler. 'Though he hated the Nazis and his civilised and fastidious temperament was outraged by their brutish methods, he remained a patriotic German.'[51] During this period, Wheeler-Bennett received a stream of other visitors, including Bruce Lockhart from London. 'The variety or notoriety of my guests, plus the fact that members of the Embassy staff often came to me from Washington for week-ends, caused me to be suspected of being a highly placed official in British Intelligence, and I became known facetiously as "operator 269".'[52]

In the autumn, Wheeler-Bennett contributed a long article to the *Virginia Quarterly Review* entitled 'European Possibilities', in which he examined the 'incongruous events' of the past two years – 'anomalies of so stupendous a character that they savour of bedlam'. 'In Russia the former President of the Communist International is executed as a Fascist, . . . in Spain a rebel movement avowedly Catholic in nature is supported by a dictator who has been engaged in persecuting the Catholic

Church . . . Political alignments and military groupings are formed of states without a basic thought in common, thrown together by the force of circumstances and the caprice of fate.' In the present day, he suggested that 'two rival constellations dominate the political horizon'. The first was the Berlin–Rome relationship, which included Hungary, 'half Spain, and an unwilling Austria'. Second, there was Britain and France with their attendant satellites, whose influence extended beyond Europe. In addition, there were the neutral states. Having examined the various relationships, he put forward four possible future scenarios: a 'show-down' between the two rival groups; a 'tacit understanding' between Britain, France and Germany that in return for a guarantee of peace in Western and Central Europe, Germany 'shall have a free hand in the East'; third, a Russo-German rapprochement; and, finally, the 'miracle of peace'. In Wheeler-Bennett's opinion, this last might yet be possible, provided – within the next two years – the gap between German and British rearmament could be narrowed. 'A war postponed may be a war avoided.'[53]

At the time that the article was written, which must have been several weeks before its publication in the autumn of 1937, Wheeler-Bennett was placing himself on the side of those who would prefer not to resort to war, provided Britain could negotiate from a position of military strength. At least one reader found his prognosis 'very gloomy'. Having met Wheeler-Bennett in Germany in 1935, Shiela Grant Duff wrote to Adam von Trott: 'What he calls the "miracle of peace" seems the only working hypothesis on which we can go on at all. It is rather defeatist to call European peace a miracle – he says the next two years are going to be the most critical in the history of Europe. But I cannot see what substantial appeasement can grow out of the mere fact of your having completed your re-armament. Unsound Machiavellianism will not keep Europe together.'[54]

By the end of the year, Wheeler-Bennett had finished *Brest-Litovsk*. His research had taken him far and wide and included working in the United States Department of State library. He had also been helped by Nicholas Oushakoff, of the Harvard Law School library, who had translated a number of documents from Russian. Describing the book as 'terribly long', Wheeler-Bennett confessed to being 'a bit exhausted after having given birth to this prodigious child! However, I hope that it will justify this parental effort.'[55] He remained in America until early 1938, by which time the European situation was worsening. On 20 February, the foreign secretary, Anthony Eden, on whom Wheeler-Bennett had placed his hopes in his *Virginia Quarterly* article, resigned in opposition to Chamberlain's discussions with Italy. There was also a growing group of politicians opposing Britain's continuing appeasement of Germany. Three weeks later, on 12 March, with the ground prepared by the Austrian Nazi Party and by Wheeler-Bennett's erstwhile riding companion Franz von Papen, who was still in Vienna, the Anschluss was effected. As a result, the German-speaking peoples of Austria and Germany were united in a Greater Germany.

After less than two months back in England, on 16 March 1938, Wheeler-Bennett set sail on board the *Queen Mary* to return to the United States. During the voyage, he became ill and the ship's doctor diagnosed a severe streptococcal infection. Although he had recovered by the time he arrived in New York, when one of his friends saw him, she described him as 'looking like death'. This was passed on to the acclaimed writer Dorothy Thompson, another journalist Wheeler-Bennett had met in Germany, who had been expelled in 1934 for her fiercely anti-Nazi line. Having taken a literal interpretation of the description, she wrote an obituary for the *Herald Tribune*.[56] 'The whole incident,' wrote Wheeler-Bennett, 'caused some perturbation among my friends in America, where I was delighted to hear that Ruth must have been deeply concerned. The newspapermen called my aged mother on the telephone in London in the middle of the night and asked if she could confirm or deny my death, but she replied tartly that if I had died she would certainly have learnt of it long before the press.'[57]

Once he was well enough, Wheeler-Bennett travelled south again to Charlottesville. He was thinking about his next book which, surprisingly after *Hindenburg* and *Brest-Litovsk*, he thought might have a North American rather than a European theme, and, owing to his fascination with the American Civil War as well as his maternal family connections, he was considering writing a book on the army of Northern Virginia. The idea proved short-lived, however. After meeting Douglas Freeman, author of the definitive four-volume biography of Robert E. Lee, published in 1934, and making a tour of the battlefields, he realised that 'any contribution I might make to the study of the army of Northern Virginia would be but feeble and superfluous'.[58]

Wheeler-Bennett's prolonged absences from Britain resulted in a decision to reduce his commitments to Chatham House. In May 1938, he wrote to Ivison Macadam, informing him that he considered it was time for somebody, and preferably a younger person, to take his place. 'So far as I can see for the next few years, my life will be somewhat divided between this country and England and even in the event of my being re-elected, my attendance could only be spasmodic and uncertain.'[59]

Wheeler-Bennett had added another American destination to his itinerary. While on a visit to Washington to stay with the British ambassador, Sir Ronald Lindsay, his wife, Elizabeth, had advised Wheeler-Bennett to go to the warmer climes of Tucson, Arizona to regain his health, giving him an introduction to a friend, Isabella Greenway. Originally from Kentucky, and a close friend of Eleanor Roosevelt, having been a bridesmaid at her wedding in 1905, Greenway had come to Arizona on her honeymoon after marrying her second husband, Colonel John Greenway, in 1922. Later, widowed for the second time, she became the state's first Congresswoman. In 1934, Greenway established the Arizona Inn as a place of respite and to create a demand for furniture built by disabled veterans of the Great War. Wheeler-Bennett's visit marked the start of a long connection with Arizona and a friendship with 'the most enchanting woman' he had ever known.[60]

Back in England by mid-August, Wheeler-Bennett watched anxiously as Czechoslovakia passed along the *Via Dolorosa* to Munich. 'It was heartrending to witness the gradual disillusionment of the Czechs as the reluctance of their French allies to aid them became more and more apparent.'[61] He had never experienced 'such mental anguish . . . I had never known one could be physically sick from humiliation and impotence'. He also confessed that he had seriously thought of emigrating to the US 'rather than remain in a country with whose national policy I was so completely at variance, with no hope of bringing about a change in it'.[62] Marking a change from his earlier belief in the 'miracle of peace', those whose company he frequented were men who were now endeavouring to stiffen the attitude of the British government 'at least to the extent of giving definite guarantees of support to France'. The dominant figure was Winston Churchill, 'a recognised leader among the dissident Tories and others in the House of Commons, Anthony Eden, Bobbety Cranborne, Harold Macmillan, Dick Law, son of Bonar, Harold Nicolson and closest of all his followers, Brendan Bracken'. Hearing Churchill speak, he came away 'strengthened and heartened'.[63]

Wheeler-Bennett was also in touch with what he called 'a ginger group', which included his friends Baffy Dugdale and Lewis Namier. They dined and lunched frequently in each other's houses and clubs and in restaurants in Soho in order to plan a strategy which they relayed back to the cabinet and Foreign Office, 'but all in vain . . . These were dreadful days, and as the late summer slipped into autumn and it became more and more apparent that the Czechs were to be abandoned to their fate, one's heart was rung for Jan Masaryk'. By the time Neville Chamberlain made his historic journey to Germany to meet Hitler in Munich, Wheeler-Bennett was thoroughly depressed. 'The last weeks of September 1938 in London will always remain with me as the lowest point to which my spirit has ever sunk. It was, indeed, in the words of St John of the Cross, "The dark night of the soul".'[64] Feeling compelled to 'do something' after Chamberlain's ill-fated announcement that he had achieved 'peace for our time' by sacrificing the geographical integrity of Czechoslovakia, Wheeler-Bennett wrote to *The Times*. As the League of Nations' high commissioner for refugees, Neill Malcolm also signed the letter, which began: 'In the midst of the natural relief and rejoicing at the withdrawal of the shadow of war in Europe and while all of us acknowledge with deep appreciation and respect the great personal effort which the Prime Minister has made in reaching a peaceful solution of the Sudeten problem, it would be wholly discreditable to us if we in the cause of peace forgot, or failed to honour, the very considerable sacrifices which the Czechoslovak people have made'. The 'pith' of the letter was an appeal for assistance for the thousands of refugees who were fleeing from the German-occupied areas of Czechoslovakia. 'Thousands of men and women in this country must feel moved to make some definite act of thanksgiving for the avoidance of war. Surely there could be no better expression of this desire than to contribute generously to the lessening of the load with which a small country has been suddenly burdened in the cause of peace.'[65] In response, the lord mayor of London, Sir Harry Twyford, opened a fund; the total amount subscribed was £318,000.

A week later, Twyford, Malcolm and Wheeler-Bennett flew to Prague to superintend the distribution of the money and discovered 'an appalling state of affairs'. All registered residents of the areas that Germany now occupied and who had fled were to be returned, which was 'tantamount to a death warrant'. To delay the order being enforced and enable them to set up a relief operation, Malcolm and Wheeler-Bennett requested an audience with General Jan Syrovy, the popular war hero and prime minister of the new Czech government. To their disappointment, the interview was 'like talking to a stone wall'. Having listened to their plea, Syrovy rejected it: 'We have been willing to fight on the side of the angels, now we shall hunt with the wolves.'[66]

Wheeler-Bennett did not stay in Europe. Earlier in the year, he had been both surprised and pleased to be asked to join the faculty of the Law School at the University of Virginia in the fall of 1938. The semester had already started but Wheeler-Bennett arrived 'primed with first hand experience' of events in Europe.[67] Unsurprisingly, Munich was a major topic of conversation and the reaction was not always favourable. 'I have never been in this country when criticism was so rife and when it was so difficult to discuss international affairs even with one's friends,' he wrote to Lord Astor in November. Foreshadowing a role he was himself to adopt, he continued: 'We are *not* popular in this country, and I think it is up to us to find out why and, if possible, to discover a remedy.'[68]

Teaching at the Virginia Law School was his first academic assignment and he approached his task 'with due awe' as someone who had never attended university himself.[69] 'On the appointed day I was received with warmth and courtesy by the Dean and assistant Dean of the Law School and conducted into a large office, light and airy. What, I asked, was I supposed to do there? The reply came: you are to be available for consul-tation by students.' However, no students came and, left in virtual solitary confinement, he spent the day writing letters, reading and waiting to be consulted, before going home. The next day, 'not a little discouraged and feeling that I was not earning my keep, I returned to my very comfortable office and to my delight I found, in the middle of my large

writing table, an envelope of the size more usually employed for an
invitation from the Queen to the Duchess to play croquet. Here, at last
I thought was someone who desired my advice and guidance.' But the
large envelope contained nothing more than an invitation to the Virginia
Glee Club on Friday night.

Once his weekly seminar session and consultations started in earnest
and his students got to know him, his office became 'something of a
rather select club'. Looking back, Wheeler-Bennett recognised the value
of the experience, 'for I was forced to collate and analyse my own
thoughts. My students were a brilliant lot and, as I write, I can see them
again as they sat around in my drawing-room, for our sessions were very
informal and supplemented by beer and sandwiches'.[70] Of his students,
those he best remembered were the prolific novelist Louis Auchincloss,
Larry Houston, one of the founding fathers of the Central Intelligence
Agency, and Franklin Roosevelt, Jr, the son of the president of the
United States.[71] As Wheeler-Bennett recalled: 'In the dear departed days
before the Second World War, there was an atmosphere of infinite charm
and leisure – a happy marriage of the formal and the familiar.' There was
no co-education and the young men wore non-matching tweed trousers
and jackets with collars and ties. 'One addressed them collectively as
gentlemen and individually as Mr So and So and they called one Sir.'
Yet beneath the formality, there was a friendly relationship between
faculty and student body. 'One might easily for example meet one's
students on the hunting field and at parties in the country. The social
life within the university was gay and frivolous, despite the fact that in
Europe and in the Orient, the portents of the coming storm had achieved
proportions a good deal larger than a man's hand in the international
firmament.'

For as long as it lasted, Wheeler-Bennett delighted in his new academic
role. Together with the dean and assistant dean of the Law School, he
had lunch at a small restaurant just outside the university grounds. 'We
would then play pin-ball to decide who should pay for the lunch. It was
that sort of age.' Putting his experience in a European context, where
war was now imminent, Wheeler-Bennett tried to 'awaken the minds of
these young men' to the problems they would face if the United States
also became caught up in the conflagration.[72]

Meanwhile, having attended lectures at Harvard, he was now being asked to speak to Bruce Hopper's government classes. In the autumn of 1938, with the Munich crisis fresh in his mind, Hopper requested Wheeler-Bennett to address his class on the situation in Europe. 'A most pleasing open countenanced, blue-eyed young man came up to me afterwards and introduced himself as Jack Kennedy.' He reminded Wheeler-Bennett that they had met in London, when his father, Joseph Kennedy, was the US ambassador. Through Hopper, it was arranged that Wheeler-Bennett would supervise the young Kennedy's Master's thesis, focusing on Britain's policy of appeasement culminating in the Munich Agreement. 'In the next few weeks, I travelled periodically from Charlottesville to Cambridge, and despite the journey and the climate, I much enjoyed my association with this attractive boy who was to be the young Knight of Camelot.' Later Kennedy's thesis was published as a book under the title *Why England Slept* (a parody of Churchill's 1938 book, *While England Slept*), and Wheeler-Bennett was presented with a copy. Thereafter the two men kept intermittently in touch.[73]

Wheeler-Bennett's *Brest-Litovsk: The Forgotten Peace*, arguably his best book, was published in November 1938. He had chosen to dedicate it to Bruce Hopper, to whom he also gave thanks in his Introduction. Other friends who received thanks included Lockhart and Namier, who was currently professor of history at Manchester University, and not forgetting his secretary, Margaret Dunk, who had laboriously typed the manuscript. Over the Christmas holidays, one of his friends, Harold Caccia, second secretary in the private office of Lord Halifax, who had replaced Eden as foreign secretary, read the book.[74] As Wheeler-Bennett later wrote, he was 'apparently favourably impressed by it, seeing a certain appropriateness in some of its contents in application to current events of the day'. According to Wheeler-Bennett, Caccia sent a minute to Halifax, warning that, with the Germans' expansionist ambitions evident since the Great War, Hitler might choose to make an attack on the Ukraine. Caccia went on to express the belief that Stalin could well be responsive to a British suggestion of support.[75] When the minute reached the desk of Vansittart, Halifax's chief diplomatic adviser, again, according to Wheeler-Bennett, he understood the intent and suggested sending a high-level cabinet member to see Stalin. However, no further action was taken. In later life, Wheeler-Bennett liked to think that his book might have had some influence in the event of an approach made to Stalin before signature of the Nazi-Soviet non-aggression pact. 'May one not wonder whether the possible adoption of the Vansittart-Caccia suggestion, in which *Brest-Litovsk* played its part, may not be numbered among the major "Ifs" of history?'[76]

An interesting by-product of Wheeler-Bennett's law seminars was an invitation in early 1939 to spend a weekend at the White House to celebrate the president's birthday on 30 January. As a birthday present, Wheeler-Bennett had brought the president of the United States a copy of his biography of Hindenburg. Their evening's entertainment was a visit to the National Theatre to see Sutton Vane's drama *Outward Bound*, the performance being given in aid of the annual campaign in support of infantile paralysis research, which always ended on the president's birthday. The following day Wheeler-Bennett spent an hour with Roosevelt in the Oval Office. His encounters with the president made him believe that 'he was incontestably one of the great figures of this century . . . he had infinite charm, the manners of an aristocrat, that is to say an amalgam of courtesy and ruthlessness and a great deal of pragmatic common sense'. According to Wheeler-Bennett, the topic that most interested the president was Munich. 'I told him all I knew, of my conversations with Beneš and with Jan Masaryk and of the fruitless mission of Neill Malcolm and myself to General Syrovy in Prague after Munich.' Although Roosevelt did not say so explicitly, Wheeler-Bennett was left with the feeling that the possibility of war 'was much in his mind'.[77]

Events in Europe were reaching a climax. On 16 March, Hitler disregarded the Munich Agreement, announcing that Czechoslovakia no longer existed. As far as Wheeler-Bennett was concerned, 'it was now no longer a question of "if" there should be a war but of "when" war would come'.[78] Although 'deeply distressed and worried', he was hopeful that Hitler's 'bare-faced brutality' would have its brighter side. 'It has certainly jolted the P.M. out of his beliefs in the fidelity of the Führer and that in itself is something, for Hell hath no fury like a disillusioned daydream! And also, by swallowing the Czechs, Hitler has incorporated in the Reich a people who for two hundred and fifty years have perfected

the art of political sabotage and this must be a factor for weakness rather
than for strength.'[79]

Meanwhile, Brüning was continuing to share his candid opinions about
the deteriorating situation, informing Wheeler-Bennett that he thought
it was a big mistake 'in a kind of panic' to have agreed to a defensive
alliance with just Poland, rather than joining all the Balkan countries
together and creating a line of resistance with Russia.[80] A month later
he was lamenting Britain's attempt to make an alliance with the Soviet
Union: 'As you know so well the mind of our Army, you will realise
better than anybody else what a shock it was to the Army. After the
[Great] War, they had only one dogma in foreign politics and that was
that Germany and Russia should never again be in opposite camps which
I think was quite right.'[81]

As always, Wheeler-Bennett remained in close touch with his mother,
sharing his highs and lows. Now aged seventy-seven, after the sale of
Ravensbourne in the early 1930s, Christina was living in a flat in Queen
Anne's Mansions, London SW1, with a companion. 'My own darling,'
he wrote from Charlottesville. 'Well Easter is over or rather Easter week
is over, which is the high point in University festivities for the year,
corresponding rather to Commem. week at Oxford. Classes stop at 10.30
on Thursday morning, April 13, which is Thomas Jefferson's birthday
and celebrated as Founder's Day and there are balls every evening until
Saturday night. Sunday is a day of farewell between the lads and their
lasses and on Monday the usual routine takes up again.' The likelihood
of war was a recurring theme: 'I do hope darling that you will not adhere
to your decision to stay in London in the event of war. It would be so
much wiser to go somewhere in the west of England – Exeter for
example . . . I really think it is the patriotic duty of everyone to get out
of London who can, because the feeding problem is going to be a difficult one. Please consider this very carefully.' He ended his letter with
the hope – but little genuine optimism – that 'the outlook will be better
next week'.[82]

As it happened, on the Founder's Day Wheeler-Bennett had described
to his mother, he had been asked to entertain the former president of
Czechoslovakia Edvard Beneš and his wife whom he had first met in the
1920s. Although Wheeler-Bennett considered him to be 'a different cup

of tea altogether' from his predecessor, Masaryk, he came 'to admire his
dogged courage in the face of adversity'.[83] Now living in exile after
Germany's 'rape' of Czechoslovakia, he had wanted to place a wreath
on the grave of Thomas Jefferson on the anniversary of his birthday. The
guest of honour at Founder's Day was Sumner Welles, the American
under-secretary of state. In view of the United States' recent recognition
of the newly established 'Protectorate of Bohemia and Moravia' in what
remained of Czechoslovakia, it was considered best that Beneš and Welles
did not meet. During the official ceremony, Wheeler-Bennett's task was
to distract Beneš and his wife with a sightseeing tour. But he miscalcu-
lated the length of time Welles would speak and when they arrived back
at the university, he observed 'with horror' that Welles was still there.
'With the speed of light I whisked Dr and Mme Beneš behind an adjacent pillar and began a voluble, introductory and doubtless wholly inac-
curate lecture on the architectural jewels of the University . . . at last the
coast was clear.'[84]

   A week later he was writing again to his mother, explaining the need
to delay his planned return to England. As far back as 1937, an invitation
had been extended both by the prime minister of Canada and the president of the United States to King George and Queen Elizabeth to visit
their respective countries. Despite the tensions in Europe, the date for
their departure had been fixed for May 1939. Momentarily, with
Chamberlain announcing a more assertive policy against the latest German
aggression, it appeared that the royal visit might be postponed. During
the period of uncertainty, Wheeler-Bennett had been unsure whether he
should return to England, as planned, or whether he should wait. 'Well
well, the best laid plans of mice and men,' he wrote. 'I know that you
will be as disappointed as I am that our reunion is thus postponed but
it's just one of the additional minor ways in which the eddies of international crises affect the lives of ordinary humble mortals . . . Isn't it
ghastly that the fate of the whole world hangs on one man's word?'
Meanwhile, he related his activities: 'I was in Washington on Thursday
and spent the night with our Counsellor, Victor Mallett. I lunched with
the Dwight Davises on Friday and then drove down to Richmond . . . That
night I was the guest speaker at the annual meeting of the Virginia
Academy of Social and Political Sciences.' He told his mother that he

had made 'a spirited case' for Chamberlain's new policy of being tough
with Hitler and that the speech 'was quite a success and a number of
people came up afterwards to tell me that they had really understood the
intricate workings of the psychology of British Foreign Policy for the
first time!!! Next weekend I am going to stay with Ted Roosevelt at
Oyster Bay and attend with him the opening of the World's Fair by the
President of the United States . . . Much, much love, my dearest one,
from your own loving, Jack.'[85]

Despite Hitler's recent renunciation of the German-Polish Non-
Aggression Treaty of 1934 and the Anglo-German Naval Agreement of
1935, as well as the finalisation of the Anschluss with Austria, it was
considered sufficiently safe for the king and queen to sail to North
America. After over two weeks in Canada, George VI and Queen
Elizabeth arrived in the United States in early June. The visit, Wheeler-
Bennett believed, 'not only strengthened immeasurably the sympathies
between the two countries but also laid the foundations of a very sincere
friendship between the King and the President which was to bear abun-
dant fruit'. Through the British ambassador, Ronald Lindsay, Wheeler-
Bennett was asked to be 'a sort of extra-equerry' at the garden party held
on 8 June at the British Embassy. 'It was the hottest day I have ever
known and I suffered gravely in my morning dress. I was attached to
Queen Elizabeth's party and all went famously, as we stopped here and
there for momentary introductions. The Queen was superb . . . She was
so utterly unlike anything they had expected; queenly but human, regal
but sympathetic. She was a revelation.'[86] As Wheeler-Bennett later wrote,
the visit of the king and queen made 'a fitting close' to his last summer
of peace. 'The most important effect of all was upon the President of
the United States . . . he quickly discovered that he had much in common
with the Queen, and that with the King he could discuss a diversity of
interests as man to man.'[87]

After the royal visit, Wheeler-Bennett returned to England with a
'strong desire' to write another book. He had rejected the idea of writing
on the American Civil War and now considered that a more appropriate
subject would be the life of Kaiser Wilhelm II, who, following his abdication in 1918, was living in exile at Doorn in Holland. 'My interest in
the German Emperor, both as an historical figure and as a personality,

had increased rather than waned over the years.'[88] To move the project forward, and with the 'storm-cones of approaching conflict' being hoisted in every capital in Europe, Wheeler-Bennett believed there was no time to be lost in meeting his subject personally. Since Bruce Lockhart had previously travelled to Doorn to write a story on the Kaiser in 1928, he agreed to accompany him.[89] When no reply was forthcoming to their official request for an interview, Wheeler-Bennett asked Crown Prince Wilhelm's youngest son, Prince Friedrich, whom he 'knew well', to take a personal letter to his grandfather. A reply came at once, inviting both Wheeler-Bennett and Bruce Lockhart to stay as the Kaiser's guests at Haus Doorn. 'It was a strange journey,' he later related. 'The Dutch countryside in that lovely summer was redolent of peace and security and prosperity; yet, to the eastward, the war clouds were gathering over Danzig, and here were we on our way to see the man who, twenty-five years before, had unkeyed the avalanche of the First World War.'[90]

Recollecting that his father had called the Kaiser a 'howling cad' with a reputation for rudeness, Wheeler-Bennett considered that 'old age and twenty years of exile had greatly mellowed him . . . his wardrobe and his English had a definite Edwardian flavour . . . once launched upon a subject – and he placed no prohibition on any subject for our discussion – he talked with fluency, animation and wit, displaying a remarkable clarity of mind and an amazing accuracy for dates, but not always such an outstanding respect for facts.' Wheeler-Bennett also recorded how the Kaiser talked of his love of England and the English (except for his cousin Bertie) and that he had been misunderstood and misled. 'He would never have gone to war if he had known that England was coming in; he had only wanted to beat the Russians!' Out of deference, Wheeler-Bennett and Lockhart restrained themselves from touching too closely on the current situation, although the Kaiser himself 'launched forth on one occasion on the subject of Lebensraum' – Hitler's ideal of obtaining greater 'living space' for the German-speaking people.

During their meeting Wheeler-Bennett noticed that 'in order to refresh his memory on a certain point he would swing round to the cupboard on his left and unlock it. There, ranged in row after row of beautifully bound red morocco volumes, each with its clasp and lock, were his diaries

from I don't know how long back. He selected the volume for 1914,
unlocked it with a key on his watch-chain, found the particular entry he
wanted and thrust it under my nose.'[91] In hindsight, Wheeler-Bennett
admitted to being oppressed 'by a sense of nightmarish unreality'. 'To
discuss all morning the events and happenings of that old world which
had crumbled in flames in 1914, and then to go back to one's rooms in
the afternoon and read in the daily papers of the increasingly inescapable
probability of an imminent repetition, was an experience which I shall
never forget.'[92] Its 'macabre motif' was epitomised by the Kaiser's farewell
remark: 'Come back and see me again next summer, if you can. But you
won't be able to, because the machine is running away with *him* as it ran
away with *me*.'[93] The Kaiser's parting gift was a signed copy of his autobiography, *Aus meinem Leben*, and some photographs which he had also
signed.[94]

Back in England, Wheeler-Bennett was offered a fresh assignment. The
new British ambassador to the United States was Philip Kerr, Lord
Lothian, whom Wheeler-Bennett had met through their mutual membership of Chatham House and other organisations. Lothian had written the
introduction to the fourth volume in the Information Series. There had
been a rift in their friendship when, in 1937, Lothian visited Germany
and was received by Hitler, Hess and Ribbentrop, and, on his return to
England, had defended German rearmament and the remilitarisation of
the Rhineland. Lothian was now proposing that Wheeler-Bennett should
be his personal assistant in Washington. 'I eagerly accepted for it marked
the healing of a breach which I had greatly regretted.'[95] As he also ascertained, his appointment had the approval of Vansittart who, since 1938,
had been chief diplomatic adviser to the foreign secretary.

On 23 August 1939, Wheeler-Bennett left Southampton on board the
French liner the SS *Normandie*. 'It was not a pleasant voyage. We were
a very mixed bag. War was now accepted as inevitable . . . The atmosphere was one of near hysteria, assisted to some extent by the fact that
we were blacked out at night.'[96] Arriving in New York five days later,
he met up with his friends there, including Ham Armstrong and Dorothy
Thompson; she had recently added to her journalistic record by cham-
pioning the cause of a seventeen-year-old German Jew, Herschel
Grynszpan, the unwitting instigator of Kristallnacht in November 1938.

Enraged at his family's deportation from Germany to France, Grynszpan
had entered the German Embassy in Paris and shot a junior diplomat. In
retaliation, on 9–10 November 1938, an orchestrated pogrom against the
Jews in cities throughout Germany had been carried out, destroying
thousands of Jewish homes, businesses and synagogues.

While discussing the likelihood of war, Wheeler-Bennett was surprised
at the 'marked tendency to believe that, even at this late hour and despite
all our declarations to the contrary, Britain under pressure from France
would "do another Munich" and abandon the Poles as the Czechs had
been abandoned'.[97] Before taking up his assignment with Lothian, he
returned briefly to Charlottesville to spend time with Ruth. 'I like to
think that my last days of peace and of the happiness of my old life in
Virginia were ending in these pleasant surroundings.' On Sunday, 3
September, as he stood on the veranda in the early morning sunshine,
'looking out towards the untrammelled peace and grandeur of the Blue
Ridge', he heard Neville Chamberlain's voice on the radio announcing
that a state of war existed between Britain and Germany.[98]

6

The Perils of War

This is not our war . . . We should not make it ours.
We should keep out of it . . .
The frontiers of American democracy are not in Europe, Asia or Africa.
Chicago Tribune, *September 1939*[1]

When, with the blessing of Sir Robert Vansittart, Lord Lothian requested
Wheeler-Bennett to be his personal assistant in the United States, he
did not intend that he should remain by his side in Washington. Instead
he wanted Wheeler-Bennett to be his 'eyes and ears' throughout the
continent, subtly promoting the war with the American people.
Wheeler-Bennett began his new assignment by visiting friends in Chicago
and Kansas City 'to see if I could assay the general opinion of this vital
heartland of America'. Talking with everybody from newspaper proprie-
tors to university professors and businessmen, his initial finding was 'the
predominant desire' to keep the US out of the war at all costs, 'and woe
betide those who might be foolhardy enough to try to make her do
otherwise'. Back in Washington, he wrote a detailed report for Lothian,
a practice he would continue for the next year. His reports were 'always
highly confidential, often trenchant and somewhat racy in style' and gave
'a fairly comprehensive picture of the development of American opinion'.[2]
Another early assignment on Lothian's behalf was to attend a requiem
mass for the archbishop of Chicago, Cardinal Mundelein, who, as a
German-American, had been an outspoken critic of National Socialism.

The presence of a British representative would, Lothian believed, appease the Catholic Poles and Irish as well as the anti-Nazi German-Americans.

Wheeler-Bennett was also assigned to visit the British Library of Information (BLI) in New York, which had been under the direction of Angus Fletcher since 1928.[3] As an institution tasked with keeping the press and private individuals informed about life and culture in Britain, it had turned into a 'sleepy hollow' 'with a decreasing prestige and a diminishing clientele'. Wheeler-Bennett found it in 'a deplorable condition not exactly of inertia but of a total inability to grasp the idea of what to do and how to do it'. The fear of transgressing the policy of 'No Propaganda', which was a tenet of the Foreign Office's thinking since the 1920s, had resulted in 'a paralysis, the staff of the Library being afraid or unwilling to open its mouth in answer to the most harmless and general enquiry'.[4]

To revitalise the institution Vansittart had already hired Aubrey Morgan, the grandson of the founder of the Cardiff department store, David Morgan, who had settled in the United States.[5] When Wheeler-Bennett first met Aubrey Morgan he recognised the differences in their temperaments (Morgan had been 'a keen and useful cricketer' at Charterhouse and Cambridge, whereas he had been 'a duffer at games'); but the two men had literary tastes in common, both being enthusiasts for the popular adventure novels of Anthony Hope, *The Prisoner of Zenda* and its sequel *Rupert of Hentzau*. Morgan had the distinction of having married two sisters: his first wife, Elisabeth, had died of heart disease in 1934; he then married her younger sister, Constance. Both were daughters of Senator Dwight Morrow, a partner in the financial investment company J.P. Morgan and former ambassador to Mexico. (The middle sister, Anne, was married to Charles Lindbergh.)[6] Another member of their group was a former financial consultant and keen cricketer, Major Cyril Berkeley Ormerod, known as 'Bill'. Dressed like a character out of a P.G. Wodehouse novel, he became the BLI's 'eyes and ears' on Wall Street.[7] Overall direction was given by Alan Dudley, assistant director of the BLI since 1930.[8] With premises in Rockefeller Center and the telegraphic address of DIGESTION, they put together press cuttings and sent them on to the consulates. While Morgan established links with American journalists and his wife and a group of writers collated the material into a series of reports, Wheeler-Bennett kept Lothian informed of their progress.[9]

At the outbreak of war, the British Embassy staff in Washington numbered eighteen; as time passed, this 'over-taxed, over-tired' band was increased to nearly a thousand.[10] Together with Lothian, whom Wheeler-Bennett came greatly to admire, the most 'outstanding personality' of the original complement of men was Frederick (Derick) Hoyer Millar, the first secretary: 'wise and firm, he had all the virtues of the Establishment and he was always fair and of great charm'.[11] An early new arrival was John Foster, a 'brilliant' barrister who took over the duties of legal adviser to the embassy.[12] In Washington, Wheeler-Bennett stayed in the pleasant locality of Georgetown with an old friend, Keith Officer, who was currently attached to the British Embassy as the Australian first secretary, and whom Wheeler-Bennett had first met at the Melbourne Club in 1923.[13] When in New York, he continued to stay at the Chatham, recommended to him by Ham Armstrong on his first visit in the 1920s. Later, he, Aubrey and Constance Morgan rented a house on the south side of East 70th Street.

Lothian had suggested that Wheeler-Bennett visit all the consular posts to assess their strength. He therefore embarked on an ambitious itinerary, travelling from Boston to New Orleans and from New York to San Francisco. In all, he noted seventeen posts, five of which were consuls-general, and three of which were on the East Coast: 'this was barely sufficient for a peacetime establishment but totally insufficient for wartime conditions.' On his return, he produced a report for Lothian which the latter used as the basis of a paper on the reform of the consular service and its personnel in the United States.[14] In addition, Wheeler-Bennett undertook a number of speaking engagements, crisscrossing the continent. By the beginning of December – three months after the declaration of war – he had spoken in thirty-seven of the forty-eight states, addressing 'every stratum of educational institutions from the Service academies at West Point and Annapolis, the Ivy league establishments and the great women's colleges of the East, to high schools and teachers' colleges in Little Rock, Arkansas and Wichita, Kansas'.[15] On one occasion, on Lothian's behalf, Wheeler-Bennett preached a sermon in Pittsburgh Cathedral, which involved wearing a black silk robe 'so bedecked with gold bullion that I could barely stagger under it'.[16] He also got in touch with the French Information Centre in New York, whose director, Robert Valeur, and colleague, Raoul de Roussy de Sales, did not have the same aversion to disseminating propaganda as the British. Every Saturday, de Sales, a former correspondent for *Paris Soir*, met Wheeler-Bennett and Morgan for lunch to exchange news and views.[17]

As a German expert, Wheeler-Bennett remained in close contact with the Germans exiled in the United States, among whom was Heinrich Brüning. Such was their friendship that among Brüning's British and American friends only Wheeler-Bennett could call 'this austere statesman' 'Harry'.[18] Coincident with the outbreak of war, the former German chancellor had been offered the position of Littauer Professor of Government at Harvard's new School of Public Administration. Another of Wheeler-Bennett's old German friends was Paul Scheffer. Having continued to contribute a column to the *Berliner Tageblatt* until the paper's closure in January 1939, he was now actively involved in publicising the initiatives of the anti-Nazi Germans.[19] In October 1939, Adam von Trott zu Solz arrived in Washington. Since Wheeler-Bennett had first met him with Bernstorff at Stintenburg in 1935, Trott had been practising law in Germany. But as the situation had deteriorated there, he had decided to go abroad, having arranged to spend the postponed third year of his Rhodes Scholarship in China. Back in Germany at the end of 1938, he had become part of a group of Germans who were anxious to avert war and who hoped this could be achieved if Hitler were replaced as chancellor. In June 1939, Trott was visiting England. While staying at Cliveden with David Astor, a friend from Oxford, he had met a number of senior British government officials, including the prime minister, Neville Chamberlain, and the foreign secretary, Lord Halifax.[20] He also met Wheeler-Bennett again, probably due to the initiatives of Lothian, who, as secretary of the Rhodes Trust, had known Trott as a scholar in 1931.

Trott's presence in the United States was ostensibly owing to an invitation from the Institute of Pacific Relations to attend a conference at Virginia Beach as a 'Far East' expert. More importantly, while in the US, he wanted to lobby for American support of the embryonic German resistance movement. At the end of November, under instruction from Lothian, Wheeler-Bennett accompanied Trott to Virginia Beach. During the time they spent together, sometimes riding along the 'broad grey sands of the Virginia shore',[21] Wheeler-Bennett listened to Trott's pronouncements against Hitler. Back in Washington, Trott's efforts to lobby for support included the preparation of a memorandum to circulate to the State Department. The paper, largely authored by Scheffer but signed by Trott, outlined the concerns of the anti-Nazi Germans.[22] As Wheeler-Bennett noted: 'Trott urged that, for their part, Britain and France should re-state their position in the war to the effect that they were fighting against Hitler and the Nazi regime but not against the German people.'[23] By circulating the memorandum to American officials, it was hoped that the US government would pressurise the Allies to accede to this demand. But suspicions had already arisen among establishment Americans that Trott might be a Nazi spy. There was also concern that, much as he might be opposed to Hitler and Nazism, he and any fellow sympathisers fell into the category of 'ultra-nationalist' Germans who would be unwilling to return the territorial gains that Hitler's policy of expansion had already made.[24]

Wheeler-Bennett, however, was sympathetic to what Trott was trying to achieve. On 27 December, he wrote a seven-page letter to Vansittart, expressing concern that not enough was being done to encourage moderate Germans.

I have been greatly exercised of late on the subject of peace terms. It seems to me that we are possibly missing a chance – perhaps only a thin one, but still a chance – of bringing about a rising in Germany by the elements in every class who are antagonistic to the Nazi regime but who hesitate to take action before they are assured that the Allies will give generous treatment to the new Germany which they – and we – hope to achieve. Obviously we cannot make peace with a Nazi or 'shadow Nazi' government, but could we not give to those elements within Germany with whom we could make peace an indication of what our future attitude towards them is to be by making an Allied Statement of Policy that we do not intend to impose a political

To Project

dismemberment on a Germany which has purged itself of the evils of
National Socialism and, as a proof of its sincerity, has restored the
Rechtsstaat? I entirely understand that a full statement of peace terms
is inopportune at this time, but if we cannot say what we <u>are</u> going to
do, we can at least say what we are <u>not</u> going to do. I believe that a
statement of this sort would have an enormous effect in Germany if it
were made in the right way.

Wheeler-Bennett went on to point out the obvious danger that Germans
might turn for support to the Bolshevik Soviet Union.

old anti - Bolsh. bogey

In point of fact, I think that the possibility of a Germany combined
with Russia on the basis of National Bolshevism is not altogether
impossible. The German people are standing at the crossroads, hesi-
tating whether to turn to the West or the East. By tradition, culture
and inclination they tend towards the West but desperation may drive
them Eastwards. The very hatred of Britain which is today so violent
is partly due to the fact that, in our propaganda, we have harped too
much upon the note that the German people have been misled by
Hitler and not enough upon what the West has to offer the German
people when they have rid themselves of Hitler. I do not believe that
the people themselves wish to turn towards Russia but they will
certainly do so rather than surrender to a humiliating peace.

To Project

Wheeler-Bennett also suggested that a statement might be made from
the German side and that Heinrich Brüning was the only person who
could make such a statement. 'As you know I am in very close touch
with him and on intimate terms of friendship.'[25]

He supplemented his letter with a four-page memorandum and two
further pages on what could be done to restore the Rechtsstaat.
Reminding Vansittart that Chamberlain had emphasised that Britain was
not fighting against the German people 'but against a tyrannous and
foresworn regime', the memorandum suggested that 'the present struggle
is a War for the Liberation of the German People, and in the struggle
the Democratic Powers have an ally within Germany itself in those high
patriots of every class and calling who reflect the fundamental decency

of the German People. These elements, more numerous and powerful than may be supposed, have a common aim with the Democratic Powers in destroying the Nazi regime and in restoring in Germany a Reign of Law (a Rechtsstaat) which will ensure to the German People their ancient liberties.'

Wheeler-Bennett concluded the memorandum by urging Vansittart to consider that it was, 'therefore, to the interests of the Democratic Powers that these elements within Germany should be strengthened and encouraged to the point where they themselves can take the initiative'. General terms, he said, were not sufficient

to convince completely a German People already rendered incredulous by the memory of what they honestly believe to be the betrayal of the Fourteen Points by the Treaty of Versailles, and, while it is realized that a full statement of peace terms would be inopportune at this moment, it is also true that a more definite assurance is necessary before the elements within Germany antagonistic to the regime can feel themselves justified in taking the momentous and perilous step of rising against their national government. They cannot be expected to risk all in the common cause without being 100% certain that the new Germany, which they will help fashion, will receive both justice and generosity.[26]

At the same time, Trott was writing to David Astor, currently working as a journalist for the *Observer* newspaper. Enclosing a copy of Wheeler-Bennett's memorandum, he commented: 'he understands, as you will soon discover, one essential role of Germany probably better than anyone in your country at the moment . . . He should be very carefully listened to.'[27]

Vansittart, on the other hand, was wary of showing any enthusiasm, noting to Alex Cadogan, permanent under-secretary for foreign affairs:

I think, in view of the position that he [Wheeler-Bennett] holds, we shall have to be rather careful how we reply to this, because what we say may go further. I am inclined for the present to send him merely an interim reply, saying that I have read his letter and enclosure with interest and am thinking the matter over . . . If any further reply is considered necessary, I think it would have to be very carefully drafted. The impression left on my mind on a first reading of this communication is that Wheeler-Bennett is too optimistic as regards Germany . . . This leads him to over-rate the potentialities of German moderates, who, to my mind, today either do not exist or have very little effective influence.[28]

Cadogan's handwritten response to Vansittart suggested that it might be worthwhile considering issuing a statement:

I don't know whether it would be of any use to announce that we should be ready to enter into a Conference with another German Govt (without at the moment defining its complexion) on the basis of principles of settlement already indicated – righting of wrongs done to Austria, Czechoslovakia, and Poland, etc. A process of question and answer through underground channels might give us an idea of what would be possible in the way of a new regime in Germany.

Cadogan hoped, however, that it would not lead to another incident of the kind that had embarrassed the British in early November, when British agents had met supposed German officers in the Dutch town of Venlo, who said that they were plotting against Hitler but were actually working for the Gestapo.[29] When Vansittart replied to Wheeler-Bennett in February, true to his own initial thinking, his 'interim letter' promised nothing: 'Thank you very much for your letter of the 27th December last enclosing a memorandum on the subject of peace terms. I have read the letter and memorandum with great interest, and I am thinking the matter over. It is of course a very big subject, which requires careful thought.'[30]

At the same time, Halifax had sent a copy of Wheeler-Bennett's letter and memorandum to Neville Chamberlain, prefaced by the remarks 'which you may care to see'.[31] Unfortunately, Wheeler-Bennett's plea coincided with the appearance of a story of a peace plan being thrust into Halifax's hands by a Danish businessman, Kai Pless-Schmidt, which had also been given to Ribbentrop.[32] As the war entered a more deadly phase, the idea of negotiating with moderate Germans was forgotten,

while Vansittart and his colleagues turned their attention to the deteriorating situation in Europe. The US government was also not convinced
that supporting a German resistance movement was going to pay the
necessary dividends. Disillusioned by the response he had received, Trott
left New York, travelling first to California and then back to Germany.
Wheeler-Bennett wrote him a farewell note: 'First let me wish you, in
every sense, the greatest of good fortune in the aim which we have in
common. May it be achieved sooner than we hope, but, in any case,
eventually!' Mindful that Trott had had to deal with Americans who
were suspicious of his intentions, he praised his forbearance. 'I would
like to say how much I admire your courage and determination
under very trying circumstances. I hope that under similar conditions I
could match you in them, but I am pretty sure I couldn't.'[33] Back in
Germany, Trott attempted to work from within, having secured a
position in the Political Intelligence Department of the German Foreign
Ministry.

By the beginning of 1940, Wheeler-Bennett had travelled so much that
he was exhausted and was glad to take a break over New Year in Virginia,
despite the very cold winter (with a reported temperature of 5 degrees
Fahrenheit below zero and sixteen inches of snow). He was no longer
renting a house, but had secured a furnished bed–sitting room, 'so that at
least I have some place to return to, but at the present time this is the
only home I have on either side of the Atlantic'. Although he was on
'indefinite' leave from the university, he had been allowed to keep his
office in the law faculty 'so that I have some place for my books'. He
also spent time with Ruth Risher, living what he called a triangular
'peripatetic' existence between Virginia, Washington, D.C. and New
York. Not surprisingly, as he informed Lockhart, who had been assigned
to work in the Central Europe and Balkans section of the newly formed
Political Intelligence Department (PID), based in Woburn Park,
Bedfordshire, his project to write the life of 'the poor old Kaiser' had
been shelved.[34] Instead, he had been working on an official book of 'war
aims', which Lockhart viewed with some scepticism, warning about 'the
various cranks who have pet schemes for the reformation of the world.
Federalisation is the new slogan. God knows whether it will ever be
possible.'[35]

While assuring Lockhart in a long letter, written on 29 January, that his book would not be 'a vehicle for any crack brained scheme to hasten the millennium', Wheeler-Bennett wanted to share some thoughts on the future. Still thinking about his conversations with Adam von Trott, Wheeler-Bennett pursued the same theme as in his December letter to Vansittart. 'Once the Nazis have gone, we should conclude a peace of co-operation and not of vindictiveness. Clearly, there can be not the slightest return to a Munich mentality. We cannot make peace with a Nazi or "shadow Nazi" regime. The first move for peace must come from the German people themselves by giving tangible evidence that they not only are prepared to destroy National Socialism from within, but that they have already taken constructive steps to do so.' He went on to describe some of the difficulties he was facing in trying to galvanise support for the war in the isolationist-minded United States: 'As you can imagine, the life of a belligerent in this very "neutral" country is not all beer and skittles. For the first time, I have felt an alien in America, and this is not a very pleasant experience for one who has as great an affection for and as close an affiliation with this country as I have. All Englishmen are suspect as propagandists and the degree of suspicion varies from frank hostility to guarded sentiments amongst one's friends.' Estimating that Americans were '98% anti-Hitler', he said that it was difficult to assess how many were 'pro-British'. Undoubtedly, he said, the proportion

is very large, but certainly not as large as the anti-Nazi opinion. People feel they can be 'anti' and still have no danger of being dragged in, but once they become 'pro' they have a fear that their isolation may be endangered. The propaganda phobia is quite astounding, though recently there have been reactions against it, because the state of mind created by this fear of believing anything seen in print or heard over the radio is actually affecting the public reaction to commercial advertising!

Wheeler-Bennett lamented to Lockhart that the Nazis had got the upper hand in terms of propagating their side of the story: 'Our friends the enemy have been clever in their approach in a whispering campaign. They have admitted frankly that their propaganda frequently lies, but they claim the same degree of mendacity for the reports put out by the British and thereby impress upon those with whom they are in contact that nothing can really be believed. This, of course, is playing into the hands of the isolationists and still further confusing an already bewildered public opinion.' In Wheeler-Bennett's view, Britain's failure to make any very clear pronouncement of war aims had led to 'the fairly wide-spread belief that this war is really one of rival imperialisms'. He therefore thought it would be 'of immense value if some one on the Allied side could repeat each month that we do not demand an inch of territory from the enemy; that we have no desire whatsoever to bring about the economic or political destruction|| of the German people, and that all we are fighting for is to put an end to a "tyrannous and fore-sworn regime", to use the Prime Minister's own words, which has forced a system of violence upon Europe. This cannot be too greatly or too frequently emphasised in this country.' Finally, writing to Lockhart, he expressed concern about his own prospects:

> I have been wondering very much in recent weeks whether I should not be of greater use at home than here. As you know, I came back at the end of August on the expressed advice of Van[sittart], who felt that my special knowledge of this country would be best used here rather than at home. But I believe that by the summer my usefulness here may well have been exhausted and that I could do better work at home. I have thought of writing to Van direct about this, but I wonder if you could sound out the ground for me and see if he feels that there is a place for me in your outfit, or perhaps in the Ministry of Information, though I would infinitely prefer to be with him and with you. I shall not write to him until I hear further from you on this subject, and shall, of course, be guided by your joint wisdom. Although this is rather a lonely 'outpost of empire' I don't want you to feel that I am in any sense running away from it. I simply feel that perhaps my specialised knowledge of this country and of Germany might perhaps be more useful at home than here . . . Please write me again in answer to this . . . in these days one's close friendships come to have more and greater meaning.[36]

Whether Lockhart wanted him back in England or not, Wheeler-Bennett was kept busy in America, undertaking more speaking engagements at a range of institutions which included Women's Clubs, Knights of Columbus and Rotary Clubs, always delivering the same message: Britain was determined to fight for its just cause. But there remained a fine line between advocating the war and adhering to the 'No Propaganda' policy. Writing to Sir Frederick Whyte, head of the American Division of the Ministry of Information in London in February 1940, Lothian maintained that 'whilst No Propaganda is still our watch word so far as the United States is concerned, this does not mean that we are not doing our best to make accurate information on our aims and actions available to those who are misinformed'. He went on: 'While as I have emphasised above, I continue to be opposed strongly to lecturers in general, I am impressed by the value of the work of such an assistant as John Wheeler-Bennett, now on the Library establishment as a consultant and spending a portion of his time there, his great value is that he keeps contact with a considerable number of interests and people and speaks at a number of gatherings of students of international affairs.'[37]

As the phoney war became the real war, another assignment for Wheeler-Bennett was to travel to California to contact the British actors living there, some of whom had written to the British Embassy 'rather vaguely' offering their services, to encourage them to continue to do what they could to retain interest in British war charities. As Lothian had at once realised, British actors in the United States formed 'a powerful nucleus' in a community that might otherwise be left 'to the mercies of German propagandists'.[38] One British actor whom Wheeler-Bennett knew personally from his days at school at Malvern was Brian Aherne, who had made his debut in 'talkie' films in 1931 and was currently starring in a film version of A.J. Cronin's 1939 story *Vigil in the Night*.[39] Through Aherne, Wheeler-Bennett met the elder of the British film colony, C. Aubrey Smith, who agreed to host a meeting of British actors. 'It was a strange experience to see in the flesh those deities of the screen whom one had so often enjoyed on film.' Among them were Ronald Colman, who had recently starred in the film version of *The Prisoner of Zenda*, the Australian Errol Flynn, and Charles Laughton, who had lately received acclaim for his role in *The Hunchback of Notre Dame*. According to Wheeler-Bennett, they were all anxious to help but were 'slightly disappointed when they found I couldn't give them all daring jobs in Intelligence'. But they succeeded in raising money for various charities and encouraged their American counterparts to do the same.[40]

On 16 April 1940, a week after the Germans had begun their invasion of Denmark and Norway, Wheeler-Bennett was speaking at Brown University, Providence, Rhode Island. Three weeks later, at dawn on 10 May, German troops crossed into Belgium and Holland. That night, Chamberlain resigned as prime minister and Winston Churchill assumed the office. The following day, Wheeler-Bennett was speaking at Princeton, describing the ensuing weeks as 'a veritable "cauchemar du diable". Isolated in New York, dependent for our news on the alarmist and emotional reporting of the American media, the almost maddeningly calm, detached broadcasts of the BBC and official telegraphs from London, which, when intelligible at all, were vastly out of date, Aubrey Morgan and I were a prey to anxiety and frustration.'[41] Amidst the crisis, however, there was always the opportunity to make new friends. In the summer of 1940, Foster brought Isaiah Berlin to dinner. 'I fell at once under the spell of his brilliant intellect.'[42] So impressed was Wheeler-Bennett with the Oxford philosopher – seven years his junior – that when Berlin's proposed job in Moscow fell through he asked him to join their mission in Washington, which Berlin did the following year.

A highlight of Wheeler-Bennett's calendar was the visit in June 1940 of the president of the United States to the University of Virginia. His son, Franklin, Jr – Wheeler-Bennett's pupil – was due to receive his law degree and the president had agreed to give the Commemoration address. On the same day – at midnight, 10–11 June – Italy declared war on Britain and France. Wheeler-Bennett recalled listening to a 'frenzied oration' by Mussolini. Roosevelt's address, given a year before his historic meeting with Winston Churchill at Placentia Bay, Newfoundland, was an early indication of where the American president's sympathies lay:

On this day, 10th June, 1940, the hand that held the dagger has struck it into the back of its neighbour. On this 10th day of June, 1940, in this University, founded by the first great American teacher of democracy, we send forth our prayers and our hopes to those beyond the

seas who are maintaining with magnificent valour their battle for
freedom . . . We will extend to the opponents of force the material
resources of this nation; and at the same time we will harness and speed
up the use of those resources in order that we ourselves in the Americas
may have equipment and training equal to the task of any emergency
and every defence.[43]

*FDR
June 1940*

When Wheeler-Bennett heard these words he felt a shock of excitement 'which passed through me like a shot of adrenalin. This was it; this
was what we had been praying for – not only sympathy but pledges of
support. If Britain could only hold on, until these vast resources could
be made available to her, we could yet survive and even win the war.
It was the first gleam of hope.'[44] As the president was due to leave, he
recognised Wheeler-Bennett from their weekend at the White House
and arranged for him to drive in his motorcade back to Washington,
whence Wheeler-Bennett was flying on to Oklahoma to speak at the
university. 'In this august company my driver Joe, who was bursting with
pride, and I zoomed over the 120 miles to Washington with the greatest
ease . . . Never have I caught an airplane with greater comfort and less
anxiety.'[45]

Shortly afterwards, Wheeler-Bennett was back in Virginia to attend
the annual session of the Institute of Public Affairs. The principal speaker
was to be Lothian but the date was not propitious. When, on 17 June,
it was clear that the battle for France was lost, Wheeler-Bennett had to
take Lothian's place. His speech, made *ex tempore*, was Wheeler-Bennett's
own call to arms: 'Tonight my country stands alone, alone – before the
embattled might of totalitarian Europe, Nazi Germany rooted in hatred
and cruelty and perversion, and Fascist Italy standing forth at last in her
true colours, wearing a suit of tarnished blackmail and with the bar-
sinister upon her shield. Tonight, for the first time in many years, your
country sees an unfriendly Power established on the far shores of the
Atlantic. France, immortal and glorious France, has fallen at our side.'

To please his more critical listeners, who were opposed to perpetuating
an anachronistic empire, Wheeler-Bennett adopted the theme of resur-
rection and purification as he felt was illustrated by John Milton in his
Areopagitica, defending free speech in England during the Civil War: 'not
degenerated or drooping to a final decay, but casting off the old and

wrinkled skin of corruption, to outlive these pangs and wax young again, entering into the truth of prosperous virtue, destined to become great and honourable in these later ages.' Of all the tributes he received for his speech, Philip Lothian's – 'Well done, Wheeler-Bennett' – gave him the 'greatest pleasure and gratification'.[46]

After the fall of France, the strategy emanating from the British Embassy in Washington, and supported by Winston Churchill, was to convince the Americans that Britain's survival was vital to the security of the United States while continuing to highlight the heroism of Britain's determined stand against Germany. To assist with their work, Churchill set up a new intelligence organisation British Security Coordination (BSC). Under the direction of the Canadian soldier and spymaster Sir William Stephenson, who operated under the codename 'Intrepid', it worked in parallel with the BLI. Over the next few months, Wheeler-Bennett witnessed a welcome change in American public opinion: 'I recall particularly an address Philip [Lothian] gave to the Yale alumni in which he laid the facts boldly and brutally before his listeners. Under Hitler's control, he told them the seas would never be open to all as under British or American control. If the Nazis gained possession of the British fleet the security which Britain and America had enjoyed for the last hundred and twenty years would disappear.'[47] This shift in approach heartened Wheeler-Bennett. Although still wanting to be back in England 'to share the exaltation of the miracle of Dunkirk and the preparations for resisting invasion', he felt 'a new tranquillity of mind'.[48]

In August, he took a month's 'working' leave. Rumours of an imminent German invasion of Britain were rife and, if they proved accurate, he preferred to be in England. If no invasion took place, he wanted at least to gain first-hand experience of the situation at home so that he could continue to address American audiences on the subject. Since early August, the Germans had been attacking shipping in the Channel in earnest, strafing the coastline. On 13 August – known as Eagle Day – the German Luftwaffe's all-out offensive against the RAF began. Wheeler-Bennett arrived in England two days later. Having been absent for a year, he delighted in seeing his old friends, especially those at the Foreign Office, including Vansittart, Alec Cadogan, Orme 'Moley' Sargent, who like Cadogan, was a permanent under-secretary of state for foreign affairs, Charles Peake, head of the News Department at the Foreign Office and chief press adviser at the Ministry of Information, and the cartoonist Osbert Lancaster, who was working in the press censorship bureau.[49] Wheeler-Bennett also met the new minister of information, Duff Cooper, who had replaced John Reith, as well as spending time with Harold Nicolson, who had become parliamentary private secretary to Cooper, and Ronald Tree, the Anglo-American MP, who was also PPS to Cooper.[50]

In addition to his duties at PID, Lockhart had been appointed liaison officer to the Czechoslovak government-in-exile and so Wheeler-Bennett renewed his friendship with Masaryk and Beneš. A highlight of his visit was an 'unforgettable talk' with Winston Churchill, who 'catechised' him about public opinion in America. With the Battle of Britain reaching its climax in the skies, Wheeler-Bennett was one of many listeners when Churchill paid tribute to the RAF fighter pilots in the House of Commons on 20 August: 'The gratitude of every home in our Island, in our Empire, and indeed throughout the world, except in the abodes of the guilty, goes out to the British airmen, who, undaunted by odds, unwearied in their constant challenge and mortal danger, are turning the tide of the World War by their prowess and by their devotion. Never in the field of human conflict was so much owed by so many to so few.'[51]

To supplement his personal knowledge, Wheeler-Bennett felt compelled to visit Dover. While he was there, a German Stuka strafed the coast. As he was about to leave, he came under direct shell-fire, necessitating a half-hour wait in a public shelter. 'I realised how much worse shelling was than bombing. It was, I found, a greater strain to the nerves and its accuracy made it the more frightening.'[52]

Before returning to the United States, Wheeler-Bennett spent the weekend of 7–8 September at Ronald Tree's Palladian home at Ditchley in Oxfordshire; later, Tree was to place it at the disposal of Churchill as an alternative to Chequers 'when the moon was high' and the prime minister's official residence was too easy a target for German bombers.[53] On this occasion, the other house guests included Duff and Diana Cooper, as well as the managing director of the investment bank Lazard's, shortly to become the head of the British Food Mission in Washington, Robert (Bob) Brand.[54] In such elegant settings 'war seemed a very long way away'. Unknown to the assembled guests, in the first of fifty-seven consecutive sorties, approximately three hundred German bombers assisted by over six hundred fighter planes had taken off from airfields in Belgium and northern France and were shortly to begin in earnest the aerial bombardment of London. The assault continued until early evening, to be followed by another attack by 250 bombers which lasted until the early hours of the following morning.[55] At Ditchley, towards midnight, the butler came to announce that the invasion had commenced. When nothing further happened, the guests went to bed, waking the following morning to hear news of the commencement of what the British people were to call 'the Blitz'.

Back in London on Sunday evening, Wheeler-Bennett dined with Neill Malcolm. During dinner a bomb fell, setting an adjacent house on fire. 'I walked back through the blackout with fires on either hand and the patter of shrapnel very audible . . . it seemed curious to be in Picca-dilly in evening clothes and carrying a gas-mask while death and destruc-tion rained down about me but somehow no more incongruous than the whole atmosphere which I found in London at this time. It was one of restrained euphoria. The glory of the Dunkirk miracle was still an influence charged almost with the supernatural.'[56] Each subsequent night, the capital was bombarded, leaving Wheeler-Bennett to note frequently in his diary: 'bad raid.' Since the lease on his flat at Albany had expired, he had rented a house in Bolton Street, off Piccadilly. But when this was hit by a bomb, he moved to the Ritz Hotel, whose doors never closed throughout the war. 'Their response was generous and magnifi-cent,' he observed since they let him leave two suitcases there indefinitely and guaranteed him a bed at a fixed rate, be it a courier's room in the attic or a suite overlooking Green Park. 'It was a kindness I have never forgotten.'[57] While in London, Wheeler-Bennett had a medical examina-tion in case, at the grand age of thirty-eight, he might be passed fit to enlist, but his heart was not considered strong enough for army require-ments. He therefore abandoned all thoughts he might have had of a military career, even in an emergency.

Wheeler-Bennett returned to the United States, leaving by sea from Merseyside on 12 September. By 15 September, the tide had turned against the German Luftwaffe, forcing Hitler to postpone Operation

Sea Lion – the invasion of Britain – and later to give orders to prepare for war against the Soviet Union instead. Although the threat of invasion receded, the Blitz continued until the following May. By late September, Wheeler-Bennett was back in Washington, breakfasting with Philip Lothian, who appeared to be 'greatly fatigued'. Soon afterwards the British ambassador himself returned for a visit to England. Meanwhile, acting as Lothian's representative, Wheeler-Bennett's work was undergoing a subtle reorganisation. Contrary to the initial planned use of the British Library of Information as an institution from which they could issue speedy press releases, it was decided that relations with the media should be separated from the BLI and a new parallel organisation set up, the British Press Services (BPS). As Lothian had argued, in a dispatch to London 'the word "service" produces a benevolent reaction in America. We do not wish to be accused of making overt plans to "influence" the press.' Alan Dudley was appointed director, leaving operational direction in the hands of Morgan and Wheeler-Bennett. 'It is important to avoid giving the impression that a vast new organisation is being started,' Lothian continued in his dispatch, 'and Mr Dudley, whose unassuming personality covers real administrative ability, is well known and liked by the considerable number of journalists who have been in the habit of consulting him at the Library.'[58]

On 31 October, Wheeler-Bennett was given formal notification that he had been appointed to the post of assistant director of the BPS.[59] As he later recalled, the establishment of the BPS was the first effort towards providing a public-relations service 'which aimed to serve the curious many rather than the enquiring few'.[60] With office space on the forty-fourth floor of the RCA Building at 30 Rockefeller Plaza, close to the BLI and BBC, Wheeler-Bennett and his colleagues were well placed to be in regular contact with the American broadcaster NBC, whose offices were in the same complex. The offices of CBS and various newspapers were nearby. Although the service's budget was generous, source material was sparse, initially consisting only of a 'well-thumbed' *Who's Who* and some reference books which Wheeler-Bennett provided from his own library. In the early days, he and Morgan were frequently working sixteen to eighteen hours a day. Later, their ranks were strengthened 'by some

distinguished reinforcements': in November 1940, René MacColl arrived
in New York with his formidable track record that included working
for the *Baltimore Sun*, the *Daily Telegraph* during the Spanish Civil War,
and the RAF press-relations unit in France.[61] Other talented Britons
'marooned' in the United States at the outbreak of war were added to
the workforce. These included Commonwealth Fund students and the
society heiress Lady Daphne Straight.[62] Wheeler-Bennett's work and that
of his colleagues was to continue to give research material to journalists
so that they could meet their deadlines, as well as providing a reference
service for editors and commentators to help them prepare their bulletins.
Another task was to facilitate the travel of American journalists who
wanted to report on the war from Britain, as well as maintaining regular
contact with the growing body of Americans who favoured intervention.
Originally formed as the Century Group, its members took the name of
the 'Fight for Freedom' committee and their offices were also in the
RCA building.

[handwritten margin note: Michael Straight's mother]

Much to Wheeler-Bennett's regret, Lothian did not live to enjoy the
fruits of his work in the United States, either in terms of the relationship
he had developed with the US administration or with the BPS/BLI.
Having returned from England in late November, after Roosevelt had
won an unprecedented third term as president of the United States,
Lothian optimistically told waiting pressmen: 'The first half of 1940 was
Hitler's year. The second half, we think is ours . . . England needs planes,
munitions, ships and perhaps a little financial help.' But, suffering from
uraemia (chronic renal failure) Lothian's health was rapidly deteriorating.[63]
Soon afterwards, Wheeler-Bennett was helping him with a speech he
was to give to the American Farm Bureau Federation. 'I have done. I
have endeavoured to give you some idea of our present position and
dangers, the problems of 1941, and our hopes for the future,' he drafted.
'It is for you to decide whether you share our hopes and what support
you will give us in realising them.' The speech became Lothian's valedictory. As a Christian Scientist, he refused conventional medical treatment
and died during the night of 11–12 December. His death 'meant more
than I can express,' Wheeler-Bennett later wrote. 'I have never known
a chief whose inspiration spurred one on to greater heights than one
thought it possible to achieve.'[64]

Lothian's replacement was the former foreign secretary Lord Halifax. He arrived in Washington at the end of January 1941, bringing with him Wheeler-Bennett's 'old friend' from the Foreign Office, Charles Peake, who Wheeler-Bennett considered did not immediately exhibit the right approach when dealing with 'any but the most sophisticated Americans'. Evidence was provided by Peake's failure to advise Halifax against accepting an invitation from the Philadelphia Hunt Club to go foxhunting. As Wheeler-Bennett recollected, such a 'caper' did not send the right message to Americans, whose admiration of Britain was based on its 'much advertised austerity'.[65] As a result of the changed situation, Wheeler-Bennett was spending more time in New York managing the BPS. A monitoring service had also been set up, presided over by Jack Rennie, who had originally been recruited to work for the consulate in Baltimore and was later to become head of MI6.[66] In January 1941, Isaiah Berlin returned to Washington also to work for the BPS. His particular brief was 'to supply details of the British war effort to the press and other media connected with various social groups and religious minorities, such as labour unions, Jews, and some of the smaller Christian denominations'.[67] As amateurs and 'proud of it', this eclectic gathering of men and women continued to prepare studies for the press who wanted greater analysis of the news, as well as talking points for those Americans who wanted to speak on Britain's behalf. One of their most valuable colleagues was Dr Alfred Wiener, who had assiduously been gathering anti-Semitic Nazi literature. Having fled from Germany to Amsterdam, he spent the war in the United States, later moving to London, where he established the world-famous Wiener Library.[68]

As Wheeler-Bennett himself observed, at government level, the United States had been inching towards greater assistance. In Roosevelt's December 1940 'fireside chat', he had declared that the interests of the Allies and of the United States were the same and that the US would become the 'great arsenal of democracy'.[69] In his State of the Union speech on 6 January 1941, the president pledged 'full support' for the Allied cause and the Lend-Lease Bill – granting the US the right to supply munitions to 'any country whose defence the President deems vital to the defence of the United States' – was put before Congress.[70] Subsequently, German and Italian credits in the US were frozen and their respective consular offices were closed. A patrol was set up in the Atlantic and all German and Italian vessels were seized. Finally, the US government occupied Iceland for purposes of defence.[71] In March 1941, as Britain rejoiced at the defeat of the Italians in North Africa by General Wavell and his small army, the BPS received a visit from Duff Cooper's PPS, Ronald Tree. Describing Wheeler-Bennett and Aubrey Morgan as 'remarkable' men, Tree recorded that their approach was in sharp contrast to the rather moribund attitude towards dissemination of information favoured by civil servants. As a result of their briefings, he said, the leading New York columnists, particularly commentators on military affairs, were 'going away satisfied'.[72]

However, much as they might favour giving aid, a large proportion of Americans remained strongly opposed to declaring war on the Axis Powers. Of these isolationists, the most influential organisation was the America First Committee, headquartered in Chicago. Many of its members were Wheeler-Bennett's friends, most prominently General Robert Wood, head of Sears, Roebuck and the national chairman of America First, and Janet Ayre Fairbank, its vice-chairman. Shortly after Lothian's death, Wheeler-Bennett and Morgan had been invited to Chicago to address the organisation's executive committee. 'This curious confrontation between the archetypes of American Isolation and two representatives of belligerent Britain was conducted with the utmost urbanity.' Not surprisingly, when Wheeler-Bennett asked at what point the Americans would consider it necessary to use force against the Germans, the answer came: 'When they cross the Rio Grande'.[73]

In mid-1941, when Britain's fortunes had sunk to a new low after the loss of Greece, Crete and the territory gained from the Italians in North Africa, the need for American support was even greater and consequently it was even more important to maximise the covert 'propaganda' facilities of the BLI. Following a report by Peake describing the BLI as a 'backwater', another reshuffle was effected, bringing the activities of the BPS and the BLI under one person in a single organisation, the British Information Services (BIS). The man selected as director was Sir Gerald Campbell, a respected consular diplomat, but who had little experience in information.[74] His deputy was the 'brilliant journalist' Robert Cruikshank, who had been the American correspondent of the News Chronicle

in the 1930s and most recently had worked as editor of the *Star*.[75] 'That
the BIS ever got off the ground as an organisation was largely due to his
efforts and inspiration,' recalled Wheeler-Bennett.[76]

An added bonus of life in America was his continuing friendship with
Aubrey and Constance Morgan, who often invited him to spend the
weekend at the Morrows' family home in Englewood, New Jersey. On
one occasion, Constance's sister, Anne, and Charles Lindbergh were
visiting from Europe, where they had taken up residence after the kidnap
and murder of their young son in 1932. Wheeler-Bennett had the opportunity to spend many evenings with these fierce isolationists and supporters
of America First, 'arguing, debating and fundamentally dissenting in the
most amicable fashion'.[77]

At the end of June 1941, Wheeler-Bennett spoke again at the Institute
of Public Affairs at the University of Virginia. He encouraged his audience to 'hold fast' to their belief in Britain.

> Have confidence in our victory; have faith in our future . . . for without
> your help in the battles of transport and production can come neither
> victory nor peace. Without your help, Europe is condemned to the
> long night of Nazi domination, and the remainder of the world to
> constant threat and peril. Let this not be written in history. Let it be
> written rather that with your help we seized the moment; that with
> your help we were in time; that out of our reverses, we snatched
> victory; that out of victory we created liberty; that out of liberty we
> fashioned happiness.[78]

In July, shortly after the startling news of Germany's invasion of the
Soviet Union, Wheeler-Bennett returned to London with Campbell to
'sell' him 'to the powers that be' in terms of arguing for an expansion
of their organisation. This meant arranging meetings with 'half the
Cabinet' including Churchill, Anthony Eden, who had replaced Halifax
as foreign secretary, and Duff Cooper. Wheeler-Bennett also secured an
invitation for Campbell to have a private lunch with the king. Their
arrival in London coincided with a heightened awareness that the key to
Britain's survival involved winning over American public opinion and so
substantial funding for the BIS was agreed. In an aside, Wheeler-Bennett

noted that the date for Campbell's farewell dinner at the Savoy was 15 July, the day on which Churchill had chosen to make changes in his government by replacing Duff Cooper with Brendan Bracken as minister of information; Harold Nicolson was to be replaced as PPS by Ernest Thurtle. Never one to be cowed by potential social embarrassment, Wheeler-Bennett happily let the invitations to the two departing men stand while extending further invitations to the new appointees or, as he put it, to both 'the quick and the dead'.[79] During his stay, he saw that the worst of the Blitz was over, 'but the scars remained. Wherever one went, in whatever quarter of London, there were stark shells of burnt-out or bomb-shattered houses, or mere holes in the ground where great masses of scarlet "fire-weed" were already blooming.' Wheeler-Bennett also travelled to Manchester, Sheffield and Birmingham, where he found much the same spirit as in London: 'great courage but great weariness, amounting to exhaustion'. Food supplies were just adequate. 'Spam we were grateful for as an evidence of Lend-Lease, if for nothing else.'[80]

While in London, Wheeler-Bennett had discovered that changes were being made in the organisation of the Political Intelligence Department (PID) and that Lockhart had been asked to become the director-general of the new covert Political Warfare Executive (PWE) as distinct from the equally covert Special Operations Executive (SOE). Whereas SOE was in charge of organising and equipping the resistance movements, PWE (or PID as it was still called as a cover) was to focus on disseminating overt propaganda to enemy and occupied countries. Familiarly referred to as 'PeeWee', its officials were known as 'Peawits'.[81] Although Wheeler-Bennett still wanted to return to London to work with Lockhart, the time was not yet right and he duly went back to the United States to take up an appointment to the staff of the UK Ministry of Information Services in the US.[82] His salary was to be £950 a year, backdated from 1 June 1941. In his letter of appointment, it was made clear that the post was temporary and 'carries no right to permanent appointment or promotion, nor to pension or gratuity on its termination'. For the duration of his tenure, he was subject to all the general rules applicable to the civil service.[83] On the day of his departure, 4 August 1941, he lunched with Lockhart, Tree and David Bowes-Lyon, Queen

Elizabeth's younger brother, who was working for SOE, in the Ministry of Economic Warfare.[84]

Wheeler-Bennett was as yet unaware that a momentous change was taking place in the Anglo-American relationship. Unknown to any of those present at Wheeler-Bennett's farewell lunch party, Winston Churchill was already crossing the Atlantic on board the *Prince of Wales* to meet Roosevelt in the harbour at Placentia Bay, Newfoundland, on board the USS *Augusta*. Together the two men would agree the principles of the Atlantic Charter, which, although the United States was yet to enter the war formally, established a vision for a postwar world. As Churchill later noted, the fact that Roosevelt had agreed to include in the document the expression of a desire to see peace established 'after the final destruction of the Nazi tyranny' was 'astonishing'.[85] In November 1941, after the sinking of the American destroyer *Reuben James*, with the loss of 115 Americans, the restrictions imposed by the Neutrality Act, which forbade US citizens from entering combat zones and US personnel from travelling on belligerent vessels, were lifted. The interventionists were 'jubilant; the isolationists almost frantic,' Wheeler-Bennett later wrote.[86] Support was also coming from unexpected quarters. Once the Germans turned on their erstwhile allies in the Soviet Union, the Communist Party of America became 'as wildly interventionist as it had been previously uncompromisingly isolationist'.[87]

To give even greater publicity to the 'gallantry' of Britain's war effort, as he later recalled, 'someone' in the American media suggested to the Ministry of Information in London that some 'heroes' should be sent from England to tour the United States. As a result, 'imperative instructions' arrived from the minister of information, Brendan Bracken, to give their proposed visit as much publicity as possible. The contingent included representatives from the Royal Navy, Army and Air Force. Arriving in Montreal, they flew to Newark. Both Wheeler-Bennett and Morgan were part of the publicity team while Bill Ormerod was 'the inspirational genius'. A high point was a traditional parade along Broadway: 'the motorcade ploughed its way through bright sunshine and clouds of ticker-tape'. Later the heroes were the guests of Darryl Zanuck of Twentieth Century-Fox who had arranged for Duke Ellington to perform for them at the Radio City Music Hall. The finale was a reception at the old Madison Square Garden in front of an estimated seventeen thousand people. 'The organ pealed; a chorus led the great audience in passionate renderings of "God Save the King", "The Star Spangled Banner", "There'll always be an England" and "America".'[88]

Meanwhile, Wheeler-Bennett had been keeping up his contacts with the film world. In New York, he first met 'that fabulous figure', Alexander Korda — 'a genius with a touch of magic in his conceptions and direction'. With his actress wife, Merle Oberon, Korda lived in Los Angeles in the Beverly Hills suburb of Bel Air, 'where only the great abide'. A naturalised British citizen from Hungary, in 1932 he had founded London Films. At the outbreak of war, he was working on an Arabian fantasy, *The Thief of Bagdad*, (released in 1940). The production of such major movies was becoming increasingly difficult in Britain so he cashed in his life-insurance policies to finance a low-budget drama about Britain's air power called *The Lion Has Wings*, starring Merle Oberon as the wife of an RAF wing commander played by Ralph Richardson. The cast included the future James Bond author, Ian Fleming, as an 'unnamed character'. Korda, however, realised that if he wanted to continue making films he would have to move to Hollywood. As a friend of Churchill, he had accepted the prime minister's suggestion that he should make 'patriotic' films which would subtly influence American public opinion in favour of Britain. As later became apparent, his offices in Los Angeles and New York also served as a cover for British secret agents working in neutral America.[89] During one of Wheeler-Bennett's visits to Hollywood, Korda invited him to dinner to talk to some of the 'top brass' of the film world. 'Alex had certainly surpassed himself and had gathered in the top brackets of Hollywood tycoonery. Even the fabulous Sam Goldwyn had consented to come, a rare event I was told, and with him were the leading lights of Paramount, Twentieth Century-Fox, Columbia, United Artists and other great concerns.' After dinner, Wheeler-Bennett gave his speech, describing 'the courage, the patience and the steadfast resolve' of the British people. As a result, they 'dug down into their pockets and the evening was a profitable one for British War Charities'.[90]

On 25 November 1941, Wheeler-Bennett was assigned the prestigious task of addressing the cream of the American military: the Corps of

Cadets at the Military Academy at West Point. The theme was all too familiar:

> This is no small enterprise upon which we are embarked. It is not just the survival of Britain, or the security of the United States, or the restoration of France which is at stake, it is no less a thing than the future of mankind. My country and yours are engaged today in opposing, each in our respective spheres, the imposition of a monstrous tyranny upon the world. We are defending, again each in our own manner, the basic faiths of our fathers, and of ourselves. It is our avowed purpose that this Nazi menace to our common heritage of a 'deathless attachment to freedom' shall be destroyed, and that, from our common effort, there shall emerge from the wrack of war, a world in which we and our children can live free, fearless and secure. It is for this reason that we must be, and shall be, victorious.

Sitting down, Wheeler-Bennett heard 'the briefest silence', followed by a standing ovation.[91] His exertions had again taken a toll on his health. Even before making his speech, he was feeling ill and dizzy. Back in New York, he went to see the doctor. Suffering from nervous exhaustion, he had the symptoms of serious anaemia and the doctor diagnosed that he had oscillating blood pressure, which produced an imbalance in the heart action and accounted for his faintness. It was a condition that had dogged him all his life but had apparently only just been recognised. As a result, he spent the first week of December in hospital. Discharged on Sunday, 7 December 1941, Wheeler-Bennett returned to the house he was sharing with Aubrey and Constance Morgan. As he later recalled, they were listening to a symphony on the radio when the broadcast was interrupted to announce that the Japanese had attacked the US fleet at Pearl Harbor. Later in the evening Wheeler-Bennett and Aubrey Morgan went to Times Square where a huge electric bulletin was displaying the news. 'There was no great excitement . . . people just stood there silently watching for the latest tidings of a disaster, the magnitude of which was, of course, still unknown to them.' Both men recognised that with 'the advent of America as a fully fledged belligerent, we should be victorious'.[92]

7

Political Warfare in America

Yet if the hands of youth should ever rake
The ash of our sad time, it holds a friend,
Whose heart was in the cause all warmth will make
Its own until the end.

Robert Vansittart[1]

Once the United States entered the war, the system for disseminating information in New York was reorganised. Curiously, as Wheeler-Bennett noted, the new phase in Anglo-American relations did not open 'on a note of complete amicability . . . all information on the war should now, it was thought, be imparted to the American public by American agencies and it was pretty clearly implied that the American public would from now on be interested only in American exploits'. To this effect a bill was passed designating all those who worked for non-American public relations agencies as 'foreign agents'. As a result, Wheeler-Bennett and his colleagues had to register with the Department of Justice to be finger-printed, and all the material they wished to disseminate had first to be sent to the Department of State.[2] Privately, Wheeler-Bennett was thinking about his relationship with Ruth Risher, whom he had continued to visit intermittently in Charlottesville. Now that America was at war, she would be joining one of the women's services and could be sent 'God alone knew where'. Although they had not yet become engaged, they had 'an understanding' that they would get married.[3]

Throughout early 1942, Wheeler-Bennett was again hoping to return to England, preferably to work in the Political Warfare Executive (PWE) under Lockhart. 'I have now served on the American front – and in one sector of it – for rather more than two and a half years,' he wrote to Lockhart in May, 'and I am getting very stale . . . I think I have exhausted my usefulness here, and can legitimately ask to be transferred to some other branch of the service.'[4] If he were to stay in the United States, he wanted to be able to capitalise on his knowledge and experience of both the US and Germany. This would mean working in collaboration with General Bill Donovan, Roosevelt's personal envoy and co-ordinator of information, whom Wheeler-Bennett had known during the interwar years.[5] 'I could return to England for two or three months to "learn the business" and then come back here,' he wrote to Lockhart, advising him that Donovan had often expressed a desire for them to work together and had asked to see various memoranda relating to Germany. 'I have sat in with his people on various occasions for technical consultation. I have also a number of old friends among the journalists and professors on his staff, and I think I can honestly say that both he and they trust me. At the same time, I have close contacts with the other United States' government agencies for propaganda and information.'[6] Soon after the letter to Lockhart, the US intelligence services were reorganised. In June, two new agencies were set up: the Office of Strategic Services (OSS), of which Donovan was made director, and the Office of War Information (OWI), which had responsibility for overt as opposed to covert propaganda. British Security Coordination (BSC), still under Stephenson, (known as 'Little Bill' to distinguish him from 'Big Bill' Donovan), became an umbrella organisation representing all British intelligence organisations in the United States.[7]

When Wheeler-Bennett returned to London in the summer, Lockhart offered him the choice of either joining PWE as 'adviser on European affairs' to a new British Political Warfare Mission in the United States or of becoming head of an American division based in London. Much as Wheeler-Bennett had been wanting to return to England, he now changed his mind, telling Lockhart that his 'intimate knowledge of the personalities in the United States' meant that he had more to contribute in Washington. 'It is a difficult and somewhat embarrassing task to assess one's own qualifications and I hope you will acquit me of any intention of self-praise,' he wrote to Lockhart, explaining his reasons.[8] The head of this new UK mission, based in Washington DC but with an operational centre in New York, was to be David Bowes-Lyon, to whom Wheeler-Bennett would be responsible. 'I wish you to divide your time between London and the US in such measure as may prove most beneficent to both,' advised Lockhart.[9] His salary remained £950 per annum.[10] His colleagues were Russell Page, later an acclaimed landscape gardener, and Leonard Miall, who had joined the BBC's European Service in 1939 and had been seconded to PWE.[11]

While in London, Wheeler-Bennett witnessed the formal denouncement of the 1938 Munich Agreement in parliament on 5 August 1942. The event 'was free from all dramatics and received but little publicity. It was accomplished in the most unemotional, almost prosaic, tradition of British parliamentary procedure.' Moreover, as he noted, the chamber in which it was made was very different from the one in which Chamberlain had been 'so hysterically acclaimed on his departure for Munich, and so glowingly eulogized on his return'. After one of the worst and final nights of the Blitz on 10–11 May 1941 the House of Commons chamber was 'now an empty shell, open to the sky, mute witness to the bombing'. As a result, ordinary parliamentary proceedings were moved to the House of Lords, which had also been damaged, but whose chamber remained intact.

Wheeler-Bennett was sitting in the Officials' Gallery with Lockhart, who had played a vital role in obtaining recognition of the Czechoslovak Provisional Government. The exchange had been prearranged: Sir Derrick Gunston, Conservative MP for Thornbury in Gloucestershire, rose to ask whether the British government still felt bound by the terms of the Munich Agreement.[12] Since Churchill was en route to Moscow to inform Stalin that Britain could not as yet open a 'second front' in Europe to relieve the pressure on Russia, it was the foreign secretary, Anthony Eden, who responded, stating that the Munich Agreement had been destroyed by the Germans. Afterwards Wheeler-Bennett toasted the event with House of Commons sherry with Lockhart, Eden, Jan Masaryk and the Conservative MP Gerald Palmer, together with Count Edward Raczynski, the ambassador of the Polish government-in-exile. 'Thus was the Ghost of Munich laid to rest, and an inglorious chapter in British history was closed with honour.'[13]

Once back in the United States, Wheeler-Bennett outlined what he believed his new duties should be. 'Primarily of course the duty of an Adviser is to advise,' he wrote to Bowes-Lyon. 'I consider myself to be at your immediate disposal for any consultation, which you might find necessary and timely.' In addition, he considered that he would have to keep in contact with the various European Regions of the American agencies, which included the OSS and the OWI, 'and to establish with them as complete a degree of confidence and collaboration as possible . . . To so influence the politics of these regions as to keep them as nearly as possible in line with those of P.W.E.' Finally, he would embody the 'fruits' of his findings in a series of reports to London.[14] By September, Wheeler-Bennett was established in his new job, writing cheerfully to Lockhart the first of many letters he was to send over the next eighteen months:

> It seems appropriate that the first letter to be written from the New York office of the British Political Warfare Mission in America should be to the Director General of the P.W.E.!! I herewith send the parent body the respectful salutation of its newest sub-dependency! In actual point of fact, I think the idea of a New York office is a good one, as it is quite necessary to provide a *pied-à-terre* for our team working with O.W.I. here. It has, moreover, the additional advantage of providing a home for me – but that is more or less incidental! Anyway, here we are; a staff of seven, including myself and the other 'hired help' – and for the rest, – *nous verrons*.[15]

Wheeler-Bennett was critical of the style and approach of the OWI under the direction of the well-known news reporter – but inexperienced administrator – Elmer Davis[16] compared to that of the OSS under the efficient former soldier Donovan. 'How far it is possible to achieve anything with O.W.I. in its present state of inconceivable muddle-headed disorder, I am not yet prepared to say, but my hunch is that very little can be achieved there without drastic internal reforms and purges. At the moment, its meetings have the appearance of being a cross between the early days of the MoI [Ministry of Information] and the more fevered sessions of the Social Revolutionaries of the Right in Petrograd!!' Since Wheeler-Bennett was friendly with Donovan, he preferred dealing with the OSS: 'there is something refreshingly conservative about O.S.S. which, though partaking in nature somewhat of the sedate, nevertheless gives one a feeling of solidarity, experience and a general awareness of what they are after. I get the impression that they have their feet considerably more firmly on the ground and their heads considerably less in the clouds than the poets and pundits of O.W.I.' Aware of the rivalry between the two organisations, Wheeler-Bennett felt strongly that 'we of the Mission should not enter into the internecine intricacies of the Battle of Washington, but should maintain officially an impartial and objective attitude toward all parties. As a mission it is our job to co-operate with all American agencies which are active in the conduct of political warfare.'[17] Once a working relationship with OWI and OSS had been established, he said he enjoyed 'immensely' working with highly intelligent men 'who combined the practical experience of diplomacy with the wide range of academic learning'.[18]

Wheeler-Bennett's duties still involved maintaining contact with the refugees who came to the United States from Europe. In time he established a survey of the foreign-language press which included Serbs, Croats, Slovenes, Italians, Germans, Hungarians, Arabs, Poles and Czechs. Those who interested him most were the Germans 'and there were many of them, good and bad'.[19] One of these was Ernst 'Putzi' Hanfstängl, an art connoisseur; as a former Nazi supporter in the 1920s and early 1930s, he provided information about the inner workings of the Nazi hierarchy, 'together with their intrigues, peccadilloes, sex lives, etc'. His suggestion to put an end to the war was almost laughable: if Goering were to be given the Order of the Garter, he would overthrow Hitler and end the war.[20]

In early 1943 a *froideur* arose with Brüning. Wheeler-Bennett believed the reason was their divergent opinions following the Allied decision, formally agreed between Churchill and Roosevelt at Casablanca in January 1943, that Germany's surrender had to be unconditional.[21] Soon after the conference, Wheeler-Bennett spent the weekend with Brüning at Harvard.

I had found Brüning greatly depressed as to the course of the war and resentful of the official British attitude towards Germany, condemning the formula of Unconditional Surrender and the heavy bombing. I thought him wrong when he alleged that a German victory was still possible and I attempted to disillusion him when he sought to emphasise the difference between a National Socialist State and a 'New Germany'. It was essential, I told him, for the elements in Germany who claimed to be anti-Nazi to eliminate Hitler, destroy the Nazi state and re-establish the Rechtsstaat and then comply with Unconditional Surrender before they could expect leniency from the Allies. The day had long passed when the overthrow of the Third Reich could be followed by a negotiated peace with a new German regime. This made him very angry, and he told me I had become a chauvinist.

To this, Wheeler-Bennett responded that he was a realist.[22] Subsequently, Brüning lamented that he was no longer on good terms with Wheeler-Bennett. 'War often destroys old friendships,' he wrote in 1945.[23]

Not long after his Harvard altercation with Brüning, Wheeler-Bennett wrote another of his many memoranda, this one entitled 'The New American Appeasement'. A decade previously he had been urging his listeners at Chatham House to accept that Germany had to be allowed to 'make its own bed' domestically. As he had told Brüning, subsequent bitter experience had made him think otherwise. 'The wisdom behind the Casablanca formula is clear. An obvious attempt has been made to obviate the mistake of 1918, and to deprive the Germans of any future opportunity of again making the world believe that they surrendered under false pretences. No blandishments, such as those contained in Woodrow Wilson's Fourteen Points, have been dangled before them.' Whoever was in charge when Germany surrendered would have no illusions, he said. 'They must throw themselves upon the mercy and justice of the United Nations.' No institution could be trusted '*per se* with the task of government before the process of the political and ideological "de-lousing" of Germany has been completed'.

What Wheeler-Bennett found challenging (and what people in Britain were largely unaware of) was the difference of opinion between the United States and Britain. As he continued in his memorandum, although

1 John Wheeler-Bennett, 'Royal Biographer', 1950s. He always wore a carnation in his button hole.

2 John and Clement with their father John Wheeler-Bennett, CBE, JP. Clement was fourteen years John's senior and hence a remote figure.

3 Christina Wheeler-Bennett. After his father's death Wheeler-Bennett was left 'a large fortune' and so he and his mother travelled 'East to the Orient' in 1927.

4 Ravensbourne - Wheeler-Bennett's family home in Keston, Kent. There were servants, gardeners and a chauffeur.

5 John Wheeler–Bennett when a young man. In the 1920s and 1930s, he lived at Albany, the 'most comfortable and desirable bachelor's quarters in London' where 'the strangest variety of persons forgathered'.

6 One of the many people Wheeler–Bennett met was Italy's Fascist dictator, Benito Mussolini, who, he said, did not have Hitler's 'black heart ... he was a human being with all the failings and few of the virtues thereof'.

7 John Wheeler-Bennett's marriage to Ruth Risher, University of Virginia Chapel, Charlottesville, 26 March 1945. When he first saw her, he told his mother 'That is the girl I am going to marry!'

8 John Wheeler-Bennett (wearing a trenchcoat, centre of the front row) at the Institute for Pacific Relations Conference, Virginia Beach, November 1939. Also in the front row (second from the right) is Adam von Trott, executed in Germany for his part in the 20 July (1944) plot to assassinate Hitler.

9 Garsington Manor, Oxfordshire, the Wheeler–Bennetts' home for over thirty years. At first Ruth said she did not like Elizabethan houses.

10 John and Ruth Wheeler-Bennett at Garsington, 1960s. He adopted a traditional 'Squire' of the manor role, and dressed the part, said his friend Bruce Lockhart – 'smart corduroys in Newmarket boots, an open shirt with scarf round the neck'.

11 Malvern College Centenary, July 1965: Wheeler-Bennett with the bishop of Worcester, the Rt Reverend Lewis Charles-Edwards; former prime minister Harold Macmillan, OM, PC is behind.

12 The Queen Mother meeting the headmaster, Donald Lindsey, with Wheeler-Bennett.

13 Sir John Wheeler-Bennett – the portrait drawn by Juliet Pannett for his 70th birthday.

British people 'to a great extent' accepted the necessity of 'unconditional surrender',

> it is far from being the case in the United States, where the tendency towards appeasement is apparent on both the Right and the Left. It is not yet generally accepted in America that the German Army must be destroyed, not only as a military but as a political and an economic factor; that the industrial power of Germany must either be reduced to helotry or rendered nugatory for an extended period; that neither the forces of reaction nor of liberalism in Central Europe can be recognised as viable under law before they have proved their sincerity in accepting the decencies of international life; and that the German people, though admittedly the first victims of Nazi terrorism and persecution, have, by their passive condoning or active complicity in the subsequent acts of Nazi aggression, forfeited the right to a place in the European comity until such time as they have been purged of the disease and madness which has ravaged the soul of Germany and precipitated the deaths of millions.[24]

Another twenty-five-page document, entitled 'The Making of Peace', enabled him to re-examine themes familiar to him since his early writings on the aftermath of World War I. Already, Wheeler-Bennett was anticipating the process of peace-making. 'In the penultimate stages of all great wars,' he wrote, 'there arises a wave of soul-searching and consideration as to how peace will come about, and what shall be its nature. The impatient idealist, the avid imperialist and the prosaic economic "planner" jostle one another for a position in the forefront of public consideration; the idea of peace in the abstract becomes news. And, behind this façade, grinding slowly as the Mills of God, the professional diplomatists draw their own plans and blue-prints.' In conclusion, he opined: 'never has the test of British statesmanship been more searching, but, equally, never has there been a greater and more inspiring challenge to its genius. For Britain will occupy a unique position in the discussions which precede the settlement. She will be among the judges who condemn the Axis Powers but, in a sense, she and her institutions, her traditional policies and her way of life will also be on trial, arraigned before the bar of her own allies.' The section titles of this extensive paper included: 'Some Errors of the Armistice'; 'Some Errors of the Peace Treaty'; 'Some Problems of the Future'; 'The International Organisation of the Post-War World'; 'The Treatment of Germany'; 'The Future of Italy'; 'The Reorganisation of Europe'; 'The Treatment of Japan and the Reorganisation of Asia'; and 'Anglo-American Relations'. Once again, he expressed views in accordance with the established line: there was to be 'no treating' with the Axis Powers except on the basis of unconditional surrender. He also recognised that, 'by reason of her geographical position, and her vital interests, Britain cannot divorce herself from Europe'.[25]

A further study anticipated 'What to Do With Germany' once the war was over:

> There can rarely have been a major war in which the interest of at least one set of belligerents was so definitely centred on post-war problems. From the very beginning of this war – and indeed long before it began – discussion in Britain turned again and again on the perplexing question of 'What to do with Germany?' There was general agreement from the outset that the Nazi regime must be defeated and destroyed, but beyond this point little progress of clarification was made by reason of the fact that none could agree on a common policy for the morrow of victory . . . There should be a complete occupation of Germany for an unspecified period, the cost of which should be borne by Germany . . . in the course of occupation Germany should be completely disarmed, militarily, industrially and politically . . . at the conclusion of the period of occupation Germany should be admitted to any existing European organisation on equal political and economic terms (with the exception of armaments).[26]

Yet another memorandum in connection with 'peace feelers' emanating from various quarters in Germany recapitulated Wheeler-Bennett's knowledge of Adam von Trott zu Solz, who, since joining the German Foreign Service in 1940, had been overtly performing the duties of a Nazi official with dedication, while covertly remaining in touch with those Germans who opposed Hitler. The group with which Trott was most closely identified was the Kreisau Circle (named after the estate of one of its leading members, the lawyer Helmut Graf von Moltke). Like Goerdeler and others, they opposed Nazism and their discussions focused on the character of the German state after the fall of Hitler, ever hopeful that some accommodation might be made with the Allies.[27] As Wheeler-Bennett wrote in his paper: 'Freiherr Adam von Trott zu Solz may be destined to play an interesting part in the possible efforts to make a non-Nazi – or perhaps more accurately, a non-Hitlerian – peace offensive.' He proceeded to give some background information, pointing to the fact that when Trott was at Oxford in the early 1930s he had 'imbibed a certain degree of Anglophile sentiments, made a number of friends and contacts, and was indeed exceptionally popular, largely because of a charm and sense of humour unusual in a German'. Wheeler-Bennett also highlighted the fact that Trott was a protégé of Count Albrecht von Bernstorff, the counsellor of the Germany Embassy in London in the late 1920s and early 1930s, and that he personally had first met Trott when staying with Bernstorff at Stintenberg.[28] Wheeler-Bennett then detailed Trott's later career, practising law in the town of Cassel, his visits to Britain and the United States in 1939 and return to Germany to join the German Foreign Service. Basing his judgement on his past conversations with Trott, Wheeler-Bennett endorsed the view that Trott was genuinely anti-Nazi. Unaware of the direction the German resistance movement would take, Wheeler-Bennett concluded by contradicting his opening remarks and suggested that 'the part which Adam von Trott will play in the future may not be a spectacular or even an important one'.[29] When Wheeler-Bennett's colleagues in Whitehall received the paper, they did not consider on this occasion that it added much to their previous knowledge.[30] As was clear from the paper and as evidenced by the freeze in his relations with Brüning, Wheeler-Bennett was now convinced that all 'peace feelers' would come to nothing.

Wheeler-Bennett's continuing presence in the United States meant that he saw more of Ruth Risher. Having been commissioned in the American Red Cross after Pearl Harbor, she had spent most of 1942 training either in Washington, D.C. or New York. But, as they both realised, once trained, she would be posted abroad. Instead of their preferred option – that she should be posted to Europe and based in London – she was ordered to take up an appointment in Cairo. Before her departure, the pair spent their last evening together with the Morgans at a Broadway theatre watching the hit musical *Oklahoma*, starring Alfred Drake and Joan Roberts. On Easter Sunday, 25 April 1943, Wheeler-Bennett accompanied Ruth to Pennsylvania Station to put her on the train to Washington. 'In these unromantic and sordid surroundings we "plighted our troth".' Wheeler-Bennett gave her a gold ring with a Hittite seal, bought in Aden on his first visit 'East' in 1927 and which he had been wearing as a signet ring. They did not see each other again for two years.[31]

Soon afterwards, Wheeler-Bennett was back in England for a 'refresher' course on the German situation. Lockhart was suffering from a severe skin condition and was recuperating in Scotland so Wheeler-Bennett took the train to visit him. They had a 'superb view' of the Cairngorms, but it rained for most of the weekend, which left 'ample time' for talking. As Lockhart recorded in his diary, Wheeler-Bennett shared his feelings about the different attitude towards the war in the United States, and told him that although the country was united against Japan, the same determination to defeat Germany did not exist. 'The war in Europe is remote; even the soldier has little idea what he is fighting for in North Africa. There is always the danger that the American armed services will rebel against the policy of "Germany first, then Japan".'[32]

In London, Wheeler-Bennett discovered that, under Lockhart's super-vision, PWE had overcome some of its teething problems, which had included competing influences from a trio of ministries – the Foreign Office, the Ministry of Information and the Ministry of Economic Warfare. Instead, it had been agreed that the Foreign Office, through the foreign secretary, Anthony Eden, should be the 'first among equals'. PWE had also moved premises from the Foreign Office to Bush House, occupied by the BBC. Since its role was to undermine the morale of the enemy and to sustain a spirit of resistance in enemy-occupied coun-tries, 'a voluntary agreement' had been reached with the BBC that gave policy control over all foreign broadcasts to Axis territories to PWE.[33]

Back in New York, though declaring himself 'perfectly happy', Wheeler-Bennett was again feeling that he had spent 'quite enough of the war out of England and was eager to make a contribution at home.'[34] Lockhart pledged that he might be able to accommodate him in six months 'or perhaps less'. Until such time, Wheeler-Bennett was to continue to report to him in London and to Bowes-Lyon in Washington, dividing his time between the UK and the United States 'in such measure as may prove most beneficial to both'.[35] Bowes-Lyon added his own humorous touch to Wheeler-Bennett's duties: 'He will rise early in the morning, reaching the office not later than nine a.m., put in a full day's work allowing a period of one hour for luncheon and will retire to bed early. He will be seen rather than heard and will indulge sparingly in the consumption of liquor and generally behave in a fashion befitting an English gentleman in a foreign country.'[36]

Part of Wheeler-Bennett's brief was to continue to write his regular 'personal and most secret' letters to Lockhart, which he generally copied to Bowes-Lyon and Alexander Halpern at the British Security Coordination office.[37] Uppermost in his mind was his continuing concern that the Americans – preoccupied with the forthcoming presidential election in which Roosevelt was standing for an unprecedented fourth term – might go back on their agreement to demand unconditional surrender, a theme he was to pursue in future correspondence:

> Though I have been here only a week, I have seen sufficient evidence to convince me that we are faced with a very serious situation in this country, as regards policy in general, foreign policy in particular, and my own microcosm of the German refugee in detail. To begin with, the coming battle for the Fourth Term dominates all public thinking and interest. All questions of foreign policy, and especially of political warfare, must be considered against this background, and, while this was apparent from London, it is a hundred per cent clearer and more emphatic here.

In addition, there had been a perceptible deterioration in US-Soviet relations, leading to discussions regarding the adoption of a more lenient attitude towards Germany. 'The anti-Russian feelings which were apparent before I left, and which I discussed with you in London, have flamed again in a fresh blaze of frenetic fury, not unmixed with fear.' As

he went on to say, there was talk of abandoning the policy of 'unconditional surrender' and of accepting a deal with more moderate German
elements, as represented by General Gerd von Rundstedt, Field Marshal
Blaskowitz, General Halder and Baron von Weizsächer, all of whom
favoured suing for peace before total defeat and argued that it was necessary to keep 'the nucleus of a German Army intact as a potential bulwark
against the Bolshevik Bogey'.[38] Support for this proposal, Wheeler-
Bennett said, was coming from 'well-meaning' Germanophiles, German
refugees who were naturally in favour of a 'soft' peace and isolationists
who wanted to concentrate on the war against Japan, as well as 'extreme'
Republicans who were more concerned about the Soviet Union's possible
domination of Europe. Blaming the 'Vermin Press', which he described
as 'subversive and fascist', for exploiting the present Russian phobia,
Wheeler-Bennett continued: 'Now it would be foolish to believe that
all this talk and public foolishness means that this country is officially
contemplating a separate peace. It is not. It does, however, indicate the
kind of tense political background against which the electoral primaries
will be taking shape in the Spring . . . we must be prepared for an inten-
sification of this kind of thing from now on.'[39]

In another letter he described the American attitude towards their
allies as

> a most curious psychological phenomenon – a manifestation of ambiva-
> lence! In the West they desire the defeat of the Germans, but they
> don't want it to be at the hands of the Russians. On the other hand,
> they don't want to incur heavy casualties in bringing it about them-
> selves! Similarly in the East they exhibit scepticism as to our intention
> to continue the war against Japan after the defeat of Germany, and yet,
> in a sense, they would infinitely prefer to encompass the defeat of Japan
> without our assistance, and thereby make their influence permanent in
> the Pacific area.[40]

In the midst of such concerns, Wheeler-Bennett and his colleagues had
'a hectic week' at the beginning of September, when the prime minister,
Winston Churchill, who had been in Canada for the 'Quebec' Conference,
visited the United States accompanied by his 'top brass', including minister

of information Brendan Bracken. At Harvard University Churchill received
an honorary degree. Although Wheeler-Bennett considered that Churchill's
speech there was a 'tour de force' – in the way that it informed American
youth that there was 'no halting place at this point in the war' – he
remained concerned that the strength of the Anglo-American relationship
was based on the personalities of Churchill and Roosevelt. 'While this is
all very well for now, there is no guarantee that these good relations will
continue on the same felicitous footing once this personal element is no
longer present.' Italy's impending armistice with the Allies was also the
subject of intense rumour, and he told Lockhart of a conversation he had
had with General von Reichenau in the spring of 1934:

> We were sitting in the little room on the corner of the Bendlerstrasse
> and the Landswehr Kanal which Schleicher always used, and Reichenau
> was talking quite openly in general terms of 'the next war'. He said
> that Germany had lost the last war because she had had to dissipate her
> military strength in bolstering up her allies whom he described as a
> collection of 'rotting corpses'. In the next war Germany did not want
> allies but benevolent neutrals, who would be of value without proving
> a burden. I asked him about Italy, and he replied with the greatest
> scorn: 'I do not count upon Italy, but of this you can be sure; which-
> ever side Italy begins the war on, at its close she will be found fulfilling
> her historic role as the Whore of Europe!'[41]

Rumours also abounded that the Soviet Union might be on the verge
of making a separate peace with Germany, leaving Wheeler-Bennett on
the side of those not wishing to jeopardise Britain's relationship with the
Russians.

> We cannot ignore the fact that we and the Russians are a part of
> Europe, and have a direct primary stake in the future of the Continent,
> while America's interest in Europe can only, at best, be indirect and
> secondary. Nor can we neglect the possibility that we shall be vitally
> dependent on Russian collaboration in Europe in the event of a
> restricted American participation in post-war reconstruction, or of
> the withdrawal of the Americans from the scene altogether . . . The

anti-Russian feeling here is growing apace, and I only hope that in the course of the forthcoming tripartite conversations [due to take place in Moscow between the foreign secretaries of the USA, the UK and the Soviet Union in October] some formula can be found which will allay at the same time the American suspicions of Russian political and ideological expansion in Europe and the Russian suspicions of American schemes for the stabilization of European reactionary forces.[42]

In order to determine what Germany might do, Wheeler-Bennett tried to 'think' himself into the minds of some of the German generals he had known. 'I would surrender to Russia on the 1941 frontier (presumably including the land offered to the Soviet Union by the 1939 secret protocol of the Nazi-Soviet Non-Aggression pact, i.e. the Baltic States – Estonia, Latvia and Lithuania – and eastern Poland) and appeal to Moscow against the West. Of course it would be a gamble but Germany's position today is so bad that she has little to lose by gambling.' In his analysis, Wheeler-Bennett considered that if Germany were to attempt to make peace with the Soviet Union, it would be 'considerably more alluring to the Army than Unconditional Surrender, and they could always bank on dividing the allies. Unless the Americans and we can succeed in getting an agreed policy with Russia toward Germany we may lose the war politically, though we win it militarily. For unless the war results in the elimination of the military caste and machine in Germany we shall not have won a 100% victory.'[43] Although Wheeler-Bennett's imaginary scenario did not materialise, the fear that Stalin would make a separate peace with Hitler remained strong in British official circles until the end of the year.

In yet another paper, entitled 'The Future of Russo-Japanese Relations', Wheeler-Bennett tried to predict what the Soviet Union's future policy towards Japan might be. 'The fact that Russia is not at war with Japan is a source of much suspicion in certain circles in Britain and America and is certainly a major cause of the Russo phobia so prevalent in the United States.' Much, he considered, would depend on how the Soviet Union felt it was going to be treated by Britain and the United States. For example, he suggested that if the Soviet Union 'feels that Britain and the United States are prepared to thwart her ambitions in Asia, she may refuse to co-operate in the defeat of Japan and may even use her influence to maintain that country as sufficient of a national entity to be used by Russia in the future against any Sino-American bloc that may be formed.'[44]

As the date approached for the third 'Moscow Conference' due to start on 18 October between the UK's foreign secretary, Eden, the US secretary of state, Cordell Hull, and the Soviet Union's foreign minister, Vyacheslav Molotov, Wheeler-Bennett grew more confident of the outcome. 'There seems to be every effort on the part of Russia to be accommodating,' he wrote to Lockhart. 'There is no doubt, to my mind, that Russia is at the cross roads in foreign policy. Her preference is for collaboration with the Americans and ourselves in knocking out the Germans and the Japanese once and for all, and in keeping the peace of the world after the war. If, however, for any reason this proves impossible of realisation, she will pursue her own line of policy and play a lone hand in Europe and Asia – and if that happens, God help us!'[45] During the conference, Wheeler-Bennett noticed that Stalin had appeared in public wearing the uniform of a marshal of the Soviet Union. 'This is to me highly significant and marks the public passing of Uncle Joe from the phase of the peasant revolutionary leader to that of the established military potentate. Sartorial changes have often had their significance in revolution. Do you remember,' he asked Lockhart, 'when Hitler abandoned the Party uniform for morning dress on public occasions during the period in which he was trying in the early days of the regime to impress his peaceful intentions on the world at large?'[46]

Meanwhile, Wheeler-Bennett was continuing to meet his usual complement of refugees, all hopeful that the changing situation would work to their advantage and, in the case of the aristocrats, restore them to their former positions. 'My engagement book looks like a section of the Almanac de Gotha! Archduke of Austria, the Dukes of Bavaria and Württemberg – pale shadows of a dead past, they come to see me, each cherishing a new hope that at last the winter of his discontent may be made glorious by some summer sun!'[47] In general he was not impressed with their calibre: 'I suppose there are comparatively few people who have seen as many political refugees and exiles of enemy origin as I have during this war, and I have probably become embittered as a result, but I have reached the conclusion that not one of them is worthy to return

to any position of importance after the war. I have talked with all of
them from the top to the bottom, from the Right to the Left, from
Archdukes to Communists, and I assure you that they are Bourbons,
every one of them, incapable of learning or forgetting anything.'[48] In his
opinion, Masaryk stood 'practically alone among them as a man of vision
and statesmanship, a man who understands the past mistakes of European
politics and is willing to profit by them. If every government-in-exile
had a Jan Masaryk in it there might be some hope for the peace of
Europe.'[49] Wheeler-Bennett was also tired, complaining to Lockhart that
he had had no leave, 'as my original plans were unavoidably changed by
the arrival of the PM and Brendan in this country'. He wanted two to
three weeks off at the beginning of November, before returning to
England in December to assume his position as European adviser, 'and
then come back here for a month or six weeks in June or July of next
year. If one can look ahead so far, just to get the hang of what is going
on. I have a hunch that things will be popping in odd places this winter
and I want to be in London when that happens. So please will you take
the necessary action. I shall be most grateful.'[50]

Lockhart secured what Wheeler-Bennett wanted both in terms of his
leave and his return to London. In November, he left for a holiday at
the Arizona Inn, going on to California. Since this meant interrupting
his weekly information bulletins to Lockhart, he promised a 'monster'
letter on his return.[51] By the end of the month he was back in the office:
'I "resume my pen" – as the Victorians would say – after a three weeks
interval, in considerably better fettle than when I last wrote to you. I
greatly enjoyed and benefited form my week's rest in Tucson, where I
lay in the sun, read books and did very little else, and then went to
California, where for a further week I became technical adviser to Paramount Pictures Inc, for the making of their stupendous, colossal, etc.,
new masterpiece entitled "The Rise of the Nazi Party."' The script for
the latter project had originally been sent to the British Embassy and
Wheeler-Bennett had been asked to comment on it. As a result of his
finding numerous factual errors, his services had been requested as a
'co-director in all but name'. With his enjoyment of the arts, Wheeler-
Bennett found it 'deeply interesting' to see how a film was made from
start to finish; he also came to understand how easy it was for a movie

director to become 'intolerable'. 'There is something god-like in sitting in a chair watching a scene and then saying expressionlessly: "We'll have that again, please." '[52] To play Hitler, Paramount had found a former comedian, Bobby Watson, whose physical resemblance to the Führer had secured him the part; Goering was played by a blond butcher 'of grotesque proportions' while Goebbels was played by a 'thin-faced little hair-dresser'.[53] 'It is, I think, a good picture and will have a salutary effect here. I was able – at considerable cost to Paramount, I may say – to have certain scenes re-taken on a more accurate basis and to inject into the script a substantial smearing of the German Army which I found to be sadly lacking in the original.'[54] The film, directed by the Australian John Farrow, was released the following year – 1944 – under what Wheeler-Bennett called the 'unduly vulgar' title of The Hitler Gang. 'Such was my first experience as a film director. I enjoyed it immensely.'[55]

Since Wheeler-Bennett had only returned from California the day before Thanksgiving when everything was closed, he confessed that he had not 'had much opportunity to gather any gossip', but as far as he could see the general feeling regarding the outcome of the Moscow Conference was 'satisfactory. It would appear that a real step forward has been taken in dissipating the mutual distrust which existed between Russian and American official circles.'[56] A week later Wheeler-Bennett was lamenting the lack of interest in the mind of the American citizen, and even in the 'above average' mind, regarding the 'tremendous happenings' in world affairs. Not only had the foreign secretaries met in Moscow, but it had officially been revealed that the first meeting of 'the Big Three' – Churchill, Stalin and Roosevelt – had subsequently taken place in Tehran at the end of November. It was Roosevelt's first meeting with Stalin and the first time Stalin had left Soviet territory for over twenty years. During their discussions, the date for the opening of the second front in Europe, indefinitely deferred by Churchill in 1942, was finally 'approximately decided'.[57]

Although Wheeler-Bennett had hoped to start work in England with Bruce Lockhart at his office at Bush House in the new year, he was 'doomed to frustration'. Having planned to fly home, instead of making his usual sea crossing, before Christmas, he had developed an 'agonising' earache and temperature. 'I have little clear recollection of what immediately followed but, thanks entirely to the kindness of Leonard Miall, who took charge of the situation with masterly efficiency, the next thing I knew I was in the Manhattan Ear, Nose and Throat Hospital, having been operated on for a mastoid infection and feeling very weak and ill.'[58] Once he was well enough to move, Aubrey and Constance Morgan took him to their home in Englewood, where he was 'cosseted and spoiled'. On New Year's Day, he wrote to Lockhart, himself subject to recurrent bouts of ill health. 'This letter is to wish you the best of everything for 1944, and particularly a complete return to good health and no more relapses. Scotland has seen enough of you in 1943; allow England to have a chance this year.' He went on to describe his own illness:

> I could do with some of these good wishes myself, in point of fact. As you may have heard through official channels I was 'stricken' – as the newspaper headlines invariably say about anyone – on the very eve of my departure for England with an infection of the ear which required an operation within twenty-four hours and drastic sulpha treatment in order to avoid a more serious operation on the mastoid. Fortunately this preventative treatment worked but can you imagine what might have happened if all this occurred twenty-four hours later in a plane with the air pressure of 12,000 ft altitude. The after effects of this drastic treatment are such as to knock me out completely for some time to come – I'm just crawling about with a stick now – and all thought of travel by sea or air is postponed indefinitely. Indeed my doctor, who had always opposed my going back just now in view of the fact that I originally left England after pneumonia and haven't wintered there for eight years, is now emphatic that I can't leave before the early summer.

As Wheeler-Bennett realised, plans for returning to England as Lockhart's 'personal intelligence officer' had to be put to one side. However, if he had to stay in the United States, he favoured moving over to work directly with Stephenson and Halpern. 'There is no doubt that I have exhausted any direct usefulness I may have had with the Mission here – I am no propagandist, and I know it. On the other hand, my political intelligence work has, I believe, been useful . . . This work . . . could be carried on very much more effectively under the auspices of Bill Stephenson and Alex Halpern, and there will be an increasing need for it in the crucial presidential election year ahead of us.' He formally resigned from the Political Warfare Mission 'in order to seek a transfer of myself and my work to this other aegis when I recover from my illness'. He also promised that he would continue to write his weekly 'gossip letter' and to send material to David Bowes-Lyon in Washington.[59] On the same day, he wrote to Bowes-Lyon, saying that the time had now come for him 'to bow myself out gracefully from the ranks of the Mission. Indeed, I have felt for some time that the clipping service on German material, with which I furnished Washington, did not constitute a major contribution to the war effort, and this was virtually all I did for the Mission, since more and more of my time became occupied with political intelligence.' He repeated what he had told Lockhart, that if he could make the transfer 'my own field of operations would be greatly widened.' Instead of working alone, 'I should have the inestimable advantage of working in constant contact with Alex Halpern, whose knowledge and experience is prodigious'.[60]

After further recuperation in California, staying with friends of the Morgans, Dick and Eleanor Griffith, Wheeler-Bennett was back in New York in April 'with at least a 75% clean bill of health, with every expectation that the balance will be made up in due course'. His stay on the West Coast had depressed him. As the Americans began to tire of the war, their isolationist sentiments were increasing. Part of the problem was the failure of the authorities to explain to the American people why they were fighting in Europe. Yet again he had detected a 'growing fear and suspicion of Russia and a desire not to be contaminated'. Issues regarding India and Palestine were making people say that they did not wish 'to sacrifice their sons and their money to maintain British imperialism'. There was a feeling that the administration in Washington 'has no vestige of an idea where it is going or what it wants to do'. As a result, he advised Lockhart that, while American troops overseas were bewildered, people at home were disgruntled. As he had been told: 'Never in her history has America been called upon to make so great an effort in manpower and production. This can only be justified on one of three grounds: defence of our homeland; conquest of territory; in defence of an ideal. We are not defending our homes; we want no territory and there is darned little sign of an ideal.'

This attitude left Wheeler-Bennett feeling discouraged at Britain's prospects at the close of hostilities. 'It seems almost inevitable that the Americans will not be prepared to take an active role in any security organisation.'[61] He also painted a gloomy picture of Roosevelt's waning popularity among the groups of immigrant 'hyphenated' Americans: 'The Finns and Poles have turned against him on account of the Russians; the Italian vote in New York and Chicago, which has always been anti-monarchist, is disgruntled at our retention of the House of Savoy and particularly of the person of the King and the Prince of Piedmont.'[62]

In addition to detailed letters, Wheeler-Bennett was continuing to write papers addressing themes in a postwar world. 'Some Aspects of the German Problem' – a supplementary memo to his earlier 'What To Do With Germany', written the previous May – displayed some of his old fondness for the German people: 'At the close of the war we still have in the heart of Europe a Germany with not less than sixty-five million inhabitants. It will be a defeated Germany; a Germany whose cities will have been shattered, whose military power will have been broken and whose territory is completely occupied by the forces of the victors. The Third Reich will have followed the First and Second into the shadows of defeat and for a time the world will sigh with relief.' He believed, however, that the Germans were

a great people with great qualities – good and bad – and Germany is inherently a great country. To deny this is to deny truth, to underestimate the gravity of the problem before us . . . Perhaps the most difficult aspect of the German problem is the kind of Germany which we ourselves wish to see as ultimately emerging in Europe. We know the kind of Germany we do not wish to see . . . The fatal error of the Treaty of Versailles was that it left a Germany full of hatred and resentment without completely depriving her of the means by which this passion might be translated into action. The fatal error of the period between the wars was that we consistently appeased the wrong Germans. At the close of this war, Germany will have been defeated even more conclusively than in 1918. Her humiliation will be the greater and her resentment the more bitter. This time, however, there will be no shadow of excuse for leaving her in any condition save that of complete military impotence; nor should there be in the future any valid reason for appeasing any Germans 'good' or 'bad'.[63]

By the end of April, Wheeler-Bennett was ready to return to Britain. Before doing so, he spent a few days in Canada. In Ottawa, he had 'a long useful talk in the department of external affairs'. He also gave a talk to the Civil Affairs School at Kingston, which left him with the impression that Canada 'now regards herself as a small power, independent in thought and policy both of the UK and of the US'. [64] Back in England, all attention was fixed on opening the second front in Normandy. Without being able to predict the outcome, Wheeler-Bennett envisaged four possible scenarios: 'that we have an initial success and are able to crumple the enemy defences, subsequently advancing without too much difficulty; that after a blood bath, we are able to overcome enemy resistance; that the operation bogs down; that the operation is a failure and we are forced to withdraw.' He put success or failure in the context of American public opinion:

It should not be overlooked in London that these people are emotional to a degree and mercurial in their emotions. They are capable of overnight changes of national feeling which are incredible unless witnessed. It must also be remembered that just as the whole tempo of war has been speeded up here so has the growth of war weariness in America been increasingly rapid. The country is tired of war and particularly of the European war; the people are good for one tremendous effort in the Invasion but it must be a successful effort or their enthusiasm will dwindle away and be replaced by apathy and ultimately by downright revulsion.[65]

After spending virtually all of the war in the United States, Wheeler-Bennett reported for duty on the seventh floor, Centre Block, Bush House in the Aldwych on 8 May 1944 to begin working for PWE. Among the men and women he was to spend time with over the next year, Wheeler-Bennett noted 'a forcing ground of gifted aptitude, a dynamo of creative power'. His colleagues included Richard Crossman, the future MP, who had joined the civil service at the outbreak of war, Duncan Wilson, a former curator of the British Museum, who became a career diplomat, Ralph Murray of the BBC and Con O'Neill, who had worked in the army's Intelligence Corps before joining the Foreign Office; all were men Wheeler-Bennett remembered with affection. He also became friends with the historian Alan Bullock, who noted the difference between those who worked on the upper floors of Bush House and those (like Bullock himself) who laboured on the lower floors (mostly in the cellars), where the BBC's European Services maintained their own form of 'resistance movement'.[66] Other friends included Peter Ritchie Ritchie-Calder, the Scottish author and journalist, and the director of PWE's Plans and Campaigns department; the lawyer Eric Sachs; the journalist and film critic Dilys Powell, whose knowledge of Greece involved her overseeing propaganda in 'occupied' Europe; and the author David Garnett. 'Rarely can a galaxy of intelligence have so remarkably fulfilled their early promise.' Working directly with Lockhart for the first time, Wheeler-Bennett considered that he was 'an excellent and inspiring chief endowed with extraordinary insight', even if on occasion he was a little too 'brusque with his staff'.[67]

Wheeler-Bennett now had three appointments. As in New York, he was designated European adviser to PWE. His second position was with the European Advisory Commission (EAC), established after the third Moscow Conference, to study the postwar political problems of Europe. Britain's representative was the diplomat William Strang, assistant under-secretary of state for Europe throughout most of the war. To begin with, meetings were held at Lancaster House.[68] His third position was as 'number 2' to the British political adviser at the Supreme Headquarters Allied Expeditionary Force (SHAEF), set up in Teddington, south-west London at the end of 1943. As he later wrote, these jobs were interesting because working at SHAEF involved planning for the government of those areas of Germany that would come under British occupation, while working with the EAC involved the unconditional surrender and postwar control of the German state, 'and the future of Germany interested me greatly'. Wheeler-Bennett's official title was assistant director-general, which – as it amused him to note in his memoirs – gave him the equivalent rank of an assistant under-secretary in the Foreign Office and a brigadier or rear-admiral at SHAEF.[69]

Meanwhile, he continued to define the tasks of 'political warfare' in the context of German militarism. On 5 June, as a vast armada was poised to embark on the invasion of Normandy, he wrote: 'the task of P.W.E is essentially complicated and delicate. It is, in fact, the trickiest piece of political tight-rope walking which they have been called upon to do during the whole war. They must promote friction and division without committing themselves to obligations; they must create disturbance yet avoid chaos; they must set German against German, Party against Party, Nazi against Nazi, Army against Army and yet preserve an unassailable impartiality.'[70]

As the Allies successfully landed on the Normandy beaches, although with severe losses, it was evident that the tide of the war had finally turned. However, the new menace for those living in London and south-east England were the V1 bombs, launched a week after D-Day by Hitler as his 'secret weapon' in a new offensive to demoralise the British people. As a result, the minister of information, Brendan Bracken, decided to move some members of PWE to the country. He commandeered 'Little Hansteads', the house belonging to the renowned traveller Lady Yule. Located in Hertfordshire, it was halfway between Watford and St Albans and within easy access of Woburn.[71] For the first time in their lives, Wheeler-Bennett and Bruce Lockhart were living under one roof. 'It must have tried him highly,' Lockhart recalled, 'for he was tidy and methodical and horrified by the amount of papers that flowed into me.' Lockhart also appreciated the toll the work took on Wheeler-Bennett's health.

He looked tired, and every day his face became more and more like the colour of yellow blotting-paper. But he worked harder than ever. I knew that he did not sleep well, because about once a week he would retire to bed early and say that he was going to take a 'Micky Finn'. This was a powerful narcotic which took its name from the American boxer who knocked most of his opponents out for the count. But when I saw him going to sleep immediately after dinner sitting in an arm-chair and holding a glass of untouched whisky, I realised that he needed a rest.[72]

In Germany, in the wake of the Normandy landings, a new and possibly last-ditch effort to assassinate Hitler was being planned under the codename Operation Walküre. The assassin was to be the thirty-six-year-old Colonel Claus Graf von Stauffenberg, a practising Roman Catholic, who had never joined the Nazi Party and had always been opposed to its ideology, especially the persecution of the Jews.[73] The plan was to kill Hitler while he was visiting the military high command in East Prussia with a bomb hidden in Stauffenberg's briefcase. However, at a critical moment the briefcase was moved out of position so that, when it exploded, Hitler survived. One of those who succumbed to his wounds following the attack was Wheeler-Bennett's riding friend during the Weimar days, Lieutenant Hans von Brandt, who had inadvertently moved the briefcase away from where Stauffenberg had placed it near Hitler and closer to himself. Stauffenberg was caught and shot the following day with several co-conspirators. Since so many of the key players had been known to him, Wheeler-Bennett was watching events in Germany with concern, although nothing had happened to make him change his mind that Germany needed the salutary lesson of total defeat. The day after the failed coup, he was asked to give his opinion to Lord Cranborne, the under-secretary of state for foreign affairs.

> I said that in the long run it was a good thing that the coup had failed. It was regrettable that so many 'good Germans', some of whom I had known personally, and who might have played a useful part in a new Germany, had sacrificed their lives in vain, but had they succeeded the complications would have been incalculable . . . On the whole, I said, I believed that things were better as they were and that the war should end with the Unconditional Surrender of the Third Reich.[74]

A few days later he elaborated on his views: 'It may now be said with some definiteness that we are better off with things as they are today than if the plot of July 20th had succeeded and Hitler had been assassinated.' If this had happened, he believed the 'Old Army' generals would have taken over and attempted a peace move 'in which Germany would admit herself defeated and could sue for terms other than those of Unconditional Surrender'. Reports that the pope had already offered to mediate added fuel to his argument. He continued: 'By the failure of the plot we have been spared the embarrassments, both at home and in the United States, which might have resulted from such a move and, moreover, the present purge is presumably removing from the scene numerous individuals who might have caused us difficulty, not only had the plot succeeded, but also after the defeat of a Nazi Germany.'

Finally, he stated that if it was true that a number of 'more distinguished generals' together with civilians such as Schacht, the former president of the Reichsbank, and Baron von Neurath, former ambassador to London before becoming minister of foreign affairs – both of whom were known to him personally – had been eliminated then 'the Gestapo and the SS have done us an appreciable service in removing a selection of those who would undoubtedly have posed as "good" Germans after the war, while preparing for a third World War. It is to our advantage therefore that the purge should continue, since the killing of Germans by Germans will save us from future embarrassments of many kinds.'[75] As it happened, both Schacht and Neurath survived. However, Adam von Trott zu Solz, who had been sitting in Stauffenberg's flat the night before the assassination attempt, was arrested and later brutally hanged. Carl Goerdeler, slated as the new chancellor had the plot succeeded, was executed in February 1945. Count Albrecht von Bernstorff was shot in April.[76] In all, Hitler took his revenge on at least two hundred people who were allegedly implicated in the plot as a vindictive lesson against further attempts on his life.

Shortly afterwards, Wheeler-Bennett prepared another 'top secret' paper examining what might happen if Hitler died suddenly. 'The death of Hitler,' he said, 'would materially shorten the war by accelerating and facilitating surrender.' However, 'a premature termination of hostilities might prove disastrous'.

Should this occur before the Russians enter the borders of the Reich proper or while the Anglo-American armies are still west of the Rhine, the German people will have lost a second world war without having experienced the humiliation and depredations of an invasion. Admittedly they will have suffered to a far greater degree than in 1914–18, but the dictum of Frederick the Great that German wars should be

fought on foreign soil will still hold good; the legend fostered by the
German General Staff that no invading army has entered the Reich
since 1813 will still be intact. However formidable and comprehensive
the disasters inflicted on the German armies *outside* the Reich may be,
the concept of defeat will not be complete in the mind of the German
people until Allied armies have entered the Reich as invaders, and not
merely as an occupying force. Unless the impression of defeat and
conquest is implanted in the German mind beyond all manner of doubt,
the ultimate measure of victory will not have been achieved . . . To
prolong the present war unnecessarily would be iniquitous . . . on the
other hand, we have now reached a stage in the war when to bring it
to a premature conclusion would be almost as iniquitous as to prolong
it unnecessarily; for unless we achieve a complete and unmistakeable
victory – so understood by the Germans as well as by ourselves – we
shall not have won a victory at all. For these reasons, it is submitted,
it is of the most vital interest to the Allied cause that the demise of the
Fuehrer should not occur until either the Russian or the Anglo-
American armies (but preferably both of them) have penetrated well
into the territory of the Reich and have made their presence felt there
in no uncertain terms.[77]

In August came the thrilling news that Paris had been liberated. 'On
reaching the house,' recalled Bruce Lockhart one evening, 'Jack Wheeler-
Bennett turned on the radio, and we stood waiting in silence. Someone
was speaking in French, and for a moment I thought we were on the
wrong wave-length. In a second we realised. It was the voice of General
de Gaulle, speaking from the Hotel de Ville in Paris and announcing
victory, glory, and happiness to his cheering compatriots.'[78] After the
liberation, SHAEF moved from Britain to France. The offices were at
Versailles and Wheeler-Bennett was obliged to commute, going to Paris
for the first time since the spring of 1939. He returned to the Hôtel de
Crillon, overlooking the Place de la Concorde, where he had stayed
many times previously. To his regret, he realised that, since the hotel
had been used as the seat of the military tribunal of the German occupation authorities, 'many had been condemned to death in those sumptuous
public rooms in which all European society had once exercised its fancy

and indulged its pleasure'. A small compensation for the ill-effects of the war was being greeted at his favourite restaurant and bookshop almost as a 'lost son (though their only real son had been executed, I learned, in the Resistance and by the Vichy Militia)'.[79] At Versailles he found his colleagues, among them Charles Peake, established in offices bearing signs of the German occupation. The problem of having three jobs, one of which was in Paris, meant that, like everyone else in England, Wheeler-Bennett was constantly 'dead tired'. With the war drawing to an end, the documents he now wrote signalled the Allied victory. On 4 December, he wrote an advance note, to be used on 30 January 1945, drawing attention to the anniversary of Hitler's assumption of power in 1933. 'Today [i.e. 30 January], marks the twelfth anniversary of the Unconditional Surrender of the German people to Adolf Hitler and the Nazi Party. The fruits of this capitulation have brought death, devastation and disaster to millions of innocent people in other lands and to the Germans themselves complete subjection and futile sacrifice, to which is now added the certainty of total defeat.'[80]

The Horrors of Peace

Though we were now spared the perils of war, the horrors of
peace loomed all too darkly.[1]

The year 1945 did not begin auspiciously. On 20 January, Wheeler-Bennett sailed from Greenock on board the *Queen Mary* with a contingent of homeward-bound American war-wounded. His travelling companion was the Canadian diplomat Tommy Stone, a friend since the 1920s. Due to a misunderstanding, neither was aware that the *Queen Mary*'s sailing time had been brought forward by two hours. While they were happily enjoying lunch in a pub overlooking the Firth of Forth, they observed that the passenger liner had slipped her moorings. Undaunted, and pulling rank ('Was I not a titular major-general and therefore equally a titular rear-admiral?'),[2] Wheeler-Bennett secured a barge to take them to the ship. It was an experience that he would have liked afterwards to forget: 'To climb a rope-ladder up the side of the *Queen Mary* in a rough sea, wearing a fur-coat (astrakhan collar and all!), with a bottle of Napoleon brandy in the pocket, and a black chapeau Eden and encumbered by an umbrella and a brief-case has remained with me as a vision of hell which I trust never to encounter again.'[3]

The journey, beset by the worst storms Wheeler-Bennett had ever experienced and the fear that a U-boat 'wolf-pack' in the vicinity might attack, did little to restore his flagging energy. By the time he reached New York, he was suffering from exhaustion as well as a severe bout of jaundice. Yet again his doctors recommended a rest. His first thought was to go to Arizona to recuperate so that he could then marry Ruth Risher, the woman whom, ten years previously, he had confided to his mother he wanted to be his wife.[4] After her wartime service in Egypt, Ruth was back in Charlottesville; Wheeler-Bennett had not seen her since proposing two years previously in New York's Pennsylvania Station. Aubrey Morgan, also suffering from 'war strain', was already recuperating at his mother-in-law's holiday villa, Casa Manana in Cuernavaca, about an hour's drive from Mexico City and had extended an invitation to Wheeler-Bennett, as well as to Isaiah Berlin, who had also been unwell. 'I cannot describe the delight of the next few weeks . . . we sat in the gardens either gossiping, arguing or just being silent together, for our friendship is of that nature.'[5] Wheeler-Bennett was not entirely idle; while in Cuernavaca, he started a new book on the Munich Agreement, a subject that had been 'much in my thoughts during such spare time as I had for contemplation during the war'.[6]

The holiday, culminating in a five-day rail journey across North America via Laredo and St Louis, restored Wheeler-Bennett's health. Back in New York, however, his doctor gave him a severe warning against further 'overwork and brain fatigue and says that I must take things as carefully as possible in order to prevent a renewed breakdown which would, apparently, be of considerable severity'. When Wheeler-Bennett indicated that he had come to the United States to get married, the doctor signalled his approval. As he informed Bruce Lockhart five days before his marriage, he intended to 'take the plunge as soon as possible', regretting that Lockhart could not be present to be his best man.[7] On Monday, 26 March 1945, John Wheeler Wheeler-Bennett and Ruth Harrison Risher were finally married in the chapel of the University of Virginia. He was forty-two and Ruth was forty-four. 'It went off in gallant style in the midst of the most overwhelming Southern hospitality,' wrote Isaiah Berlin.[8] Wheeler-Bennett related that it was 'no ordinary wedding, because so many of our friends were on active service including the local rector whom we would have liked to perform the ceremony'. Since the university was non-denominational, they were married by a Presbyterian minister who read the Episcopalian service. In Lockhart's absence, Wheeler-Bennett's best man was his oldest friend in Virginia, Bobbie Gooch, former Rhodes Scholar at Christ Church and currently head of the Department of Political Science at Virginia. Among the wedding presents was one from Baffy Dugdale: a copy of Thomas Masaryk's book *The Making of a State*, which the author had inscribed and sent to A.J. Balfour after the Paris Peace Conference. When Balfour died in 1930, he had left it to Baffy, his niece. For the rest of Wheeler-Bennett's life, the book remained among his 'treasured possessions'.[9]

For Wheeler-Bennett, a bachelor until his early forties, marriage was a new experience which he embarked upon with commitment. In the years to come Ruth proved an ideal companion. But his close friends realised that the relationships he had built up over the years would not be the same. 'I was full of happiness,' wrote Bruce Lockhart, whose own marriage had been short-lived, 'at the thought that you would be happy and a little sad that, after the many years we have known each other, we should never again be quite so care-free as we were in the days of lesser responsibility. In other words, we shall have to mind both our language and our liquor.' Lockhart also teased Wheeler-Bennett about having to reform his breakfast regime, which normally consisted of black coffee and cigars. 'When a man reaches middle-age; nay, when a man achieves marriage in middle-age, he must make his peace with his stomach and treat it with respect.'[10] To some degree, Wheeler-Bennett did adopt a new persona: to Ruth and their new friends he was always 'John', never 'Jack', as he remained to his own family.[11] As soon as he was married, he deposited his bride 'back to mother' so that he could keep his promise to Lockhart that, if summoned to London, he would return at once. Heavy storms over the south coast of England meant that he was stranded in Bermuda for a week in beautiful weather without – for security purposes – being able to inform his wife of his where-abouts. Eventually, his host in Bermuda, the governor, Lord Burleigh, sent her a message of reassurance. A minor irritation during his stay in Bermuda was being woken at five o'clock each morning to be told that he would not be departing that day.[12]

Wheeler-Bennett reached England in mid-April. His return coincided with the news of Himmler's offer of an unconditional surrender to Britain and the United States. Since it did not include surrendering to the Soviet Union, the Allies felt compelled to reject it. 'Thereafter,' as Wheeler-Bennett recollected, 'the whole thing petered out.'[13] Later, Himmler was apprehended, posing as an ordinary German officer, by British forces in Bremen, and committed suicide before further interrogation could be carried out.[14] When Wheeler-Bennett arrived in London, he found that Lockhart was having treatment for his recurrent nervous dermatitis at the Royal Infirmary in Edinburgh, so he travelled again to Scotland to visit him. With the end of the European war so obviously in sight, the two men discussed the future world order as well as the impact of President Roosevelt's death earlier in April. As Lockhart recorded, 'Jack is of the opinion that Roosevelt's death is an advantage. He has done his job and had been failing in health badly. He would have been disastrous as a "ga-ga" President.' Wheeler-Bennett also shared with Lockhart his new fear that co-operation with Russia might 'go awry'.[15]

Back in London, Wheeler-Bennett and his colleagues heard the news that, on 30 April, Hitler had shot himself in his bunker in Berlin. A week later, word came through that the 'Unconditional Surrender of the German Armies' had been signed at Rheims in the early hours of Sunday, 6 May. Hostilities officially ceased at one minute past midnight on 8 May, known as 'Victory in Europe' – VE – Day. This also happened to be Ruth's birthday 'and for this reason VE-Day has always had an additional significance for me'.[16] Soon afterwards Wheeler-Bennett wrote another paper outlining future problems, giving voice to his recurring fear of German militarism:

> The Germans have suffered an overwhelming military defeat, a defeat as catastrophic in comparison with 1918 as was the defeat of France in 1940 when compared with that of 1870. Both the German military machine and the Nazi terror machine have been crushed and destroyed. Germany lies prostrate before her conquerors, yet she still retains the power to distil the poison of propaganda, with which it is hoped to sow dissension among the Allies and to preserve the German military legend . . . In our treatment of Germany we shall be called upon to combat these lines of propaganda and others which are not yet formed. They should be made the subject of continuous study.[17]

Although the war in the Pacific was not yet over, Wheeler–Bennett was almost out of a job. The two organisations with which he, as a member of PWE, had been involved had disappeared. After the surrender, the EAC had ceased to exist. SHAEF disintegrated when the British and US armies took up position in their respective zones of occupation in Germany. Looking back, Wheeler–Bennett was realistic about their achievements. 'Our efforts to undermine the morale of the German people were not very effective until the tide of victory had turned and we were able to demonstrate conclusively that ultimate defeat was creeping nearer and nearer.' He believed, however, that in terms of fulfilling their second objective – raising the morale of the 'enslaved' people in the occupied countries – the record of success was 'very high indeed'.[18] While Wheeler–Bennett mused on his future, domestic and international events moved 'with increasing velocity, changing all our lives'.[19] On 15 June 1945, Churchill and the National Government he had led since May 1940 resigned. When the general election was held the following month, the outcome was a landslide victory for Labour and Clement Attlee became Britain's new prime minister. On 6 August, the first atom bomb was dropped on Hiroshima; three days later another bomb was dropped on Nagasaki.

On 10 August, the BBC picked up a message from Tokyo that Japan had accepted an unconditional surrender. 'It was unofficial and unconfirmed but it set rumours aflame.' Finally, on 14 August, Wheeler–Bennett heard Clement Attlee's 'dry and unemotional voice' ('very different from Mr Churchill's rolling periods') announce the end of the war. That evening he dined with Bruce Lockhart at the Ritz, where both men were staying. 'It was a hot night and after dinner we sat out on the balcony of my sitting-room overlooking Piccadilly. Outside there was jubilation.'[20] As he later wrote, the relief at the end of the war was 'enormous'. Yet, as he realised, they had now been precipitated into the unknown benefits and perils of the Nuclear Age. 'Already one of our principal partners in victory [the Soviet Union] was menacing our chances of effecting a lasting settlement. We, the British, were exhausted physically and mentally, financially imperilled, economically insecure and with a disintegrating empire.'[21]

On Victory in Japan – VJ – Day, Wheeler–Bennett began his return journey to the United States to wind up the New York office. 'More than anything else' he wanted to rejoin Ruth to resume his married life, 'which had been so rudely interrupted'.[22] As far as Lockhart was concerned, the day and night marking the end of World War II 'were nightmares . . . Jack Wheeler-Bennett was so frightened that he would not be able to get to Victoria [station] for the crowds that he insisted on taking his luggage to Airway House at 9.30 a.m.' To make matters worse, although his train to Bournemouth did not leave until seven in the evening Jack would go to the station at five. 'In point of fact, he could have gone at any time, for the traffic was not seriously impeded.'[23] Before leaving, Wheeler-Bennett sent a farewell letter to Lockhart, with a present of vintage port.

I am about to close my third year as a member of your department – I joined it in July 1942 – and I look back over the time with a great degree of interest. The fact that you made me spend the first portion of this period working under the authority of a young man who – at my prompting – became known in Washington Society as 'Master beaux-Yeux' [Bowes-Lyon] was indeed a test of our friendship, but one which it withstood! The difficulties of this period have been more than compensated for by the pleasures of the Bush House-Little Hansteads period, the twilight of which is upon us in all its sadness of dissolution . . . I've watched with no little envy your capacity for suffering fools gladly and your ability to guide the destinies of a troupe of prima donnas with just that amalgam of ruthlessness and encourage-ment which restrains their excesses without rebuking their genius. This is the real secret of true leadership . . . There are memories which we shall share together and I shall always regard it as a great privilege to have worked under your leadership and a lasting pleasure to have lived, laughed and wept with you, both in and out of office hours. I could have had no better and no kinder chief.[24]

Lockhart was pleased to have worked with Wheeler-Bennett too: 'I owe him much. PWE was a difficult department and Jack was the one man on whose judgment and loyalty I could rely implicitly.'[25] For the next three months, Wheeler-Bennett was still officially on the books of PID. In October, after another month's sick leave due to nervous exhaustion, he wrote to Major General Kenneth Strong, the new director-general of PID, to terminate his association. 'It is with very considerable reluctance that I contemplate "running out" on the arrangement which we made tentatively in London for my activities during the next three months. I am exceedingly sorry to be thus forced to let you down . . . certainly in my present shape I am not much use for anything.' He suggested that he make a survey of the current position and prepare a report on the German-American and German refugee activities 'concerning a soft peace, recommending what if anything can be done about it. This I can complete in the course of this month, and shall then request my release.' Under the circumstances, he did not feel justified in continuing to take a salary from the department, 'and would ask, therefore, if you agree, that it be terminated forthwith. For purposes of convenience in remaining in this country for the next few months and of ultimately returning to England, I should be most grateful if I might remain as an unpaid member of the department, though, if this is considered inexpedient, I shall quite understand.'[26] Strong wrote back appreciatively:

> I am grateful for your suggestion that in view of the need to economise dollars we should discontinue your salary forthwith and I have taken advantage of this. At the same time, it will suit our books to retain you as an unpaid member of the department with the feeling that we shall always be able to turn to you if we need some special services or a contact in the United States. The fact that you are thus to remain with us for the time being will for the present anyhow relieve me of the almost impossible task of expressing myself in adequate appreciation of your services to the department, your political sense and the quality of the contribution you have made on both sides of the Atlantic.[27]

For the first time since the beginning of the war, Wheeler-Bennett felt that he was again master of his own destiny.[28] The previous year, Isaiah Berlin had written to the warden of All Souls, suggesting that he would be an ideal candidate for a chair in military history. 'His brilliant works on the Treaty of Brest-Litovsk and Hindenburg you will doubtless know . . . I do hope he will be considered if the topic ever arises. He is remarkably well informed about American politics and if ever in Oxford well worth talking to.'[29] For his part, Wheeler-Bennett had no wish to remain a civil servant; nor did he 'hanker after a professionally academic career'.[30] Instead he wanted to continue writing books, and already had two projects in hand. First, there was his book on Munich, the draft of which he had begun earlier in the year in Mexico. Second, he wanted to write a book on the failed assassination attempt on Hitler in July 1944. 'Both required much thought and careful planning, as well as copious research.'[31]

He also wanted to return to live permanently in England. But it proved less easy to cross the Atlantic than he had anticipated. Since Ruth needed to transport her possessions, they had to travel by sea and it was difficult to get a passage; furthermore, after his latest bout of illness, his doctors had yet again advised a rest. The Wheeler-Bennetts therefore bided their time, staying in a house owned by Isabella Greenway King (as she had become following her marriage to Harry King in 1939), built in the style of a Touraine château on the Connecticut coast. In this comfortable residence, Wheeler-Bennett began the second draft of his book on Munich, making use of research he had already done during the war, which included interviews with Czech exiles in the United States and Britain. Of these, Beneš had once more become president of Czechoslovakia, and Masaryk his foreign minister. It was fortunate for Wheeler-Bennett that, while living in Connecticut, their neighbours were Charles and Anne Lindbergh, Constance Morgan's sister. Lindbergh was working as a consultant to the US Air Force and Pan Am Airways and agreed to give Wheeler-Bennett access to his diaries in which he described his prewar visits to Germany on behalf of the US military to report on German aviation and the Luftwaffe.

By early 1946, the backlog of Britons returning from the United States had diminished and the Wheeler-Bennetts secured a passage on board the *Queen Elizabeth*, which was to sail on 6 February. As he and Ruth boarded, he was handed a cable from his sister, Irene. Their mother, whom Wheeler-Bennett described as 'a hopeless invalid for some years', had died at the age of eighty-three.[32] She had been a widow for twenty years. The house to which the Wheeler-Bennetts returned to live in England was Garsington Manor. During the war, Irene and Trevor had

GARSINGTON

rented it out, but now realised that, with grown-up children, they could no longer afford to stay in it. When Wheeler-Bennett heard that it was to be put up for sale, he immediately cabled his sister to say that he wanted to buy it, ignoring his wife's complaint that she did not like Elizabethan houses.[33] Installed in Garsington in April 1946, the Wheeler-Bennetts began a pattern of entertaining that they would continue for nearly thirty years. From 'southern belle', Ruth transformed herself into 'a warm and successful' English hostess, ably assisted by Ethel, a young girl from Garsington village who came to cook for them for a few weeks and was then invited to stay indefinitely.

Re-entry into England was not easy. The country was 'tired and war-weary, yet compelled to face the severities of continued wartime short-ages . . . I shall never forget the dour drabness of those years, the greyness of one's daily existence . . . food was scarce, scarcer than it had been in wartime. Bread was rationed for the first time in our national history.' Fortunately for the Wheeler-Bennetts, their supplies were supplemented by food parcels which Ruth's mother sent from America, and which they shared with their 'less fortunate friends and neighbours'.[34] As Irene recog-nised, her new sister-in-law coped extremely well. 'I have never admired anyone more than Ruth in that first winter of 1946. She was a stranger to this country, and used to a very warm house. There was no coke for central heating, there was only a very small petrol ration, and staff was hard to come by. But in spite of all this, Ruth never complained, never grumbled, never said how homesick she was, and she must have been very homesick indeed.'[35]

One of the Wheeler-Bennetts' first guests in the summer of 1946 was Moley Sargent, still permanent under-secretary of state for foreign affairs. Widely read and with a store of reminiscences and anecdotes, he provided Wheeler-Bennett with enjoyable company. 'One never talked with him without adding to one's knowledge in some unexpected way and he could be the best and funniest of companions.' Sargent's visit to Garsington had important repercussions for Wheeler-Bennett. He was still working on his Munich book, having recently been to Paris to read Duff Cooper's diaries. Currently serving as the ambassador in Paris, Cooper had famously resigned as First Lord of the Admiralty in protest at the Munich Agreement. Although Wheeler-Bennett found that the diaries helped him 'enormously', he still wanted to see the German documents, 'of which many had a direct and vital bearing on my subject' and which were being frequently mentioned in the press as a result of the trials of the senior surviving Nazi leaders taking place at Nuremberg.[36] When Wheeler-Bennett brought the subject up with Sargent, his reponse was: 'Why aren't you *at* Nuremberg?' Promising to telephone 'our man' on the prosecution team, he assured Wheeler-Bennett that the Foreign Office would arrange his passage.

By the time he arrived in Nuremberg in June 1946, the International Military Tribunal had been in session since the previous November. Since Wheeler-Bennett was there in a private capacity to gather research material for his book, initially he felt unsure how to proceed. 'I was entering here a military area where passes were *de rigueur* and regulation sacrosanct.' His fear of being a mere amateur amidst professionals was soon allayed when he met Sargent's 'man' in Nuremberg, Patrick Dean, who was from the legal department of the Foreign Office. 'The warmth and kindness with which he welcomed me indicated that Moley Sargent had given me a "good character".'[37] For the first few days, he stayed at the Grand Hotel. In the evenings, to entertain the guests, the management put on a cabaret, but, having known the 'wit and spice' of prewar cabaret, Wheeler-Bennet found the atmosphere depressing. 'There was something infinitely tragic in these underfed entertainers in their pathetic and tarnished finery, singing their songs of the pre-Nazi period with desperate nostalgia.' He was only too pleased to be 'liberated' from the hotel by Francis Biddle, former US attorney-general, whom he had known in Washington. As the senior American judge on the International Military Tribunal, Biddle had been given a villa on the outskirts of Nuremberg and Wheeler-Bennett accepted with 'alacrity' an invitation to stay there. They were joined by the prolific author Rebecca West, who was writing a series of articles for the *New Yorker*. 'The three of us made a very agreeable company.'[38]

Through Patrick Dean, Wheeler-Bennett was introduced to Sir David Maxwell Fyfe, the deputy chief of the British prosecuting team, 'an impressive and amicable figure'.[39] The two men immediately found a common interest in discussing Napoleon and the American Civil War. Wheeler-Bennett was also able to provide Maxwell Fyfe with background knowledge on those Germans on trial whom he had known from his horse-riding days at Fallingbostel – the former chancellor Franz von Papen, the financier Hjalmar Schacht and Germany's former ambassador to Britain and foreign minister under Hitler Konstantin von Neurath. 'We usually had our sessions together at lunchtime, eating off trays at either side of his desk, and he would ask me simply to talk to him of the three defendants in whose prosecution he thought I could help him. I told him all I knew, and the most minute details returned to my mind as I talked. He would sit silently, drinking it all in, now asking an appropriate question, now making a single note.'[40] When Wheeler-Bennett came to record his impressions of the courtroom and its occupants in his memoirs, he recalled that his 'primary reaction on being confronted by this rogues gallery was one of supreme satisfaction . . . while I did not entertain a deep-seated loathing for the entire German people – a mental process both senseless and fruitless – I confess to a considerable sense of gratification at seeing these leaders of a tyrannous and foresworn regime brought to book at last.'[41]

On this first visit, Wheeler-Bennett spent a week in Nuremberg. He returned to Germany again briefly at the beginning of August after a visit to Prague to see President Beneš and to consult the Czech archives about Munich. By the end of August, the evidence for and against the accused had been concluded and Wheeler-Bennett did not go to Nuremberg again until the end of September, in time for the judgments on 30 September and the sentencing on 1 October. 'I do not think anyone who was present on that occasion can ever forget the experience. There was an electric tension throughout the court-room, palpable alike in the body of the court, in the press seats and in the Visitors' Gallery which was crowded with distinguished persons as never before since the beginning of the trials.' Eleven men were condemned to death: Frank, Frick, Goering, Jodl, Kaltenbrunner, Keitel, Ribbentrop, Rosenberg, Sauckel, Seyss-Inquart and Streicher.[42] The executions took place two weeks later, with the exception of Goering, who had committed suicide the previous day.

Although invited to observe the executions, Wheeler-Bennett was glad to have refused, especially when reports circulated that, for some of the condemned men, death was not instantaneous. 'Though I should not

have considered doing so under any circumstances, I was particularly glad
not to be a witness of what proved to be an intolerably bungled affair.'[43]
Of the men Wheeler-Bennett had known, Papen and Schacht were
acquitted, and Neurath was sentenced to fifteen years in prison. Later in
the year, he visited Spandau jail in Berlin, where the remaining war
criminals were carrying out their varying sentences. He was not allowed
to speak to them, but he lunched with the commandants of the guard
and saw the fallen leaders of Germany in the exercise yard.

By spending time in Nuremberg, Wheeler-Bennett obtained additional
information for his book on Munich. Back in London, it was suggested
that he and Patrick Dean, whose service as a temporary civil servant had
ended, should write the official history of the Nuremberg Trials under
the patronage of the foreign secretary, Ernest Bevin, and the attorney-
general, Hartley Shawcross, the chief prosecutor at Nuremberg. 'We
were a sound complementary choice. Pat had the legal experience and
knowledge and I the historical expertise. Moreover we liked one another
and the prospect of working together was agreeable to both of us.'[44]
Despite the fact that they received their letters of appointment and had
several meetings with Bevin and Shawcross, Moley Sargent did not want
to lose the services of Dean and appointed him head of a newly formed
German department in the Foreign Office. As a result, although both
Dean and Wheeler-Bennett drafted chapters, Wheeler-Bennett was left
'holding the baby'. After attempting to find an international lawyer to
assist him, assuring his publisher, Harold Macmillan, as late as 1950 that
the project was 'not dead but sleeping', he was forced to abandon it.[45]
Later, Dean became chairman of the Joint Intelligence Committee which
had been founded in 1936 and was the principal intelligence
body in Britain throughout the war. Dean and his wife, Patricia, became
lifelong friends of the Wheeler-Bennetts and frequent visitors to
Garsington.

In the 1946 King's Birthday Honours, Wheeler-Bennett, like many
contemporaries, was awarded an OBE in recognition of his services
during the war. It was his first decoration. 'I am delighted with the
honour, of course, and am deeply touched at receiving so many expressions of kindness from old friends,' he wrote in response to Ivison
Macadam's letter of congratulations from Chatham House.[46]

Having settled in Britain, the Wheeler-Bennetts retained their links with the United States. Ruth went annually to visit her mother – nearly ninety – in Charlottesville. Once the Treasury regulations forbidding the expenditure of more than £25 abroad were lifted, Wheeler-Bennett began to accompany her. The University of Virginia, where he had enjoyed lecturing before the war, had changed. 'Gone were the sophisticated hair cuts of the pre-war days and in their place one saw the rather hideous crew cut and the short back and sides which were handovers [sic] from the Armed Services,' he recollected. 'There were also the long hair and straggling beards of the incipient hippy movement. The students wore blue jeans and girls were even seen on the Lawn. All this came as a considerable shock to the more elderly and conservative elements in the university community – who Bourbon like – never ceased to bemoan the good old days.' As Wheeler-Bennett noted, it did not take long to realise that beneath the new trappings of youth, the students were as 'sound, pleasant and responsive' as their predecessors.

With returning 'warriors all clamouring for an education', the student body had trebled in size. The faculty had likewise proliferated and a new age had brought procedural changes. The increase in size of the university meant it was no longer possible to retain the sense of intimacy that had existed before the war between the faculty and students: 'like the Red Queen one had to keep on running very fast in order to stay where you were'. This shift also determined whether Wheeler-Bennett could resume his 1938 position as 'lecturer extraordinary'. 'A group of my old friends in the various departments had mooted the idea of my return to the university on a part time academic basis.' But, despite his growing reputation in Britain, gone were the days when an appointment could be decided over 'a sandwich and glass of beer. It was in line with the new spirit of the times that any appointment should be mulled over by a committee, reviewed, examined and essayed by the pundits before a decision could be taken.' On this occasion, Wheeler-Bennett's candidature was rejected because he lacked the 'formal education' to qualify for an appointment. As he good-humouredly recognised, since his formal education had concluded with public school, they were justified in their view.[47]

Another employment opportunity, however, had arisen. The documents that had been used at Nuremberg were only a fraction of what had been captured and were being kept at Marburg, a university town in the American-controlled zone of Germany. In keeping with the Allied belief that the German people should themselves understand what had happened to cause both the war and their defeat, a joint decision had been taken by the Foreign Office and the United States Department of State to publish selected German archives. To undertake what proved to be an immense task, both governments were to nominate an editor-in-chief. Wheeler-Bennett was well aware of the deliberations regarding the German archives, but it came as a surprise when he was asked to be the British editor-in-chief. 'Deeply interested though I was and not a little flattered at being selected to lead the British team in this unique project, I did not jump at it at once.' Not only did he want to finish *Munich*, but, to make up for the lack of dons to meet the demands of the rising tide of new applicants at Oxford, Isaiah Berlin had put it to him that it was his 'national duty' to join New College as a temporary lecturer and tutor.

Wheeler-Bennett made a commitment to teach Philosophy, Politics and Economics (PPE) for five years. 'It proved a most entertaining experience and brought me a number of new friends.' Moreover, he at last improved his academic credentials. On realising that he did not have a degree, the university conferred an MA on him 'by decree'. At his first tutorial he was confronted by five ex-brigadiers of an average age of twenty-six. There was also a young man, Anthony Wedgwood Benn, on whom his tutorials made a lasting impression. 'He was just so interesting on these interwar years. He was the most marvellous tutor to have.'[48] Mindful of Benn's subsequent left-wing views, Wheeler-Bennett later described his former student as being 'not then what he is now!'[49] Wheeler-Bennett also held tutorials for his nephew, Rick, Clement's third child, who went up to Oxford in 1948 to read PPE. 'It was to my advantage that he was my uncle. My tutorial partner, Richard Venables [the son of Malcolm Venables, a Canon at St George's Chapel, Windsor], . . . and I found that his intimate knowledge of the *dramatis personae* made for a lively interchange between the three of us.' An added bonus was that his uncle offered his students 'very nice sherry'.[50] Another later protégé was the nephew of Wheeler-Bennett's old friend Alexander Korda, now a 'leading magnate' of the British film industry. In the early

1950s, Korda financed a commission to explore the possibility of creating a department of film and drama at Oxford. Although, as Korda's nephew, Michael, recollected, nothing much came of it, 'Oxford seldom forgets a generous donor'. When Korda telephoned Wheeler-Bennett to ask which college his nephew should apply to, Wheeler-Bennett suggested 'Magdalen as a place where a brilliant scholastic record was not necessarily a requirement'.[51]

While at New College, Wheeler-Bennett was still being pressed to take up the position of British editor-in-chief of the captured German archives. Despite his reservations, a personal letter from Ernest Bevin finally made him accept the job for two years, from 1946 to 1948, provided he could finish his book on Munich. His American opposite number was Professor Raymond Sontag, since 1941 the Sidney Hellman Ehrman Professor of European History at the University of California at Berkeley.[52] Other activities had to be sidelined. Although he had continued his association with Chatham House, the tasks that he had undertaken before the war – the *Information Bulletin* and editing the *Documents* – were no longer his concern. For a while he remained as vice-chairman of the Information Committee, but his frequent absences meant that in July 1946 he had resigned altogether. 'I find that now I am so little in London my time gets booked up very much in advance and it is really always impossible for me to attend luncheon meetings.'[53] A minor upheaval was caused when he requested the return of the furniture he had installed in his office at Chatham House for his use in his new job at the Foreign Office. This included a mahogany roll-top desk, writing table, side table, desk, armchair and a set of oak bookcases.[54]

The former premises of Radio Berlin became the operational base for work on the German archives. Although Wheeler-Bennett was pleased to return to Germany, the streets were filled with rubble and he found it 'simply impossible' to direct his driver to once familiar landmarks.[55] More friendships were cemented: Sir William Strang, with whom Wheeler-Bennett had worked at the EAC, and Christopher (Kit) Steel were both political advisers to the commander-in-chief in Berlin.[56] Another friend was the head of American Military Intelligence, Colonel Peter Rodes, whose three daughters 'cut a swathe through the ranks of the occupation personnel'.[57] One issue that needed to be resolved concerned the translation of the documents. As Wheeler-Bennett later recollected, although the selected materials were to be published in German, 'in both our countries there were too many people engaged in the study of German history whose knowledge of the language was insufficiently great to permit them to make full use of our volumes in the original'.[58] It was therefore decided to publish a parallel edition in English. 'We shall begin somewhere about the year 1937 and then come forward to the end of the Nazi regime,' Wheeler-Bennett had informed a journalist from the *Oxford Mail* in early 1947. 'I think we shall then work backwards from 1937 to the Bismarck era.'[59] In April 1947, the French government joined the project and Maurice Baumont, 'a man of delightful personality and authority', became another co-editor. Wheeler-Bennett considered him 'a far greater historian and scholar than Sontag or myself'.[60]

While in Berlin, he found time for some sightseeing, including visiting Hitler's bunker, in which the gigantic table, at which Hitler had shot himself, lay crumbling. 'I picked up a chunk of it as a souvenir, and later had it made into an ink-stand to give to Alan Bullock when he had written his great study of Hitler.' On another occasion, he went to Charlottenburg, resting place of the Hohenzollerns. Having been told that Kaiser Wilhelm's diaries had been taken there after his death in 1941, he hoped he might find a clue as to their precise location. But the trail went cold and the diaries were never found; without them, he felt he could not complete his ambition of writing the life of the Kaiser. He attended some sessions of the Allied Control Council, the body in which Britain, the United States, France and the Soviet Union had vested the sovereignty of Germany. To Wheeler-Bennett, it was 'a neat historical irony' that the hall in which the council met was where the People's Court had dispensed its rough justice against numerous opponents of the Nazi regime.[61] He sat with the British delegation, behind the military governor, General Sir Brian Robertson, whose father was the famous field marshal 'Wullie' Robertson, chief of the Imperial General Staff during War World I. His deputy was Major General Nevil Brownjohn, a former Malvernian.[62] Contrary to Wheeler-Bennett's more favourable wartime assessments of Russia, he now realised that the 'chill wind of the cold war' was beginning to blow through the council chamber as the Soviet Union found itself at loggerheads with its Allied counterparts.

Busy as he was with the German archives, finishing his book on Munich remained a priority. As Wheeler-Bennett conceded in the book's foreword, one of the difficulties he had encountered was being so close to the events he was attempting to chronicle. He had therefore tried to balance his narrative, neither writing with too much wisdom of hind-sight, nor, as he explained, emulating the prophetic Cassandra, making predictions that no one at the time believed.[63] He paid tribute to the windfall of documentation from which he been able to benefit 'thanks to the extraordinary capacity of the German official mind for committing to paper, and never destroying, the archives of an entire Government machine'. *Munich: A Prologue to Tragedy* was published in 1948. Among those whose assistance Wheeler-Bennett acknowledged were his friends Patrick Dean, Lewis Namier, who had taken up a position as professor of modern history at Manchester University, Isaiah Berlin and Aubrey and Constance Morgan (to whom he dedicated the book). Neill Malcolm, Wheeler-Bennett's 'adopted father' in the early years of his research and now nearly eighty years old, also received his thanks,[64] as did Elizabeth Morrow for her hospitality in Mexico and Isabella Greenway King for hers in Connecticut. True to the views that Wheeler-Bennett had held at the time of the agreement's signing, he concluded that Munich was a case history of political myopia 'which afflicted the leaders and the peoples of the world in the years between the wars'.

> The problem posed then is the same which confronts us now – and remains unsolved. It is not, fundamentally, a political or a technical problem; it is psychological and spiritual. Can we, with the experience of two world wars behind us, admit, both consciously and subcon-sciously, the essential truth that peace is one and indivisible; that, in our efforts 'to seek peace and ensure it', we must realize that a threat to the peace of any country is a threat to ourselves?[65]

Writing in the *Slavonic and East European Review*, the historian George Gooch applauded Wheeler-Bennett's 'stinging' criticisms. Stating that 'no living Englishman has a wider knowledge and deeper understanding of our depressing performances during the inter-war years', Gooch high-lighted Wheeler-Bennett's knowledge of the personalities involved. 'For Mr. Wheeler-Bennett, unlike Neville Chamberlain, Czechoslovakia is not a distant country of which we know little, but a virile nation with an inspiring record and a right to live.' Gooch also pointed out the similarity of his views to those of Churchill, whose first volume of his *History of the Second World War, The Gathering Storm*, had just been published. 'One is struck by the virtual identity of the conclusions of two writers working in complete independence.'[66]

After finishing *Munich*, Wheeler-Bennett divided his time more evenly between lecturing at New College and working on the German archives. 'We were rendering down between three and four hundred tons of documents into a form suitable for publication by means of informed and adequate selection.'[67] One file caused particular concern. Known as the 'Marburg File', it contained information regarding German foreign minister Ribbentrop's attempt in 1940 – through intermediaries – to encourage the duke of Windsor to leave Portugal (where he was en route for the Bahamas to take up his position as governor) for Spain so that the Germans could use him as 'part-collaborator, part-mediator, part-hostage'. The duke was unaware of the plan but had made 'indiscreet talk with neutral friends'. While the Americans and French wanted to publish the file, both Clement Attlee and Winston Churchill were opposed to this in view of potential harm to the monarchy's reputation. As Bruce Lockhart noted in his diary, 'Jack is worried': if Britain did not publish the file and the Americans did, the former would look 'very foolish'.[68] To discuss the matter with Buckingham Palace, Wheeler-Bennett and Sargent met the king's principal private secretary, Sir Alan Lascelles. The strategy adopted was to postpone its release by publishing other captured German archives first. It was not until 1957 that 'the bulk' of its contents was published.[69]

Inevitably, the emerging Soviet-American power play in Berlin had repercussions on their work. To embarrass the Soviets, without Wheeler-Bennett's knowledge, the United States chose to publish the documents relating to the Nazi-Soviet Non-Aggression Pact of 1939 unilaterally. 'This work was carried on in great seclusion, and so great was the degree of secrecy imposed upon them that no whisper of their activities reached London at any level, neither governmental nor editorial, until the completed work burst upon the world with a blaze of publicity early in 1948.' Wheeler-Bennett was 'not wholly pleased'. Not only was it a breach of editorial co-operation, but he considered that the US action was a breach of the spirit of the 'escape' clause permitting each government to publish separately any part of the documents. 'The secrecy of their operation implied a lack of confidence in both the Foreign Office and in me, and also some measure of disagreement between Ray Sontag and myself as to whether the documents should be published. Nothing could have been further from the truth.'[70] With the Cold War 'in full swing', the two men put the episode behind them and continued with their work. In Berlin the situation was fast deteriorating, as the Soviet Union tightened its control over its zone of occupation. The final break occurred when Britain, France and the United States introduced a new Deutschmark; the Soviet authorities responded with their own reformed currency which they intended to introduce throughout Berlin. On 24 June 1948, all land and water traffic was halted. To counter this Soviet blockade, the Western countries instituted a massive and historic airlift lasting 323 days.

At the same time, there were sinister developments in other countries, notably Czechoslovakia. In the 1946 elections, the Communist Party had won a majority in the Czech lands, although Slovakia was left in the hands of the Democrats. In February 1948, the Communists seized control of the whole of Czechoslovakia. Out of loyalty to Beneš, Jan Masaryk had remained in the government, with the intention of waiting for a suitable opportunity to resign. On 10 March he was found dead on the pavement outside his apartment in the Foreign Ministry, having apparently committed suicide by jumping out of his bathroom window. Wheeler-Bennett believed that he had been murdered by the Communists, 'who had learned of his plans for escape and feared that, if successful, he would establish a rallying point in London or in America for the enemies of the new regime'. Wheeler-Bennett regarded his relationship with Masaryk as one of his most special friendships. For the rest of his life he treasured two volumes particularly – one was a selection of Masaryk's broadcasts; the other was a copy of Bruce Lockhart's memoir of him with the inscription 'For Jack Wheeler-Bennett, who loved Jan and was loved by him'.[71]

During the Berlin blockade, Wheeler-Bennett was preparing to hand over his editorship to a suitable successor. Recognising the volume of material still to be edited, the Foreign Office appointed two men to the position: James Joll, whom Wheeler-Bennett knew through his association with New College; and James Marshall-Cornwall, a distinguished general and military attaché in Berlin in the 1930s who, like Wheeler-Bennett, had witnessed the rise of National Socialism at first hand.[72] The new editors' first decision was to remove the original German documents to England. In early July 1948, Wheeler-Bennett was in Berlin to hand over his editorship to Joll and Marshall-Cornwall, who immediately asked him if he would remain as historical adviser (a position he held until 1956). For this visit he had been furnished with an official letter 'To Whom It May Concern', signed by Moley Sargent, informing the reader that he was travelling to Berlin 'on official business' and requesting that Wheeler-Bennett be afforded 'all facilities compatible with the regulations in force'.[73] As he drove around the city for the last time, while maintaining that Berlin had never charmed him like Paris or New York, he felt compelled to admire the Germans' toughness in their now beleaguered city. 'For the first and only time I experienced that feeling of shared comradeship which President Kennedy expressed some years later in another and similar crisis: "Ich bin ein Berliner".'[74]

No sooner was Wheeler-Bennett back in England than another academic avenue opened to him. Late in 1948, he heard rumours that plans were being discussed for the establishment of a new college at Oxford for graduate studies in international affairs under the benefaction of a Frenchman, Antonin Besse, for which purpose a council had been formed under David Maxwell Fyfe's chairmanship. Although Wheeler-Bennett had not met Besse, he liked what he had heard about him. 'I have always had a partiality for those tycoons and merchant princes who had made their fortunes in a world in which daring and adventure, ruthlessness and integrity and an indomitable faith in themselves were the predominating elements. After all my father had been one of them.' While acknowledging that his father had not operated on the same scale as Besse, who had made his fortune in the incense market in the Middle East, he considered that Besse and he 'had much in common and that we talked the same language'.[75] Besse's gift of one and a half million pounds and desire to see mature students come to Oxford from the Continent and overseas made possible the foundation of St Antony's College.[76]

The choice for the first warden fell on William Deakin, whom Wheeler-Bennett had met during the war when Deakin was working for SOE under Bill Stephenson in the United States.[77] Wheeler-Bennett considered that his qualifications for heading up a new college were ideal:

> He was courageous and it was a time for courage; he could be subtle and it was the moment for subtlety; he was wise in the ways of men – and of universities – and it was a season for wisdom. He had learned the gentle art of diplomacy and the fierce craft of partisan fighting [in Yugoslavia]. Both were to stand him in good stead. He knew when to be tough, when to be pliable and when to seek compromise. He had the capacity to command unswerving loyalty . . . he belonged amongst those chieftains for whom one would willingly 'bleed and die'.

To Wheeler-Bennett's 'intense surprise', with an eye to his wide circle of contacts, Deakin asked him to become one of the college's Founding Fellows.[78] As he recollected, the invitation had been made 'on the sword knot of friendship. My diffidence of academic qualification he dismissed with the encouraging words. "You've watched history being made at close quarters, you've even taken part in it; you can teach others about it." And that was that.'[79] Deakin also drew on other friends and teaching associates. James Joll became the sub-warden and Geoffrey Hudson, former Fellow of All Souls and an expert in Far Eastern studies, became another Founding Fellow.[80]

St Antony's opened its doors in the Michaelmas term of 1950. Housed in a former Anglo-Catholic convent in the Woodstock Road, it was 'conveniently opposite the Horse and Jockey, a pub of some repute'. In his capacity of Founding Fellow, Wheeler-Bennett gave two seminars a week, one on twentieth-century Germany and the other on 'the Influence of the Military on German Policies during the years between the wars'. This last topic was based on research for his next book, *The Nemesis of Power*. Although Wheeler-Bennett had first thought to write about the abortive 20 July plot to assassinate Hitler, he realised that what he really wanted to explore was 'the tragic and futile culmination of a whole period of history'. To fulfil this objective, he would have to write about the role of the German army in politics from its defeat in November 1918 to the surrender in 1945. With a wealth of literature still emanating from Germany as well as his own German interwar experience to draw on, he considered himself well placed to write a book that was both 'scholarly and readable'.[81] He wrote to his publisher, Harold Macmillan: 'We agreed, I think, that just one more book on the Plot of July 20th would be a waste of time.'[82] Macmillan wrote back enthusiastically: 'Of course we will publish your new book.'[83]

But there was a significant gap in his knowledge which related directly to the period leading up to the 20 July assassination attempt. As Wheeler-Bennett was vividly aware, the key conspirators, guilty of 'anti-Nazi sentiment', had been eliminated. A few, however, had survived. Of these, Dr Otto John had been a legal adviser to Lufthansa, working in the same department as (and influenced by) Klaus Bonhöffer. Together with his younger brother, Pastor Dietrich Bonhöffer, whom Wheeler-Bennett had known since his days as a Lutheran pastor in London, Klaus Bonhöffer was a prominent member of the 'Freiburg Circle', consisting mainly of professors from Freiburg University. Like the Kreisau Circle, their objective had been to destabilise the Nazi regime by overthrowing Hitler. After the plot failed, both Klaus and Dietrich had been executed.[84] In the immediate aftermath, Otto John's brother, Hans, another conspirator, was also caught and executed, although Otto escaped. Having taken a Lufthansa flight to Madrid, he reached Lisbon and was brought to England and to the attention of Bruce Lockhart, who gave him a job in PWE's covert propaganda section.[85] After the war, John had been transferred to the prisoner-of-war section and given the job of interrogating and segregating important German prisoners.

When, through Lockhart, Wheeler-Bennett met Otto John, he found him to be 'gemütlich' (agreeable), with a 'delightful sense of humour' and an ideal source for his research. Both men shared a conviction that the German army should never again be allowed to establish its supremacy. John had recently married an opera singer of Jewish descent, Lucie Manen, who had come to England to sing at Glyndebourne in 1934 and settled in London. During the ensuing months, the Wheeler-Bennetts and Johns were in frequent touch. In the autumn of 1949, both men were involved in the trial of another high-ranking German, Field Marshal Erich von Manstein, charged with 'neglecting to protect civilian lives'. Proceedings took place before a British court in Hamburg and the prosecuting lawyer was Sir Arthur Comyns Carr.[86] As at Nuremberg, Wheeler-Bennett benefited from a two-way flow of information with Comyns Carr, who asked questions 'about the German army, and was greatly interested when I talked about the book I was writing on this subject. He was very helpful in opening up the archives of the court to me.'[87]

To secure Otto John's literary collaboration, Wheeler-Bennett offered either 'to go fifty-fifty on the whole transaction, that is to say, I would undertake to give you one half of any advances which Macmillan may make to me on the delivery of the MS [manuscript] and also one half of all the royalty payments which may subsequently accrue'. Alternatively, he suggested giving John a larger lump sum, which he would recoup on the subsequent sales of the book. 'In these days of "Battle, Murder and Sudden Death" it is impossible to foresee what the fortunes of a book may be, however good it is!' Wheeler-Bennett intimated that he thought it best if the actual writing were left to him.[88] John readily agreed to the arrangement to split the royalties.

> I think it is most useful for you if I do send you my comments together with my notes referring to the subject. I have hired a German typist to copy all the handwritten comments of the Generals . . . I am now dictating my own notes made in the course of the many discussions which I had with the Generals on the subject . . . Besides I have notes on comments made by Generals during interrogations on their own political attitude from 1918–1949. These I think are most important for your work.[89]

When Otto John later suggested publishing this long memorandum, Wheeler-Bennett discouraged him on the grounds that it was 'too big for an article and too short for a book. Even as two articles you would probably not get more than ten guineas for it. On the other hand, it is worth considerably more than that to me as a piece of research.' He offered to give John fifty guineas as remuneration for its use as well as promising that 'full acknowledgement will, of course, be made to it and to you in every way'.[90] Not long after starting work on their joint enterprise, instead of continuing the process of becoming a naturalised British citizen, John decided to return permanently to resume his legal practice in the newly established West German Federal Republic.[91]

Over the next few years, Wheeler-Bennett remained in touch with John, continuing to benefit from his introductions. In October 1950, Wheeler-Bennett thus secured an interview with the new president of West Germany, Theodor Heuss. As with his visit to Kaiser Wilhelm in 1939, Wheeler-Bennett's fame as the biographer of Hindenburg preceded him. He became concerned, however, when he heard that Heuss had offered John the job of heading the recently established Federal Office for Internal Security (Bundesamt für Verfassungsschutz), the equivalent of MI5. 'I was aghast. My poor friend, I felt, had walked into a political quicksand which would gradually engulf him.' As Wheeler-Bennett realised, in the new Germany, the old establishment was reasserting itself and the survivors of the 20 July conspiracy 'were at a discount'. Otto John had already made enemies among ultra-patriotic Germans in high places, including the chancellor, Konrad Adenaeur.[92] Not only had he worked for the defeat of Germany during the war, on behalf of Britain he had interrogated senior surviving German officers, including Manstein, who was now regarded by the younger generation as the 'paladin of honour'.[93] Writing later, with hindsight of his subsequent fate, Wheeler-Bennett lamented that John took such an exposed position, putting his reputation at risk.

Throughout 1951, Wheeler-Bennett was working on *Nemesis*, sending John the draft chapters. The approach he took consisted of his usual detailed narrative, supplemented by footnotes. In keeping with the tone he had adopted towards the German resistance in his various memoranda prepared for PWE, he affirmed his belief that the unconditional surrender of the Germany army was imperative. His assessment of the German resistance movement and Adam von Trott zu Solz did not go beyond

what he had said in his 1943 memorandum. He also chose to highlight
Trott's and Moltke's strong nationalist aspirations. 'Both, for example,
though they deplored the spirit of the Munich Agreement and the subsequent dismemberment of Czechoslovakia, expressed strong anti-Czech
sentiments, and from neither was there forthcoming any indication that
a "de-nazified" Germany would be prepared to forgo Hitler's annexation
of Austria and the Sudetenland. Indeed it was hinted that Britain and
France might well reward the conspirators, if successful, with the return
of Germany's former colonial possessions.'[94] While admitting that, had
the putsch of 20 July succeeded, there would have been pressure on the
Allies to negotiate an end to the war, which would undoubtedly have
saved lives, he again echoed his PWE memos:

> One must not allow a sense of humanity, nor of historical hindsight,
> to obfuscate political vision. To have negotiated a peace with any
> German Government – and particularly one which had come into
> existence as a result of a military revolt – would have been to abandon
> our declared aim of destroying German militarism . . . Had the Allies
> succumbed to the temptation to reach a negotiated settlement with
> a 'new Germany' there would have been no Unconditional Surrender
> at Rheims and no formal recognition by the Germany Army of its
> Unconditional Defeat. The objectives for which the youth of the
> world had been sacrificed would not have been fulfilled; nor would
> the Allies have provided themselves with the opportunity to draw
> upon a clean page the blue-print of what they believed should be the
> future Germany.[95]

Wheeler-Bennett also criticised the German officers for not having
stood up to Hitler in the mistaken belief that, if the situation got out
of hand, they could oust him. Even those who were anti-Nazi were
'not 100 per cent so. They wished to secure, for the benefit of the
Reichswehr, all that could be gained to advantage from the Nazi movement, while dominating and controlling its policy. They were still
dreaming in their blindness of a martial State in which the masses,
galvanized and inspired by modified National Socialism, would be
directed and disciplined by the Army.' Although they may have had it

in their power to counter Hitler's rise to power in January 1933, 'they did not wish to do so'.[96]

While Wheeler-Bennett was working on *Nemesis*, Alan Bullock, his friend and colleague at St Antony's, was writing his detailed biography of Hitler and the two men frequently discussed their respective subjects. Much to Bullock's surprise, since his book was going to be published first, Wheeler-Bennett 'put in my way unpublished material which any other historian would have felt it entirely legitimate to keep for his own use. Such was John Wheeler-Bennett's practice of friendship.'[97] Wheeler-Bennett was also back in touch with Brüning, but the warmth had gone out of their relationship. The former chancellor had been vehemently opposed to the International Military Tribunal in Nuremberg and had refused to assist with the testimony against the Nazi regime.[98] In the autumn of 1952, Brüning accepted an appointment to teach political science at the University of Cologne and returned to Germany from the U.S. He had also been writing his memoirs but eventually stopped work on them, leaving several incomplete manuscripts. Unable to play the role of 'elder statesman' in Germany due to disagreements with Adenauer, Brüning later left the country and settled permanently in the United States.[99]

On 2 February 1952 Wheeler-Bennett wrote to Otto John to tell him that he had finished *The Nemesis of Power*. 'Is there a new spirit abroad in Germany,' he asked in his conclusion, 'or is this merely "where we came in" in the repetitive history of the Germany Army in politics?'[100] Prior to sending the manuscript to the publishers, he made one more visit to Germany to check some final details. As before, he and Ruth stayed with Otto and Lucie John in Cologne. He was distressed to see that John had aged considerably and 'was nervous and depressed'. The strain of his job was compounded by the fact that he had not been able to shake off the taint from his past assistance to the British during and immediately after the war, leaving Wheeler-Bennett with the impression that he was 'nervous and depressed'.[101] Although he described John's memorandum as 'invaluable' in a footnote in *The Nemesis of Power*, perhaps to protect him, John was not among those he mentioned 'with particular gratitude' in his Foreword. Among those he did list were his new friends at Oxford, James Joll and Allan Bullock, as well as Bill Deakin and, as usual, Lewis Namier, 'whose wisdom, criticism and

counsel have ever been to me a source of pleasure and improvement'.[102]
He also thanked Alfred Wiener, whom he had met in New York during
the war and in whose library he had worked. Finally, he expressed his
gratitude to his niece, Juliet, who, together with another young woman,
Dorothy Bonnaire, had worked as his secretary. Absent from the list of
those he thanked was Neill Malcolm, who died at his London home in
December 1953, aged eighty-four.

The Nemesis of Power: The German Army in Politics, 1918–1945 appeared
in the autumn of 1953, by which time the memoirs of several key players
had also been published, most notably Franz von Papen. Wheeler-
Bennett's book had been too far advanced for him to make use of Papen's
diaries and he concluded that they did not add much anyway to what
the former German chancellor had said during his interrogation at
Nuremberg. Otto John described the book as 'the most authoritative
book available on the nature and the working of the German military
hierarchy'.[103] Alan Bullock noted that it was 'well-received' in Britain,
but caused 'a storm of controversy in Germany', with offence being taken
at the blame that Wheeler-Bennett had placed on the German generals
for their failure to stop Hitler. His views on 'unconditional surrender'
also upset those who believed not enough support had been given to the
German resistance movement.[104] At the time of publication, Wheeler-
Bennett's Nemesis was widely read and 'highly regarded as the definitive
work on recent German political developments'.[105] George Messersmith,
whom Wheeler-Bennett had known in Germany in the 1930s, said the
book gave 'the most accurate and interesting' picture of the 'disintegration of morale' in the German army.[106] 'It really is a magnificent work,'
Harold Nicolson wrote in his diary in early 1954.[107]

9

High Honour

Royal biography, like matrimony, is not to be entered into unadvisedly or lightly, but reverently, discreetly, advisedly, soberly and in the fear of God.[1]

In August 1952, a few months after the untimely death of George VI, a conversation with Harold Nicolson opened another door to Wheeler-Bennett. Nicolson and his wife, Vita Sackville-West, were staying at Garsington not long after publication of his biography of George V. 'I am not, I think,' Wheeler-Bennett later wrote, 'a man of unusually precipitate reactions but as I read Harold's splendid book for the first time I felt my imagination kindled by a desire for emulation.' As a staunch royalist, 'the prospect of writing the life of one's sovereign and combining this with the narrative of one's own times and illustrating the role and responsibility of the monarch in these great events held for me at that moment the highest ambition in life'. Sitting with Nicolson in the sunlit loggia at Garsington, he shared his thoughts. 'I can't think of anything more fascinating than to do for George VI what you've done for his father. I'd give anything to do it.' Nicolson's only immediate response was 'Would you?' and the subject was not raised again.[2]

During the ensuing months, Wheeler-Bennett was still finishing *The Nemesis of Power*, tutoring at St Antony's and working at the Foreign Office. Then, in November, he received a request to call upon Sir Alan Lascelles, who, after the death of the king, had remained private secretary to the new queen. Asked 'hypothetically' whether he would be prepared

to write the life of King George VI, Wheeler-Bennett answered with a
'resounding "yes"'. 'I left the Palace in a state of some bewilderment . . . I
had a persistent feeling in my bones that the job would be mine.' Soon
afterwards, he was informed that the queen mother would receive him
at Buckingham Palace on 17 December 1952. Yet again, the question
of writing the late king's biography was put hypothetically. Once more
Wheeler-Bennett replied in the affirmative. According to his memoirs,
it was not until the new year that the request was formalised and he
received a written warrant as a royal biographer. An official announcement was made in the press on 9 February 1953.[3] 'No one was better
suited to become a royal biographer,' noted Alan Bullock. 'He had the
instincts of a courtier as well as an officer, and understood the restricted
and inhibiting world in which royal personages were required to live,
and could talk to them as human beings.'[4]

Unlike the official biography of King George V, which was 'dichoto-
mized' between the king's private life, covered in 1941 by John Gore,
and his public life, covered by Nicolson in 1952, Wheeler-Bennett was
undertaking to write about King George VI both as a sovereign and as
a man, as well as giving the background to the events that occurred
during his reign. For such a task, the queen gave him unrestricted access
to the Royal Archives in Buckingham Palace and at Windsor Castle.
Included in his source material would be the diaries of King George V
and Queen Mary as well as various personal letters, the king's diaries and
official correspondence; also available for consultation were cabinet
minutes, documents and memoranda. 'I was given an absolutely free hand
– nothing, so far as I know, was ever withheld from me of either a
public or a private nature . . . it was made known by the Queen that
all who had had association with her father in any capacity should
make me free of their correspondence with him and share their recollections, whatever their nature might be, with me.'[5] On a practical
note, the queen permitted him to use the Pine Room in Buckingham
Palace 'where the security was good and I could leave things lying
about'.[6]

For the next few years, with his 'much loved and highly efficient'
niece Juliet employed as his secretary, Wheeler-Bennett happily worked
on the royal biography. As with his earlier works, he employed his 'triple

formula' of reading the published works of the period, consulting the
documents and talking to as many people who had known the king as
possible. On several occasions, Wheeler-Bennett was the guest of the
queen and the queen mother at their separate residences, as well as having
the opportunity to talk to Prince Philip and Princess Margaret about
'their very different relationships' with the late king. From the duke of
Windsor, whom he saw in both London and Paris, Wheeler-Bennett
learnt about the early lives of the princes and their schemes to 'torment'
their tutor, Mr Henry Hansell, a former teacher at Ludgrove prep school.[7]
The duke of Windsor also 'evinced a decided inclination to discuss with
me the events of the abdication, etc., and this I studiously avoided as I
am not really concerned with the events preceding the event. The subject
of my study comes into them only indirectly and the less I discuss them
with the Duke of Windsor the better.'[8] From Mary, the Princess Royal,
he heard about their youth and how, as a young boy, 'Bertie' was obliged
to write with his right hand rather than his left, which was his natural
instinct, 'though she could not be sure whether the change had been
enforced by Hansell or not'.[9] Wheeler-Bennett was also received by
Queen Mary, before her death on 25 March 1953.[10] 'Kindness, co-
operation and enjoyment were everywhere.'[11]

In addition to members of the royal family and personal friends, in
order to be able to write about the king's public life, Wheeler-Bennett
needed to meet the politicians who had been involved with him. Top
of his list was Winston Churchill, prime minister from 1940 to 1945 and
currently prime minister again after defeating Clement Attlee in the 1951
general election. In March 1953, through Bill Deakin, Wheeler-Bennett
met Churchill's private secretary, Jock Colville, who put in a request for
him to have 'five minutes' with the prime minister 'in order that he may
ask you one or two questions about King George VI. If you were willing
to do this I think it would be very helpful to him.'[12] However, seeing
Churchill at this time was easier suggested than done. A tentative appointment had to be cancelled because of Queen Mary's funeral. Churchill
then fell ill. Then there was the new queen's coronation in June. Meanwhile, Wheeler-Bennett's research followed a set routine. 'On Monday
or Tuesday we would drive up to London to stay at Albany,' recalled
the Wheeler-Bennetts' cook, Ethel, who was able to attend Constance

Spry's cookery classes – paid for by her employers – while 'Mr John' worked at Buckingham Palace.[13] In London, Wheeler-Bennett enjoyed lunches and dinners at his various clubs – Brooks's, Pratt's and the Beefsteak – with an ever-increasing circle of friends, which invariably included the numerous people he wanted to meet to discuss the king's life. With no children of his own, he enjoyed the company of his siblings' children. Of Clement's three, he had developed a close relationship with the youngest, Rick. Irene's elder daughter, Mary, had married a South African barrister, Walter Stanford, in 1945 and moved to Cape Town. Juliet was happily occupied as her uncle's secretary and David was working in the Gold Coast (Ghana) Administrative Service.

In October, Wheeler-Bennett wrote again to Colville, affirming that he would 'suit his time to the Prime Minister's and would come to see him anywhere and at any time convenient to him'.[14] Colville therefore repeated the request to Churchill:

> Mr W–B is most anxious to have ten minutes or a quarter-of-an-hour with you because so much of the late King's Reign was intimately connected with you and you are bound to figure largely in the work. He has written to me himself about this and I have also received pleas to submit the request to you from personal friends of Wheeler-Bennett's such as Sir Orme Sargent, Sir Alan Lascelles and Bill Deakin. Sir Alan Lascelles says that he knows The Queen would be very much obliged to you if you would agree to see him as She naturally wants Her Father's Life to be as good as it can possibly be made.[15]

All the same, the meeting had still not taken place when Wheeler-Bennett set sail for the United States in the new year.

On his US itinerary was a visit to the Roosevelt archives at Hyde Park, the president's former home in New York on the Hudson River, preserved as a National Historic Site, and where on 10–11 June 1939 the king and queen had spent the weekend before continuing their royal tour to Canada. Arriving in 'a blizzard of snow', Wheeler-Bennett had been invited to lunch with Roosevelt's widow, Eleanor, who was living in a cottage in the woods above the family estate. When their meeting was over, 'she bade me farewell in a most kindly way'. Wheeler-Bennett's conclusion was that 'she has greatly matured since the President's death and has acquired grace and poise. She has become a personality in her own right.'[16]

Back in England in the summer, 'after eighteen months persistent effort', the meeting with Churchill finally took place at Chartwell on 12 August 1954. At nearly eighty, the prime minister was no longer the man who had led Britain to victory in World War II, but Wheeler-Bennett noted that 'his eye is still an undimmed blue and in his flashes of fire he is very great indeed'. He found, however, that Churchill's conversation was 'disconnected and even rambling, passing from one subject to another with disconcerting elision and skipping from reign to reign and from sovereign to sovereign with the bewildering rapidity of a young ram!' Regarding George VI, as Wheeler-Bennett recorded in his interview notes, the prime minister 'delivered a general panegyric on his virtues, but otherwise contributed only two points of major interest. The first was that, quite two weeks before the Abdication took place, [the prime minister] Stanley Baldwin had said to him in the course of a conversation on the general situation: "I think the Yorks can do it", thereby indicating that even at that early date he foresaw the necessity of a change of monarch.'

The second point of interest was Churchill's insistence that, once the king had overcome his disappointment at not having Lord Halifax as prime minister, 'never since the days of my ancestress, Sarah, Duchess of Marlborough, and Queen Anne, has there existed such a degree of intimacy between subject and sovereign as I achieved with King George VI'. Churchill went on to describe how, soon after the Tuesday luncheon meetings between sovereign and prime minister became established, 'the King dispensed with service at the table and insisted on serving Winston himself – or rather, trying to. "For I could never allow my Sovereign to wait upon me, and so when he placed meat and potatoes before me, I insisted upon performing a like service for him!" '[17] The visit to Chartwell paid further dividends since Churchill granted permission for Wheeler-Bennett to see all the manuscript letters from the king in his possession. Immediately afterwards, he wrote to Colville, thanking him for arranging the meeting which 'bore fruit so very pleasantly and successfully . . . I enjoyed our talk immensely.' In addition, there was 'a wealth of valuable background material to be derived from the PM's reminiscences'.[18]

Another key figure to be interviewed was the former Labour prime minister Clement Attlee, whom Wheeler-Bennett admired despite his own Conservative leanings. He also considered 'most impressive' Eamon de Valera, the Irish prime minister – or Taoiseach – 'who had not scrupled to shed both British and Irish blood to achieve the independence of his country'.[19] Describing their meeting, Wheeler-Bennett noted that he had 'a feeling that the vanity of the Celt was not wanting in his character', so he began the interview by praising de Valera's military dispositions when he occupied Boland's Mill during the Easter Rising in 1916. 'After all, with a hundred men he prevented a considerable force of British troops from marching from Kingston to Dublin, and inflicted heavy casualties upon them.'[20]

In view of the late king's membership of the Guild of Sovereigns, dubbed 'the royal trade union', Wheeler-Bennett travelled abroad to meet numerous fellow monarchs. These included King Michael of Romania and Queen Wilhelmina of the Netherlands, 'the longest reigning monarch' in Europe who had succeeded to the throne in 1890 and abdicated in favour of her daughter in 1948.[21] He also spoke to George VI's uncle by marriage King Haakon of Norway, as well as to King Peter of Yugoslavia, whom he met at Claridges in 1956. To capture the atmosphere of the king's 'never-to-be-forgotten visit in June 1943 to the recently belea-guered island fortress'[22] of Malta, he travelled to Valetta. The governor was Lord Mountbatten, who, as a second cousin of the late king, had known him 'all his life'. As an aside, in the notes of his interview with Mountbatten, Wheeler-Bennett could not refrain from recording that 'all the fairies were present' when Mountbatten was born at Windsor in 1900. 'He was gifted with good looks, a fine physique, a good sense of humour, fluency of expression, a fine intelligence, considerable charm, outstanding physical, and no little moral, courage, indefatigable energy and great ambi-tion. As against this he is intolerant of criticism and of fools, ruthless – even, I should say, to the point of cruelty – something of an intriguer, very vain and avid of admiration.' During his stay, Mountbatten 'was kindness itself to me both as a host and as a source. I found him a most agreeable companion. But he could also be a very dangerous enemy.'[23]

In the later stages of his research, Wheeler-Bennett had the opportu-nity to see Harry Truman who, with his wife, was visiting Europe.

Invited to breakfast at the Savoy, he wanted to record the former president's recollections of meeting George VI at Plymouth in August 1945, when the new US president had visited the king on board HMS *Renown* and the king had returned his call on board the USS *Augusta*. Their discussions included questions of general interest, more especially whether the president 'ever lost any sleep, either at the time or subsequently', at having given the order to drop the first atomic bomb on Hiroshima. 'Not a wink,' came the reply. 'It was my plain duty and I did it.'[24] As Wheeler-Bennett recorded after their meeting: 'Mr Truman was simple and delightful . . . when he says that he has given his record to history and to hell with the critics and professional historians, he means it in the best possible sense. He has rested his case before the bar of time, and is content to await the ultimate verdict.'[25]

Throughout the 1950s, the Wheeler-Bennetts were enjoying life in the English countryside. Since coming to Garsington, Wheeler-Bennett had adopted the traditional role of 'squire of the manor' in the village. As Lockhart had noted after one of his early visits: 'He dresses curiously for the part – smart corduroys in Newmarket boots, an open shirt with scarf round the neck and yellow or khaki jacket like a U.S. officer's battle jacket. Adopts benevolent feudal attitudes towards village, goes to church twice on Sundays.'[26] Wheeler-Bennett had also taken a particular interest in promoting the sporting side of village life, attending the local football and cricket matches. In 1949, the Garsington Sports Club had been founded, of which he became the first president. Three years later, there was an opportunity to acquire the site for use as a playing field, which, with the construction of a pavilion, would bring together all the village sports – cricket, football, tennis and darts – at one location. As recollected by the Wheeler-Bennetts' cook, Ethel, they needed to raise £500: 'It was decided that anyone who gave 10 guineas or more was entitled to life membership of the sports club.'[27] Since then, Wheeler-Bennett had helped to organise the annual cricket match between locals and the 'President's XI', of which he was the captain and Rick the vice-captain. 'I can't remember who won. I fear it was the village every time,' recalled Rick. 'In the early days the match was played on a field near the Manor with a dizzying slope which allowed the bowler at the relevant end to launch the ball out of the sun! The milking herd was cleared out of the field for the day. It required skill to pick the ball out of the nettles in the outfield or from the embrace of a meadow muffin.'[28]

In view of Wheeler-Bennett's wide-ranging connections, the list of the sports club's vice-presidents included a galaxy of celebrities and friends, their number eventually reaching 'a century'. As a governor of Cuddesdon Theological College since 1955, he had met the principal, Robert Runcie, later to become archbishop of Canterbury, whom he recruited for the President's XI.[29] Another recruit from Cuddesdon was Oliver Twisleton-Wykeham-Fiennes. As related by Juliet, at a match in 1955 he was playing cricket when Vic Ruffels, from the village, broke his finger. Juliet offered to drive him to the hospital and Twisleton-Wykeham-Fiennes accompanied her. So began a romance which led to their marriage a year later.[30] The following year, Ruffels married Ethel. Although no athlete, Wheeler-Bennett was happy to field, which meant staying in the deep, perched on his shooting stick. On one historic occasion, recorded for posterity by Rick as 'THE CATCH!',

> the ball was struck towards him in a gentle parabola. We watched in horror. Rising slightly from his shooting stick, Jack met the ball with his hands before his face, staggered under the impact and held on to it, undamaged. Having established he was unhurt, we couldn't make too much of his catch for fear of indicating surprise that he had caught it. Ruth, who found in cricket many similarities with baseball, was not inhibited in her delight and made up for our reserve with uncricketlike cheering.[31]

An annual dinner became part of the ritual, with Wheeler-Bennett speaking in addition to a distinguished visitor, who would inevitably be enrolled as a vice-president.[32]

Busy as he was with the life of George VI, Wheeler-Bennett was pursuing other interests. Since leaving Malvern, he had repeatedly turned down suggestions that he might become involved with his old school. While he was immersed in his royal research, his old school friend Errol Holmes, who had become a renowned cricketer, playing for Oxford University, Surrey and England, suggested that he become a member of

Malvern's Governing Council. 'I repeated that I wasn't interested and had little relish for administration and committee work.' Undaunted, Holmes told him that there was a new headmaster, a historian, Donald Lindsay, and invited Wheeler-Bennett to an Old Malvernian dinner in April 1954 to meet him. 'Because I felt guilty and contrite about my cavalier treatment of someone whom I really liked very much, I consented and in due course we met for dinner at the Café Royal.' To begin with, Wheeler-Bennett considered it a 'dreary' occasion, with 'conversation rarely rising above the level of "Well old boy, long-time-no-see!"' His disappointment vanished when the headmaster responded to a toast to his health, earning Wheeler-Bennett's praise as one of the 'best *ex tempore* speakers I have ever listened to'. With the ability of an actor manqué, Lindsay 'soothed the fears of the Philistines with glowing tributes to the school's past and present athletic triumphs, . . . spoke in praise of the standards of scholarship, resisting the temptation to suggest that they might be higher, . . . then, venturing on more dangerous ground, said boldly that public school education should provide opportunities for the athlete and the scholar and also for the artist, the boy who could seek and find expression in the world of arts and craftsmanship': that an interest in music, drama, painting, sculpture or photography was not something 'different', to be ashamed of, but rather that it was to be accepted as part of school life.[33] Wheeler-Bennett was delighted. 'Here was someone who talked my language and shared my belief that in a public school the needs and interests of mind and body were catered for in balance and perspective . . . From that first confrontation I knew that Donald Lindsay was my man and that I was prepared to support him to the nth degree.'

In later life, he recorded that he never changed his first impression and that Lindsay proved himself to be 'one of the most inspirational leaders in the public school world of today'. Talking to Errol Holmes after the dinner, 'somewhat shamefacedly' Wheeler-Bennett apologised for his earlier gracelessness. '"If your offer's still open, I'd like to become a Member of the School Council," I said. "You're as good as in," was Errol's reply.'[34] Elected to the Governing Council in 1955, he was 'suddenly projected into the top level of direction of a great public school. It was an experience I have never regretted.' The council's chairman was Admiral Sir William Tennant, who had organised the embarkation of the Allied armies at Dunkirk in 1940, as well as being on the planning staff of Operation Overlord prior to the Allied invasion of Normandy in 1944. 'I liked him immensely and learned much from him which was to stand me in good stead.'[35]

Wheeler-Bennett had not abandoned other writing projects. When, in 1955, the historian A.J.P. Taylor, a Fellow of Magdalen College, asked him to contribute to a volume of essays which he and Richard Pares were collecting to present to their mutual long-term friend Lewis Namier, Wheeler-Bennett agreed to submit two essays, the first on two 'great' German soldiers, Erich Ludendorff and Wilhelm Gröner, the second consisting of some personal recollections of the Kaiser incorporating a description of his 1939 interview with him, delivered as the 'Leslie Stephen Lecture' at Cambridge.[36] His study of Ludendorff and Gröner demonstrated Wheeler-Bennett's ability to evaluate positively men who were undeniably the 'enemy' during World War I.

When Wheeler-Bennett turned his attention to the royal biography, he had assured Otto John that he would not forget his 'old German friends'. However, although he remained 'Historical Adviser to the Foreign Office Project for publishing the captured German Foreign Ministry Archives', his interest in contemporary Germany was waning. In July 1954, he received the surprising – and somewhat embarrassing – news that John had defected to East Germany. It was a bizarre event that interrupted what had been a regular, if slightly dwindling, correspondence between the two men. Much as Wheeler-Bennett wanted to think the best of his friend, three days after his disappearance John's voice sounded out on East Berlin's Deutschlandsender radio, 'slow at first, then normal: he had defected to "establish contact with the Germans in the East" and because "Nazis are reappearing everywhere [in West Germany] in political and public life . . . Possibilities for German reunification . . . must at least be tried out.'[37] Wheeler-Bennett was mystified. 'The whole episode seems to me an extraordinary one and I hope that some day it will all be straightened out,' he later wrote to their mutual friend, Prince Louis Ferdinand, who had worked with Otto John at Lufthansa and, as Kaiser Wilhelm's grandson, had once entertained ideas of restoring the German monarchy.[38]

In 1957, Wheeler-Bennett's brother, Clement, died. With a gap of fourteen years between them, the two had never been close but his relationship with Clement's son, Rick, was strengthened by the event. They would lunch frequently at Brooks's, or dine at Pratt's, feasting on potted shrimps and dover sole. As a banker, Rick Wheeler-Bennett looked after his uncle's finances and assisted in organising a personal annuity for his retirement.[39] His wife, Joan, daughter of the Harvard professor and distinguished classicist Eric Havelock, shared Wheeler-Bennett's literary interests, and he enjoyed suggesting books that she should read. 'We discussed J.D. Salinger's *Catcher in the Rye* and then he sent me another of Salinger's books, *Franny and Zooey*,' she recollected. He also sent her a regular supply of American novels and when she and Rick visited Garsington, he would sit with her and talk about what she had been reading.[40] Inside the manor, Ethel continued to work faithfully. Although never actually on the staff, her husband, Vic, played an important role in looking after Garsington. As Wheeler-Bennett's nephew David noted, Vic 'had all the practical skills and countryman's knowledge that Jack lacked'. Despite his town manners, Wheeler-Bennett enjoyed a Saturday morning ritual of cutting wood. Dressed appropriately in a heavy donkey-jacket or lumberjack's shirt, and accompanied by Vic (and sometimes his nephew David), he would 'lead the attack on any tree that needed to be lopped or felled, or any undergrowth that needed clearing. At about 11 a stop would be made for tea (laced with rum in winter). Jack may not have cut very much wood himself, but he enjoyed the feeling of physical work, and of being with others who were working hard.' No doubt, his nephew surmised, it was a form of relaxation from the 'nose-grinding business' of writing. 'Certainly he enjoyed the chat, the gossip, and the company.'[41]

After two and a half years, having conducted over two hundred interviews, as well as research at Buckingham Palace and in the Royal Archives at Windsor, Wheeler-Bennett was ready to start writing his biography of King George VI. 'When at length I sat down at Garsington to the actual writing of my task I had a very clear impression of the man in whose life and times I had been immersed.'[42] As he admitted, before beginning his research, he had considered that the king was 'something of a colourless if worthy figure'. But he had found that far from being 'insipid', he was 'a vivid personality, with a wealth of pragmatic common-sense, foresight and good judgement'. Together with humanity and a sense of humour, 'sense and sensibility may be said to epitomise his character'.[43] Aware of the assignment, the press had been keeping an eye on his progress. 'Mr John Wheeler-Bennett, the 52 year-old historian, has got well under way with his story of King George VI,' noted the *Oldham Evening Chronicle* in 1955. 'He works at Garsington Manor, his Elizabethan home near Oxford. There he sometimes shuts himself in his study for days going over details again and again. He is a stickler for accuracy. When working he refuses to receive any callers. Even his wife may only interrupt him in an emergency.'[44]

As Wheeler-Bennett was only too well aware, there were issues during the king's lifetime that remained controversial, and his narrative was diplomatic in dealing with these. When describing the abdication crisis, he made use of the contemporary account 'written in the Duke of York's own hand, a simple and poignant chronicle depicting vividly his thoughts and sufferings', and preserved in the Royal Archives at Windsor.[45] He had also benefited from hearing Queen Mary's account of the duke of York's 'agony of mind' at this time, and he found himself being critical of George V's 'policy of refusing to allow his second son to be initiated even into the ordinary everyday working of government'.[46] One issue that particularly interested Wheeler-Bennett was the duke of Windsor's appointment to the British Military Mission in Paris at the outbreak of the war. Initially, he believed (as did many others) that the duke had chosen to go to Paris rather than serving as a civilian under the regional commissioner for civil defence for Wales. In the later stages of his research, however, he came across a newspaper article citing the duchess of Windsor's assertion in her memoirs that the duke would have preferred to stay in Britain.[47] Wheeler-Bennett was anxious to determine who had decided to send the duke to Paris. In correspondence with the cabinet secretary, Sir Norman Brook, he was informed that it had been the king's decision to send his brother abroad, which he duly recorded.[48]

Another sensitive subject which he needed to document was the treatment George VI had received for his stammer from the Australian speech therapist Lionel Logue, who had also treated Wheeler-Bennett. One of the first letters Wheeler-Bennett had sent after being commissioned to write the biography was to Logue in February 1953, reminding him that he himself 'was a patient of yours some twenty-five years ago and [have] ever been grateful that the cure which you effected then has continued almost without set-back to this day'.[49] Although Logue was unwell and died in April, his eldest son, Valentine, provided access to his father's papers and case notes, which Wheeler-Bennett later acknowledged as being 'of the greatest help'.[50] He also sent Valentine the galley proofs for approval, adding as an aside: 'I can never forget or be too grateful for the change which he wrought in my own life.'[51] Describing the king's affliction, Wheeler-Bennett could have been narrating his own experience.

Mr Logue's approach was both physical and psychological. His presence and personality inspired confidence . . . Those who sought his professional advice felt immediately that not only did he believe in his own power of healing but he was able to inspire them with a similar belief both in him and in themselves. With a complete understanding of his own subject, he knew that the stammerer's first fear was of seeming 'different' from others. His first objective, therefore, was to convince his patient that stammerers were entirely normal people with a perfectly curable complaint.[52]

As each section of the biography was made ready, Wheeler-Bennett sent it to Alan Lascelles, who, although now retired as the queen's private secretary, had served both as assistant private secretary and private secretary to George VI throughout the 1930s and 1940s and who, by his own admission, knew the late king 'perhaps even better' than his brothers did. 'I would pounce on it as eagerly as poor Captain Brown, in Cranford, used to pounce on Mr Boz's instalments of The Pickwick Papers. I would take it home, armed with my sharpest blue-pencil, keenly looking forward to using it.' Alas, Lascelles said, his blue pencil 'nearly always remained unblunted . . . such emendations as I have had to suggest were almost invariably the correction of typists' errors.' Lascelles had been concerned that, while portraying George VI in his role as king, Wheeler-Bennett might not 'get on to his canvas the likeness of the man himself . . . if he did not do this, his book, in my opinion, would be relatively worthless'. Reading through the first few chapters, Lascelles had his doubts dispelled and grew confident that 'the portrait was going to be a true one'.[53] At the same time, Wheeler-Bennett was sending selected chapters to other friends and associates. Among these, Sir Norman Brook was an instant admirer: 'I hope you will allow me to say how very good these chapters are . . . I read them avidly, and with the greatest possible interest . . . I do congratulate you most sincerely.'[54]

While he was writing the book, Wheeler-Bennett enjoyed the entertainment value of the palace stories he was able to share. On one occasion, while dining with Lockhart and Moley Sargent, he regaled them with 'an amusing account' of his visit first to see the queen at Balmoral, and then to see the queen mother at her private residence at Birkhall, in Aberdeenshire. While he was at Balmoral the queen did not mention her father's biography until the last morning of his stay, when she took Wheeler-Bennett for a long walk. As Lockhart related:

> Jack, who was not dressed nor shod for such a walk and was more or less 'beat' when he got back to Balmoral, collected his suitcase and drove over to Birkhall. The Queen Mother promptly took him for an afternoon walk as long as his morning walk with the Queen. When they returned to the house, Jack wilted visibly. The Queen Mother said to him: 'Did my daughter, by any chance, take you for one of her walks this morning?' Jack admitted that she had. 'Then,' said the Queen Mother, 'champagne is the only remedy.'[55]

His friends considered that writing a royal biography had had a beneficial effect on his stammer, which occasionally resurfaced. As noted by Bruce Lockhart, 'now that he has full confidence in himself, he rarely, if ever, stammers.'[56]

Preoccupied as Wheeler-Bennett was with his book on King George VI, he continued with the activities that he always enjoyed most. Christmas and the New Year heralding 1958 were spent in Charlottesville with Ruth's family. In February, he returned to Malvern to open the new Grundy Library, named after a former headmaster. In April, he lunched at 10 Downing Street with Harold Macmillan. Following the disastrous invasion of Suez in 1956, Anthony Eden had resigned, which meant that Wheeler-Bennett's friend and publisher, chancellor of the exchequer under Eden, had succeeded him as prime minister in January 1957. In July, there was a visit to Glyndebourne to see Rossini's *Comte*

Ory. Wheeler–Bennett also found time to lecture at the NATO Defence College in Rome and as usual lunched and dined at his various clubs in London.

King George VI: His Life and Reign was published on 13 October 1958, Wheeler–Bennett's fifty-sixth birthday. A note preceding the narrative described how 'in an enterprise of this magnitude one's gratitude is infinite to all those who have by word or deed given aid and succour in greater or lesser degree; one's regret is also profound that, because of dictates of space, it is impossible to thank each individually'.[57] Wheeler–Bennett's first impulse had been to dedicate the book to Harold Nicolson. But Nicolson rightly realised that this would be inappropriate, advising him that the queen mother 'might think that if the book were dedicated to someone outside the magic circle, it would in some way render it lay, irreverent, or even plebeian'. Wisely, Wheeler–Bennett had bowed to Nicolson's 'superior judgement', having assured him how much he recognised 'the immense amount of help and kindness which you have given . . . it would have been perfectly easy for you – and indeed perfectly understandable – having completed the course yourself, to sit back and watch the next man come down over the hurdles'.[58]

On the day of publication, a lunch party was held at the Savoy and Sir Alan Lascelles gave his own accolade, describing his 'sustained' correspondence with Wheeler–Bennett over the past four years. 'In one of my letters, I remember, I hinted that the autumn of 1958 might be rather late for the publication of his Life of K.G. VI. With quiet dignity he rebuked me, pointing out that, in the very nature of things, the authorised biographers of royal personages must sit long upon their eggs.' Lascelles went on to describe their association, concluding with the 'verdict – for what it is worth – that Jack W–B has written a great book – a book that will be not only a notable contribution to contemporary history, but will also be a worthy memorial to a Sovereign to whom his subjects owed far more than the great majority of them ever realised'.[59]

Excluding notes and index, the book ran to over eight hundred pages, rivalling Wheeler–Bennett's lengthy biography of Hindenburg, written two decades previously. It was his first major non-politico-military work and it gave his profile as an author a new slant. No longer would he be referred to just as a military historian; he was now a royal biographer too. 'Six years of my life had been consumed in the most fascinating task which I have ever undertaken.'[60] What had impressed him most about George VI 'were, first, his deep humanity and his interest in the welfare of his peoples, and secondly, the amazing way in which he grew into his office. None could have been more reluctant to assume the Crown and yet none has sustained the burden of sovereignty with greater dignity none more worthily than he.'[61] On 18 December, after clearing out his papers, Wheeler-Bennett noted in his diary: 'leave B[uckingham] P[alace] for good (!)'[62]

In general, the reviewers were charitable towards a book that inevitably had to have the blessings of the royal family. While describing it as 'enthralling', the *Christian Science Monitor* pointed out that Wheeler-Bennett had not been able to escape 'the jargon and cant of British writings about the British royalty. One of the reasons for this is that the biography of George VI appeared sooner after his passing than is usual with British Kings and Queens.' Whereas Harold Nicolson's biography had been published sixteen years after George V's death, Wheeler-Bennett's had appeared a mere six years after that of George VI. 'The cutting of this period by a half seems to have the disadvantage of making the biographer more wary of offending the susceptibilities of the subject's relatives and of making the historical perspective less sure. It has the advantage that the period and events covered by the biography are fresher in the minds of readers.'[63] A widely published review by John K. Hutchens described the book as 'judicious . . . the tone is reverent, the style stately, the footnotes and indeed the book as a whole is so detailed as to suggest that its author had in mind a time capsule as he went about his labours'.[64]

Crane Brinton in the *New York Herald Tribune* wrote: 'John Wheeler-Bennett writes of both man and sovereign a long, admirably documented, soberly but not dully written biography. Mr Wheeler-Bennett never, of course, debunks, never even gets close to the journalist informality of much contemporary biography. On the other hand . . . this book in no sense embalms George VI.'[65] Reflecting on his achievement and the reaction to the biography, Wheeler-Bennett realised that there were aspects he had not fully explored out of deference to the feelings of the royal family. By his own admission, he had not wanted to get drawn into discussions with the duke of Windsor about the abdication, which the queen mother regarded as an 'agonising interlude in our history', preferring simply to highlight sympathetically George VI's position.[66]

Of those whom Wheeler-Bennett had interviewed, one of the first to offer criticism was Mountbatten, who had read the serialised version in the *Daily Telegraph*. His complaint related to the credit that Wheeler-Bennett had given to Winston Churchill as First Lord of the Admiralty in ordering the fleet not to demobilise after the test mobilisation in the summer of 1914. Mountbatten was anxious to point out that his father, Prince Louis of Battenberg, the First Sea Lord, should instead have been acknowledged. Wheeler-Bennett apologised at once. 'I should be greatly saddened if anything which I have written could be construed, even by implication, as falling short of the tremendous admiration which I have always had for Prince Louis and of which I have spoken to you on a number of occasions.' He went on to explain that the misunderstanding had arisen 'from the difficulties of compression in extracts in the book', and assured Mountbatten that, in the next impression, the misunderstanding would be corrected by making it clear that it was under Prince Louis's authority that the fleet had been kept in a state of preparation.[67]

Within a year, *King George VI* had become the most requested book in public libraries, followed by Field Marshal Montgomery's memoirs and Boris Pasternak's *Doctor Zhivago*.[68] After its publication, Wheeler-Bennett had temporarily busied himself responding to the 250 letters of congratulations, which he recorded having received. To celebrate the book's success he gave cheques for £10,000 to the niece and nephews he knew best, Juliet, David and Rick.[69]

In the 1959 New Year Honours list, Wheeler-Bennett received a knighthood for his biography of the late king. On 4 February, he was appointed to the Royal Victorian Order. Since it would be some time before a biography of Queen Elizabeth would be commissioned, Sir Michael Adeane, Lascelles's successor as the queen's private secretary, suggested that some advance research might be undertaken.[70] As a result, on 11 February 1959, Wheeler-Bennett was appointed historical adviser to the Royal Archives, with special responsibility for seeing that a report was made and filed of every official interview, audience or contact with the queen so that, in due course, material would be available for her official biographer. Among the many people he contacted was Anthony Eden, prime minister in 1955 after Churchill's resignation. Wheeler-Bennett's letter was the first of more than three hundred that the two men would exchange over the next fifteen years.

My Dear Sir Anthony,

As you may know, The Queen has appointed me to be Historical Adviser, Royal Archives, with the specific job of collecting and collating material and information about the early years of Her Majesty's life and reign. This appointment is to facilitate the task of the future official biographer of The Queen by providing him (or her) with as much contemporary evidence as possible on this early period.

As, it is to be devoutly hoped, this official biography will not be written for another fifty years, my task, as I see it, is to obviate the recurrence of the lack of material which existed, for example, on the early years of Queen Victoria's reign at the time of her death, when all the sources of contemporary information had also died . . .

It is in this connection that I am writing to you. Your impression of The Queen during the time when you were, first her Secretary of State for Foreign Affairs, and later her Prime Minister would be of great importance and interest to her future biographer and if you would consent to give these to me you would be greatly aiding me in the task which The Queen has assigned to me.[71]

Eden responded warmly, recollecting their 'talks of the 'thirties' and inviting the Wheeler-Bennetts to visit him and his wife, Clarissa, at their home in Wiltshire.[72]

At the same time as recording interviews about the queen, Wheeler-Bennett was engaged in writing another biography. Not long after finishing *George VI*, he had been requested by the widow and son of Lord Waverley (John Anderson), who had died in January 1958, to write his life.[73] As a British civil servant and politician, he had served as a minister under Neville Chamberlain and as home secretary, lord president of the council and chancellor of the exchequer under Winston Churchill, earning him the sobriquet 'the Home Front Prime Minister'. Wheeler–Bennett agreed to write his life, provided he was given access to the relevant official documents dating from 1938 to 1945, whereupon ensued a series of discussions between Norman Brook, Anderson's principal private secretary between 1938 and 1942, and other members of the government regarding such access. Eventually the decision was taken that, 'without having a complete run over all the archives', Wheeler–Bennett could go ahead, provided they retained the right to scrutinise the draft of the biography if official help was given.[74]

Although Wheeler–Bennett's heart was evidently not in this project as it had been in George VI, he set about the task with his usual dedication. One of its more enjoyable aspects was visiting prominent people associated with his subject's life. Since Waverley had been under-secretary of Dublin Castle, Wheeler–Bennett went again to meet Eamon de Valera, who had become president of Ireland in June 1959. 'President de Valera received me at the old Vice-Regal Lodge, now the President's House. He was most cordial taking me by both hands.' As a courtesy, Wheeler–Bennett presented him with a copy of George VI, 'calling his attention to the passage on page 731 in which I had said that the present formula of April 1949, which regularized the new relationship of the nations of the Commonwealth to the Crown, was really, in all essentials, Dev's old formula of External Association . . . Dev was delighted, purred like an old cat and laughed heartily.'[75]

In addition to researching Waverley, Wheeler–Bennett was taking on new assignments and giving up others. After 1957, he no longer taught at St Antony's, but his continuing help to the college resulted in his election to an honorary fellowship in 1961. In addition to being a governor of Cuddeson Theological College, he became a governor of Radley College near Oxford, as well as of Lord Williams's Grammar School in Thame. In 1959, he resumed his membership of the Council of Chatham House, and became a Trustee of the Imperial War Museum, a connection which, as Joan Wheeler–Bennett recalled, he relished. 'He was always anxious for us to attend every new exhibition.'[76] Two years later he took up an equally rewarding tenure as chairman of the Council of Management of the Ditchley Foundation, established in 1958 by the philanthropist Sir David Wills to promote Anglo–American dialogue and the study of international relations.

In the summer of 1959, Otto John reappeared in Wheeler-Bennett's life. When he returned to West Germany over a year after his 1954 disappearance, the German authorities refused to believe that he had been drugged and abducted, as he now maintained. Instead, he was put on trial for treason and sentenced to four years' hard labour. After his early release in July 1958, John wanted to re-establish contact with Wheeler-Bennett, not only because of their past friendship but because of their prior arrangement to share the royalties of *The Nemesis of Power*. Characteristically, Wheeler-Bennett was keen to honour their agreement.

> Let me say at once that I have not forgotten, nor have I in any way abated my gratitude to you for the great help which you gave me when I was writing the *Nemesis of Power*. The latter part of the book would have been poor polo stuff without your aid. Nor have I forgotten the arrangement which I made with you nine years ago to recompense you for this help by sharing with you the profits of the book. I am very glad now to be able to discharge this debt.[77]

In due course, he meticulously worked out what was due and the sum of £1,405 .4s. 10d was transferred to Lucie John's British bank account.[78] Whatever Wheeler-Bennett privately thought of Otto John's disappearance, he did not challenge his explanation. For his part, John wanted to share his feelings with an old friend, expressing his bitterness at not being permitted to come to England. 'You can well imagine what a bad time I have been through the last five years, first with the Russians and then here,' he wrote from Germany. 'I soon afterwards had a real breakdown from which I am gradually recuperating.'[79] Although the two men continued to correspond, Wheeler-Bennett's interests now extended well beyond Germany. Over the next decade he was to make his mark not only as a biographer and historian but as a lecturer and academic.

10

The Sixties

The young in revolt against the standards, conventions and traditions of their parents and the parents in bewildered resentment at this defiance of their authority.[1]

John and Ruth Wheeler-Bennett embarked on 'the Sixties' as unaware as were their contemporaries that they were entering an unprecedented era of social upheaval. While the decade was memorably 'swinging', with people generally optimistic that the period of postwar austerity was over, a rebellious mood was taking hold throughout Europe and the United States, polarising relations between the old and the young. As a middle-aged man who had had an essentially Edwardian upbringing, Wheeler-Bennett took this new challenge in his stride, adopting a benevolent attitude to youthful discontent. Throughout the decade, he continued with his rigorous schedule of work, combined with the usual round of travelling and entertaining. His friend and publisher Harold Macmillan was still prime minister and Wheeler-Bennett's position as adviser to the Royal Archives ensured a valued and continuing contact with the royal family.

After nearly fifteen years at Garsington, the Elizabethan manor had become a home that he and Ruth loved. In pride of place in the hallway was the T'ang horse bought in China with Neill Malcolm in 1929. 'Ruth's domain was the drawing room. She made it extremely pretty and feminine, a marvellous backdrop for flowers,' recalled

Wheeler-Bennett's nephew David Heaton. Her other private space was
the small ground-floor room overlooking the famed ilex trees and the
lake which she called 'the morning room'. 'Otherwise the rest of the
house was in Jack's style, in furniture, pictures, books and ornaments.
He had a huge collection of silver, porcelain, signed photographs and
memorabilia of every sort and kind, all known and cherished.' Wheeler-
Bennett's special preserve was his study where he did most of his writing,
and where documents, transcripts, drafts and proofs 'proliferated in seemly
opaque disorder, transparent and orderly only to Jack'.[2]

Since her arrival in England, Ruth had perfected the art of being a
hostess. 'She had enormous American southern charm,' recalled Juliet.
'Both she and Jack had this gift of making you feel you were clever.'[3]
They were not 'cocktail-party people . . . their main form of entertaining
was the small lunch party, on Sunday, to introduce weekend visitors to
local friends and acquaintances, people with whom they would have
something in common, carefully stage-managed.' On 25 June 1960, they
held a 'splendid' garden party. 'The world and his wife were there, there
were strawberries, there was music and there was champagne,' recalled
David, who met his future wife, Joan Lainé, the only daughter of Edward
and Phyllis Lainé of Guernsey, at Garsington.[4] In return for their staff's
loyal service, Wheeler-Bennett gave them birthday presents, having made
a note of the relevant dates in his diary, and brought souvenirs from
abroad. Vic Ruffels kept a collection of alcohol miniatures which, with
Wheeler-Bennett's contributions, rose to number over three thousand
bottles. During the owners' absences Vic and Ethel Ruffels moved into
the house to undertake a thorough spring-clean. After a particularly
severe winter in 1962/63, they received an antique silver platter as thanks
for their care of Garsington.[5] Each Christmas Ruth would prepare 'a
score of personalised carrier-bags of food and drink for those who helped
in the house or garden, which Jack would deliver'. As his nephew David
observed, 'they may have reminded him of the similar visits his mother
had made in Keston when he was small.'[6]

In the early 1960s, Wheeler-Bennett was working on the life of John
Anderson, Viscount Waverley, sending his draft to Norman Brook. 'To
tell you the truth I send these chapters to you with some trepidation,'
he wrote in February 1960, 'for I'm not at all sure that I've been

successful either in telling the story or in giving a picture of the man. There is so very little first hand material and one is so dependent upon the recollections of others, who, with the best will in the world, are but fallible.'[7] Brook responded with four pages of polite notes, and Wheeler-Bennett was pleased to know that what he had sent 'passes muster'.[8]

As a member of Malvern's Governing Council, he had become involved with the production of a history of the college, to be published by Macmillan. Having declined to write the book himself for 'health reasons', he agreed to contribute a foreword. The senior history master, Ralph Blumenau, was entrusted with the main narrative. Since Blumenau was not an Old Malvernian, to reassure traditionalist 'OMs', Wheeler-Bennett had agreed to supervise the writing of the text. During their association, Blumenau formed an unusual opinion. 'Like me,' he noted in his diary on 30 June 1961, '[Wheeler-Bennett] is a bit ill at ease *à deux* and at the beginning of a party.' On another occasion, he saw the strength of Wheeler-Bennett's relationship with Ruth, observing that 'W-B' was 'a bit shy, but not when his wife is there'. As result of their association, Blumenau developed a lasting love of vodka. 'When I went to see him at Garsington to discuss the book, he offered me vodka to drink, prefaced by the remark: "It's a wonderful drink, it doesn't give you a hangover." It was the first time I had drunk vodka and have continued to do so ever since!' In hindsight, and recalling how kind Wheeler-Bennett had been to him, Blumenau was pleased that his supervisory role did not lead to any material changes to the college history.[9]

When, in August 1961, Anthony Eden, recently elevated to the peerage as the 1st Earl of Avon, requested 'active help and suggestions' on the manuscript of his forthcoming second volume of memoirs, Wheeler-Bennett felt obliged to decline. 'I feel immensely honoured and deeply touched that you should consider me a suitable collaborator in the writing of your second volume of memoirs. I appreciate this very much indeed and shall always recall it with pleasure.' However, he did not consider it possible to accept.

The reason is that, when I return from my holiday in September, I shall be very fully occupied with the correction of my proofs of John Anderson's life and the revisions which are always inevitable at this stage. As soon as this is over I have to leave for the United States to fulfil some engagements there and to take a rest which my doctors have been urging upon me for some time. Ruth and I will be spending Christmas with her old mother in Virginia and will not be back in England before the Spring. I am terribly sorry, therefore, that I shall not be able to give you the help you require and I greatly regret this.[10]

Avon responded with understanding. 'I am of course disappointed, but I had hardly dared hope that you might be sufficiently free.'[11]

John Anderson, Viscount Waverley was published on 27 September 1962, dedicated to Ruth 'with love'. The reviews were mixed. Although he had not been 'over-blessed with a richness of written material', H.B. Boyne in the *Daily Telegraph* believed that Wheeler-Bennett had still managed to write a comprehensive study of Anderson's life. The book was, he said, a 'carefully researched biography, more absorbing, one might even say more romantic than many a novel'.[12] Robert Blake, tutor in politics at Christ Church, Oxford and a frequent guest at Garsington, wrote sympathetically in the *Sunday Times*: 'It is a tribute to Sir John Wheeler-Bennett's genius as a biographer that he has brought vividly to life this cautious figure who to most of us stands like some granite statue swept for ever by the east winds that moan through the grey squares of Edinburgh.' Although the book ran to four hundred pages, Blake said that it was 'not a page too long'.[13]

Anthony Sampson in *The Observer* called it 'the perfect Establishment Biography', noting that the list of acknowledgements included the queen and the prime minister and 'no plain Misters', but the subject 'failed to come to life'.[14] Donald McLachlan in the *Sunday Telegraph* said that Wheeler-Bennett would have written a better biography in ten years' time, 'because we are too close to the living'.[15] A letter of congratulations from Sir William Wylie, law adviser to the Irish government in 1919, elicited a grateful response: 'I wanted to get the Irish picture right, for anyhow Irish relations of that period have always fascinated me. That you find what I have written satisfactory is of immense satisfaction and gratification to me, for you really know what happened in those years.'[16] A later reviewer, D.N. Chester, the warden of Nuffield College, Oxford, who had known and worked with Anderson, considered that the book was 'not up to the high standard we have come to expect from Wheeler-Bennett. The author is probably not very interested in administration and on occasion, one suspects that he did not find his task quite a labour of love . . . I do not think Wheeler-Bennett's book either explains [Anderson] adequately or quite does him justice . . . But . . . Anderson is not an easy subject for a biographer.'[17]

Soon after publication, Wheeler-Bennett wrote to thank Norman Brook for his help: 'I know how great was your admiration and liking for John Anderson and I am delighted to have measured up to your standards of what a biography of him should be, because one of my primary objects in writing the book was to satisfy you. . . . I am so very conscious of the help and guidance which you have given me through my task and I know full well that without your aid I could not have written the book at all.'[18]

As Wheeler-Bennett's stature as a historian grew, he never forgot those with whom he had shared so much during the war. Bruce Lockhart was still trying to make a living by writing, but was constantly in debt. In September 1962, Wheeler-Bennett sent him 'a handsome cheque' which temporarily relieved his financial anxieties. 'He said he owed much to me,' Lockhart noted in his diary.[19] At home, when not writing, Wheeler-Bennett enjoyed reading. 'He would sit puffing his pipe with a book and a dog,' recalled Rick, 'he loved big dogs, boxers' – one of which was named Rhett after a supposed resemblance to Clark Gable.[20] One book Wheeler-Bennett read was by a young historian, Alistair Horne, entitled *The Price of Glory: Verdun 1916* which the author had sent him, eliciting a four-page handwritten letter in response. 'Needless to say I've got well into it at once and have been proclaimed "anti-social" by my wife as a result! You have done a wonderful job. The book reads as excitingly as a novel and yet has tremendous weight of authority.' When, a few years later, Horne wrote a sequel, *The Fall of Paris*, Wheeler-Bennett once more commended the 'clarity and sustained excitement of the narrative'.[21]

In 1962, Wheeler-Bennett came to the end of his 'specific historical job' (of recording interviews of those who had known the queen in her early life) as the queen's historical adviser. Expressing the queen's gratitude for his valuable labours, Michael Adeane informed Wheeler-Bennett that, although there was no immediate work to be done, the queen still wished him to act as her historical adviser and that he was to keep a 'foothold' in Buckingham Palace.[22] Enclosed with Adeane's letter was a pair of signed photographs of the queen and the duke of Edinburgh. Wheeler-Bennett, who was going through another bout of ill health, responded that he would 'cherish and preserve' the photographs for the rest of his life. 'I should also be very grateful if you would assure Her Majesty of the happiness it has afforded me to serve her as Historical Adviser, and how glad I shall be to continue in this office according to her wishes. Would you also please tell Her Majesty that, once I have regained my health – and I hope to do so fully after my period of rest – I shall be only too glad to be once again at her disposal.'[23]

Wheeler-Bennett's next project was a revised edition of *The Nemesis of Power*. Since its initial publication in 1953, the book had been reprinted twice in 1954 and again in 1956 and 1961. In 1963, Harold Macmillan had endorsed its contents by sending the book to the president of the United States, John Kennedy, for his birthday in May, just before a scheduled state visit to West Germany. Remembering Wheeler-Bennett's tutelage, Kennedy commented in his letter of thanks to Macmillan: 'Since my university days, I have always had the highest esteem for Wheeler-Bennett and his ability to portray the sweep of history and to capture the special role of individual character.' He also appreciated the irony of reading a book which was critical of the German army's past role at such a moment in his own duties: 'I am not sure that this is precisely the book that [the chancellor] Dr Adenauer would recommend that I read on the eve of my journey to Germany but I am most grateful for your gift.'[24] A month later, Kennedy made his historic speech of solidarity with the German people, in defiance of the Soviet Union's erection of the Berlin Wall, claiming: 'Ich bin ein Berliner' (I [too] am a Berliner). Five months later – on 22 November – he was assassinated, leaving Wheeler-Bennett, who had visited him in the White House the previous year, to mourn 'personally at his tragic death'.[25]

During the decade since *The Nemesis of Power* was first published, considerable fresh material had appeared and, as Wheeler-Bennett recollected, his publishers 'very properly desired me to take into consideration the large quantity of additional supplementary evidence which appeared in Germany in memoirs and in documentary form during the years since the book was originally published'. While maintaining that there was nothing new in this material to change his conclusions, he accepted that certain 'corroborative details' needed recognition. He was still feeling 'exhausted' after spending six years on the king's life and also working on Anderson. 'To plunge again into the field of German politics was a daunting prospect and one on which I did not think I could embark single-handed.' He therefore asked Bill Deakin to suggest a research assistant. Deakin recommended an emerging historian, Anthony Nicholls, a Research Fellow at St Antony's specialising in modern German history. When Wheeler-Bennett met Tony Nicholls (who, like many postwar friends, addressed him as 'John'), he at once 'took to him' and they entered into a 'pleasurable' partnership. Wheeler-Bennett acknowledged that it was beneficial for him 'to get the reactions of a younger man with an historian's perspective toward personalities and events which I had known at first hand'.[26]

In his preface to the second edition of the book, he described how the German army had been 'reborn' and then corrected himself to high-light that there were two German armies 'because the Soviet Union and the Western Powers have vied with one another in rearming their German allies'. Taking as his starting point the formal creation of the Federal German Army (Bundeswehr) on 12 November 1955, he said there had been 'the opportunity to observe its impact on German politics during the last eight years. The position of the so-called "People's Army" in East Germany is of less importance. Despite its apparent regard for old traditions — even down to the goose-step — it is, like other institutions in that sad satellite, the product of an alien regime, which can be expected to wither at the root the moment Soviet protection is removed from it.'

Wheeler-Bennett also differentiated between the new German Republic at Bonn and the old one at Weimar, observing that the current 'prospects were brighter'. 'The relative positions of the new Republic and the new Army are very different from those which pertained in 1919. Then a nation in political confusion was forced to rely on the army as a pillar of support against anarchy. By skill and evasion the Officer Corps avoided committing itself to a whole-hearted defence of the Republic and escaped responsibility for Germany's defeat and her subsequent hardships,' he wrote. 'In the form of the Federal Republic, Western Germany had been transformed with a remarkable rapidity from an abjectly defeated nation to a sovereign State allied to three of her erstwhile victors.' With a life-time's experience behind him, Wheeler-Bennett was cautiously opti-mistic. 'One hopes that the grounds for such optimism are not misplaced. The position which the Federal Defence Ministry has obtained in federal politics during the last eight years must warn us against taking the Army's role too lightly. In a country where military questions are of such impor-tance, the Army and its political leadership are bound to form a very influential part of the administration.'

Discussing the material which had surfaced since the first edition, he stood by his earlier conclusions.

> During the last few years a great deal of work has been done, both in Germany and elsewhere, on recent German history, with especial emphasis on the failure of the Weimar Republic and the tragedy of the German opposition to Hitler. I have found much that is interesting in these accounts, but I have had no cause to alter my interpretations of either the Army in German politics between the two world wars or of the role played by the military in the opposition to Hitler.

Citing Gerhard Ritter's book *Carl Goerdeler und die deutsche Widerstands-bewegung* (Carl Goerdeler and the German Resistance Movement), published in Stuttgart in 1954, Wheeler-Bennett upheld the view that Germany had had to be defeated unconditionally and made no reference to his own thoughts in early 1940 of a peace plan:

> Lastly, a word on the German opposition to Hitler. Some distinguished Germans – Dr Gerhard Ritter, for example – have been angered by my suggestion that a victory for the German opposition in 1938 or 1944 might not have been an unmixed blessing for the Germans and for Europe. I think we should ask ourselves two questions when considering this problem. First, could the conspirators have provided Germany with a system of government suitable for a modern industrial society? Second,

were the opposition circles capable of building a Germany which would be able to take its place in the community of nations without provoking international conflict? So far as internal policy is concerned I do not feel that very many of the opposition showed themselves able to come to terms with the twentieth century. Dr Ritter himself remarks that German political parties and trade unions owed their reappearance after 1945 largely to the influence of the occupying powers – striking tribute, one would think, to the allied policy of re-education upon which so much contempt has been lavished. As to the international question, one can hardly do better than turn to Dr Ritter's own excellent biography of that most intelligent and courageous conspirator, Carl Goerdeler. What Dr Ritter has to tell us about Goerdeler's European scheme does not leave an impression of acute statesmanship. It is worth remembering that when Goerdeler approached Vansittart in the spring of 1938 with proposals for a European settlement, he included as a matter of course the cession of the Sudetenland to Germany.

Most of what Wheeler-Bennett had to say that was new appeared in the preface, although, where possible, he amended the text elsewhere 'if it seemed to me that my version had been proved inadequate'. But, for technical reasons – 'the method of photographic reproduction used in this edition' – it was 'impossible to conduct a wholesale revision'. He was, however, 'satisfied that the text as it stands represents a fair inter-pretation of the German Army in politics from 1918 to 1945 and that this area of the past still deserves careful study by both the Germans and their allies'. He amended the bibliography to include 'the most important recent publications'. In addition to *The Rise and Fall of the Third Reich* by William Shirer, the American correspondent for CBS who was in Berlin during the 1930s, he added a number of German works: Ritter's book on Carl Goerdeler, as well as Erich Raeder's *Mein Leben* (My Life), Wilhelm Gröner's *Lebenserinnerungen* (Life's Recollections) and Annelise Thimme's political biography of the foreign minister Gustav Stresemann, who had died in office in 1929. Hans Rothfels, professor of modern history at the University of Tübingen, who had spent much of the war in the United States at Brown University and the University of Chicago, had expanded his short book on the German opposition, first published in 1948, and this new edition was also cited in Wheeler-Bennett's revised bibliography.

Wheeler-Bennett's thanks to his research assistant, Tony Nicholls, were generous. 'To his great ability and indefatigable effort, and to the meticulous accuracy of his research, I am deeply indebted. I am also most grateful to him for the pleasure which I have derived from our association in this project.'[27] The revised edition of *The Nemesis of Power* was published in July 1964. Its publication made less of an impact this time, but it retained its status as a classic. As Hugh Trevor-Roper wrote in the *Sunday Times*: 'It is, by its very detail, a fascinating book, and by its scope a majestic book, and by its scholarship, an illuminating book.'[28] Harold Macmillan, who resigned as prime minister in 1963, commended 'the extraordinary erudition which makes all our amateur efforts seem puerile in comparison'.[29]

In 1964, Wheeler-Bennett was invited by the president of the University of Arizona to become a visiting lecturer (and then full professor) of history and politics in the graduate school of the history department. The appointment was annual on the basis of one semester. Since writing books remained his major interest and commitment, Wheeler-Bennett's continuing role as an academic was still a surprise. 'In my early years I never had the slightest desire or ambition to teach anybody anything. It all happened "contrariwise", as Tweedledum might have said to Twee-dledee.'[30] The invitation to Arizona began 'a pattern of travel' which he and Ruth, already regular visitors to the United States, 'clung to' for the rest of his life: 'we would cross the Atlantic in one of the Queens, surrendering ourselves for four and a half days to the blissful and welcoming warmth of the Cunard Line service.' Every year he would consult his nephew Rick, who managed his finances, before booking their first-class passage. 'Can I afford it, dear Boy?' he would ask. Rick always assured him that he could.[31] The Wheeler-Bennetts would first stay in New York with friends, notably Patricia and Patrick Dean, who, before moving to Washington as British ambassador, was serving as permanent representative to the United Nations. They then travelled to Charlottesville to spend Christmas with Ruth's family.

I look back over a long vista of dinner-parties, supper parties, drinks parties and (regrettably because I hate the stuff) egg-nogg parties at

which we would see our many friends old and new. These gatherings
would be held in splendid old houses of red brick or more recently of
white clapboard in the front yards of which would often be an illuminated Christmas tree . . . The rooms would be warmed by open fires
of cedar and pine and hickory which purveyed an aromatic scent
through the house and the dining room table would be laden with 'the
makings' for sandwiches – piles of new bread and crocks of butter and
platters filled with slices of such succulent cold delicacies as peanut fed
sugar cured ham, roast turkey and beef and tongue and fried chicken
– one of the most delectable dishes in America, which by set tradition
has to be eaten in one's fingers. Another delectable 'bonne bouche'
might be a chafing dish of scalloped oysters which have to be eaten to
be believed . . . On other evenings groups of carol singers would roam
the colonnades of the University and would be welcomed into the
Professors' pavilions there to be heartened and sustained with hot spiced
punch. Midnight Mass was celebrated in both the Episcopal and Roman
Catholic churches on Christmas Eve and was well attended; on the day
after Christmas there was a Meet of the fox hounds at Farmington
Country Club.[32]

Shortly after the New Year celebrations in Charlottesville, the Wheeler-
Bennetts would board the *Crescent* for New Orleans to take the *Sunset
Special* of the Southern Pacific Railroad – famous for the quality of its
service – and head towards Arizona. In many ways, he found this the
'best part' of the trip, with the ambling journey to Arizona, across the
width of Texas, and the experience of 'stepping out into balmy night air
perfumed with the scent of the blossom of orange and lemon and grape-
fruit trees'.[33] By the time Wheeler-Bennett returned to stay for the duration of the semester at the Arizona Inn, his old friend Isabella Greenway
King had died but her children greeted the Wheeler-Bennetts warmly.
Ruth also became 'addicted' to the ambience of the Inn, 'with its devoted
service, pink washed cottages, verdant lawns . . . rivalling the Oxford
colleges . . . and its flower beds ablaze with candytuft violas, California
poppies and ranunculus, cheek by jowl with an amazing variety of cacti
and succulents'. During their visits, they were often joined by friends
from all over the United States, including Aubrey and Constance Morgan,
who had retired to their home in Washington state.[34]

Lewis Douglas, the US ambassador to Britain after World War II, had been an influential figure in Wheeler-Bennett's appointment at the University of Arizona and the two men had become close friends. 'Lew Douglas was one of the most remarkable men. Born the son of a wealthy copper mining family in Arizona, he served with courage in WWI. Afterwards he learnt the family business from bottom up, working on the pit face.' To copper mining he had added cattle ranching, finance and politics as well as a keen interest in education. For six years he was a Congressman until, in 1933, Roosevelt appointed him director of the budget. Since 'politics were meat and drink to Lew', the two men got on famously. Wheeler-Bennett also admired Douglas's physical bravery: he was suffering from worsening cancer, which necessitated numerous operations although 'he never permitted this, nor the disability inflicted by the loss of the sight of one eye sustained in a fishing mishap to impair his enjoyment of life. He was little short of heroic.'[35]

When Wheeler-Bennett had first visited the university in 1938, it had a student body of about five thousand and was distinguished for its schools of mining, engineering and agriculture and the outstanding reputation of its polo team, 'which I was informed had been founded and endowed by the famous stage and film star Will Rogers, whose two sons were alumni of the university'.[36] When he returned, the student body numbered some twenty-seven thousand, with schools of liberal arts, law, economics, history, drama and journalism, all of which were of a 'high quality and standard'. On the polo ground, where he used to watch games with Isabella Greenway (as she then still was), a school of medicine and a teaching hospital were destined to be built 'second to none in that part of the country'.

Wheeler-Bennett's appointment in Tucson was his first postwar academic posting at an American university:

> the authorities were not unnaturally a little uncertain as to how it would work. The head of the history department, a kindly, shy, cautious man, was torn between the dangers of my being rent in pieces by the pack of young wolves to which I was to be thrown and the risk that they themselves might prove too receptive of the sophistication in scholarship, the Machiavellian subtlety of western intellectualism of

western Europe which I was supposed to represent . . . I was therefore brigaded with a delightful professorial eccentric, James Donohoe, a devout Catholic with delicious Hibernian wit, humour and frivolity.

Not surprisingly, any fears proved groundless. Wheeler–Bennett found the graduate students of a high standard. 'I think I can honestly say that over the years I have never corrupted their approach to historical study.'[37]

He was once more discussing a long-term project: the writing of Avon's official biography. When Avon first broached the subject in the summer of 1964, Wheeler–Bennett had accepted with the proviso that the biography would not be written during Avon's lifetime. He also insisted that a shortlist should be drawn up of 'younger men, as well as "those of riper years", who might write the biography'. Avon was in poor health following an unsatisfactory operation over a decade previously to remove gall stones, during which his bile duct had been damaged. Wheeler–Bennett – sixty-two in October – was only five years his junior and had his own health problems. Putting himself at the top of the list, he also suggested Freddy Birkenhead, aged fifty-seven, 'an excellent and experienced biographer but perhaps too near my own age bracket'; third, he put Robert Blake, aged forty-eight, 'well known to you and whom I esteem as the best of the younger historian biographers'. Last, he put forward the name of Anthony Nicholls, who at thirty was 'as yet untried but whom I regard as having great promise as a coming historian. Were I to do the book I should certainly enlist his assistance. It would seem,' he concluded, 'that this age span would take care of all eventualities and would provide you with an acceptable biographer at any time!'[38] Expressing the view that 'fate will so handle matters that you will have ample time to do it after I have shuffled off this mortal coil,' Avon initially wanted to keep the issue of 'the junior alternative open for a year or two'.[39] Birkenhead had just written the biography of Lord Halifax, and, much as Avon liked his work, he did not think it appropriate to use the same biographer.

This new assignment meant that henceforward the two men kept in regular touch. Every so often Avon would write to Wheeler–Bennett to suggest that he visit him at his home in Wiltshire to view new material which he had assembled for 'The Biographer's File'. 'There is, as you no doubt guess, a large quantity of material available for the biographer which has not been used by me for a variety of reasons,' he wrote in July 1964. 'There are phases like the early years in the army in the First World War.'[40] A year later Avon was writing: 'Certainly we must meet soon and have a talk about many things, including the biography.'[41] They continued to discuss their mutual writing projects.

Having been encouraged by Wheeler-Bennett to write a series of portraits of 'the many fascinating figures whom you have known in your long career' under the working title 'Great Contemporaries',[42] Avon sent him an early draft of a portrait of Beneš. 'It is, of course, only a cock-shy, and, as you will see, mingles diplomatic comments with personalities.'[43] Wheeler-Bennett was critically enthusiastic: 'I think that as a basis it is excellent and what it needs is, as you suggest, a certain amount of "personalization". By this I mean the inclusion of some material of the "I said to him" and "he replied" nature. This will give the intimate and familiar touch which the reader will like to have and I am sure you will be able to recall some anecdotes.' In addition to the 'Great Contemporaries' Avon already had in mind, who included Maxim Litvinov, the Soviet Union's 'roving' ambassador during the Stalin period, and John Gilbert Winant, the US ambassador to Britain during much of World War II, Wheeler-Bennett suggested Jan Masaryk, and asked Avon whether he could recall 'any intimate details' of his meeting with Hitler and Ribbentrop.[44] But Avon's enthusiasm for this project was overtaken by events and the volume was never completed.

In 1964, Wheeler-Bennett became chairman of Malvern College's Governing Council following the death of the previous incumbent, Admiral Sir William Tennant. 'I was somewhat shaken by the expressions of confidence by my fellow Council members,' he confided. During his three-year tenure, the school was going to celebrate its centenary in 1965. As it happened, the actual centenary – 25 January – fell on the day after Winston Churchill's death. 'We celebrated our Centenary today,' Blumenau recorded in his diary, 'notwithstanding the thoughts about Churchill that were with us throughout the day and to which Wheeler-Bennett, in his remarks, gave worthy expression – that we owe it to him that our schools can carry on today as centres of learning and free enquiry.' To mark the occasion, *A History of Malvern College*, which, under Wheeler-Bennett's supervision, Blumenau had been working on for nearly four years, was published.[45] Mindful that he had not enjoyed his own schooldays, in his foreword Wheeler-Bennett singled out some 'surprising features' of the school system. 'For while the Public Schools have in the past claimed to be the leaders of our society, they have themselves been led by it; and while they have been thought to be a privileged and separate section of the community, they have so often reflected its essential characteristics and trained their pupils to meet the particular needs of the day.'[46]

This preliminary celebration was followed by three days of events in July. In preparation, assisted by his vice-chairman, Philip Nicholls, Wheeler-Bennett delegated the 'nuts and bolts' of the organisational work. His major personal responsibility was the guests of honour: Harold Macmillan, who visited the school on the first day, together with the bishop of Worcester, the Rt Reverend Lewis Charles-Edwards. On the third day, Queen Elizabeth the Queen Mother 'graciously consented to visit us' (Ruth ably taking her place when it came to rehearsing Her Majesty's arrival). In between these prestigious visits, there was a gala dinner, a cricket match, 'jollifications of all sorts and a display of fireworks'. As chairman, Wheeler-Bennett opened the proceedings to an audience of about two-and-a half thousand visitors, parents and boys, packed into 'what I was assured was the largest marquee in Britain'. Harold Macmillan spoke, passing 'with measured pace through the chronicle of the school' and ending 'with a laudation of the public school system and its place in the history of our country'. Recalling the day's events, Wheeler-Bennett praised Macmillan, his friend for thirty years, as

the most elegant, accomplished and effective orator in Britain to-day – certainly I know none greater – and it is a joy not only to hear him but to watch his performance. It is a masterly display of every kind of rhetorical variety. Always eloquent, he can ring the changes on wit and humour, on pathos and emotion, on a roaring call of leadership and on a subdued note of nostalgia. His technique of constructing a speech is itself a work of art. Persiflage, historical perspective, and a deep and convincing sincerity of purpose all find their place in a delicately designed pattern, and one delights in it as in the work of

a master-craftsman. He could have been a great actor; as it is he is
Britain's last great statesman.[47]

The visit of the queen mother on Saturday, 24 July was the 'final
climacteric of the celebrations'. As the bright red royal helicopter appeared
above Bredon, the sun broke through the clouds. Once it had landed,
'out of it stepped the one person who never fails to radiate that wonderful
combination of dignity and fun, which endears her instantly to all, and
places everyone immediately at their ease,' Wheeler-Bennett recalled.
'She enchanted us all of all ages,' having always 'the right word whether
of interest, appraisal or encouragement, for everyone she met'. During
the visit, the queen mother had made one stipulation: to have tea alone
with the prefects. 'To those of us outside, it seemed as if the proceedings
within the tea tent were hilarious in the extreme, peals of laughter and
bursts of unalloyed merriment. The difficulty was not to keep the thing
going but how to "break it up."' As Wheeler-Bennett recollected, 'the
agitated commander of the helicopter besought me to intervene because
of the schedule and, greatly daring, I entered the tent by the back way.
I was gaily waved away by Queen Elizabeth who was obviously enjoying
it all as much as anyone and was keeping everyone in fits of jollity,
having placed even the shyest under the spell of her charm.'[48] Finally, at
the third request, the queen mother left.

   After seeing Malvern's centenary through, the Wheeler-Bennetts
'withdrew in a state of considerable exhaustion to Ireland'.[49] In 1967, he
handed over the chairmanship to Admiral Sir Deric Holland-Martin.
Having inherited a Governing Council that included several seventy year
olds, two eighty year olds and one ninety year old, before vacating the
chair, Wheeler-Bennett was 'brutal', persuading the more senior members
to retire while retaining the services of 'those who were clearly assets',
such as General Sir Nevil Brownjohn, a friend since Berlin after the war,
and Bernard Weatherill (also known as Jack), future speaker of the House
of Commons, but overall reducing the average age of the body's membership to the late fifties. Henceforward, there was a tacit understanding that
the retirement age should be seventy.[50]

Throughout the 1960s, much as Wheeler-Bennett was enjoying his
teaching at the University of Arizona, he had not forgotten that he had

been rejected as a lecturer by the University of Virginia in the 1950s due to his lack of formal academic qualifications. He was accordingly gratified when, in 1966, he received an invitation to give a series of three Page-Barbour lectures, some of the most important events in the institution's academic fixture list.[51] His credentials had much improved in the interim. His books *Munich: A Prologue to Tragedy*, *The Nemesis of Power* and *King George VI* had enhanced his reputation. He had taught at New College, Oxford and been awarded an MA as well as an Honorary DCL by Oxford in 1960, and had become an Honorary Fellow of St Antony's the following year. Although none of his academic awards or publications had added to his 'formal education', he believed he had become 'eminently respectable'. He was, however, 'a little daunted when I found myself following in the footsteps of Lord Bryce, T.S. Eliot and W.H. Auden'.

His chosen theme was the position of the crown and the sovereign in the government of Britain and the constitutional evolution of the Empire and the Commonwealth. Not only did the series of lectures give him the chance to explain to an American audience the importance of the British monarchy, but also to show that 'our imperial record was not really so pernicious and oppressive as most Americans believe it to have been'. As the queen's historical adviser and a member of her household, Wheeler-Bennett was precluded by tradition from writing or talking formally about the sovereign or the monarchy. Before embarking on the subject, he therefore consulted his friends at the palace: in addition to Michael Adeane, the queen's private secretary, he approached the Lord Chamberlain, Lord Cobbold, and Burke Trend, who had succeeded Norman Brook as cabinet secretary in 1962. 'As a result Queen Elizabeth II "graciously consented" (I was given to understand not unwillingly) to allow me to deliver my lectures under the title of "The Crown, the Empire and Common-wealth."' The lectures were 'well received' and he was pleased to note that 'they have [since] been used with advantage in the history graduate schools at various American and Commonwealth universities'.[52]

Meanwhile, Wheeler-Bennett had begun another huge project, suggested to him by Harold Macmillan, which was a study of the postwar world in the context of World War II. Feeling that it was too much to do on his own, he had again enlisted the help of Tony Nicholls, who had worked on the revised edition of *Nemesis*. Since their earlier collaboration, the two men had stayed in touch, lunching either at St Antony's

or at the Luna Caprese, one of the popular Italian restaurants off the
Banbury Road in Oxford. The title they agreed upon – *The Semblance
of Peace* – was taken from a quotation by W.B. Yeats:

> Civilization is hooped together, brought
> Under a rule, under the semblance of peace
> By manifold illusion.[53]

Divided into two parts, 'War and Peace' and 'No War – No Peace',
Wheeler-Bennett intended to write thirteen chapters, and Nicholls
nine. The narrative embodied some of Wheeler-Bennett's postwar
cynicism.

> The gentle art of peace-making has greatly changed since the days of
> grace and elegance at Vienna. Even the Peace Conference of Paris
> subscribed to the conventional standards of diplomacy – despite what
> followed. At least for a while we enjoyed the Semblance of Peace and
> indeed became all too wedded to it for our own good – hence the
> diplomatic defeat of the West at Munich in 1938 and the collapse of
> France two years later. But since the termination of hostilities with
> Germany and Japan in 1945 the world has enjoyed only the very flim-
> siest illusion of peace.[54]

Since he was frequently in touch with Avon over 'The Biographer's
File', Wheeler-Bennett benefited from the opportunities afforded to
discuss various aspects of wartime history: 'At the Tehran Conference [in
November–December 1943], it seems that the main strategic differences,
between Mr Churchill on the one hand and Stalin and President Roosevelt
on the other, hinged on the possible entry of Turkey into the war. Is
it,' he went on to ask Avon, 'your impression that the Soviet Government hindered this occurrence, or do you think that it was a forlorn
hope anyway?' Avon readily responded:

> At the Moscow Conference [in October 1943], the Russians were
> eager to get Turkey into the war. Their enthusiasm cooled, perhaps in
> part because they feared that such an event might divert British forces,

which they would rather see used on the Western front. I do not think
that this issue was a main strategic difference at Tehran. In general, my
recollection is that Moscow was the most successful of our Three
Power meetings, with Tehran less so and Yalta least so. This was not
on account of any merits of the participants, but because as the tide
turned in favour of the Russians, so they became more difficult.[55]

In their correspondence the two men were invariably solicitous as to
their respective states of health. After going into hospital for some tests
in June 1966, Wheeler-Bennett gave Avon a progress report of his
ailments (and then excused himself for being so explicit): 'They have
found out what is wrong and can at any rate treat it. It appears that I
have an angina condition and also some major degree of diverticulitis.
Both of these can be "contained" (as we used to say about the Russians!)
though I don't think there is any cure for either! The net result is that
I have to live carefully and rest a good deal.'[56]

The 1967 Arab-Israeli war, which resulted in Israel's occupation of
part of Sinai, was a major concern. 'How splendidly the Israelis have
fought and with what courage and initiative,' Wheeler-Bennett enthused
to Avon. 'It will be a terrible thing if they are robbed of their success
as a result of diplomacy.'[57] The two men were also discussing a suitable
biographer for the former chief of the Imperial General Staff, Field
Marshal Sir John Dill, who, as chief of the British Joint Staff Mission in
Washington, had played a significant role in fostering the Allied relationship before his early death in 1944.[58] Meanwhile, Avon was pleased with
the progress Wheeler-Bennett was making on 'The Biographer's File'. 'I
am so grateful to you for having done so much "homework",' he wrote
in August, 'and for being willing to do more! This will all be of the
greatest help to the biographer.'[59] Busy as Wheeler-Bennett was, he had
declined an invitation to contribute to a history of Chatham House,
although promising 'to give any help I can to whomever you appoint
to write the history'.[60]

In 1967, Wheeler-Bennett was invited to return to the University of
Virginia as 'scholar-in-residence' for the fall semester, a 'much coveted'
teaching position. Wheeler-Bennett's predecessors in the role included
'old friends': the jurist and lawyer Arthur Goodhart and Sir Robert

Menzies, former prime minister of Australia and an 'outstanding authority on constitutional law'. His close friend and former colleague Hardy Dillard was then the dean. 'We were the only survivors of that faculty of eight members which I had joined in 1938.'[61] In the same year, New York University had secured Wheeler-Bennett's services, 'with the splendid title of Distinguished Professor of History, the adjective being applicable to the title and not the holder personally'.[62] As Wheeler-Bennett was pleased to note, the president of the university was Dr James Hester: in 1947, he had been the Rhodes Scholar from Princeton University to Pembroke College, Oxford and Wheeler-Bennett had supervised his PhD on German-American relations after World War I. Twenty years later, Hester transmuted his relationship 'from that of friend and ex-pupil to that of friend and employer'. Much to Wheeler-Bennett's delight, he had married Janet, one of the three beautiful daughters of Colonel Peter Rodes, former head of American Intelligence, whom he had met in Berlin after the war.[63]

The atmosphere at New York University presented a greater challenge to Wheeler-Bennett than anything he had experienced either in Virginia or Arizona. By the time he started lecturing at NYU, the wave of protest sweeping across the country was at its height. 'Be it remembered that in the mid-sixties the generation which had been born into the atomic age was approaching man's estate and throughout the world a large number of them were becoming increasingly disenchanted with the condition of affairs in which they found themselves,' he later wrote. 'Students were disgruntled by what they perceived was the menace of nuclear war with its paradoxical corollary that the sole guarantee of world peace lay in this self-same menace and the terror it evoked.'

Wheeler-Bennett believed that the young were 'contemptuous of their elders' and the 'mess' that they had seemingly made of international relations 'which had resulted in two devastating world wars in a half century'. Furthermore, 'there was no sign that the statesmen and leaders of the world had greatly profited by the experiences of the past. The generations were therefore divided, leaving parents unable to understand the ideals and motives of their progeny.' As he now discovered, it had not taken long for 'this conflict of generations' to infect the world of learning. It was particularly 'virulent' in the United States, where universities were congested 'with a flood of returning warriors who, in their turn, gave place to the new generation of war babies'.[64]

The situation on college campuses was exacerbated by the prevailing doctrine of 'Publish or Perish' to which the faculty members were subjected: if they did not produce something in print at least once a year, their jobs were in jeopardy. 'Hence there were long corridors of offices, the doors of which were closed to students while the occupants slogged away at their masterpieces.' As a result, students felt neglected. 'Doubtless many excellent works resulted from this intellectual servitude, but it cannot be denied there also emanated, in my own field, for example, a host of the dullest historical and biographical productions and an ever-growing ocean of unreadable articles in learned journals.' There were other pressures: the Vietnam War and compulsory military service, which divided the student world between doves and hawks – those who refused to believe in the 'domino theory' and regarded US involvement in Vietnam as another imperialist venture in which they could justifiably refuse to become involved, and those who did their duty 'honourably and bravely'. As a result, the world of student youth was 'in a ferment, a fierce and heady brew in which frustration and revolt, ideals and ideology, cynicism and honest belief, punitive violence and contempt for authority, protest and cannabis, a general lack of spiritual discipline and a strong sense of guilt, a deep unhappiness and insecurity were inextricably commingled'.[65]

Before taking up his appointment in New York, Wheeler-Bennett had received some dire warnings: 'that I ran the risk of being insulted, execrated, denied a hearing and even subjected to physical violence. I was assured that any previous experience I might have gleaned of American university life would be of little or no worth to me in the jungle conditions in which I should now be steeped.' Subsequent experience did not bear out such apocalyptic expectations: 'I can only say that from the first moment of my joining the History Dept of NYU . . . I met with nothing but kindness and good fellowship from my faculty colleagues and from my graduate and undergraduate students.' Although Wheeler-Bennett had agreed to take two seminar sessions a week of two hours each in both the graduate and undergraduate schools and had specified that there should be no more than twenty students in each, he was now informed, to his consternation, that sixty-seven graduates and around fifty undergraduates had signed up. 'I have rarely experienced a more exhausting experience than a two-hour period of instruction on this numerical scale.' Later he was able to reduce the class sizes but never to fewer than twenty. As he wrote to Avon at the beginning of March, it was 'a most entertaining and rewarding job. The American youth may be ill-informed but they are very ready to be taught the truth!'[66]

Wheeler-Bennett was also pleased to be receiving a 'handsome salary' and to be 'nobly' housed. 'A really splendid pent-house had been given us on the twenty-fifth floor of the One Fifth Avenue hotel, a short walk from the history department at 19 University Place, with a magnificent view over Washington Square, still bearing graces and memories of Henry James, and beyond this, across a range of architectural cromlechs, which, in the early morning sun, took on the appearance of Minoan palaces, to a straight vista southwards which terminated in the Statue of Liberty, sunlit by day and flood-lit by night.'[67] As regular churchgoers, he and Ruth worshipped at the nearby Church of the Ascension, where Wheeler-Bennett was pleased to note that the decoration above the altar had been painted by the father of his old friend Ham Armstrong, who, now in his late seventies, was still editing the Council of Foreign Relations' journal, *Foreign Affairs*. Armstrong's father had also designed and executed a stained-glass window, the subject of which was the youthful Christ in the Temple among the Scribes and Pharisees. 'He was depicted as standing at the foot of a flight of steps with one foot a step or two higher than the other and Ham had often told me of the hours during which he had posed in his father's studio, standing bare-footed and clad in an Edwardian nightgown, with one foot resting on a crate of oranges to get the proper stance. I never passed that window without thinking of Ham's suffering in the cause of art and religion.'

Looking back on his time at NYU, Wheeler-Bennett recorded that never in his academic career had he met with 'a more stimulating and stimulatory challenge than these sessions presented nor have I enjoyed anything more . . . Now I was face to face with the nitty-gritty of student life, meeting for the first time a class of student to whom an education was a life's ambition' and for which they were prepared to make sacrifices. He had found that he could only hold a graduate seminar in the afternoon or evening because in the morning his students were working in a variety of jobs so that they could afford to listen to their 'Distinguished Visiting Professor' later in the day. He believed this gave him a special obligation: the students were buying an education and so he felt morally bound 'to give of one's best in selling it to them'. Unlike in Virginia, he had an 'ecumenical' group of students, the majority of whom were Jewish, some Anglo-Saxon with 'Black, Chinese, Spanish, French, Russian and German, a Greek or two and not least of all two Irish Nuns from a teaching order in New Jersey, of whom one was doing a doctoral thesis on "British and American Privateering during the Revolutionary War"'. As with his other teaching appointments, Wheeler-Bennett enjoyed encouraging 'bright youngsters'. On one occasion, he suggested to one of his students, who had written a 'wholly excellent' essay on Raymond Poincaré's foreign policy in the 1920s, that he should enter it for the *New York Times*'s $100 essay prize in modern history. 'Judge then of my pleasure when, some weeks later, in reading my morning paper, I found that his essay had not only won the prize but that it had been specially commended.'[68]

As a visiting professor, he had one great asset over his American peers: he was not subject to 'the rule of Publish or Perish', and so could afford the luxury of 'an ever open door', through which passed many young men and women, 'while outside it looked like a dentist's waiting room'. In addition to discussing their studies, Wheeler-Bennett regarded the consultations like 'hours in the confessional while they rattled on about their souls and their bodies, their sex life and their drug life, perversion and draft-dodging, their hopes and fears and dreams'.

Early one morning, Wheeler-Bennett was woken 'by a hideous cacophony of sound, partly human and partly metallic'. Looking out of the living room window, he saw the building in which he was shortly to take an undergraduate class surrounded by a cordon of students beating kitchen utensils, 'while chanting slogans and battle cries, some of which were pretty obscene. In due course I went to take my class. I had never crossed a picket line before but I was determined to do so; recognising some of my students among the pickets I greeted them cheerily with as much *sang froid* as I could muster. They grinned and let me through.'

By the afternoon, the 'rebels' had seized the elevators and immobilised them, preventing Wheeler-Bennett's ascent to his eighth-floor office. As a result, teacher and students assembled in the furnace room of one of the dormitories. 'It was grimy and very hot; by right of age and authority I possessed myself of the only chair and they sat around on the concrete floor.' Recalling this incident in later life, Wheeler-Bennett appreciated the vote of confidence in his teaching that the gathering represented. Within a week the strike had petered out.

Wheeler-Bennett realised that, as an Englishman in New York, he was a novelty:

> they liked my English accent, or at least were tolerant of it, liked my monocle and were always asking, like children, to be shown how it was used, they appreciated my sense of humour which was of the dead pan variety and they realised that because of my age and experience, I had something to offer them. Moreover I had been knighted and this also intrigued them. Was I then a nobleman? Was I an intimate – perhaps even a distant relation – of the Royal Family? Were the copper bracelets, which I wore against neuritis, anything to do with my being a knight? They were therefore respectful and there rapidly grew up a hard core of young disciples, a sort of Praetorian guard, who would have protected me from any trouble had there been a need for it and some of whom took the course two or three times even though they could only gain credits for it the first time.

Describing himself as decidedly 'square', he treated his students as friends of a younger generation and made 'no attempt to be anything but my natural self with my usual semi-frivolous approach to life . . . Drawing on my near half century of research and writing, I gave them the essential facts of the period they were studying – 20th century Europe, the Orient and the Commonwealth – richly larded with stories and descriptions of the leading performers in the cast, and also personal experiences and adventures of my own.' He made his classes even more interesting by 'hopping about' in his historical recitals, 'relating the past to the future and the present to the past in an effort to illustrate the futility in which many of their generation indulged that the study of history was "irrelevant" to the problems of the present day'.[69]

Wheeler-Bennett could certainly impress them with his first-hand reports. 'Sir,' a student once said. 'I have come to the conclusion that I have to choose between Jesus Christ and Leon Trotsky. What would you advise me to do?' 'I have never had the privilege of meeting Jesus Christ,' Wheeler-Bennett replied, 'but I did have a long talk with Trotsky and I don't think I should advise you to follow him.'[70]

Although NYU experienced its share of student violence, Wheeler-Bennett attributed the fact that it never got out of hand to the deans and the president, James Hester. 'He projected its image in a manner unequalled in its history.' By developing housing facilities and raising educational standards, he attracted students from all parts of the country until the university became the largest private institution of higher education in America, with an estimated student body of forty thousand and a faculty of four thousand. 'Well might it be said of him as of Pericles that he found his Athens of brick and left it of marble.'[71]

The Wheeler-Bennetts' sojourns in the United States always involved stopping in Virginia to see Ruth's family. Since the Avons wintered in Barbados, they extended an invitation to them to break their journey and spend a few days at their house, Villa Nova, which the Wheeler-Bennetts did for the first time in the winter of 1967 en route to Charlottesville. In January 1968, Ruth's mother, Martha Risher, died, aged ninety-three. Having lost his own parents decades before, Wheeler-Bennett considered that no man could have been more fortunate in his mother-in-law.

> Mrs Risher was one of those rare people who are absolutely natural and sincere. She was wise and compassionate and very discerning, with the most heavenly sense of humour. Born in North Carolina under the shadow of the defeat of the Confederacy and the grotesque depravities of the Reconstruction, she had married young and become a widow at forty. She had brought up her family, a girl and two boys, under difficult circumstances and with amazing success. I am of course prejudiced as regards Ruth, but am also devoted to her two brothers, Dan and John. I have never felt so honoured as when I joined Mrs Risher's family. She became a mother to me also and was

loved as such. I shall never forget the mischief of her smile nor the warm giggling quality of her laughter. I shared Ruth's sense of loss and sorrow to the full.[72]

Throughout this period, in addition to corresponding regularly with Avon, Wheeler-Bennett maintained a close relationship with Harold Macmillan, whose wife, Lady Dorothy, had died in 1966. The interest in their respective publications was mutual. During one of Wheeler-Bennett's visits to New York, Macmillan had sent him the galley proofs of his second volume of memoirs, *The Blast of War*.[73] Not surprisingly, Wheeler-Bennett was full of praise. 'I cannot tell you how much I admire your style, the marshalling of your material, and the way in which you keep the reader on the edge of his chair.'[74]

At the same time, *Brest-Litovsk* was being reprinted in paperback and Wheeler-Bennett had written a new foreword, drawing attention to the continuing shadow that the Peace of Brest-Litovsk 'cast in the middle years of the Second World War – and beyond'.[75] Wheeler-Bennett's publishers, Macmillan, had also agreed to issue a collection of his earlier writings and lectures in book form, under the title *A Wreath to Clio*. The first section, 'British Studies', included his Page-Barbour lectures on Crown and Empire delivered at the University of Virginia. The second section, 'American Studies', consisted of three essays reflecting his lifelong interest in the American Civil War. It began with a paper on his mother's cousin, 'A.P. Hill: A Study in Confederate Leadership', which he had given as a lecture at the Virginia Military Institute in 1960.[76] The other two pieces, 'Gettysburg' and 'The Trent Affair', were articles he had published in *History Today*. Finally, in 'German Studies', he included his contributions to A.J.P. Taylor's collection of essays presented to Lewis Namier, as well as his 'Twenty Years of Russo-German Relations, 1919–1939', which he had written for *Foreign Affairs* in October 1946.[77] The concluding chapter was his 'Call to Arms' in 1940 when he had addressed the Institute of Public Affairs, standing in for the ambassador, Philip Lothian, at the University of Virginia on 17 June 1940.[78]

Despite the book's eclectic contents, the reviews were favourable. As noted in the *Times Educational Supplement*: 'It can hardly be said that Sir John has woven these 12 studies into a single wreath, as the title of his book implies. But he certainly offers Clio and his readers some charming blossoms.'[79] Geoffrey Barraclough in the *Guardian* suggested that perhaps Wheeler-Bennett's style was no longer in fashion:

> As the professionalisation of history gathers pace, the inspired amateur tends to be edged out. Sir John Wheeler-Bennett is in no sense an amateur. But, in spite of his honorary fellowship at Oxford, he is not an academic historian either. This, and a long experience of public affairs, explains the peculiar qualities (and perhaps – dare I say it? – the limitations) of his writing. For one thing, he does not despise style and, sometimes, an almost Churchillian rhetoric. For another, he freely confesses in an age of flat sociological analysis to an abiding interest in 'the effect of human personality upon history.'[80]

Not long afterwards, Wheeler-Bennett gave substance to just such a belief when he agreed to edit a series of memoirs by men who had worked with Winston Churchill. The book had been instigated by Jock Colville, Churchill's former principal private secretary, in discussion with Avon, to rectify factual errors which they believed were to be found in Lord Moran's recently published *Winston Churchill: The Struggle for Survival* (1966).[81] Among the contributors was Norman Brook, created Baron Normanbrook in 1963, although he did not live to see the book, *Action This Day: Working with Churchill,* in print. Wheeler-Bennett wrote a brief introduction, pointing to the 'unique historical value of the book, for, as a collective result of their individual writings, the portrait which they jointly offer is one of a man conceived on grand and magnificent lines, displaying fortitude and magnanimity and vision, yet with the engaging frailties of personality which make him an essentially human character'.[82]

While Wheeler-Bennett was working on *The Semblance of Peace*, he was continuing to benefit from Avon's insights. In August 1968, he sent him chapter fourteen, 'The Road to Potsdam', in which he described Churchill's deteriorating relationship with Stalin, compared to the warmth which existed between the Soviet leader and the American president, Franklin Roosevelt, 'on which I shall be very delighted and grateful to receive any criticisms, comments, strictures, etc. which you may feel moved to make'.[83] Avon's response was candid:

My only comment is a general one, but it is, I think, of some
substance.

Events at that time may now seem to have been in black and white,
but at the time grey was the prevailing colour. For instance, Winston
was by no means as consistently convinced of predatory Russian intentions as is implied here. Sometimes he was, but other times, particularly
at meetings with Stalin or the Big Three, this was not so . . . the truth
is that Winston was not the cold, calculating type, as Stalin was; also
his position was weak. The Lepidus of the party. All of this does not,
of course, excuse FDR, who was, I fear, not well disposed to the British
Empire. All I would suggest, as a result of these reflections, is that it
would be prudent, and I am sure historically correct, to put a little
more water in your wine in proclaiming Winston's attitude towards
the Russians. At this time he was more often right than wrong, which
is good enough and more human than unbroken rectitude.[84]

Wheeler-Bennett could not help but agree with such forthright comments:
'I accept most readily the advice which you most wisely extend. I will
certainly water down the bit about Winston, not by taking anything out,
but by inserting something on the other side . . . This will, I think give
a more balanced portrait.' Wheeler-Bennett was also mindful of present
events. In August 1968, the Soviet Union had invaded Czechoslovakia,
suppressing a period of liberalisation. 'Those poor Czechs,' he continued
in his letter to Avon.

It is too ghastly that almost exactly thirty years after Munich they should
again be invaded in the name of legality and without redress. I fear
that this Russian operation will be considerably more brutal than the
rather 'covert' occupation by the Reichswehr in 1938. I am deeply
distressed about it all, and the saddest part is that it makes nonsense of
all our hopes that a change of policy (if not of heart) was in process
in Moscow . . . if they treat a friendly communist state with this brutality,
what would they do to the capitalist neighbours if the spirit moved
them? It is altogether, horrible. [85]

Busy writing his own books, Wheeler-Bennett was well aware that
numerous others were being published both on the key players and the

main issues of the war. In 1968, the debate over the German resistance movement came to the fore on both sides of the Atlantic with the publication of Harold Deutsch's *The Conspiracy against Hitler in the Twilight War*. A Fulbright scholar in Germany in the late 1950s, Deutsch had traced the fortunes of Adam von Trott zu Solz when he visited Britain and the United States in 1939 to lobby for support against Nazi rule. Drawing upon Wheeler-Bennett's revised *The Nemesis of Power* and Hans Rothfels's book on the German opposition, he alluded to the time that Wheeler-Bennett had spent with Trott in 1939 and the fact that, when writing *Nemesis*, Wheeler-Bennett had not mentioned his own lobbying attempts on behalf of the anti-Nazi Germans. 'Mystifying, in view of his pronounced part in the affair, is the divergence between Wheeler-Bennett's role in it and his later one as a historian. In the latter capacity he gives no hint of having inside knowledge or of having been involved personally in any way.'[86]

In the same year, *Troubled Loyalty*, a biography of Trott by Christopher Sykes, who had previously written on the maverick soldier Orde Wingate, was published. During his research, undertaken at the instigation of Trott's family, Sykes had questioned Wheeler-Bennett about his friendship with Trott. In conversation, Wheeler-Bennett was more forthcoming than he had been in *Nemesis* about his personal views, telling Sykes that he had never believed the allegations made against Trott – that he was a Nazi spy or pro-Soviet – and that he 'respected his honourable intentions'. To explain the fading of their friendship, he said that he had looked 'with increasing misgiving on Trott's political ideas . . . [Trott] frequently expressed admiration of Neville Chamberlain and deplored the influence of Winston Churchill', who was advocating a firmer line against Nazi Germany.[87] It was the same concern that had eventually ruptured the deep friendship between Shiela Grant Duff and Trott after Munich.[88] Trott's apologists were critical of Sykes's book and his supplementary article in the December issue of *Encounter* magazine, 'Heroes and Suspects: The German Resistance in Perspective', which appeared to belittle the courage of the conspirators.[89] The point at issue concerning Wheeler-Bennett's role was whether, through his friendship and possibly his influence, more could have been done by the British government to support the anti-Nazi Germans. David Astor, editor of the *Observer*, and Trott's friend since Oxford in the 1930s, certainly thought so and he blamed Wheeler-Bennett for letting Trott down, suggesting that 'he was the British friend in whom Trott had the highest hopes and that those hopes were misplaced'.[90]

Wheeler-Bennett rose to his own defence in a letter to *Encounter*, repeating the British government's official line and omitting any reference to his own 'peace terms' letter to Vansittart in late 1939:

> Astor suggests that there might have been a *coup de main* against Hitler during the war, had the British and US governments given support and encouragement to the German Resistance Movement. He goes on to attribute to me a substantial measure of responsibility for the fact that this support and encouragement was not forthcoming . . . At no time – before, during, or after the War – was I in a position to exercise the kind or degree of influence which Mr. Astor ascribes to me . . . I believed then, and I believe now, that . . . once hostilities had begun, it was essential that Germany be defeated in the field and compelled to surrender unconditionally – whatever government might be in control of Reich policies at the time. It was essential that there should be no recurrence of the 'stab-in-the-back' exculpatory fallacy. I also believed and still believe that any plot against Hitler must succeed of itself and would have been less likely to do so with Allied support or promises for the future. Real or alleged foreign interference can only strengthen national resistance.[91]

He elaborated these opinions in a review of the American edition of Sykes's book, now entitled *Tormented Loyalty*, repeating much of what he had said in the August edition of *Encounter* – that the allegation that he was responsible for the failure of the German resistance movement by withdrawing support at a 'crucial' moment was 'false'. Although he conceded that Trott was anti-Nazi, he also pointed out that Trott hoped that a 'de-nazified' Germany could retain Hitler's prewar territorial acquisitions, which would not have been acceptable to the Allies. Had he had anything like the influence that Astor suggested, it 'would certainly have been cast against the pursuit by the British government of so impractical a policy as giving pledges in advance – particularly of a territorial nature

– in support of an anti-Nazi conspiracy. It seemed to me absolutely necessary that the conspirators first give evidence of success before anyone entered into negotiations with them.'[92]

Astor was not prepared to let the matter rest and the *pro* and *contra* arguments appeared in the pages of *Encounter* throughout 1969. Referring to the memorandum enclosed with Wheeler-Bennett's 1939 letter to Vansittart, Astor wrote:

Sir John Wheeler-Bennett is mistaken if he believes that he never thought the German opposition might take successful action against Hitler, once war had broken out. His official memorandum (dated 28 December 1939) speaks of 'an ally within Germany itself . . . more numerous and powerful than may be supposed . . . [with] a common aim with the Democratic Powers in destroying the Nazi regime.' He is also mistaken in suggesting that he always believed outside help unnecessary or undesirable. In the same document he says 'these elements within Germany should be strengthened and encouraged' and speaks of the 'essential preliminary assurance' that they needed from the Allies.

Furthermore, if he had no influence, 'why, then, did he write his memorandum?'[93]

The debate over Trott's role and the German resistance movement was to continue, but what had most bearing on Wheeler-Bennett's reputation was not so much that he might have changed his opinion for what he considered to be the greater good of the war effort, but that he seemed reluctant to admit that he had at one time held opposing views, albeit in a more benign political climate. During the 'phoney war' the situation was different from the one in the spring of 1940 and subsequently, when the manifestation of the German desire for *Lebensraum* and its attendant brutalities was plain for all to see. In support of Astor, Anthony Howard, editor of the *New Statesman* and a columnist on the *Observer*, described Wheeler-Bennett's change of heart as 'one of the most nimble political somersaults the corridors of power can ever have seen'.[94] That he had chosen not to reveal his early friendship with Trott when writing (or revising) *The Nemesis of Power* seemed to point towards a

conscious decision to distance himself from Trott. Deutsch's explanation
was probably closest to the truth. Wheeler-Bennett, he said, was writing
his book 'when anti-German sentiment was still strong in Britain, and
his reticence may reflect a desire to remain silent on his own intimate
share in these events'.[95]

For the rest of his life, Wheeler-Bennett held fast to the opinion that
the Allies could not afford to repeat the 'fatal mistake' of World War I,
when, prior to the armistice, correspondence between the German chancellor, Prince Max of Baden, and the US president, Woodrow Wilson,
had led the Germans to believe that the peace terms would be more
lenient than those eventually imposed by the Treaty of Versailles.[96] It
was a view later endorsed by Anthony Nicholls:

> Trott's attempts to get a separate peace with Britain (and later the USA)
> were rightly seen as highly dangerous for the solidarity of the United
> Nations Alliance. The Western powers feared for some years during
> the war that Stalin might be tempted to do a deal with the Nazis to
> get them out of the Soviet Union, and any sort of arrangement, which
> would have satisfied Trott and his colleagues, would rightly have
> been seen as betrayal in Moscow. By the same token British (and by
> 1944 American) public opinion would not have accepted any peace
> with Germany that did not involve the unconditional surrender of
> German forces.[97]

Finally, as Alan Bullock pointed out: 'John Wheeler-Bennett's views
were the product not only of many years of research and reflection on
"the German problem", but of longer and closer first-hand acquaintance
with German politics and German politicians and soldiers (over more
than twenty years) than any other Englishman could claim.' Bullock also
emphasised that 'no Englishman had worked harder to secure greater
understanding and support abroad for the hard-pressed German Government before Hitler came to power'. Moreover, the 'further period of
research and reflection involved in producing, after the War, three more
major works on Germany did not lead him to change his views'.[98]

Undaunted by the exchange with Astor, Wheeler-Bennett was contemplating future projects. In February 1969, he had written to Avon, telling

him that he had received an invitation from the chancellor of the Order
of St Michael and St George, Viscount William De L'Isle, via Jock
Colville, to write the life of the former chief of the Imperial General
Staff, Lord Gort. 'It's an interesting life to write and by 1970 the Cabinet
papers etc for 1940 (e.g. Dunkirk et al) will be freed under the 30 years
rule.'[99] Avon was unenthusiastic. 'I would not have thought that Gort
was worth your while. His career was essentially military,' he advised. 'I
would have thought Dill an infinitely more interesting soldier to write
about.'[100] Since he had been privy to Avon's search for a suitable biographer of Dill (which, after Bernard Fergusson, author of a 'portrait' life
of Field Marshal Earl Wavell, had included an approach to the military
historians John Terraine and Michael Howard), Wheeler-Bennett was
immensely flattered. 'I think it would be a fascinating life to write . . . I
must say I'm very much attracted by the idea,' he replied, suggesting that
he hoped Dill's son 'might find me an acceptable biographer. I am
certainly an admirer.'[101] But, as he was to discover after two years'
preliminary research, all Dill's papers had been burnt and there was no
primary source material. 'I'm really disappointed at the complete lack of
personal material on Dill – or of his own writing. One cannot, I believe,
write a biography entirely on second-hand opinions and official
documents.'[102]

Wheeler-Bennett still had to finish *The Semblance of Peace*, and in
September received Avon's remarks on his treatment of the Cold War
in chapter twenty-two. 'It is, I suppose,' commented Avon, 'the distinctive mark of the historian that, having assimilated a vast quantity of
material, he can stand back and present a coherent and convincing
account of the whole. This you do admirably in the present chapter,
which I much enjoyed.' As usual, he had a few points of criticism. 'I
think you are hard on Herbert Morrison,' he said. After being home
secretary in the coalition government during the war, deputy prime
minister under Attlee after the war and leader of the House of Commons,
Morrison was briefly foreign secretary, until the Conservatives won the
1951 general election. As Avon explained: 'He came to the work at the
end of a long period at other offices and I think was tired. . . . the
eyesight of one eye was defective, or nearly so, and he found much
reading very difficult. He told me this himself and complained, not

unjustly, of the amount of paper he was expected to read at the Foreign Office.'[103] Such was their friendship that Wheeler-Bennett was glad to have Avon's criticisms, 'which are always so cogent and valuable. I will mitigate my comments on Herbert Morrison.'[104]

By the end of the 1960s, Wheeler-Bennett and his academic colleagues had weathered the early student protests in the United States, although the spectre of the Vietnam War still hung over them. 'We are all waiting, with some trepidation,' Wheeler-Bennett wrote to Avon on 13 October 1969 – his sixty-seventh birthday – 'the outcome of Wednesday's Moratorium Day protest against the Vietnam War. I wonder if there is any historical precedent for a nation-wide protest against established government policy . . . it's a very odd atmosphere. Most of those concerned, whom I have met, are genuinely opposed to the war and think they should say so, but others are just out to make trouble, to disrupt civil peace . . . it is somewhat alarming!'[105] Since Wheeler-Bennett was teaching at NYU, he had to decide whether or not to cancel his classes. 'I didn't want to embarrass the Administration who would, I sensed, really prefer for there to be no classes on that day for fear of provocation but on the other hand I felt that I was in a somewhat different position from that of my colleagues and, after considerable searching of heart, I let it be known that I would hold my graduate seminar as usual.'

When, at lunch time, Wheeler-Bennett looked out of his window, he saw Washington Square 'crammed with a monster crowd of students. They were well behaved and save for a few songs of revolution they were mostly silent, but not unimpressive in their hour of protest, standing there under a grey, lowering autumnal sky.' Having made his way without obstruction to his office, he found that about 80 per cent of his students, 'some looking rather sullen', were waiting. 'Again I was touched by this show of support and I made a statement to them of my position. I reminded them that I was a foreigner, and therefore a neutral. It was not my war and while I respected their right to protest peaceably, it was my duty to discharge my duty to the University, to whom I was under contract to hold this seminar for which I was in receipt of a salary.'[106]

The decade ended with the University of Virginia's celebration of its sesquicentennial anniversary in late October. Knowing that

Wheeler-Bennett had been a scholar-in-residence there, Alan Bullock, now vice-chancellor of Oxford University, asked him to represent Oxford at the ceremonies, to which delegates from universities worldwide had been invited. One of the delegates Wheeler-Bennett was pleased to meet was the University of Paris's representative, Raymond Aron, the political scientist, who, for thirty years, was an influential columnist for Le Figaro before joining L'Express.[107] The celebrations began with a candlelit reception and supper party. Other events included a football game, a 'superb' concert given by the Boston Symphony Orchestra and a magnificent banquet. The weather was 'crisp and sunny with unclouded azure skies', and Wheeler-Bennett was offered 'fraternal greetings' by the foreign seats of learning. In terms of his unconventional academic career, he considered the episode 'climacteric'. 'It was indeed pleasurable that I had been able to represent one great university, which had, with warmth and kindness received me into its midst, at the birthday ceremonies of another, which had given me such consistent and generous hospitality.'[108] And he was gratified that Ruth, to whom he had now been married for nearly twenty-five years, was with him.

11

Memories

Never was there a man with so many 'special relationships'.
Patrick Dean[1]

Sir John Wheeler-Bennett began the 1970s in good spirits. He and Ruth still relished their transatlantic voyages. *The Semblance of Peace* almost finished, Wheeler-Bennett was enjoying lecturing in the United States and entertaining his friends at Garsington. 'Our plans are that we stay here until March,' he wrote to Avon from Arizona in February, 'and then fly back to New York, where we shall be until the 28th when we sail in the *Christophoro Colombo*. This doughty vessel takes us to Lisbon and then into the Mediterranean and eventually via several Italian ports . . . to Venice. There we disembark and entrust ourselves to the Orient Express, which brings us directly to Calais, Dover and London on April 11th. Isn't this adventurous?'[2] Among their regular guests at Garsington was Harold Macmillan, who, as chancellor of the University of Oxford, was happy to accept the Wheeler-Bennetts' hospitality during the Encaenia festivities at Christ Church. 'I am afraid I am going to be a very tiresome guest,' he apologised in May 1970. 'I could almost be accused of using your beautiful home and your kind hospitality as if it were a sort of hotel. Please forgive me or tell me to go somewhere else if you prefer it.'[3]

In addition to Macmillan, Wheeler-Bennett retained numerous other correspondents, among them Avon (with whom he was still discussing 'the Biography'), Aubrey Morgan and Patrick Dean, who had recently returned from four years in Washington as British ambassador. Other friends were departing. In February 1970, Bruce Lockhart died, having never again achieved the literary fame he had enjoyed in the 1920s. After suffering a breakdown in his health, for the last few years of his life he had lived with his son and daughter-in-law in Sussex. He was, Wheeler-Bennett noted after his death, 'a delightful and faithful friend'.[4] Heinrich Brüning also died in 1970. Their friendship had never recovered from the strains placed upon it by the war and Wheeler-Bennett was disappointed when Brüning's posthumous memoirs appeared later in the year. These recollections, he said, portrayed the man he had known so well as 'unappealing, patronizing and petulant, with a strong inclination to be "too clever by half," and a pronounced tendency to place the onus of blame for his ultimate failure on every one but himself'.[5]

Wheeler-Bennett was now increasingly prone to illness. At the end of November 1970 he was writing to Avon, whose health was also poor, to explain why he and Ruth could not accept the Avons' invitation to stay with them that winter in Barbados. 'I was so sorry to have to forego my visit to you but this pneumonia business blew up rather suddenly and I really was very ill for several days . . . I know how well you under-stand the weakening effect of high fevers and I can now sympathise with you even more than I did before. They leave you feeling very washed out and "chewed stringy".' He and Ruth were also recovering from the shock of having been burgled in the autumn, when a quantity of antique family silver of great sentimental value was stolen.[6] 'It also led to the insurance companies insisting on the installation of a complex burglar alarm system which caused the Wheeler-Bennetts considerable inconve-nience,' recollected Nicholls.[7]

Ill health meant that Wheeler-Bennett had to give up teaching at New York University. Writing to Avon from the Arizona Inn in early 1971, he explained:

> The doctors here put me through a very searching series of tests, as a result of which they said very emphatically that I could not go back to New York in February to take up my assignment at New York University, but must stay in an equable climate till it had warmed up

a bit at home, when I could return. So we've had a complete change
of plan and we are staying on here till the end of February when we
shall go to Ruth's home in Virginia and then return to England in
mid-April.[8]

Both he and Ruth 'were deeply regretful' to be forced in this way to
leave old and new friends in New York. 'Moreover it was fun to have
one foot in the Bohemian surroundings of Greenwich Village and Washington Square and another in the more sophisticated social world of the
up-town 70s and 80s.'[9]

Back in Garsington for the summer, a highlight in the Wheeler-
Bennetts' social calendar took place on 11 May 1971, when the queen
mother came to have tea and plant a magnolia tree in the grounds. Since
there were no security arrangements for the royal helicopter to land in
the grounds at Garsington, it had to set down at a helipad at New
College instead and the queen mother came on to the house by car.
When it was time for her to depart, she did so from the children's
playground in the village. Ethel helped to prepare the tea and recalled:
'the whole village turned out. It was a wonderful day.' After the queen
mother had gone, tired from the day's events, 'Sir John said: "Those
policeman did a really good job. I think I'll invite them to have
some beer." So they all trooped back to the manor, young and old. I
was there getting the silver tray out and the beer mugs. Then Sir
John picked on the youngest policeman and said: "I think you should
help Ethel"!'[10]

During the summer, the Wheeler-Bennetts attended the funerals of
two more friends. In July, Brian Melland died. As the senior member of
the Historical Section of the Cabinet Office, he had greatly assisted
Wheeler-Bennett with his work on the captured German archives and
the two men had remained friends ever since. In 1969, Wheeler-Bennett
had written to the cabinet secretary, Sir Burke Trend, recommending
that for his 'admirable service to the official historians over some 20
years', Melland should be awarded a CMG or 'at least a CBE'. He
received, in fact, an OBE in June 1970.[11] Then, in August, came the
unexpected news that the renowned traveller and author Peter Fleming
had died. Only two weeks previously he had written to Wheeler-Bennett
asking for assistance with sources relating to the deception activities with

which Fleming had himself been involved during the war. 'You have only yourself to blame if I pester you for advice, since a chance word from you gave me, years ago, an entire chapter for *Invasion 1940*'.[12] Wheeler-Bennett was especially saddened by Fleming's death, at only sixty-four years of age. 'We had been friends for forty years,' he told Avon's wife Clarissa, 'and I always found him a delightful companion. I would also have said that he was one of the fittest men I have ever known. It was a great shock that he should have died so suddenly.'[13]

After the premature termination of his New York duties, it was not long before another academic avenue opened to him. In the autumn of 1971 Wheeler-Bennett was invited to return to the University of Virginia as scholar-in-residence for a second time. On this occasion, he would be attached not only to the Law School, but also to the History Department and the School of International Studies, which meant a heavy but enjoyable work schedule: two full seminars and a weekly meeting of young dons, when – mindful of the book he was writing – he discoursed on the prevailing 'semblance of peace' in the world. His students found 'this alarming and deeply interesting'.[14]

The only 'marring' incident, as he wrote to Tony Nicholls, was when, 'if you please cold sober and at four o'clock in the afternoon', he fell up some steps and broke his left ankle, 'requiring a plaster cast, crutches and a wheel chair'.[15] Their home was 'a most delightful small house', which, like much of Charlottesville, had been designed and built by Thomas Jefferson. Thanks to his broken ankle, Wheeler-Bennett was very mindful of one particular design drawback: 'If Mr Jefferson may be said to have one fault as an architect it is that he despised staircases. He regarded them as unnecessary, uneconomical and merely using up space which could be otherwise better employed.' To save space a spiral staircase led from the ground floor to the basement, where the dining room, kitchen, Wheeler-Bennett's study, in which he held his seminar sessions, and a spare bedroom were all located. 'To negotiate an oblique spiral stair is difficult at any time but it becomes increasingly so when encumbered by a plaster cast! However I became adept at negotiating it . . . pulling myself up sideways one step at a time.' He lowered or pulled up his crutches by attaching a clothesline to them. 'It worked perfectly.'[16] He refused to let the accident interfere with his routine. 'I could still drive a car with an automatic gear-shift; I became easily accustomed to my crutches and greatly enjoyed whizzing about the Law School in a wheel-chair and making myself a menace to pedestrian traffic.'[17] By the time he was ready to have his cast off, he could 'practically walk a tight rope' in his wheelchair.[18]

While he was in Charlottesville, Wheeler-Bennett received the draft chapters of *The Semblance of Peace* from Tony Nicholls. With research ranging 'over a wide field', the book had taken them both the 'better part' of five years to write. Starting with 'thoughts on peace-making' and the outbreak of World War II, the narrative ended with the origins of the UN and the coming of the Cold War. Of the book's twenty-two chapters, Wheeler-Bennett had written thirteen, and Nicholls nine. Much of what Wheeler-Bennett wrote covered familiar terrain, focusing mainly on the Paris Peace Conference, Germany and Central Europe, the trial and punishment of Nazi war criminals, the United Nations and the Cold War. He also wrote a chapter on the unconditional surrender of Japan. Nicholls's contribution included chapters on the conferences at Casablanca, Tehran, Yalta and Potsdam. A further chapter examined Germany as a divided country. So pleased was Wheeler-Bennett with Nicholls's writing that he made only a few corrections. 'I feel a nice glow of pride when people who have read the book in manuscript say that they can't tell which chapters are written by whom!!' he wrote to Nicholls in November.[19] Having decided that they would like to dedicate the book to Bill Deakin, 'to whom we both are greatly endebted [*sic*] both individually and collectively as he was responsible for our literary partnership', they then became concerned that such a gesture might compromise Deakin's relationship with the Yugoslavs, if it were interpreted as meaning that he endorsed the book's contents. Eventually, they decided that it would not upset the Yugoslavs and the book was duly dedicated to Deakin, 'with admiration and affection'.[20] In view of Wheeler-Bennett's long absences in the United States, he was well aware that the brunt of dealing with the final stages of the book had fallen on Nicholls: 'You have done nobly with it and I fear have suffered in health.'[21]

Wheeler-Bennett himself was feeling light-headed and fatigued and was suffering from 'low fever',[22] but he enjoyed watching the waxing fortunes of his wide circle of friends, as, for example, when fellow historian Alan Bullock received his knighthood in the 1972 New Year Honours. Then, in late January 1972, he heard that Irene's husband, Trevor Heaton, to whom she had been married for over fifty years, had died. As he confided to Tony Nicholls, his brother-in-law's death was 'not unexpected and [was] welcomed' because he had been suffering from Parkinson's disease.[23] He was by now reading another instalment of the proofs of Harold Macmillan's memoirs which he described as 'interminable'. Macmillan had sent him the fifth (and last) volume, to be published under the title *Pointing the Way*. In return, Macmillan was reading the proofs of *The Semblance of Peace*, which he described as 'a splendid work of great range and dignity with your usual wide knowledge. I think I can detect passages which you have not written – but I may be wrong . . . Altogether it will rank with your other books which have that rare combination of being both scholarly and readable.'[24] Before leaving Charlottesville towards the end of January 1972, Wheeler-Bennett had been invited to give the annual General Lee Memorial Lecture at the Virginia Historical Society in Richmond. He described the event – which gave him 'a splendid fee' – as 'a riot', more for what happened during the dinner before than because of his talk. 'Just as we were being served our drinks, the lights went out and in the ensuing chaos the butler swiped the odd bottle of vodka and the catering chief had a stroke.' He had found the episode 'exceedingly funny', but his hosts had failed 'to rise above it'.[25]

In Tucson for the spring semester, he and Ruth settled into their Arizona routine and the warm air improved Wheeler-Bennett's health. 'My seminar is agreeable,' he wrote to Nicholls in March, describing his students as 'pleasant, receptive, courteous, respectful, kind and funny'.[26] His appearance remained 'quintessentially English', recalled Richard Cosgrove, a member of the history faculty at this time. 'He was the last person I knew who wore a monocle without affectation . . . Sir John used a cane, wore beautifully tailored pinstripe suits, and yet was an individual utterly without pretension. In the best sort of way, he was a man of infinite charm. He put everyone at ease: friends, colleagues, students, and staff. There was not the slightest hint of arrogance in his demeanour or conversation. He was, in the best sense of the phrase, an English gentleman.' Cosgrove considered that Wheeler-Bennett was 'a great asset' to the department: 'he often displayed his extensive knowledge in the first person. In a lesser person this would have been obnoxious, a crass form of name dropping . . . His command of names, dates, and events in German history was truly encyclopaedic but it never lorded [sic] over anyone.' On one occasion, Cosgrove was designated to bring Wheeler-Bennett and the medieval historian Sir Steven Runciman to the campus. 'Sir John chatted about the humidity of Athens in the summer, how much better winters were in Cairo and other places that I will likely never see in my lifetime. It was the conversation of two historians who literally possess a global perspective.'[27]

In July 1972, while back in England, Wheeler-Bennett was elected a Fellow of the British Academy, the national academy for the humanities and social sciences, whose fellows were elected for 'distinction and achievement'. For some reason, perhaps because Wheeler-Bennett had never considered himself a serious academic, he found this accolade 'did not fit his picture of himself'.[28] While continuing to gather material for Avon's biography, it was agreed with the Avon family that Wheeler-Bennett should become one of his literary trustees, which left him 'greatly touched and honoured . . . I will gladly do this but I hope with all my heart that it will not become an "active duty" for many years to come!'[29]

After a certain amount of delay and wrangling over the cost of the American edition, resulting in an agreement to reduce royalties, *The Semblance of Peace: The Political Settlement after the Second World War* was published in the autumn of 1972. It was a huge work, running to nearly nine hundred pages, with detailed appendices, documents, notes and bibliography. In recognition of the benefits he had derived from their collaboration, Nicholls presented Wheeler-Bennett with a copy which he had inscribed: 'With gratitude and affection. To have worked together with you on this book has been a great honour and has given me tremendous pleasure. My admiration for my co-author knows no bounds!'[30] Recalling the experience thirty-five years later, Nicholls acknowledged that their collaboration was 'a wonderful experience, both as an apprenticeship in dealing with a broad sweep of international history and as a fascinating opportunity to discuss the policies and personalities of so many American and European politicians whom he knew personally'.[31]

As usual, Wheeler-Bennett had acknowledged the assistance of numerous friends, including Avon, Macmillan and Patrick Dean. During the book's gestation, several of those he wished to acknowledge had died: Clement Attlee, Alexander Cadogan, Allen Dulles, René MacColl and Normanbrook. The *Times Literary Supplement* was generous to both co-authors:

> Sir John Wheeler-Bennett has already made distinguished contributions to the study of the earlier illusion known as appeasement. With his new collaborator, who also has scholarly work on Germany in the 1930s to his credit, he has made an equally distinguished study of the later illusion and its merciful dissipation. It is a fascinating and persuasive work, heightened with much compelling drama – for instance, an eyewitness account of the Nuremberg Trial, written from notes made at the time. Not everyone will agree with the authors' interpretations, but no one will complain that the presentation of evidence is anything but clear, thorough and accurate.[32]

In the *Observer*, A.J.P. Taylor, briefly a member of the British Communist Party (of which one of his uncles was a founding member), commended Wheeler-Bennett as a historian of 'considerable distinction', but, in defence of the Soviet Union, he asserted that 'the prime motive of Soviet policy during the war and after it was fear, not domination'.[33] Gordon A. Craig, of Stanford University, wrote in the *Journal of Modern History* that the book was 'a solid and circumstantial account of Allied diplomacy in the Second World War which also provides a thorough description and analysis of the conferences of the Big Three and of the peace treaties that were concluded'.[34] Wheeler-Bennett's former colleague during the war in the Propaganda Warfare Executive, Leonard Miall, now working as controller of overseas and foreign relations at the BBC, was critical of the index and of spelling mistakes.[35]

Inadvertently, Wheeler-Bennett became embroiled in a discussion about the origin of the phrase 'Iron Curtain', generally credited to Winston Churchill during his speech at Fulton, Missouri in 1946. Wheeler-Bennett had said that it actually originated in a newspaper article by Goebbels, who predicted an 'Iron Curtain' descending in Europe in the event of a Russian victory. This elicited correspondence in the *Daily Express* suggesting that it was first used about Russia by Ethel Snowden, wife of the Labour Party's first chancellor of the exchequer, Philip Snowden, when she described her first visit there in 1920. 'We were behind the iron curtain at last,' she was recorded as saying.[36]

Despite much positive comment, *The Semblance of Peace* was Wheeler-Bennett's least popular book. As Nicholls recollected:

> One point of criticism was that we had been too unkind to the Soviet leaders. At the time the book was published there was a controversy raging over some (mainly American) 'revisionist' accounts of the Cold War which laid the blame for East-West tensions on the capitalist West, and in particular on the Truman administration. It was claimed, for example, that after the dropping of the A-bombs on Hiroshima and Nagasaki, the USA deliberately abandoned the policy of friendship and collaboration with the USSR and tried to exclude Soviet influence from Eastern Europe.

According to Nicholls, the authors had deliberately decided to set out their own account of the division of Europe as they saw it, 'rather than engage in detailed polemics against a position we felt to be fundamentally absurd'. The most they were prepared to do was to include a list of the main 'revisionist' works 'so that readers could consult them if they wished'.[37]

One of those who wrote critically was the distinguished historian Michael Howard. 'So far from coming up with anything new, the book so firmly re-states the dogmas of . . . Western light, Soviet darkness – that it might have been written at least fifteen years ago.' Acknowledging that Wheeler-Bennett had written 'as a privileged observer of events', Howard concluded that as a historian he needed more than 'passionate subjectivity in order to pronounce definitive judgements'.[38] So critical was his review, which appeared in the *Sunday Times* under the headline 'Frozen Postures', that he wrote a personal note to Wheeler-Bennett apologising for his candour. Characteristically Wheeler-Bennett replied, thanking him for his 'charming note'. 'I am sorry not to have earned the approval of as old a friend and as eminent an historian as yourself, but equally, of course, I should have been, as you suggest, deeply shocked if you had allowed ties of friendship to inhibit you in expressing disapproval.'[39] As Alan Bullock was later to point out, although they might not have addressed the revisionist argument, 'the authors did not produce an official apologia [of the British and American governments] but a highly critical account, particularly of American policy'.[40] 'Before very long,' Tony Nicholls later commented, 'most of the "revisionist" assertions proved impossible to sustain, and, by the time the Cold War ended, I think I could claim that our interpretation had stood the test of time.'[41]

At the time of publication, Wheeler-Bennett was delighted with the response. In the United States, as he told Nicholls, the book was 'making a slow but not insignificant impression', with the Washington Post describing it as 'massive, tendentious, but significant and impressive'.[42] Averell Harriman had written to say that if the book did not 'checkmate revisionism, the truth has less power than the press comfortably suppose'. George Kennan, the American diplomat, historian and political scientist, renowned for being the 'father of containment', described the book as 'one of the really great works of diplomatic history of this century'. George Backer, Roosevelt's private envoy on several assignments, called it a 'brilliant' piece of work.[43] As Wheeler-Bennett told Avon, he had heard that even President Truman 'had had an approving view of it before being stricken in his last illness'.[44]

In October 1972, Wheeler-Bennett celebrated his seventieth birthday in style, 'splurging' with a large cocktail party in the Great Subscription Room of Brooks's. 'I like the idea of being seventy,' he wrote to Avon who was absent but had sent a congratulatory telegram. 'One can sit back and reminisce and enjoy one's memories and get off all committees!'[45] Harold Macmillan proposed his health and another former prime minister, Sir Alec Douglas-Home, started off the singing of 'Happy Birthday'. There was also a royal guest, Princess Margaret, who had admired Wheeler-Bennett's 'masterly' biography of her father.[46] Rick, Juliet, David and their spouses gave 'Uncle Jack' a portrait drawn by the artist Juliet Pannett, showing him wearing the characteristic carnation in his buttonhole.[47] The directors and staff of Hatchards, where his titles were regularly displayed, gave him a leatherbound book with all their signatures to 'commemorate FIFTY YEARS of his patience with their company'.[48] His own 'staff' – Ethel, Vic, John Prior, the gardener, and other members of the Ruffels family – presented him with an aerial photograph of Garsington. 'Nothing you could have thought of', he wrote, could have given me more pleasure than this beautiful aerial photograph.'[49]

In December, the Wheeler-Bennetts once more departed for North America. Christmas was spent in Charlottesville, where Wheeler-Bennett was 'stricken with 'flu'. For his seminars at the University of Arizona, he had decided to talk to his students about 'a comparison of the evolution of the peace settlements after the two world wars'.[50] He had 'temporarily abandoned' the idea of writing a study of Philip Lothian's ambassadorship in Washington.[51]

'Very agreeable' was the news in the new year that he was to be awarded an Honorary Doctorate of Letters by New York University – James Hester was still the president there and officiated at the ceremony in June. 'In the citation . . . there were two comments which afforded me especial pleasure and gratification,' Wheeler-Bennett wrote. The first of these praised him for having been a 'cultural ambassador from Britain to the United States since the late 1930s'. The second was the concluding comment: 'Here at New York University, where, on four occasions, you have served as Distinguished Visiting Professor of History, your knowledge, your warmth of manner and your appeal as a teacher to both undergraduates and graduate students, have won our admiration and affection as a friend and colleague.'[52] Birmingham University, of which Avon was chancellor, had also bestowed an Honorary Doctorate of Letters on him, which gave him equal satisfaction.[53] 'I have been most happy to accept this honour,' he wrote to Avon from Arizona. 'I know that I owe it entirely to your recommendation, and I am filled with gratitude to you.'[54]

Meanwhile, Wheeler-Bennett was seeking to find a younger man who might take over Avon's biography if the worst befell. He still thought the best candidate was Tony Nicholls. Initially, Nicholls, who opposed the way that Avon, as prime minister, had handled Suez and who was anyway busy with his own research, was reluctant to commit himself. For Nicholls's benefit, Wheeler-Bennett explained why he himself had agreed to write Avon's biography.

First of all, he is a very old friend whom I have known and served for many years. Secondly, it is the story of my life as well as his, in that all the hopes and fears of my generation were centred on him, and through him, of the success of diplomacy and the League of Nations. Young, romantic and idealistic we may have been but Anthony was our man and he epitomized the fulfilment of our dreams. Thirdly, I do honestly regard him as the greatest of British Foreign Secretaries since Palmerston and perhaps since Castlereagh, though equally the worst PM since Spencer Percival or anyway since Liverpool, and the combination of this shining success and abysmal failure fascinates me. There is something of Greek tragedy about the whole thing in that he waited too long to be Prime Minister and then surprised all by his non-fulfilment. There is even a thought, if taken in perspective, that the failure was inherent in the success – rather like Alcibiades![55]

For all these reasons, Wheeler-Bennett said, he would like to write the biography, although he recognised that he might not write a 'good' book. 'I was pro-Suez but horrified at the mutton-headed, ham-fisted way in which it was executed. But he had the genius of statesmanship when dealing with foreign affairs.'[56] Still Nicholls demurred, leaving Wheeler-Bennett to write to Eden informing him that Nicholls was 'a non-starter'. 'He has become very much immersed in research for a major project in relation to modern German history, which will take him some time, and he is also involved in another book covering the period of the Bavarian Revolution of 1918/19, so I fear we must look elsewhere.'[57]

In the summer of 1973, Harold Macmillan was once more planning to stay at Garsington for the Encaenia celebrations, which, on this occasion, included a gaudy at St Antony's to mark the twenty-fifth anniversary of the college's foundation. 'I am so glad that you can go to this because it is an occasion to honour Bill Deakin,' Wheeler-Bennett wrote to him. 'As an original Fellow of St Antony's, I can testify that the College would never have survived its birth pangs had it not been for Bill's patience, ingenuity and initiative.'[58] In July, Wheeler-Bennett went to Birmingham to receive his Honorary Doctorate of Letters in person from Avon. He had sent an advance draft of his acceptance speech to Clarissa, in which he praised Eden as being 'our *preux chevalier*, the champion and defender of our pathetic belief in what proved to be those ephemeral shibboleths of "a war to end war" and "let us make the world safe for democracy". Though he did not succeed, we knew that it was through no fault of his, and he retained our confidence.'[59] She replied, saying that she had 'lapped up all the wonderful things' he had said about her husband but suggesting that he might add 'a bit of a message' to the graduates. 'After all, they know you are a very eminent historian, so would not some comments linking past and present, or some advice on their attitude to the past and present, not be valuable to them?'[60] Wheeler-Bennett agreed to her suggestion but still used the occasion to pay a personal tribute to Avon by explaining to his listeners why he had become a historian.

> So impressed was I by his gallant struggle for sanity in diplomacy, so imbued with the ideal which I felt to be an integral part of those policies which he favoured and pursued, that I felt impelled to chronicle the narrative of that tragic and anguished period of history which began with the blaze of euphoric, if myopic, optimism at the signing of the Kellogg-Briand Pact for the Renunciation of War in 1928, followed closely by the collapse of the Disarmament Conference and of Collective Security, the adoption of the Policy of Appeasement and the Second World War.

Thus, he said, his career as a serious historian had begun, 'born of a desire to place on record the story of what may be called the Eden ethos, together with its failures and triumphs'.[61] After the ceremony, Wheeler-Bennett wrote to Avon: 'It was a wonderful occasion and one which I shall never forget. The moment when you actually gave me my honorary degree greatly touched and moved me. I can only say "thank you very much indeed".'[62] Meanwhile, he was still gathering material for Avon's biography, while Avon was preparing to place his papers in the University of Birmingham library, but 'only on condition that this does not mean that they would be released to the public before you have had a chance to use them'.[63]

In August 1973, Wheeler-Bennett complained of being unwell, stricken again with a recurrence of that 'wretched laryngitis bug which makes me lose my voice every now and then, which is mildly disconcerting, but doubtless beneficial to my otherwise potential listeners'.[64] Once more, he approached Nicholls to see if he would be willing to take over writing Avon's biography in the event of his death, and finally secured his agreement. Suggesting to Avon that Nicholls had been 'too modest' to have his name put down when first approached, he wrote: 'I could not recommend him to you more highly . . . Personally, I should be greatly relieved at the thought of his being in charge of the project in the event of my pre-deceasing you or otherwise succeeding me should I become non compos mentis!'[65]

Avon immediately responded: 'Remote as the contingency happily is, I suppose that you could want some help from Nicholls anyway at some stage in which event it would be a great help and a saving of time to have him booked in.'[66] The next stage was to introduce Nicholls to Avon and this was accomplished in November. Wheeler-Bennett was pleased at the outcome. 'I am truly delighted that you liked Tony so much,' he wrote after their meeting, 'and felt that you could repose confidence in him. I have worked with him now for some twelve years or so and have found him not only an invaluable colleague, but a delightful companion and a man of great intellectual integrity. He is a very careful researcher and has a good facility with words, both orally and in writing.'[67] Avon then confirmed the arrangement with his literary executor, Anthony Head. 'We have been having a little discussion with John Wheeler-Bennett about mortality, i.e. what arrangements should be made against the unhappy eventuality that he could not finish work upon my biography. We have concluded that the best alternative choice would be Anthony Nicholls who was Wheeler-Bennett's co-author in "Semblance of Peace". The two men have worked together now for some twelve years so that continuity should not present any difficulty.'[68]

During his correspondence with Avon about the biography, it had emerged that the US secretary of state, John Foster Dulles, whom Avon had held responsible for the debacle over Suez, may have had a change of heart over his Suez policy in later life. Having ascertained the name of the commanding general at the Walter Reed Army Medical Center, Washington D.C., where Dulles had died in 1959, Avon encouraged Wheeler-Bennett to write to him to ask, 'for the record, whether he [Dulles] spoke to you at all of his thoughts or recollections of the Suez

Crisis in these last days of his life. From the point of view of history it is often of such great importance to know how those who have had a hand in history-making view their own record in the light of approaching death and this has always interested me greatly as a historian.'[69] The officer in question, Major General Leonard Heaton, responded at once in a handwritten letter, saying that he did 'indeed know John Foster Dulles very well during his last years. I recall only one reference of his to your question: "Perhaps I made a mistake at Suez." '[70] Although Heaton's response was not quite the 'triumph' they had hoped for, Wheeler-Bennett considered that it was 'very satisfactory from our point of view . . . [that it was] at least circumstantial if not conclusive evidence that Foster had second thoughts at the end'.[71]

While working on Avon's biography, Wheeler-Bennett had begun writing his own memoirs. Rather than embark on a one-volume account, he chose to compartmentalise his life into separate phases. In the first volume, he intended to describe 'myself when young' and up to the beginning of World War II. Such an approach meant that he could be selective, highlighting the aspects that he wished to draw attention to and omitting others. After narrating his childhood and schooldays, the main focus was his experience in Germany in the interwar years and some of his extraordinary encounters during the Weimar Republic and the early days of National Socialism. He was scathing in his criticism of the Nazi regime. If Hitler was 'black-hearted', he wrote, Goebbels was 'evil personified'. On the other hand, Goering was 'at least a human being. Brutal, ruthless and cruel, he, too, when one talked with him, could exercise his own particular kind of attraction.' Röhm was the 'most malign and dangerous of all'. This was not because of his 'promiscuous' homosexuality, but because for him the war had never ended. 'He dreamed of leading revolutionary armies, fired with the ideals of National Socialism, across a decadent Europe.'[72]

Wheeler-Bennett had agreed to edit *The History Makers* with Frank Pakenham, the earl of Longford, a British politician and social reformer. This was a series of essays on influential individuals who 'presided over and, in many cases, brought about these momentous events of the 20th century'.[73] The subjects ranged from Clemenceau – authored (at Wheeler-Bennett's suggestion) by his friend Lewis Douglas – and Woodrow

Wilson to Mao, Kennedy and President Nasser of Egypt. Wheeler-Bennett himself contributed two chapters, one on Kaiser Wilhelm II, which included material from the essay published in *A Wreath to Clio*. His other contribution was on Eamon de Valera (whose official biography Longford had recently co-authored), based on Wheeler-Bennett's meetings with him when researching *King George VI* and his life of Viscount Waverley. Other contributors included Nicholls, who wrote on the German chancellor Konrad Adenauer, William Shirer on Hitler and A.J.P. Taylor on Lloyd George.

After almost two decades, Otto John was finally allowed to come to England. To tell his side of the story of his 'abduction' to East Germany in 1954, he had written his autobiography, *Zweimal kam ich heim*. The book had been published in English, under the title *Twice through the Lines* in 1972.[74] Henceforward, the two men corresponded almost as though nothing had interrupted their friendship. In the autumn, John wrote excitedly to Wheeler-Bennett of the 'tremendous success' of one of his wife's pupils – the English tenor Peter Pears – when singing the leading part in Benjamin Britten's *Death in Venice* at the Venice Biennale.[75] Wheeler-Bennett replied enthusiastically, saying that it must have given her great satisfaction to be present at the triumph of her 'star pupil'.[76]

In the 1974 New Year Honours, Wheeler-Bennett was awarded the Knight Grand Cross of the Royal Victorian Order (GCVO), the highest rank in that particular order of chivalry, the queen's private order. He was delighted and set about responding to an estimated 250 letters of congratulations, writing from the Arizona Inn, where he was once more installed for the spring semester at the University of Arizona. 'How very kind of you and Clarissa', he wrote to Avon, 'to send me your congratulations on my "G". I am so touched and appreciative and so is Ruth. I must confess to being very pleased and proud.'[77]

He kept in touch with the political climate at home as usual. At the end of 1973, following their earlier strike in 1972, the miners had demanded a pay rise. The Conservative prime minister, Edward Heath, had refused to accede and called a state of emergency, which included a three-day working week to save electricity. In February 1974, a general

election was called. Coincidentally, Wheeler-Bennett's former pupil at
New College Tony Benn, who in the interim had renounced his title
and hyphenated name, was creating news as a politician on the extreme
left of the Labour Party, still led by Harold Wilson.[78] As Patrick Dean,
now retired from the diplomatic service, confided: 'Mr Wilson is getting
rather anxious about the Left Wing, but Mr Benn goes on his own way
regardless.'[79] Despite Wheeler-Bennett's conservative background and
establishment views, when the Conservatives lost to Labour by four seats,
he greeted the result with equanimity. 'What fun and games you have
been having in the UK,' he wrote to Tony Nicholls. 'I prophesied that
neither of the major parties would get an overall majority but I fell down
in thinking that the Tories would be the largest single party.' In Wheeler-
Bennett's opinion, Labour's four-seat margin of victory showed 'that the
electorate are disenchanted with both the Tories and Socialists and don't
trust the Liberals'. So far, he considered that Harold Wilson and the
minority government had done 'really very well, even as regards the
Budget which seems to me to be a pretty fair one'. What pleased him
was that the foreign secretary, James Callaghan, had been working
to improve Anglo-American relations, which Wheeler-Bennett considered had been 'considerably impaired as a result of Ted [Heath]'s
indifference and pre-occupation with the EEC [European Economic
Community]'.[80]

Wheeler-Bennett also enjoyed observing the power play in Washington. After winning a second term of office in 1973, President Richard
Nixon had appointed Henry Kissinger as secretary of state. But Wheeler-
Bennett did not rate him. 'The interesting thing here is how much Henry
Kissinger's image and reputation has shrunk since he became Secretary
of State. While he was a back room boy [as national security adviser,
when he orchestrated the opening up of relations between the United
States and China as well as the policy of détente with the Soviet Union]
one couldn't fault him but apparently he can't stand the lime-light and
has definitely lost his touch or so it seems.'[81] By the time the Wheeler-
Bennetts returned to England in the spring of 1974, the industrial unrest
was over, but Conservatives such as Avon were demoralised. 'The trou-
bles here have indeed fallen thick and fast so that, resist as one will, it

begins to affect one's spirits,' Avon confided in a welcome-home letter in April, 'and it is good to talk with someone who has been through what you and I have known. There are so few of us now.'[82]

Shortly after his return to England, Wheeler-Bennett was informed that he was to receive yet another honorary Doctorate of Letters, this time from the University of Arizona in appreciation 'of your long and illustrious career as a public servant, historian, scholar and teacher'. He declared himself 'overwhelmed', writing to John Schaefer, the president of the university, that his association with the institution 'has been one of the happiest in relation to my colleagues and to my students'. As it happened, the date, 18 May, on which the honorary degree was to be conferred conflicted with a prior engagement. He had already been informed by Martin Charteris, the queen's private secretary (in succession to Adeane, who had retired after twenty years), that his presentation with the insignia of the GCVO would be on the same day. Wheeler-Bennett regretted that he would have to give this priority over any other engagement. 'I am not blessed with the gift of bilocation.'[83] There was also sad news. In March, Lewis Douglas had died just before his eightieth birthday. 'Ruth and I suffered a profound sense of loss for we had loved him.'[84] Wheeler-Bennett's old friend Ham Armstrong had died in April the previous year, aged eighty, having only relinquished the editorship of *Foreign Affairs* in 1972.

Throughout this period, Wheeler-Bennett had retained his 'foothold' in Buckingham Palace as the queen's historical adviser. One bizarre query came from some Americans asking whether Queen Victoria had given Mt Kilimanjaro in Tanzania to Kaiser Wilhelm II as a birthday present. When Wheeler-Bennett put the matter to the librarian at Windsor Castle, the answer came back unsurprisingly that the story was 'apocryphal'.[85]

During that summer, much as he and Ruth guarded their privacy, they agreed to the use of the gardens at Garsington for the filming of a dramatised version of Iris Murdoch's 1962 novel *An Unofficial Rose*. Filming took place on 17 and 18 June; for the privilege of permitting approximately thirty people together with two equipment vehicles, one generator, one minibus, one catering truck, three private cars to 'nestle' in the

far corner of the stable yard, and allowing access and egress for those
vehicles belonging to the house, he was paid £40 per day.[86] As had
become customary, performances of a Shakespeare play were held on the
old grass tennis court in the summer. Once more, in late June, Harold
Macmillan came to stay for the Encaenia celebrations, writing gratefully
to Ruth afterwards: 'You know how much I appreciate your kindness
and without it I could never get through the Oxford engagements . . . many
thanks for all that you do for me.'[87]

In October 1974, Wheeler-Bennett's first volume of memoirs
was published – a slim two hundred pages. Perhaps inspired by Bruce
Lockhart's *Friends, Foes and Foreigners*, published in 1957, he chose to call
his book *Knaves, Fools and Heroes: In Europe between the Wars*. He dedicated it 'with my love' to his sister, Irene, now in her eightieth year.
For the cover, Osbert Lancaster had drawn a cartoon depicting Wheeler-
Bennett, with a carnation in his buttonhole, entering his office to be
greeted by an array of photographs on his desk of all the celebrated
people he had ever interviewed, including the Kaiser and Trotsky. As
usual, Wheeler-Bennett dispatched complimentary copies of his book to
his wide circle of friends. In this instance, top of his list was the royal
family. On behalf of the queen, immediate thanks came from Martin
Charteris, who informed Wheeler-Bennett that Her Majesty had only
had time so far to admire Osbert Lancaster's jacket, but was looking
forward to finding out more about the historical adviser to her archives.[88]
The queen mother responded graciously with a handwritten letter, delivered by hand to Wheeler-Bennett at Brooks's, commenting on aspects
of the book which rang true for her.

> The first chapter, (myself when young) reminded me vividly of the
> first war years, and nostalgic memories kept nudging my mind waiting
> to be remembered after so many years – Like you, 'I called you Baby
> Doll a year ago' (diddle dee diddle dee diddle dee) always brings a
> lump to my throat. . . . Chapter 2 is absolutely fascinating – All the
> things that one has forgotten, and yet are so terribly important for
> students of history . . . it is all brilliant, and thank you a thousand times,
> not only for writing all these fascinating & personal accounts of your
> meetings & talks with all those interesting & dubious characters (&

good ones), but also for your charming thought in giving me the book
– I am, yours ever Elizabeth R.[89]

Friends and family likewise enthused. 'I am enjoying every sentence in
it, separately and together,' wrote Isaiah Berlin. 'The brilliance and the
warm and the sparkling and scintillating quality of your mind and style
are on every page.'[90] Wheeler-Bennett's nephews were laudatory. David
described the book as 'a skilful and entertaining account'.[91] Rick praised
his 'remarkable' uncle. 'You write with sympathy and real wit. It is a
delight to follow your recollections of meetings and your uniqueness in
your surroundings both physical and temporary. You make history live,
your word pictures both thrill and chill.'[92] Rick's wife, Joan, was anxious
for more answers, particularly in relation to the accident that brought on
his stammer:

> You force the reader to guess at the mainsprings of the human being
> at the heart of it all. I do beg you to reveal more of yourself in future!
> . . . the cryptic reference to the traumatic blow that crowned as it were
> a stellar prep school career, haunted this reader – and presumably the
> writer – for the next many years. But we are left to wonder whether
> the succession of friendships in high places that were forged in the
> ensuing years went unhampered by the impediment and shyness that
> overtook the hapless lad. (Did it make you try even harder?).[93]

Newspaper reviewers were mostly enthusiastic. 'I have seldom been
more enchanted, I would have added "surprised" if the book had not
come from one in whom niceness is never surprising,' wrote Sir Colin
Coote, a former deputy editor and managing editor of the *Daily Telegraph*. 'How right you are about Brest-Litovsk! It was the supreme
example of German folly.'[94] John Raymond of the *Sunday Times* called
Wheeler-Bennett's recollections 'vivid, exciting and highly personal
annals'.[95] Donald Cameron Watt in the *Times Literary Supplement* was
more critical. Although he commended Wheeler-Bennett's 'gentleman-
scholar' attributes, it was, he said, 'perhaps, not so easy to defend Sir
John against charges of putting anecdotage ahead of analysis or of not
always having checked the accuracy of his recollections against the

archives now so readily available to historians'. The example that Watt gave was Wheeler-Bennett's suggestion that his Brest-Litovsk book had prompted Harold Caccia, at that time private secretary to the foreign secretary, Lord Halifax, to propose a change in policy towards the Soviet Union. In Watt's opinion, the change of policy had already been effected by Sir William Seeds, who had arrived in Moscow as British ambassador on 21 January 1939. 'It is, for example, not altogether easy to reconcile his account,' Watt wrote, 'with Sir William Seeds's account of his mission, with the gestures undoubtedly made towards the Soviet Union at the end of February.'[96] Max Beloff, Fellow of All Souls, noted that the publishers 'have not done you too well on the proof reading side and there are some errors in names in particular'.[97]

The most significant factual error was Wheeler-Bennett's claim that he did not return to Germany following the Night of the Long Knives in 1934 until after the end of the war, when he visited Germany twice in 1935, as noted in his appointment diaries. Although unrelated, this claim became caught up with the continuing debate about Adam von Trott zu Solz. When questioned in 1971 by the retired US air force officer Professor Henry Malone about his friendship with Trott, Wheeler-Bennett had insisted that he could not have met him in 1935, as Malone was wishing to confirm, because he did not go back to Germany after 1934 until after the war.[98] Reviewing his movements, it is not clear why Wheeler-Bennett was so adamant in offering this denial. His visits in 1935 were made en route to other destinations for his research. As an acknowledged 'German expert' and self-described 'political animal', he would have been expected to spend a few days in the country to obtain new information. Germany was preparing to host the Olympic Games in 1936 and despite the increasing brutality of the Nazi regime, not all of Germany had been affected by recent events. As Shiela Grant Duff noted after their mutual visit in September 1935, Stintenburg was 'a place apart, huge and ancient and still untouched by the Nazis'.[99]

One simple explanation is that, as someone who was constantly on the move, writing nearly forty years later, he had genuinely forgotten and had failed to consult his diaries to check. But this does not quite tally with his comment to Shiela Grant Duff in 1969, when he told her that his memory of his presence in Germany in the mid-1930s was blocked on 'psychological grounds'.[100] Another explanation is that he had been commissioned to undertake clandestine activities and thus had never mentioned returning to Germany in 1935 at the time, with the result that, in later life, his silence had become a habit; yet none of those he met during these visits, including the British ambassador, Eric Phipps, appears to have been sworn to secrecy.[101] Or perhaps, renowned as he was for his brilliant storytelling, did he think the account of his departure from Germany before the Night of the Long Knives too enthralling to moderate by revealing that he had been able to return in 1935? Unfortunately, his refusal to admit that he was in Germany in 1935, thereby refuting meeting Trott at that time, compounded the feeling among Trott enthusiasts that Wheeler-Bennett the historian, who placed such value on accuracy, was not being entirely transparent in his own recollections.[102]

At the time of publication, Wheeler-Bennett's readers were mostly unaware of such discrepancies. Malone's dissertation, which questioned his version of events, was not published until after Wheeler-Bennett's death. One reader – Keith Sutton from Port Elizabeth in South Africa – quibbled with Wheeler-Bennett's claim that Trotsky's grip on his assassin was so strong 'that it literally had to be broken after death', on the grounds that it had apparently taken Trotsky twenty-six hours to die. 'Twenty-six hours seems a long time to be in the grip of a dying man,' he had written. Wheeler-Bennett's response was imaginative: 'it may well be that it was necessary to break Trotsky's grip while he was unconscious rather than dead'. Moreover, he said that his information came from the Mexican authorities.[103] But the praise far outweighed the criticism and his next task was to finish the second volume. At the end of October, he described himself as 'unwell'. Although Wheeler-Bennett did not realise it, his next year was to be his last.

As usual the Wheeler-Bennetts planned to spend Christmas in Charlottesville and spring in Arizona. 'We are off next week (D[eo].V[olonte]),' Wheeler-Bennett wrote enthusiastically to Avon, 'and I must confess that I shall not be entirely sorry to leave this poor, distracted country for a short while and also to get into a warmer climate.'[104] Before leaving, Wheeler-Bennett had deposited the manuscript for volume two of his memoirs with his publisher. The title was *Special Relationships: America at Peace and War*. For those unfamiliar with his American heritage, he provided a detailed account of his family's origins, elucidating in the process his love of the South and special interest in the American Civil War. He went on to describe his 'more mature years', including his war service in the United States and Britain. The present volume, he wrote, 'begins with the Age of Affluence in America before the Great Depression of the thirties; it concludes on the threshold of the Nuclear Age'.[105] Appropriately, he dedicated it to his American wife: 'Ruth, with my devoted love, John'. Once again he thanked numerous friends for either reading the manuscript or checking facts. Among them were Isaiah Berlin, Harold Macmillan, Aubrey and Constance Morgan, and Tony Nicholls. Like the first volume, his narrative demonstrated his unusual ability to secure, with apparent ease, important introductions, critical for his research and for his greater understanding of the world. But, while Wheeler-Bennett continued to draw interesting pen portraits of those he had met, he said nothing about any intelligence work that many friends assumed he undertook when working with Bruce Lockhart for the Political Warfare Executive.[106]

While the book was in production, the Wheeler-Bennetts once more took up residence at the Arizona Inn. An important engagement was the Foundation Luncheon at the University of Arizona, at which Wheeler-Bennett thanked the president of the university for the honorary degree bestowed on him the previous summer. 'Please let me say how appreciative I am of the fact that I can now speak, not of "*Your* Great University", but of "*Our* Great University".'[107] However, Wheeler-Bennett's voice was troubling him. He had fallen sick with what was diagnosed as laryngitis and bronchitis 'caused (believe it or not) by a too dry climate,' he told Nicholls. 'I've had difficulty with my voice and . . . am rapidly becoming the world's most persistent and penetrating whisperer! But it is rather a bore and is bad for one's morale.' He was delighted to hear that Bill Deakin had been knighted in the 1975 New Year Honours: 'Much too long delayed, of course, but better late than never.'[108]

Shortly before returning to England in the spring, Wheeler-Bennett gave the first Fitzpatrick Lecture, at Woodberry Forest School, Virginia. Taking the theme 'On Being a Historian', it became his valedictory on his life's work: 'For one who comes from a quite respectable background, I seem to have associated with some of the most destructive and disreputable characters of modern times. The reason for this is that I am of that type of historian who likes to touch hands with history no matter how soiled those hands may be.' His conclusion embodied principles that he hoped had guided him throughout his 'fairly long life':

> We seek by our writings and teaching to mould the thinking of others along lines which we ourselves believe to be truthful and accurate. It is our duty therefore to apply ourselves with zeal and discipline and great diligence to the meticulous precision of our research and to the integrity of our teaching and writing. You will find, as I have, that it is not always given us to know the complete truth on any one of our subjects, but this must not exonerate us or discourage us from making every human effort within our power to discover the truth as best within us lies.

Perhaps acknowledging that there were times when he had been less than accurate, he continued: 'We must never forget that by our mistakes – and we are all prone to make them – we may cause others to stumble and be led astray.' His final comment raised questions he never answered: 'The failures are to be found within our own consciences and we have to live with them.'[109]

Back home at Garsington in the summer, Wheeler-Bennett was finishing his third volume of memoirs, *Friends, Enemies and Sovereigns*, describing his postwar life after his marriage to Ruth and covering the period from his forty-third birthday in 1945 to his seventieth in 1972. In addition to relating how he came to write King George VI's biography, he described his experiences at Nuremberg and as British editor-in-chief of the captured German archives. Since Tony Nicholls had worked on the revised edition of *The Nemesis of Power*, he sent him the relevant chapter of his memoirs to read: 'I hope you won't find this too much of a bore.'[110] Yet again, he acknowledged a long list of friends for their support: Harold Macmillan, Martin Charteris (who, as an amateur sculptor, was also engaged in making Wheeler-Bennett's bust in bronze),[111] Patrick Dean, Bill Deakin and, once more, Aubrey and Constance Morgan. He also included Otto John.

A lump on his neck had been found to be malignant and so to his usual routine were now added visits to St Thomas's Hospital. 'I go up to London to-morrow for further tests and treatment,' he wrote to Avon in mid-July, 'but I only anticipate being up there for a day . . . They are still searching for a satisfactory formula, which will tackle the major problem and, at the same time, keep the blood count on a proper balance. Science is wonderfully exact!'[112] Although in pain, he put on a brave face. 'I continue to make good progress, but it is slow and rather erratic. Some days I feel quite well and others like hell,' he told Nicholls.[113]

During the summer, Wheeler-Bennett had agreed to write a brief introduction for a young historian, Nicholas Reynolds, whose dissertation for his D.Phil. at Oxford on Colonel General Ludwig Beck, former chief of the German General Staff and one of the conspirators of the 20 July 1944 plot, was now being published as a book: *Treason Was No Crime*. Since Tony Nicholls was Reynolds's supervisor, Wheeler-Bennett sent him a draft 'for any criticism which you might make'.[114]

In the introduction, Wheeler-Bennett once more – and for the last time – broached the controversial subject of the German opposition, pinpointing the essential driving force for all those who dared to challenge Hitler. 'In his wholly admirable book,' he wrote, 'Nicholas Reynolds makes it abundantly clear that, whatever the varied motives for Beck's code of conduct may have been, the all transcendent element was a deep-rooted love of Germany and an essential sense of patriotism.' Ranking Beck (together with Hans von Seeckt) as 'among the military geniuses in the annals of the Germany army' and as the man who became the 'keystone of the arch of the Conspiracy, the figure, universally respected by conservatives, democrats and socialists alike, to whom nearly all of them looked to lead the new Germany which should follow the assassination of Hitler and the elimination of the Nazi regime', Wheeler-Bennett put Beck's earlier support for Hitler in context: 'Beck saw Hitler not as the radical tyrant which he became but as the conservative nationalist which he pretended to be.' True to his belief that the German army could not be considered blameless, he pursued a familiar theme: 'Beck was not alone in being beguiled by those cajoleries to which many Germans of the Right assented under the incredible belief that when they had got what they wanted from Hitler they could dispose of him in their own time.'

Having written hundreds of thousands of words on the subject himself, in this final statement of his views on Germany Wheeler-Bennett was passing on the baton of his life's work to future historians. 'This tragic chronicle of human frailties and human courage, of self-delusion and the gradual, irresistible, compelling revelation of evil is told by Nicholas Reynolds with a wealth of fascinating detail and of high drama.'[115]

Wheeler-Bennett had now started on a fourth volume of memoirs. This was to include his experiences and impressions of China and Japan in the 1920s, some recollections of Malvern, the founding of St Antony's and, as the working title suggested, 'Things I Have Left Out'.[116] He was intending to include an essay on his 'longstanding' devotion to the works of Anthony Hope. Recalling an amusing story about the filming of *The Prisoner of Zenda* in 1937 told to him by the actor Raymond Massey (who had played the part of Black Michael) while they were both staying at the Arizona Inn, he wrote to Massey. He also wrote to David Niven and Douglas Fairbanks, who had played the roles of Fritz von Tarlenheim and Rupert of Hentzau respectively, wanting confirmation. The story he wished to verify was whether the 'dignity' of the coronation procession to the Cathedral of Strelsau was 'wrecked during rehearsal by the passionate attachment' that was conceived by Black Michael's charger for the mare ridden by King Rudolph/Rudolph Rassendyll.[117]

That June he was not well enough to welcome Macmillan to Garsington for his usual visit for the Encaenia celebrations. Instead, as Macmillan advised, he was 'sitting quietly' in his garden in glorious sunshine,[118] although the 'inundation' of Ruth's nephew and nieces and great-nephews and great-nieces all demanded 'both one's time and one's strength'.[119] Wheeler-Bennett celebrated his seventy-third birthday on 13

October. He did not acknowledge publicly how ill he was, but the cancer had taken hold. 'I've had rather a horrid summer, having been in and out of hospitals most of the time with a rather acute case of anaemia', he wrote on his birthday to Donald Lindsay, who had retired as head-master of Malvern College in 1971, 'which necessitated a series of blood transfusions, pills and injections. I have been recuperating here most of the summer and am just beginning to get into circulation again now that I am filled with other people's blood!'[120] 'He looked like a new man,' commented Ethel when he returned to Garsington after a spell in hospital. Even so, he realised that his strength was ebbing.

At the end of October, Wheeler-Bennett wrote to Avon: 'My Dear Anthony, It is with the greatest regret that I write to tell you that it is the opinion of my doctors, with which I must most reluctantly concur, that I have neither the energy nor the stamina required to shoulder alone the physical demands which would be made of me as your biographer.' He proposed a formal collaboration with Tony Nicholls: 'We work together well as a team, as witness our collaboration in "the Semblance of Peace", and our views, though separated by nearly a generation, have enough in common to be mutually stimulating.'[121] Avon, who had also been unwell, replied at once: 'I think your decision is an eminently wise one.'[122] Wheeler-Bennett seemed greatly relieved, genuinely thinking that he would still be able to help write the biography: 'I am confident that, between us, Tony Nicholls and I can give you satisfaction. I know how gratified he will be to learn of the confidence which you repose in him.'[123]

When *Special Relationships* was published on 13 November (with Juliet Pannett's portrait of Wheeler-Bennett on the cover), a celebratory lunch was held at the Dorchester. Such occasions were now a struggle. Wheeler-Bennett stayed at Brooks's while Ruth stayed either at Brown's or at the University Women's Club in South Audley Street. On this occasion, Ruth was concerned about leaving her husband to make his own way to his room, so she entreated the taxi driver to assist him.[124] 'I have been rather under the weather,' Wheeler-Bennett wrote again to Lindsay in mid-November, in a communication intended to clarify some of his recollections about Malvern. Describing the effect of the drugs and painkillers that he had to take as slowing him up 'somewhat in my cerebral processes', he said that he was still hoping to be well enough to make his annual visit to Arizona in January.[125]

Meanwhile, the visits to St Thomas's in London continued. On 24 November, Wheeler-Bennett told Avon that he was going into hospital 'for a few days tomorrow, for some tests, but hope to be back by the weekend'.[126] By early December, he was forced to admit that he was dying. Telling Ruth and Irene that he wanted so much to live because there was still so much to do, he came to accept the future with stoicism. 'I look upon death not as an enemy but as a friend,' he told his sister and his wife.[127] With meticulous detail, he planned his funeral, expressing a desire for a memorial service to be held in London.

John Wheeler Wheeler-Bennett died on 9 December 1975 aged seventy-three. Ruth was at his bedside. His wish that his coffin would be carried on a hay cart drawn by four black horses from central London was considered impracticable. The funeral service was held at Garsington Church. Juliet's husband, Oliver Fiennes, now dean of Lincoln, conducted the service, offering this prayer: 'Eternal Father, we thank thee for all those good lives which, touching our own, have increased our knowledge of thee, and here do we especially give thanks for the life of John, our brother, for his gallantry and resilience in illness, his skill and power in scholarship, his friendship for all of us, and many others of many nations, his gentleness in all things.' The queen mother sent a wreath of flowers.

The memorial service was held on Wednesday, 21 January 1976 at noon. Instead of St James's Piccadilly, as Wheeler-Bennett had requested, the service was held in St Margaret's, Westminster in order to accommodate a greater number of people. The queen was represented by her private secretary, Sir Martin Charteris, and the queen mother by hers, Sir Martin Gilliat. Princess Margaret attended in person. The gathering of over five hundred people included the archbishop of Canterbury and three former prime ministers: Harold Macmillan, who read the lesson, Sir Alec Douglas-Home, now Lord Home of Hirsel, and Edward Heath. The earl of Avon was represented by his son, Viscount Eden.

Friends and colleagues from the various phases of Wheeler-Bennett's life attended: the warden of St Antony's, Raymond Carr, and his wife;

the former warden, Sir William Deakin, and his wife; Donald Lindsay and his wife; as well as the new headmaster of Malvern, Martin Rogers; and many fellow historians, including Isaiah Berlin, Hugh Trevor-Roper, Michael Howard and the young historian whose work Wheeler-Bennett had praised, Alistair Horne, as well as Wheeler-Bennett's friend and collaborator Tony Nicholls. Patrick Dean gave the memorial address: Ruth's 'great loss', he said, was felt 'so deeply and by so many people both here and overseas. For surely there was no-one who knew, and was known so well, not only by almost every one of the leading figures of the present century, but by a host of others in every walk of life.' At Wheeler-Bennett's request, the Lord Chamberlain's Office provided a trumpeter from the Blues and Royals who played Purcell's *Trumpet Tune and Air*.[128]

Friends, Enemies and Sovereigns was published posthumously in 1976. Indicative of the achievement Wheeler-Bennett rated so highly – his status as royal biographer – he had chosen to dedicate 'with humble duty and by gracious permission' his third volume of memoirs to Her Majesty Queen Elizabeth the Queen Mother. This gesture was, as the *Virginia Quarterly Review* suggested, 'typical of this loyal son of England and friend of the United States'.[129] The foreword was written by Harold Macmillan, who acknowledged Wheeler-Bennett's ability to charm 'not only Kings, Presidents and Prime Ministers (and so won their confidence and their confidences) but also the girl behind the counter and the man behind the bar . . . Club porters were as glad to see him as ambassadors and statesmen. When he came into our publishing office he brought with him an atmosphere of kindliness which was felt by all with whom he had to deal.'[130] Macmillan could not help but regret that, entertaining as the three volumes of John Wheeler-Bennett's memoirs were, 'they are too discreet. I would have liked to see on record some of the extraordinary tales with which he could fascinate us.' He acknowledged that Wheeler-Bennett probably judged rightly in deciding what material to include. 'There is a gulf properly fixed between the frivolity of the spoken word and the decorum of the printed text.'[131] In a later tribute, Alan Bullock suggested that 'those who know the author only from his books will, alas, have little idea of the qualities of a personality which will be remembered and loved as long as any of his friends survive'.[132] Irene described her brother as 'a very remarkable person, as well as the dearest, warmest, funniest and most lovable . . . beloved by the highest and the lowliest'.[133]

In faraway Tucson, Arizona, five years after John Wheeler-Bennett's death, a library alcove was dedicated to his memory at the Arizona Inn. Patrick Dean read a tribute which the queen mother had sent for the occasion, in which she remembered 'with gratitude and admiration his skill and dedication as an author and his brilliance as an historian. He combined too, those rare qualities of kindness, wisdom and under-standing, and all who knew him fell under the spell of his personality.'[134] Harold Macmillan was unable to be present but he contributed a set of all the books Wheeler-Bennett had written and his firm had published over a forty-year period since *Hindenburg* in 1936. Aubrey Morgan, introduced by Lewis Douglas's widow, Peggy, recalled Wheeler-Bennett's 'Aladdin's cave' of anecdotes: 'Talking to John was one of the most exciting things in my life.'[135]

John Wheeler-Bennett was never a household name but, in the mid-twentieth century, he knew virtually everyone who was. 'The list of those present at his Memorial Service,' observed his nephew Rick, 'is testimony to the circles in which he operated from Royalty down-wards.'[136] Since he had not needed to earn his living, from an early age he had been free to choose to become a historian. 'The rewards of our calling are rich and golden,' he had said shortly before his death.[137] Despite intermittent poor health, hard work and the discipline of his research accorded him high status as a member of the intellectual establishment. 'He was brilliantly intelligent, an enterprising journalist, a courageous adventurer, a gifted writer, one of the best-informed people in Europe, well-connected and wonderful company,' wrote historian Sir Michael Howard.[138] As Harold Macmillan acknowledged, Wheeler-Bennett may have been 'an amateur for he was self taught; but, in accu-racy and imagination, and also power of writing, he ranked very high among the professionals'.[139] A generation after his death, the headmaster of Malvern College, Hugh Carson, instituted the Wheeler-Bennett

Society for sixth-form students.[140] The Sir John Wheeler-Bennett History Prize, established at Malvern College from a gift in his will, is awarded annually.[141]

As a young man, Wheeler-Bennett virtually created the new early twentieth-century academic discipline of 'international relations'. He pioneered the study of contemporary history – as historian and observer – when, as Alan Bullock remarked, 'an interest in the history of one's own time was looked at askance in the universities, [and] anything after 1914 [was] referred to scornfully as "politics"'. Well before projects in recording oral history became fashionable, he showed what could be done 'in the way of collecting and using oral evidence'.[142] 'I am a historian who delights in the touch of original material,' he said in his memoirs, 'even as a devout medieval worshipper might derive inspiration from contact with pieces of the True Cross.'[143]

To this day, the Information Service he founded remains an essential department of Chatham House. During World War II, Wheeler-Bennett's role as a civil servant, working in 'political warfare', was notable. Publicising the war in Europe when the United States was neutral, he frequently addressed hostile audiences of die-hard isolationists, anxious to keep aloof from another global conflict. As he later confided to Tony Nicholls, he felt that the Americans to whom he was speaking in 1940 'regarded me as somebody on a sinking ship. They were sympathetic, but it was as if they were waving me goodbye.'[144]

Wheeler-Bennett could be described as an exponent of the 'great man school of history' espoused by the nineteenth-century historian Thomas Carlyle. Winston Churchill, prime minister throughout most of World War II, epitomised that sort of 'great man', enabling Wheeler-Bennett to endorse the view that 'the steadfastness and the irrefragable determination of one man' was necessary for the survival of Britain at that time. 'The Man and the Hour had met.'[145] Given his focus on personalities, he was less interested in documenting social and economic trends, which, in the post-war world, were beginning to attract a new generation of historians. Having grown up with the fear of the German menace, he found it hard to conceive of a peaceful Europe once the pusillanimity of the League of Nations had been exposed. He was right that the world would continue to be turbulent but initially wrong about the cause. The fear expressed in the epilogue of *The Nemesis of Power* that there might be another revival of German militarism did not materialise. As noted by Richard Overy in his introduction to the republished *Nemesis of Power* in 2005, postwar Germany 'soon shed the legacy of German military imperialism and it has never revived'.[146] As Wheeler-Bennett came to recognise, the Soviet Union, which he thought would have a pivotal role to play in Europe, became the new enemy. His early fear of German aggrandisement meant that, like many others, he remained fiercely critical of the prewar appeasers, expressing no sympathy for those Britons, who, alarmed by the continuing Bolshevist threat and mindful of the horrors of World War I, did not want to go to war with Germany in early 1938. A man of his times, Wheeler-Bennett's views were shared by many, including his long-term friend Anthony Eden, the first Earl of Avon, and Winston Churchill.

Wheeler-Bennett's books provide a valuable insight into contemporary thought. *Munich: A Prologue to Tragedy* remains an important study of a much debated aspect of Britain's foreign policy. Wheeler-Bennett's biography of Hindenburg sets the scene for the dénouement between the German Establishment and the rising power of National Socialism, as does *The Nemesis of Power*. For its originality of subject matter and depth of research alone, *Brest-Litovsk: The Forgotten Peace* is an enduring work for scholars wishing to understand the motives behind the diplomatic moves made by the Soviet Union and Germany at the end of World War I. As Wheeler-Bennett wrote, 'the very prominent place which the Treaty of Brest-Litovsk holds in world history [is] a fact which has hitherto been generally unrealized'.[147] A high point was his authorship of *King George VI*, which, more than fifty years after publication, was a principal source for the award-winning film, book and play, *The King's Speech*.

During Wheeler-Bennett's lifetime, the 'age of security' into which he was born passed into one of 'euphoric fantasy', when his early dreams of world peace 'proved to be but a chimera'. The Cold War between the United States and the Soviet Union meant that towards the end of his life he felt that the world had reached 'the nadir of irony in that our main guarantee of world peace lies in our knowledge that even the victor is vanquished in a nuclear war'.[148] 'It is, of course, a sad comment on the standard of our contemporary morals and ethics, that we accept with relief and gratitude a state of affairs which permits "conventional" warfare almost as a humanitarian activity, even when it assumes the bitter ferocity and recurrence of the Middle East struggle,' he wrote in the conclusion to *The Semblance of Peace.* 'There is, indeed, a strange impression of our having struck a bargain with Fate, but the nightmare which rides our dreams, as we teeter on the razor-edge of uncertainty, is – how long will this bargain hold?'[149] All of Wheeler-Bennett's adult life was spent with the world at war, recovering from war or fearful of the outbreak of war; even so, he was prepared to adapt, to take what gave him most pleasure and share it with his wide and varied circle of friends. 'Amid this gloom,' he wrote in the epilogue to his third published volume of memoirs, 'there are compensations and one clings to them.'[150]

Notes

Abbreviations

BIS	British Information Services
BL	British Library
BLI	British Library of Information
BSC	British Security Coordination
COI	Coordinator of Information
EAC	European Advisory Commission
HM	Harold Macmillan
IB	Isaiah Berlin
JEWB	Joan Ellen Wheeler-Bennett
JWWB	John Wheeler Wheeler-Bennett
OSS	Office of Strategic Services
OWI	Office of War Information
PWE	Political Warfare Executive
RA	Royal Archives
RBL	Robert Bruce Lockhart
RCWB	Richard (Rick) Clement Wheeler-Bennett
RIIA	Royal Institute of International Affairs
RRWB	Ruth Risher Wheeler-Bennett
SANT	St Antony's College
SHAEF	Supreme Headquarters Allied Expeditionary Force
SOE	Special Operations Executive
TNA	The National Archives
UB	University of Birmingham
WB	Wheeler-Bennett

Chapter 1 The Undertow of History

1 JWWB, *Friends, Enemies and Sovereigns*, p. 170.
2 John Wheeler Wheeler-Bennett, CBE, JP (1840–1926). Director of Metropolitan
Railway and other companies, high sheriff of Kent 1923–24. In his memoirs JWWB
says that his father was sixty-four when he was born but this was evidently an error
for sixty-two. Rumours that JWWB was the illegitimate son of Kaiser Wilhelm II
appear unfounded. The only time a liaison could have taken place was when the
Kaiser visited Britain for Queen Victoria's funeral in early 1901 and for Edward

VII's coronation in June 1902. It seems that this rumour only surfaced when JWWB went to Germany and his physical resemblance to one of the sons of the Kaiser was noted. See Chapter 4 below.

3 Clement Wheeler-Bennett, MRCS, LRCP 1913, MA, MB, BCh 1914, RNVR (1887/8–1957).

4 (Constance) Irene Heaton *née* Wheeler-Bennett (1895–1980). Quotations are from her unpublished memoirs, private collection.

5 Sir Joseph Flavelle (1858–1939). Born in Ontario, he made his fortune in the meat-packing business. Chairman of the Imperial Munitions Board, he was given a baronetcy in 1917. JWWB to Richard Garnett, 14 March 1973, D11, WB papers, SANT, Oxford. Canada Packers is now part of Maple Leaf Foods.

6 JWWB presented this report, which he described as 'very favourable', to Chatham House. After the 1917 revolution, Prince Dolgorouki led various monarchist conspiracies against the Soviets; returning to Russia in disguise, he was caught and executed in 1927.

7 JWWB, 'China Going P & O's', D13, WB papers, SANT, Oxford.

8 Irene Heaton, unpublished memoirs, private collection. Margaret Kennedy (1896–1967), novelist. Her first published novel was *The Ladies of Lyndon* in 1923; her most famous novel was *The Constant Nymph* (1924). Irene says she was 15 when she wrote *The Season*, but if JWWB was five at the time she would have been only 11.

9 *Ibid.*

10 JWWB, *Knaves, Fools and Heroes*, p. 5. He means Napoleon's Imperial Guard.

11 *Ibid.*, p. 173.

12 JWWB, *Special Relationships*, p. 13. Mary Johnston (1870–1936). *The Long Roll* had just been published in 1911.

13 JWWB, *Knaves, Fools and Heroes*, p. 3.

14 *Ibid.*, p. 7. The Balkan Wars (1912–13); present in the field of battle were all the sovereigns of the Allied states, Ferdinand of Bulgaria, Peter of Serbia, George of Greece and Nicholas of Montenegro.

15 JWWB, *Knaves, Fools and Heroes*, p. 5.

16 JWWB, 'China Going P & O's', D13, WB papers, SANT, Oxford.

17 JWWB, *Knaves, Fools and Heroes*, p. 6. Emperor Kaiser Wilhelm II of Germany (1859–1941); Emperor Franz Joseph I of Austria (1830–1916).

18 *Ibid.*, p. 7. He says 'for a twelve year-old' but he was not 12 until October 1914.

19 Archduke Francis Ferdinand of Austria (1863–1914).

20 JWWB, *Knaves, Fools and Heroes*, p. 7.

21 The five signatories pledged to recognise and guarantee the independence and integrity of Belgium. It has since been debated whether the obligation 'to protect' required them to go to war. British propaganda at the time emphasised that they were indeed bound to do so once Germany had violated Belgium's neutrality. France's alliance with Russia was agreed in 1894. The Entente Cordiale was signed between Britain and France in 1904. After the signing of the Anglo-Russian Entente in 1907, the alliance was called the Triple Entente.

22 JWWB, *Knaves, Fools and Heroes*, p. 9.

23 *Ibid.*

24 The Alexandra Hotel was demolished in the 1950s to make room for Agriculture House, demolished in 1993.

25 JEWB to the author, 20 Aug. 2007.

26 JWWB, *Knaves, Fools and Heroes*, p. 10.

27 *Ibid.*, p. 12.

28 See Errol Holmes, *Flannelled Foolishness*.

29 Blumenau, *History of Malvern College*, p. 87.

30 JWWB, *Knaves, Fools and Heroes*, p. 5. Alexandre Dumas, père (1803–70), French novelist and playwright, whose most famous books were the Musketeer series and

The Count of Monte Cristo; George Henty (1832–1902), author of over eighty historical novels, for example, *With Clive in India* (1884), *Redskin and Cowboy* (1896), *With Buller in Natal* (1901); Nicholas Breton (1545–1626), poet and satirist.

31 JWWB, *Knaves, Fools and Heroes*, p. 12. Edward Gibbon (1737–94). William Coxe (1747–1828), *Memoirs of the House of Austria* (1807).

32 JWWB, 'Groves of Academe', D17, WB papers, SANT, Oxford.

33 Blumenau, *History of Malvern College*, p. 89.

34 F.S. Preston, quoted in Blumenau, *History of Malvern College*, p. 89.

35 JWWB, 'Groves of Academe', D17, WB papers, SANT, Oxford.

36 *Ibid.*

37 Out of 2,833 Malvernians who served in World War I, 457 were killed and over 1,100 were mentioned in despatches or otherwise honoured. Blumenau, *History of Malvern College*, p. 90.

38 JWWB, 'Groves of Academe', D17, WB papers, SANT, Oxford.

39 Blumenau, *History of Malvern College*, p. 89.

40 JWWB, 'Groves of Academe', D17, WB papers, SANT, Oxford.

41 *The Malvernian*, 145, Dec. 1917, pp. 584–85, 598.

42 JWWB, 'Groves of Academe', D17, WB papers, SANT, Oxford.

43 JWWB, *Special Relationships*, p. 16. Woodrow Wilson (1856–1924), president of the United States 1913–21.

44 The Discussion Society is now called the Wheeler-Bennett Society. The first meeting was in March 1920.

45 JWWB also says that another senior boy, Dikran Kouyoumdjian (1895–1956), later Michael Arlen, was his fagmaster, but he had left Malvern in the summer of 1913 and JWWB did not arrive until the summer of 1917. Rajendra Sinhji (1899–1964). See JWWB, *Knaves, Fools and Heroes*, p. 136.

46 George Courtauld (d. 1980).

47 Errol Holmes (1905–60).

48 JWWB, 'Groves of Academe', D17, WB papers, SANT, Oxford. He later became chairman of Malvern College's Governing Council.

49 Irene Heaton, unpublished memoirs, private collection; JWWB, *Knaves, Fools and Heroes*, p. 13.

50 JWWB passport, loaned to the author by the Very Reverend Oliver Twistelton-Wykeham-Fiennes.

51 Irene Heaton, unpublished memoirs, private collection; JWWB makes no reference to this first voyage either in his unpublished memoirs or in *Knaves, Fools and Heroes*. The trip he made on behalf of the League of Nations was in 1922–23, by which time he was twenty and not eighteen – see next chapter.

Chapter 2 Youthful Illusions

1 JWWB, *Friends, Enemies and Sovereigns*, p. 170.

2 *The Beacon*, Dec. 1921.

3 RBL, *Giants Cast Long Shadows*, p. 60.

4 JWWB, 'Reminiscences', D16, WB papers, SANT, Oxford.

5 *Ibid.* William Ewart Gladstone Murray, DFC, MC (1893–1970), publicity director, League of Nations 1921, 1922, publicity manager, Radio Communications Co. Ltd 1922, 1924, director of public relations, BBC, Information and Broadcasting 1924–35. He is not to be confused with the Australian professor Gilbert Murray (1866–1957), founder of the League of Nations Union, whose daughter married Arnold Toynbee.

6 JWWB, 'Reminiscences', D16, WB papers, SANT, Oxford. Vernon Bartlett (1894–1983).

7 Dr Trevor Braby Heaton (1886–1972), Dr Lee's Reader in Anatomy and Student of Christ Church.

8 C.E. Carrington, rev. Mary Bone, *Chatham House: Its History and Inhabitants*, p. 47. The BIIA had developed out of a meeting in Paris in May 1919 convened by Lionel Curtis (1872–1955), who argued that the various delegations at the Paris Peace Conference had greatly benefited from being able to exchange information not only between diplomats but also between experts and that it was important to continue this kind of exchange of views. The joining fee was one guinea, annual subscription two guineas.

9 Inaugural meeting, 5 July 1920, quoted in *Rules and Lists of Members 1920–25*, p. 11, RIIA Archives.

10 BIIA certificate of candidate for election, 4/WHEE, RIIA Archives.

11 JWWB, *Knaves, Fools and Heroes*, p. 14. Major General Sir Neill Malcolm, KCB, DSO (1869–1953), British Military Mission, Berlin, 1919–21, GOC Malaya 1921–24. The other three were Anthony Eden, Robert Vansittart and Lewis Namier.

12 JWWB, 'Reminiscences', D16, WB papers, SANT, Oxford. The Chanak affair contributed to the downfall of Lloyd George.

13 JWWB, *Special Relationships*, p. 51.

14 *Ibid.*, p. 19.

15 *Ibid.*, p. 20. After the end of the Civil War, the men who had served in the Confederacy were disenfranchised; to maintain their standard of living, it became common for aristocratic families to take in lodgers. Johnston left JWWB part of her Civil War library.

16 Hamilton Fish Armstrong (1893–1973), managing editor 1922–28, editor, *Foreign Affairs* 1928–72. Author of *Hitler's Reich: The First Phase*, Macmillan, New York, 1933. JWWB writes of him as a much older man, but he was only in his early thirties when they met.

17 JWWB, *Special Relationships*, p. 24. Alfred Emanuel Smith (1873–1944). He secured the Democratic nomination in 1928 but lost the election to Herbert Hoover. William Gibbs McAdoo (1863–1941). His second wife was the daughter of Woodrow Wilson. John W. Davis (1873–1955).

18 *Ibid.*, pp. 25–26. In most US states, prohibition lasted from 1922 to 1933. A 'speakeasy' was a place that was used for selling and drinking alcohol. The term comes from a patron's manner of ordering alcohol without raising suspicion – a bartender would tell a patron to be quiet and 'speak easy'.

19 Memorandum on the Information Department, 4/WHEE, RIIA Archives.

20 Memorandum on the Policy of the Information Service on International Affairs (ISIA), 4/WHEE, RIIA Archives.

21 Lt General Sir George Macdonogh, GBE, KCB, KCMG (1865–1942).

22 Oliver Sylvain Baliol Brett, 3rd viscount Esher, FRIBA, FRSL, MBE, GBE (1881–1963).

23 Arnold J. Toynbee (1889–1975), British historian, whose greatest work was a twelve-volume analysis of the rise and fall of civilisations, *A Study of History* (1934–61).

24 Baffy (Blanche) Balfour (1890–1948) was married to Edgar Dugdale. She was the daughter of Arthur Balfour's brother, Eustace, and a committed Zionist.

25 Sir Lewis Bernstein Namier (1888–1960), born in the Ukraine, educated at Balliol College, Oxford. Until his death in 1960, Namier read and offered feedback on everything JWWB wrote. See Alan Bullock, 'John Wheeler Wheeler-Bennett 1902–1975', *Proceedings of the British Academy*, LXV, 1979, p. 801.

26 JWWB, *Knaves, Fools and Heroes*, pp. 13–14. Anthony Eden, 1st Earl Avon, KG, MC, PC (1897–1977).

27 *Ibid.*, p. 16.

28 The phrase 'Weimar Republic' is an invention of historians. At the time, the new republic called itself the 'Deutsches Reich', translated as the 'German Reich' rather than 'Empire'.

29 JWWB, *Knaves, Fools and Heroes*, p. 20. Gustav Stresemann (1878–1929), chancellor and foreign minister 1923, minister of foreign affairs 1923–29.

30 Edgar Vincent, 1st Viscount D'Abernon, GCB, GCMG, PC, FRS (1857–1941). British ambassador in Germany 1920–25 and credited with being the 'godfather' of Locarno. See also Lord Vansittart, *The Mist Procession*, p. 276. JWWB must have met Max Hoffman during this visit (October 1925 – the date in his passport) since Hoffman died in July 1927.

31 The Locarno Treaties were seven agreements negotiated by the foreign ministers of Britain, Germany, France, Belgium, Italy, Poland and Czechoslovakia. The chief negotiators were Austen Chamberlain, Britain's secretary of state for foreign affairs (1924–29), his French counterpart, Aristide Briand, and Gustav Stresemann, the German foreign minister. The terms included an undertaking between Germany, France and Belgium not to attack each other, with Britain and Italy acting as guarantors. Germany also accepted her western frontiers; while not accepting her eastern frontier, the government promised not to try to change it by force.

32 Neill Malcolm, introduction to *The Reduction of Armaments* (1925).

33 Alan Bullock, 'John Wheeler Wheeler-Bennett 1902–1975', *Proceedings of the British Academy*, LXV, 1979, p. 801.

34 JWWB, *Knaves, Fools and Heroes*, p. 17.

35 Alan Bullock, 'John Wheeler Wheeler-Bennett 1902–1975', *Proceedings of the British Academy*, LXV, 1979, p. 800.

36 C.E. Carrington, rev. Mary Bone, *Chatham House, Its History and Inhabitants*, pp. 47–55. The BIIA moved to St James's Square in 1923. Lord Meston (1885–1943).

37 Macdonogh to Lord Meston, 5 April 1927, 4/WHEE, RIIA Archives. It is not clear why he wrote to Meston when Malcolm was chairman.

38 JWWB, *Knaves, Fools and Heroes*, p. 17. Harold Nicolson and Isaiah Berlin also had rooms at Albany.

39 Alan Bullock, 'John Wheeler Wheeler-Bennett 1902–1975', *Proceedings of the British Academy*, LXV, 1979, p. 802.

40 John Buchan, 1st Baron Tweedsmuir, PC, GCMG, GCVO, CH (1875–1940); during World War I he worked for the British War Propaganda Bureau and as a correspondent for *The Times*. He wrote over a hundred novels, short stories and non-fiction books, the most enduring being *The Thirty-Nine Steps* (1915). He later became governor-general of Canada (1935–40), dying in office.

41 Sir Anthony Hope Hawkins (1863–1933); Baroness Emmuska Orczy (1865–1947).

42 'Merchant's Large Fortune', *The Times*, 29 July 1926. His age was erroneously stated as seventy but he was 85 or 86. Duties of £200,000 still left a considerable sum (for example, when Arthur Balfour died his estate was estimated at £76,433).

Chapter 3 International Traveller

1 Unless otherwise indicated, all JWWB quotations in this chapter are from his unpublished memoir, 'The Gorgeous East', D13/D15/D16 WB papers, SANT, Oxford. JWWB wrote these recollections when he was in his early seventies, i.e. over forty years after the events described.

2 Sun Yat-sen (1866–1925), Chiang Kai-shek (1887–1975). The latter, JWWB said, was 'ultimately fated to die some half a century later as the ruler of the miniscule state of Taiwan'.

3 Princess Beatrice (1857–1944), Prince Henry of Battenberg (1858–96); Beatrice's niece Victoria married Prince Louis of Battenberg, the parents of Earl Mountbatten (1900–79).

4 Suzanne Lenglen (1899–1938). She won thirty-one Grand Slam titles, including the Ladies' Singles at Wimbledon six times. She withdrew from Wimbledon and amateur tennis in 1926, reportedly because she had unknowingly kept Queen Mary waiting

in the Royal Box for her appearance in a preliminary match. Informed of her error, which some attendees considered an insult to the monarchy, she fainted. King Gustav V of Sweden (1858–1950). He was the last Swedish king to intervene directly in politics.

5 The Mamelukes were descended from freed Turkish slaves. Mameluke sultans ruled Egypt until it was conquered by the Ottomans in 1517; Mehmet (also written Muhammad) Ali (1769–1849), Governor of Egypt from 1805 until 1848, founded a dynasty that ruled Egypt until 1953.

6 1st Baron Lloyd of Dolobran, PC, GCSI, GCIE, DSO (1879–1941).

7 King Fuad I of Egypt (1868–1936).

8 Lady Alexandra 'Baba' Curzon (1904–95), Captain Edward Dudley ('Fruity') Metcalfe, MVO, MC (1887–1957). They later became neighbours and friends with JWWB in Oxford. They were divorced in 1955.

9 Ferdinand I, tsar of Bulgaria (1861–1948). He abdicated in favour of his son in 1918.

10 James Henry Breasted (1865–1935). JWWB calls him Charles but that was the name of his son who wrote his father's biography. Sir Alan Gardiner (1879–1963), Howard Carter (1874–1939).

11 Henri Cosme (1885–1952), counsellor, 1927–29, and later ambassador 1938–44 at the French Embassy, Peking. Raymond Poincaré (1860–1934), French prime minister 1912–13, 1922–24, 1926–29, and president, 1913–20.

12 The Washington Naval Treaty of 1922 was the cornerstone of naval disarmament between the world's largest naval powers, the USA, Britain, France, Italy and Japan, and was designed to maintain the status quo in the Pacific. The combined British and American foreign concessions in Shanghai, known as the Shanghai International Settlement, were administered by the Shanghai Municipal Council, staffed by individuals of all nationalities, including Britons, Americans, New Zealanders, Australians, Danes and Japanese. Chinese members were not permitted to join the council until 1928.

13 The Bund (from the Urdu word *band* meaning embankment) is a stretch of embanked riverfront in Shanghai which was part of the International Settlement.

14 Rodney Gilbert (1889–1968), author of *The Unequal Treaties: China and the Foreigner* (1929) and *What's Wrong with China*, 1926.

15 Report on visit from 10 May to 1 June 1927 from Hon. Sec. to the committee of management, D2, WB papers, SANT, Oxford. No record remains of his report for the consul-general although it is likely that he used much of the same information in his report to the Committee of Management. In the latter document JWWB says that he went under armed escort to the divisional headquarters to see the commissioner for foreign affairs, Mr Quo Tai-chi (who later served as ambassador in London and Washington). 'The Commissioner was in Nanking conferring with Chiang Kai-shek but I had a long and interesting conversation with his deputy and his Director of Publicity, Mr Kwok. They seem confident that the Nanking government has come to stay and that the Hankow government has ceased to exist.' The account of JWWB's meeting with Chiang Kai-shek comes from his unpublished memoirs, D13/15/16, WB papers, SANT, Oxford.

16 Report on visit from 10 May to 1 June 1927 from Hon. Sec. to the committee of management, D2, WB papers, SANT, Oxford.

17 Sir Miles Lampson, later 1st Baron Lord Killearn, GCMG, CB, MVO, PC (1880–1964), British minister to China 1926–33, later high commissioner (then ambassador) to Egypt and the Sudan 1934 ('36)–46.

18 John Marquand (1893–1960). Mr Moto was a Japanese spy.

19 Report on visit from 10 May to 1 June 1927 from Hon. Sec. to the Committee of Management, D2, WB papers, SANT, Oxford.

20 *Ibid.*
21 *Ibid.*
22 The first military aviators to complete the journey at the end of June 1927 were Albert A. Hegenberger and Lester J. Maitland in the *Bird of Paradise*. The prize for the 'Dole Air Race' was awarded to two civilian aviators in August.
23 Chester H. Rowell (1867–1948). He was editor of the *Fresno Republican* newspaper (founded by his uncle) 1898–1920; he was editor of the *San Francisco Chronicle* 1932–35. Report on Leave Abroad from Hon. Sec. to the committee of management, Lt General Sir George Macdonogh, Chairman, Aug.–Sep. 1927, C3, WB papers, SANT, Oxford.
24 Georgy Chicherin (1872–1936), commissar for foreign affairs 1918–30 (in succession to Trotsky). The USA did not recognise the USSR until 1933 although economic ties remained. In 1917, Woodrow Wilson had broken off relations following the October Revolution due to non-payment of debts and seizure of American property in Russia. JWWB did not elaborate on the conditions.
25 Salmon Oliver Levinson (1865–1941). In his memoirs JWWB calls him Charles.
26 JWWB, Report on Leave Abroad from Hon. Sec. to the committee of management, Lt General Sir George Macdonogh, Chairman, Aug.–Sep. 1927, C3, WB papers, SANT, Oxford.
27 Senator William Borah (1865–1940), prominent Republican Senator and attorney, also noted for his isolationist views and oratorical skills.
28 JWWB, Report on Leave Abroad from Hon. Sec. to the committee of management, Lt General Sir George Macdonogh, Chairman, Aug.–Sep. 1927, C3, WB papers, SANT, Oxford.
29 *The Nation*, quoted on dust jacket.
30 Tony Venison, 'Enigma with an Italian Manner, Gardens of Garsington Manor, Oxfordshire', *Country Life*, 18 March 1982.
31 David Heaton, 'Garsington Manor 1928–1982', unpublished memoir, 1994, private collection.
32 JWWB, 'Renunciation of War', letter to the editor of *The Times*, 26 June, 1928, p. 12.
33 JWWB, *Knaves, Fools and Heroes*, pp. 164–65. The Kellogg-Briand Pact or Pact of Paris was nullified by the 1931 Japanese invasion of Manchuria, the 1935 Italian invasion of Ethiopia and the German invasion of Poland in 1939. However, as a multilateral treaty, it remains part of the body of international law and is the legal basis for the notion of a crime against peace.
34 *Ibid.*, p. 166.
35 *Ibid.*, p. 158.
36 Ralph Wigram, CMG (1890–1936). Churchill described him as 'a great unsung hero'.
37 Bertrand de Jouvenel (1903–87) was one of a number of Frenchmen promising moral and financial support to the recently established Institut pour L'étude du Fascisme. Geneviève Tabouis (1892–1985) escaped from Bordeaux in 1940. She began her career by writing articles about the League of Nations.
38 Hon. Sec. Report to Lt General Sir George Macdonogh on Activities from 26 Aug. to 6 Oct. 1928, C3, WB papers, SANT, Oxford.
39 JWWB, *Knaves, Fools and Heroes*, pp. 116–17.
40 *Ibid.* Wheeler-Bennett's 'four great ladies' were 1. Princess Stéphanie of Belgium, crown princess of Austria (1864–1945); 2. Archduchess Elisabeth Marie of Austria (1883–1963) whose father, Crown Prince Rudolf of Austria, was found dead after a suicide pact with his mistress, Baroness Mary Vetsera at the Imperial hunting lodge at Mayerling when Marie was five; 3. Katharina Schratt (1853–1940); 4. Frau Sacher.

41 *Ibid.*, p. 119. Frau Sacher died in 1930.

42 The Hon. Harold Nicolson, KCVO, CMG (1886–1968). He had arrived in Berlin in October 1927, having been demoted as counsellor in Tehran and sent to Berlin as chargé d'affaires, where he was later reinstated as counsellor. He resigned this position in September 1929 and went to write for the *Evening Standard*, later becoming Labour MP for West Leicester 1935–45. JWWB says he was chargé d'affaires when he first met him. See *Knaves, Fools and Heroes*, pp. 20, 23.

43 General Hans von Seeckt (1866–1936); in his memoirs, JWWB says he also asked to see General Max Hoffmann (1869–1927): see *Knaves, Fools and Heroes*, p. 23. But, as noted, Hoffmann had died in July 1927 and Nicolson did not arrive in Berlin until October 1927. General von Seeckt had been forced to resign in 1926 after permitting Kaiser Wilhelm's eldest grandson, Prince Friedrich-Wilhelm, to attend army manoeuvres in the uniform of the old Imperial First Foot Guards without prior government approval. The description is so detailed that the meeting must have taken place at some point although JWWB does not mention it in his report to Lt General Sir George Macdonogh. Nicolson does not mention JWWB in his unedited diaries for the years 1927 to 1929. See Nicolson Diaries, Balliol College, Oxford.

44 JWWB, 'Men of Tragic Destiny: Ludendorff and Gröner', *A Wreath to Clio*, p. 141.

45 JWWB, *Knaves, Fools and Heroes*, pp. 26–27.

46 JWWB, Hon. Sec. Report to Lt General Sir George Macdonogh on Activities from 26 Aug. to 6 Oct. 1928, C3, WB papers, SANT, Oxford.

47 Further report by Hon. Sec. to Lt General Sir George Macdonogh, C3, WB papers, SANT, Oxford.

48 Philip Henry Kerr, 11th marquess of Lothian, KT, CH, PC (1882–1940); later British ambassador to the United States, 1939–40.

49 *Documents on International Affairs*, RIIA, Oxford University Press, 1928–34.

50 A thousand miles of track already linked Moscow and Cheliabinsk in the Urals; from there, Witte's railway pioneers began in 1891 to construct a track across Siberia to Vladivostok, which ranked as one of the world's greatest engineering feats. After the 1895 Sino-Japanese War, with French assistance, Russia gave China a large loan; following the 1896 Treaty of Friendship, China allowed the Russians to construct a railway, later known as the Chinese Eastern Railway, through the north of Manchuria, linking up with the Trans-Siberian Railway; it was completed in 1904.

51 Thomas Creevy (1768–1838). John Wilson Croker (1780–1857) was famous for introducing the word 'conservative' in 1830. Charles Greville (1794–1865); his brother Henry (1801–72) also kept a diary.

52 Sir Hugh Clifford, GCMG, GBE (1866–1941), Governor of Straits Settlements, high commissioner in Malaya, 1927–30.

53 Dwight Davis (1879–1945), American politician and tennis player. Manuel L. Quezon (1878–1944), second president of the Philippines, first president of the Commonwealth of the Philippines. Emilio Aguinaldo was regarded as the first president; however, he was not recognised as such by the United States. Sergio Osmena (1878–1961).

54 Emilio Aguinaldo (1869–1964), first president of the Philippines 1899–1901. In return for his life he was obliged to recognise the sovereignty of the United States over the Philippines. See JWWB, Report 16 April to 2 May 1929, C3, WB papers, SANT, Oxford.

55 *Ibid.*

56 Sir Robert Ho-tung (1862–1956). Jardine, Matheson & Co., founded by William Jardine and James Matheson in 1832, made early profits through opium, but withdrew from the trade in 1870.

57 Manchuria was invaded by the Japanese in 1931, Peking in 1937. This was the last time JWWB met Powell. During World War II when the Japanese took over the Settlement, he was arrested and died in the notorious Ward Road gaol in Shanghai, known as the 'Alcatraz of the Orient'.

58 See also JWWB, *Knaves, Fools and Heroes*. Colonel Max Bauer (1875–1929) was the only person to be infected with smallpox in the region, hence the suspicion that his infection might have been deliberate.

59 Wang Cheng-T'ing is not to be confused with the defecting Nationalist leader Wang Ching-Wei, who headed the Japanese puppet government in Nanking during World War II.

60 Prime minister Osachi Hamaguchi (1870–1931).

61 Emperor Hirohito (1901–89), 124th emperor of Japan. His Japanese name was Emperor Showa (meaning the era of Enlightened Peace). Regent of Japan Dec. 1921, emperor 1926. In 1921, he had travelled to Europe, the first Japanese crown prince to do so.

62 T'ang dynasty (seventh to tenth centuries AD). During the T'ang dynasty the number of actual horses in China grew to 700,000. Anthony Nicholls recollected seeing this horse at Garsington Manor in the 1960s; Nicholls to the author, 2006.

63 Leon Trotsky (1879–1940). The book JWWB refers to must be Trotsky's *The History of the Russian Revolution to Brest-Litovsk*, published by the British Socialist Party in 1919. The three-volume *History of the Russian Revolution* was not published until 1932.

64 JWWB, *Knaves, Fools and Heroes*, p. 15.

65 Joseph Stalin (1878–1953), general secretary of the Communist Party of the Soviet Union's Central Committee 1922–53.

66 When JWWB returned to Moscow in 1935, Trotsky's participation in the Revolution had been expunged from the official record.

67 John Reed (1887–1920). In his memoirs, JWWB says that only Reed's heart is buried there. See JWWB, D16, WB papers, SANT, Oxford.

68 Paul Scheffer (1883–1963) was accused of being a Nazi spy involved with Soviet grain sabotage. Walter Duranty (1884–1957), British journalist and Moscow correspondent of the *New York Times*. His award of the 1932 Pulitzer Prize remains controversial due to his reporting of the 1933 Ukrainian famine.

69 Rt Hon. Sir Horace Rumbold, 9th Bt, PC, GCB, KCMG, KCVO (1869–1941), British ambassador in Germany 1928–33.

70 Richard von Kühlmann (1873–1948), German secretary of state for foreign affairs 1917–18.

71 Otto Meissner (1880–1953) was head of the Office of the Reich President from 1929 to 1937. After 1937, his role in the Nazi regime was a minor one. Adolf Hitler (1889–1945) became a German citizen in 1932.

72 JWWB, 'Thirty Years of American-Filipino Relations, 1899–1929', *Journal of the RIIA*, 8 Sept. 1929, pp. 503–21.

73 See JWWB Diary 1969, D1, WB papers, SANT, Oxford.

74 Egon Erwin Kisch (1885–1948). Both he and Namier were active Zionists.

75 Sir Robert (Hamilton) Bruce Lockhart (1887–1970), diplomat, banker, editor, author; Political Intelligence Department, Foreign Office 1939–40; British representative with provisional Czechoslovak government, London 1940–41; deputy under-secretary of state, FO and director-general, PWE, 1941–45. See RBL, *Giants Cast Long Shadows*, pp. 58–70 and RBL, *Diaries* I and II.

76 RIIA Reports 1926–31, pp. 25–26, RIIA Archives.

77 Ivison Macadam, OBE, secretary, RIIA to JWWB, 23 June 1930, 4/WHEE, RIIA Archives.

78 Clause 15, Schedule of Bye-laws. 'Any member contributing a sum of not less than £1,000 to the Institute . . . shall be deemed to be and be recorded as a Founder and

as such shall be entitled to all the privileges of membership during his life and shall be exempt from payment of any subscription.' It appears that JWWB continued to pay an annual membership fee.

79 JWWB, Report to Chatham House, circulated Oct. 1930, C3, WB papers, SANT, Oxford.
80 JWWB, *Knaves, Fools and Heroes*, p. 17.

Chapter 4 The Tragedy of Weimar

1 JWWB, *Knaves, Fools and Heroes*, p. 35.
2 *Ibid.*, pp. 32–33.
3 Eric D. Weitz, *Weimar Germany*, p. 121.
4 JWWB, *Knaves, Fools and Heroes*, p. 33.
5 *Ibid.*, p. 35. Hermann Müller (1876–1931), chancellor 1920, 1928–30. As foreign minister, he had been one of the signatories of the Treaty of Versailles.
6 Gustav Stresemann (1878–1929) had also been chancellor and foreign minister in 1923. He was co-winner of the Nobel Peace Prize in 1926 and became foreign minister under Müller in 1928. Wilhelm Gröner (1867–1939), minister of defence 1928–32. See JWWB's sympathetic portrait in 'Men of Tragic Destiny: Ludendorff and Gröner', *A Wreath to Clio*, pp. 133–66.
7 JWWB, *Knaves, Fools and Heroes*, pp. 34 and 36. Franz von Papen (1879–1969), member of the Catholic Centre Party, chancellor of Germany 1932. Kurt von Schleicher (1882–1934), chancellor 1932–33.
8 General (later Field Marshal) Walter von Reichenau (1884–1942). He died of a heart attack.
9 JWWB, *Knaves, Fools and Heroes*, p. 31.
10 *Ibid.*, p. 34. Hjalmar Schacht (1877–1970). He did not join the Nazi Party but helped raise money for it and was among the 'war criminals' tried at Nuremberg.
11 *Ibid.*, p. 35. Ernst Torgler (1893–1963) later worked for the Nazi Propaganda Ministry. Carl von Ossietzky (1889–1938) was arrested at the end of February 1933. JWWB and Knickerbocker went to visit him in the Papenburg concentration camp; in May 1936, suffering from tuberculosis, he was transferred to hospital where he remained in custody until his death.
12 *Ibid.*, p. 38. Heinrich Brüning (1885–1970), chancellor 1930–32.
13 *Ibid.*, p. 39.
14 Norman Ebbutt (1894–1968) was expelled from Germany in 1937.
15 D'Arcy Gillie wrote for the *Manchester Guardian* (not the *Daily Telegraph* as JWWB states), Fredrick Voigt (1892–1957), correspondent of the *Manchester Guardian* in Berlin, 1920–33. He moved to Paris and was back in London by 1934. With his journalist wife, Margaret Goldsmith, he collaborated on a biography of Hindenburg in 1930. Hugh Carleton Greene (1910–87). He was the brother of Graham Greene. He did not start freelance journalism until 1933, becoming *Daily Telegraph* correspondent in February 1934.
16 Hubert Renfro Knickerbocker (1898–1949) published six books in German and wrote columns in two major German newspapers, the *Vossische Zeitung* and the *Berliner Tageblatt*. He circulated in the highest German political, social and cultural circles. After the Nazi takeover in 1933, he was deported and reported on Germany from outside the country. JWWB wrote the introduction for his book *Will War Come to Europe?* (1934) He died in a plane crash over India: 'His untimely death was an irreplaceable loss both to his many friends and to the world of international journalism where his integrity and ability were deeply respected.' JWWB, *Knaves, Fools and Heroes*, p. 18.

17 Edgar Mowrer (1892–1977) won the 1933 Pulitzer Prize for his reporting on the rise of Hitler. In 1932, he and JWWB worked together on a book, 'Germany Turns the Clock Back' – 'the author of it is not so much I as Mr Wheeler-Bennett himself': Mowrer to Miss Dunk, 23 July 1932. But they had difficulty in finding a publisher. D2, WB papers, SANT, Oxford. JWWB also says William Shirer (1904–93), author of *The Rise and Fall of the Third Reich* (1960), was in Berlin but he did not arrive until September 1934, leaving Germany in 1940; Frederick (not William, as JWWB writes) T. Birchall won the 1934 Pulitzer Prize for unbiased reporting from Germany. Elizabeth Wiskemann (1899–1971) arrived in Berlin in 1930; she was arrested and expelled by the Gestapo in 1936. The Taverne was a popular restaurant.
18 JWWB, *Knaves, Fools and Heroes*, p. 41.
19 *Ibid.*, p. 15. Sir Robert (later Lord) Vansittart GCB, GCMG, PC, MVO (1881–1957). No documents remain among JWWB's papers of what he reported to the Foreign Office. During this time he was often back in London and it is possible his reports were verbal. As his diaries indicate, he frequently met Neill Malcolm.
20 JWWB, 'The End of the Weimar Republic', *Foreign Affairs*, Jan. 1972, p. 358.
21 See JWWB, *Information on the Reparation Settlement, Being the Background and History of the Young and the Hague Agreements 1929–30*, in collaboration with Hugh Latimer (a colleague and contributor to the *Bulletin*).
22 In his posthumously published memoirs, Brüning claims that he deliberately pursued inflationary policies and allowed the economic crisis in Germany to force the Western Allies to abolish reparations. As a friend, JWWB took a more sympathetic view of Brüning's actions. See Heinrich Brüning, *Memorien*, and Nicholls, *Weimar and the Rise of Hitler*, p. 150.
23 JWWB and Latimer, *Information on the Reparation Settlement*: Sir Charles Addis (1861–1945), former London manager of the Hong Kong and Shanghai Banking Corporation and member of the British Delegation on the Committee of Experts for Reparations in Paris, wrote the Foreword. 'The authors have set out clearly and comprehensively the tangled story of Reparations . . . the general reader who seeks to understand the tortuous course of the Reparation controversy could not do better than turn to this soberly compiled, well-documented record,' noted the *Times Literary Supplement*.
24 JWWB, *Knaves, Fools and Heroes*, p. 43. See Nicholls, *The Weimar Republic and the Rise of Hitler*, p. 108.
25 JWWB to Ivison Macadam, secretary, Feb. 1931, 4/WHEE, RIIA Archives.
26 JWWB to chairman of Information Committee, RIIA, Luxor, 6 March, 1931, 4/WHEE, RIIA Archives.
27 JWWB to Neill Malcolm, 30 April 1931, C3, WB papers, SANT, Oxford.
28 JWWB, *Knaves, Fools and Heroes*, p. 43. Ernst Röhm (1887–1934).
29 *Ibid.*, Frederic Sackett (1868–1941), US ambassador to Germany 1930–33. Konstantin von Neurath (1873–1956), German ambassador to Britain 1930–32, minister of foreign affairs 1932–38.
30 Hans Luther (1879–1962), chancellor 1925–26, president of the Reichsbank 1930–33.
31 JWWB, *Knaves, Fools and Heroes*, p. 47.
32 Pierre Laval (1883–1945), prime minister of France 1931–32, 1935–36, 1942–44.
33 JWWB, *Special Relationships*, p. 39. Sir Willmott Lewis (1877–1950) first went to China in 1899 to cover the Boxer Rebellion, and became Washington correspondent for *The Times* in 1920.
34 Neill Malcolm, Introduction, *Disarmament and Security*.
35 JWWB, *Disarmament and Security*, p. 355. He dedicated the book to his friend Carlton Elliott Früchtnicht. The name Elliott appears frequently in his diaries but it is not clear who he was.

296 to pp. 68–73

NOTES to pp. 68–73

36 JWWB to HE General Sir David Campbell, KCB, ADC Palace Malta, 14 April 1932, C3, WB papers, SANT, Oxford.

37 JWWB to Macadam, 26 April 1932, writing on RIIA notepaper, 4/WHEE, RIIA Archives.

38 Sir Evelyn Wrench (1882–1966), editor of *The Spectator* 1925–32; also founder of the English-Speaking Union in 1918.

39 Count Albrecht von Bernstorff (1890–1945). From 1923 to 1933 he was in London at the German Embassy. Implicated in the 20 July 1944 plot, he was imprisoned and killed in April 1945.

40 Eric D. Weitz, *Weimar Germany*, p. 122.

41 JWWB, *Knaves, Fools and Heroes*, p. 48.

42 *Ibid.*, p. 49.

43 André Tardieu (1882–1945), prime minister of France 1930 (twice), 1932. He lost this election and was succeeded by Edouard Herriot. See 'The German Claim to Equality of Rights in Armaments', H[ugh]. L[atimer]., *Bulletin of International News*, RIIA, 9:6, 15 Sept. 1992, for contemporary discussion.

44 See Nicholls, *Weimar and the Rise of Hitler*, p. 157 for an explanation of Brüning's loss of political support in Germany.

45 JWWB, *Knaves, Fools and Heroes*, pp. 51 and 54.

46 JWWB to H.R. Knickerbocker, 31 May 1932, WB papers, SANT, Oxford.

47 JWWB, *Knaves, Fools and Heroes*, p. 53. There were also personal reasons for Brüning's dismissal, especially in relation to his proposed enquiry into improper grants of Eastern Aid (*Osthilfe*) to Colonel Oskar von Hindenburg's landowning friends. See Patch, *Heinrich Brüning and the Weimar Republic*, p. 291 and RA/PS/GV/C/P/586/228. Memorandum by Mr Breen, press officer, British Embassy, Berlin, October 1935.

48 JWWB, 'The German Political Situation', address to RIIA, 20 June 1932, *International Affairs*, 11:4, July 1932, p. 460.

49 Edgar Mowrer to JWWB, 1 July 1932, D2, WB papers, SANT, Oxford.

50 JWWB, *Knaves, Fools and Heroes*, p. 56. The dinner was hosted by Gottfried Treviranus, a loyal member of Brüning's cabinet.

51 JWWB to Macadam, July 1932, 4/WHEE, RIIA Archives.

52 JWWB to Dr Erwin Planck, Staatssecretär, 25 Sept. 1932, WB papers, SANT, Oxford.

53 JWWB, *Knaves, Fools and Heroes*, p. 56.

54 JWWB to H.R. Knickerbocker, 2 Dec. 1932, D2, WB papers, SANT, Oxford.

55 Sir Victor Mallett, GCMG (1893–1969), British diplomat and author. He was a godson of Queen Victoria.

56 RBL, *Diaries* I, 17 Nov. 1932, p. 236.

57 JWWB, *The Wreck of Reparations: Being the Political Background of the Lausanne Agreement 1932*, Walter Layton, 1st Baron Layton, CH, CBE (1884–1966).

58 *The Times*, 24 Sept. 1929.

59 *The Times*, 10 April 1933. The Anglo-German Association was dissolved in 1935. As a Jew, the marquess of Reading (1860–1935) resigned in April 1933 in protest at Hitler's policy of persecuting the Jews.

60 See JWWB, 'Men of Tragic Destiny: Ludendorff and Gröner', *A Wreath to Clio*, for JWWB's evaluation.

61 JWWB, 'The End of the Weimar Republic', *Foreign Affairs*, Jan. 1972, p. 369.

62 JWWB, *Knaves, Fools and Heroes*, p. 57.

63 In the November 1932 elections the Nazis won 196 seats compared with 230 in July and 288 in March 1933. See Nicholls, *Weimar and the Rise of Hitler*, p. 198.

64 JWWB, 'The W-B Armaments Plan, 1.10.32', B13, WB papers, SANT, Oxford.

65 JWWB, *Knaves, Fools and Heroes*, p. 64. JWWB to Papen, 19 Oct. 1932, D2, WB papers, SANT, Oxford.

66 JWWB, letter to *The Times*, 'Disarmament. The German Claim to Equality', 15 Nov. 1932.

67 JWWB to Brüning, 15 Nov. 1932, D2, WB papers, SANT, Oxford.

68 JWWB, *Knaves, Fools and Heroes*, p. 64. And see 'The W-B Armaments Plan, 1.10.32', B13, WB papers, SANT, Oxford.

69 Sir John Simon, later 1st Viscount Simon, GCSI, GCVO, OBE, PC (1873–1954).

70 H.R. Knickerbocker to JWWB, 11 Jan. 1933, D2, WB papers, SANT, Oxford. Note: Knickerbocker dated his letter 1932 but JWWB responds on 13 January 1933, thanking for his letter of the 11th. A common error at the start of a new year!

71 Hermann Goering (1893–1946), William Frick (1877–1946).

72 JWWB, *Knaves, Fools and Heroes*, p. 69. In his memoirs JWWB describes watching the procession but he had an operation in England on 20 January and his diary does not indicate that he visited Germany before Knickerbocker wrote to him on 16 February: see Diary 1933, D1, WB papers, SANT, Oxford.

73 H.R. Knickerbocker to JWWB, 16 Feb. 1932, D2, WB papers, SANT, Oxford.

74 In *Knaves, Fools and Heroes*, p. 70, JWWB says he was dining with Knickerbocker on the night of the Reichstag fire (27 February), but his diary indicates that he did not arrive in Germany until 28 February: see Diary 1933, D1, WB papers, SANT, Oxford.

75 JWWB, 'The New Regime in Germany', address to RIIA, 21 March 1933, *International Affairs*, 12:3, May 1933, pp. 313–26, also in B31, WB papers, SANT, Oxford.

76 Joseph Goebbels (1897–1945), Rudolf Hess (1894–1987).

77 JWWB, *Knaves, Fools and Heroes*, p. 72.

78 Ninety-four Social Democrats voted against; twenty-six were either under arrest or in hiding. Although, even after the Reichstag fire, the Communists were allowed to stand in the Reichstag elections, they were arrested and so the Social Democrats were the only ones with a vote against the Nazis.

79 JWWB, *Knaves, Fools and Heroes*, p. 75.

80 Hindenburg, quoted in JWWB, *Hindenburg*, p. 448.

81 *Ibid.*, p. 448. Hitler was forty-four in April 1933.

82 JWWB, 'The New Regime in Germany', address to RIIA, 21 March 1933, *International Affairs*, 22:3, May 1933, pp. 313–26. Not mentioned in diary. See also JWWB to Harold Macmillan, 14 June 1965, D11, WB papers, SANT, Oxford.

83 JWWB, *Knaves, Fools and Heroes*, p. 170. There is no record of these comments in his speech; perhaps they occurred during question time.

84 *Ibid.*, p. 77. JWWB 'was never conscious of anything magnetic or hypnotic in his personality'. JWWB to Harold Macmillan, 14 June 1965, D11, WB papers, SANT, Oxford.

85 JWWB, *Knaves, Fools and Heroes*, p. 78.

86 JWWB to Baron von Neurath, 3 April 1933, D2, WB collection, SANT, Oxford. He was succeeded as foreign minister by Joachim von Ribbentrop. He joined the Nazi Party in 1937 and was awarded the honorary rank of Obergruppenführer in the SS.

87 JWWB to H.R. Knickerbocker, 27 April 1933, D2, WB papers, SANT, Oxford.

88 Horst Wessel (1907–30), author of the lyrics of the Nazi song 'Die Fahne Hoh' (Raise High the Flag).

89 As related by RBL, Diaries I, 16 June 1933, p. 258.

90 Papen, quoted in JWWB, *Knaves, Fools and Heroes*, p. 72.

91 *Ibid.*, p. 74.

92 *Ibid.*, p. 81.

93 *Ibid.*, p. 121. Englebert Dollfuss (1892–1934), chancellor of Austria 1932–34; called the 'Millimetternich' because he was so short.

94 RBL, *Diaries I*, 26 Aug. 1933, p. 270. Henry Vincent (Harry) Hodson (1906–99), editor of *The Round Table* 1934–39, Director of the Empire Division of the Ministry of Information 1939–41, editor of the *Sunday Times* 1950–61, provost of the Ditchley Foundation 1961.

95 JWWB, *Special Relationships*, p. 41. Claud Cockburn (1904–81). Cockburn later suggested that much of the information for *The Week* was leaked to him by Vansittart. See Claud Cockburn, *In Time of Trouble*.

96 JWWB, *Special Relationships*, p. 28. The exact dates are unclear.

97 Averell Harriman (1891–1986) President Roosevelt's special envoy to Europe, also US ambassador to the Soviet Union 1943–46 and Britain 1946.

98 JWWB, *Special Relationships*, p. 43. In his memoirs JWWB calls the NRA the National Reconstruction (rather than Recovery) Administration. General Hugh Johnson (1882–1942).

99 Emil Nagy de Vamos (1871–1956). He was not foreign minister as JWWB says but minister of justice 1923–24 and served as vice-president of the Christian Social Alliance and of the Association of Hungarian Foreign Affairs. He is not to be confused with the Hungarian communist and future leader, Imre Nagy (1896–1958).

100 JWWB, *Knaves, Fools and Heroes*, p. 122. Several buildings comprise the Ballhaus-platz; the room where the Congress of Vienna was held was in a different building from the chancellor's office and so JWWB's account of Dollfuss attempting to escape through a door that had been blocked up seems mistaken. The Congress of Vienna (1814–15) was when the major European powers decided to redraw the political map of Europe after France's defeat and the end of the Napoleonic Wars.

101 Dr Thomas (Tomas) Masaryk (1850–1937), president of Czechoslovakia 1920–35.

102 JWWB, *Knaves, Fools and Heroes*, p. 131.

103 Office of the President of the Czechoslovak Republic to JWWB, Prague, 17 Jan. 1934, private collection.

104 JWWB, *Knaves, Fools and Heroes*, p. 133.

105 Details from JWWB diaries, D1, WB papers, SANT, Oxford.

106 Camille Chautemps (1865–1963), prime minister 1930, 1933–34, 1937–38, 1938. Edouard Daladier (1884–1970), prime minister 1933, 1934 (seven days), 1938–40.

107 JWWB, *Knaves, Fools and Heroes*, p. 168.

108 *Ibid.*, p. 169. The riots of 6 February 1934 are rather more complicated than JWWB indicates in his memoirs. Gaston Doumergue (1863–1937), prime minister 1913–14, 1934, president 1924–31.

109 *Ibid.*, p. 170.

110 Louis Barthou (1862–1934), prime minister 1913, foreign minister 1934. He held many other ministerial appointments. He was succeeded by Pierre Laval (1883–1945). JWWB writes as though he was there but his diary indicates that he did not go to Paris until 21–23 February 1934. See Diary 1934, D1, WB papers, SANT, Oxford.

111 Originally formed in 1925 as the Saal-Schutz (Assembly Hall Protection), under Himmler's leadership in 1929 it was renamed the Schutzstaffel (Protection Squad); the SS grew to become the most powerful organisation in the Third Reich. Heinrich Himmler (1900–45), military commander (*Reichsführer*) of the SS and leading member of the Nazi Party. The Storm troopers (SA), co-founded by Ernst Röhm (1887–1934), played a key role in Hitler's rise to power.

112 Quoted in Patch, *Heinrich Brüning and the Weimar Republic*, p. 304.

113 JWWB, *Knaves, Fools and Heroes*, p. 88 and JWWB, *Nemesis of Power*, p. 317 n. 2. JWWB never divulged details of Brüning's escape because 'other people were involved'; JWWB to Mrs Rosemary Meynell, 4 Feb. 1975, D12, WB papers, SANT, Oxford. When Brüning came to London, *The Times* (15 June 1934) reported his presence, indicating that he would be returning to Germany 'in a few days'.

114 JWWB, Introduction to H.R. Knickerbocker, *Will War Come in Europe?*, pp. v–xi.

115 Quoted in Franz von Papen, *Memoirs*, p. 307.

116 JWWB, *Nemesis of Power*, p. 319.
117 See *The Times*, 19 June 1934.
118 JWWB, *Hindenburg*, p. 461.
119 JWWB, *Knaves, Fools and Heroes*, p. 91, JWWB gives the date of 28 June for his
    dinner with Papen's adjutants; it must have been before that because he arrived in
    Lausanne on the 27th. The purge began on 29–30 June. It was kept secret until 13
    July, when Hitler used the expression 'The Night of the Long Knives' (from a
    popular song) to describe what had happened, by which time JWWB had returned
    to London (on 3 July). Diary 1934, D1, WB papers, SANT, Oxford. Röhm was
    executed on 2 July. After the purge, under Himmler's leadership the SS replaced
    the SA as the dominant force in Germany. According to JWWB, *Knaves, Fools and
    Heroes*, p. 92, he did not return to Germany until 1945 'with the full force and
    authority of a representative of an occupying power'. He in fact returned twice in
    1935 and thereafter not until 1946.
120 Hindenburg, 2 July 1934, quoted in JWWB, *Hindenburg*, p. 464.
121 *Ibid.*

Chapter 5 Twilight

 1 Robert Vansittart, 'Envoi', quoted in RBL, *Giants Cast Long Shadows*, p. 9.
 2 See *Knaves, Fools and Heroes*, p. 92, where JWWB describes his room at the Kaiserhof
    as having been searched; information was later given to him that had he been there
    he would have been killed.
 3 Mary Stanford *née* Heaton, correspondence with the author, 4 Jan. 2000.
 4 Juliet Fiennes *née* Heaton to the author, 28 August 1999.
 5 Alan Bullock, 'John Wheeler Wheeler-Bennett 1902–1975', *Proceedings of the British
    Academy*, LXV, 1979, p. 810.
 6 As told by JWWB to his niece Mary Stanford, letter to the author, 4 Jan. 2000. It
    is not clear how or why he obtained his Papal audiences.
 7 See JWWB, *Knaves, Fools and Heroes*, photograph, dated 25 February 1935, opposite
    p. 57.
 8 *Ibid.*, p. 81. The chronology in *Knaves, Fools and Heroes* is misleading. He did not
    return to Paris but to Luxor: see Diary 1935, D1, WB papers, SANT, Oxford.
 9 JWWB, *Knaves, Fools and Heroes*, p. 93 (with one exception – that about King
    George VI).
10 *Ibid.*, p. 98. He writes as though he interviewed Hoffmann while researching *Brest-
    Litovsk* but, as noted, Hoffmann had died in 1927 and so JWWB must have been
    referring to his visit in the mid-1920s.
11 *Ibid.*, p. 96.
12 *Ibid.*, p. 95. JWWB's recollection of his conversation with Richard von
    Kühlmann.
13 *Ibid.*, p. 97.
14 RBL, *Diaries* II, p. 13.
15 Count Ottokar Czernin (1872–1932), imperial foreign minister of Austria-Hungary
    1916–18; JWWB, *Knaves, Fools and Heroes*, p. 99.
16 *Ibid.*
17 Sir Walford Selby, KCMG, CB, CVO (1881–1965), PPS to the secretary of state for
    foreign affairs 1924–32, envoy extraordinary and minister plenipotentiary in Vienna
    1933–37. George Messersmith (1883–1960), US minister to Austria 1934–37.
18 JWWB, *Knaves, Fools and Heroes*, p. 123. He says he made his last prewar visit to
    Austria on his way to Moscow, 'it being impossible for me to take the more direct
    route through Germany'. As noted, he returned from Moscow via Germany, where
    he stayed between 1 and 4 July; he went again to Austria in the autumn and also
    to Berlin. Diary 1935, D1, WB collection, SANT, Oxford.

19 JWWB, *Knaves, Fools and Heroes*, p. 125. Duke Max of Hohenberg was sent to Dachau; he died in 1963.

20 *Ibid.*, p. 100. William Bullitt, Jr. (1891–1967), first US ambassador to the Soviet Union 1933–36. Maxim Litvinov (1876–1951), people's commissar for foreign affairs 1930–39. His Jewish ancestry and pro-British/French leanings meant that he was 'purged' by Stalin and replaced by Vyacheslav Molotov, who negotiated the Nazi-Soviet Non-Aggression pact.

21 *Ibid.*, p. 101. Karl Radek (1885–1939).

22 *Ibid.*, p. 103. There were rumours that Radek lived on until the 1950s.

23 JWWB in Moscow from 21 to 29 June; Berlin 1 to 4 July 1935. Diary 1935, D1, WB papers, SANT, Oxford. William E. Dodd (1869–1940), US ambassador in Berlin 1933–38. Paul Scheffer became editor in April 1934 after assurances from Goebbels that the paper would not have to print Nazi propaganda. He resigned in December 1936.

24 Shiela Grant Duff, *The Parting of Ways*, p. 190.

25 *Ibid.*, p. 96. Adam von Trott (1909–44). The Nuremberg Laws were passed in mid-September 1935. Sir Basil Newton, KCMG (1889–1965), counsellor, Berlin 1930–35, minister 1935–37, minister to Czechoslovakia 1937–39.

26 Trott to his father, 18 Oct. 1935, as quoted in Henry Malone, *Adam von Trott zu Solz: The Road to Conspiracy against Hitler*, p. 467 n. 146. '*Ausserdem war noch ein besonders interessanter englischer Schriftsteller da, der gegenwärtig ein Buch über Hindenburg schreibt.*' JWWB claimed not to have met von Trott at Stintenberg in 1935 on the grounds that he did not return to Germany after 30 June 1934 (Malone interview, 12 May 1971, quoted in Malone, *Adam von Trott*, p. 466 n. 146). JWWB told Christopher Sykes that he met Trott when he was an 'undergraduate', i.e. in 1933 (at Stintenberg); Sykes, *Troubled Loyalty*, p. 307 n. 47 and D2, WB papers, SANT, Oxford. He also said that if his memory served him correctly he first met Trott in 1938; *New York Review of Books*, 11 Sept. 1969. JWWB did meet a great number of people and it is possible he did not remember exactly when he met Trott, but his 1935 diary clearly states 'Go Stintenburg' on 28 September. Further corroboration for the 1935 date is provided by Shiela Grant Duff, interview with Malone, 29 April 1971, quoted in Malone, *Adam von Trott zu Solz*, p. 466 n. 146 and Shiela Grant Duff, *The Parting of Ways*, p. 96.

27 Eric Phipps to HM the King, from British Embassy, Berlin, 16 Oct. 1935, memorandum prepared by Mr Breen, press officer at the British Embassy, RA PS/PSO/GV/C/P/586/227 and 228. Sir Eric Phipps, PC, GCB, GCMG, GCVO (1875–1945), British ambassador to Germany 1933–37. Phipps's meeting with JWWB was on 4 October 1935; Diary 1935, D1, WB papers, SANT, Oxford.

28 Heinrich Brüning, *Briefe und Gespräche*, 22 August, p. 83 and note October, p. 94.

29 JWWB, *Hindenburg*, p. 448.

30 *Ibid.*, p. ix.

31 *Ibid.*, p. x.

32 Namier to RBL, as recorded in RBL, *Diaries* I, 28 Aug. 1936, p. 354.

33 Alan Bullock, 'John Wheeler Wheeler-Bennett 1902–1975', *Proceedings of the British Academy*, LXV, 1979, p. 801. Harold Macmillan (later Lord Stockton), OM, PC, FRS (1894–1986), prime minister. Until reaching ministerial office in 1940, he worked in the publishing firm founded in 1843 by his grandfather and brother. After his retirement from politics he presided over the firm's international expansion.

34 George Messersmith to Mr D.N. Heineman, Vienna, 25 Jan. 1937, George S. Messersmith papers, MSS 109, Special Collections, University of Delaware Library (digitalised).

35 JWWB to Macadam, 25 March 1936, 4/WHEE, RIIA Archives.
36 Thomas Jefferson, 3rd president of the United States (1743–1826). He achieved distinction as a polymath, with talents as a statesman, architect, horticulturalist, archaeologist, palaeontologist, author and inventor. He founded the University of Virginia.
37 JWWB, *Special Relationships*, p. 54. JWWB says this was in the spring of 1935 but it has to have been in May 1936 since neither he nor his mother was in the US in May 1935. Ruth Risher Wheeler-Bennett (1900–91).
38 *Ibid.*, p. 32.
39 Flavelle lived until 7 March 1939. JWWB was a pallbearer at the funeral.
40 JWWB, recorded by Baffy Dugdale, *The Diaries of Blanche Dugdale, 1936–47*, p. 34.
41 W.T. Stead (1849–1912). He died on the *Titanic*.
42 JWWB, WB papers, SANT, Oxford.
43 JWWB to Miss Cleeve, 18 Jan. 1937, 4/WHEE, RIIA Archives.
44 Theodore Roosevelt, Jr (1887–1944). Governor-general of the Philippines (1932–33).
45 JWWB, *Special Relationships*, p. 47. Alice Roosevelt Longworth (1884–1980).
46 JWWB, *Knaves, Fools and Heroes*, p. 103. Lev Davidovich Trotsky (1879–1940).
47 *Ibid.*, p. 106. JWWB donated the signed copies to the library of St Antony's College, Oxford. He says he returned the following day to see Trotsky. His diary has only one entry, with an appointment at 4.30 on 11 September 1937; Diary 1937, D1, WB papers, SANT, Oxford.
48 Carl Friedrich Goerdeler (1884–1945). Had the 20 July 1944 plot succeeded, he would have served as chancellor. He was executed on 2 February 1945. He had been working to overthrow Hitler, enlisting the help of numerous co-conspirators.
49 Heinrich Brüning, *Briefe und Gespräche, 1934–1945*, p. 153.
50 JWWB, *Special Relationships*, pp. 55–56.
51 *Ibid.*, p. 69.
52 *Ibid.*, p. 55. It is not clear who gave JWWB this name.
53 JWWB, 'European Possibilities', *Virginia Quarterly Review*, 13:4, autumn 1937, pp. 481–500.
54 Shiela Grant Duff to Trott, 6 Nov. 1937, quoted in *A Noble Combat*, p. 290.
55 JWWB to Macadam, 30 Dec. 1937, 4/WHEE, RIIA Archives.
56 Dorothy Thompson (1893–1961). In 1939, *Time* magazine called her and Eleanor Roosevelt the two most influential women in the USA.
57 JWWB, *Special Relationships*, p. 49. JWWB puts the date as 1936 but according to his diaries it was 1938; on 25 April he noted in his diary: 'Death by Dorothy T.' Diary 1938, D1, WB papers, SANT, Oxford.
58 JWWB, *Special Relationships*, p. 53.
59 JWWB to Macadam, 31 May 1938, 4/WHEE, RIIA Archives.
60 JWWB, *Special Relationships*, p. 50. Isabella Greenway King (1886–1953), married first Robert Ferguson, who died in 1921; then Colonel John Greenway in 1922, who died in 1926; finally, Harry O. King in 1939.
61 JWWB, *Knaves, Fools and Heroes*, p. 137.
62 JWWB to Otto John, 18 May 1950, D8, WB papers, SANT, Oxford.
63 JWWB, *Knaves, Fools and Heroes*, p. 138. Sir Winston Churchill, KG, OM, CH, TD, PC, DL, FRS (1874–1965), prime minister 1940–45, 1951–55.
64 *Ibid.*, p. 139.
65 JWWB, letter to *The Times*, 5 Oct. 1938. The editor admitted that he had received some seven hundred letters on the subject.
66 General Jan Syrovy, quoted in JWWB, *Knaves, Fools and Heroes*, p. 144.
67 JWWB, *Special Relationships*, p. 59.
68 JWWB to Lord Astor, from Farmington Country Club, 15 Nov. 1938, 4/WHEE, RIIA Archives.

69 JWWB, D20, WB papers, SANT, Oxford.
70 JWWB, *Special Relationships*, p. 59.
71 Louis Auchincloss (1917–2010). He wrote a novel a year while working as a lawyer. Lawrence Houston (1913–95), Franklin Roosevelt, Jr (1914–88). Others were Tony Bliss, administrator of the Metropolitan Opera, and Marshall Field, heir to a Chicago fortune.
72 JWWB, D20, WB papers, SANT, Oxford.
73 JWWB, *Special Relationships*, p. 35. John F. Kennedy, *Why England Slept* (1940).
74 Harold (later Baron) Caccia, GCMG, GCVO GCStJ (1905–90).
75 JWWB, *Knaves, Fools and Heroes*, p. 107. See FO 371 23677.721, TNA.
76 JWWB, *Knaves, Fools and Heroes*, pp. 107–08. The British ambassador, Sir William Seeds, was already making approaches to the Soviets in February before Hitler disregarded the Munich Agreement in March.
77 JWWB, *Special Relationships*, p. 62. He spent the night of 29–30 January at the White House.
78 *Ibid.*
79 JWWB to Macadam, 22 March 1939, 4/WHEE, RIIA Archives.
80 Brüning to JWWB, 13 April 1939, *Briefe und Gespräche*, p. 244.
81 Brüning to JWWB, 18 May 1939, B9, WB papers, SANT, Oxford.
82 JWWB to his mother, 16 April 1939, WB papers, SANT, Oxford. He later moved her to Droitwich.
83 JWWB, *Knaves, Fools and Heroes*, p. 134. Edvard Beneš (1884–1948), first and longest-serving foreign minister 1918–35, president of Czechoslovakia 1935–38. JWWB first met Beneš in 1924.
84 *Ibid.*, p. 147.
85 JWWB to his mother, 23 April 1939, WB papers, SANT, Oxford. These are the only two surviving letters he wrote to his mother. JWWB says that he had already evacuated her to Droitwich (*Knaves, Fools and Heroes*, p. 139) but these letters are still addressed to her at Queen Anne's Mansions.
86 JWWB, *Special Relationships*, p. 63. Rt Hon. Sir Ronald Lindsay, PC, GCMG, GCB, CVO (1877–1945), ambassador to Germany 1928–30, ambassador to the United States 1930–39. He was replaced by Lothian.
87 JWWB, *King George VI*, p. 385.
88 JWWB, 'Three Episodes in the Life of Kaiser Wilhelm II', *A Wreath to Clio*, p. 178.
89 JWWB says in his memoirs *Knaves, Fools and Heroes*, p. 175, that RBL had been received several times by the emperor but Lockhart records how, in 1928, the Kaiser refused to see him because he was 'very frightened' of journalists. RBL, *Diaries* I, p. 74.
90 JWWB, *A Wreath to Clio*, p. 179 and *Knaves, Fools and Heroes*, pp. 175 and 179.
91 *Ibid.*, p. 185. After the war, JWWB attempted to trace what had happened to the diaries; he never found them (p. 190).
92 JWWB, *A Wreath to Clio*, p. 181.
93 Kaiser Wilhelm II, as quoted by JWWB in *ibid.* and in *Knaves, Fools and Heroes*, p. 188.
94 JWWB, *Knaves, Fools and Heroes*, p. 188. Wilhelm II, *Aus meinem Leben*, 1859–88, Berlin and Leipzig, 1927. Signature dated 16.VIII.1939, donated by JWWB to the library of St Antony's College, Oxford.
95 JWWB, *Special Relationships*, p. 67.
96 *Ibid.*, p. 68. The *Normandie* never sailed again. Pending conversion to a troopship in 1942, she caught fire and was scrapped in 1946.
97 *Ibid.*, p. 69.
98 *Ibid.*, p. 70.

Chapter 6 The Perils of War

1 *Chicago Tribune*, Sept. 1939, quoted in Nicholas John Cull, *Selling War: The British Propaganda Campaign against American 'Neutrality'*, p. 34.

2 JWWB, *Special Relationships*, p. 71. When JWWB came to write his memoirs, he was disappointed to find that his reports were not among the Lothian papers and felt they must have been 'purged'.

3 Sir Angus Fletcher, KCMG, CBE (1883–1960), director, BLI 1928–41.

4 JWWB, *Special Relationships*, p. 74.

5 Aubrey Morgan (1904–85). He and JWWB remained friends for life.

6 Constance Morrow Morgan (1913–95). Charles Lindbergh (1902–74), aviator, author, explorer. Having flown non-stop from New York to Paris in 1927, he used his instant fame to help promote commercial aviation. Anne Morrow Lindbergh (1906–2001), also a pioneering aviator and author. Between 1935 and 1941, after the kidnap and murder of their son, they had been living in Europe. There were fiercely 'isolationist' until the Japanese attack on Pearl Harbor.

7 Sir Cyril Berkeley Ormerod, KBE (1897–1983), director of public relations, BIS 1945–62. He played representative cricket.

8 Sir Alan Dudley, KBE, CMG (1907–71), assistant director, BLI 1930–40, director, BPS and BIS 1940–42. See Cull, *Selling War*, p. 60.

9 JWWB, *Special Relationships*, p. 76.

10 *Ibid.*, p. 86.

11 Sir Frederick Hoyer Millar (later Lord Inchyra), GCMG, CVO (1900–89). JWWB probably first met him in the 1930s because he was assistant private secretary to the foreign secretary 1934–38.

12 Later Brigadier Sir John Galway Foster (1904–82); see JWWB, *Special Relationships*, p. 86.

13 Sir (Frank) Keith Officer (1889–1969). JWWB says he first met him in 1923 in Melbourne. However, from 1919 to 1924 Officer was political officer in Nigeria; he may have been on leave in Melbourne at the time. See *ibid.*, p. 85. Officer later served in Tokyo, Moscow and Chungking.

14 *Ibid.*, p. 78. Lothian did not live to see his report implemented but as a result the number of consular personnel was increased.

15 *Ibid.*, p. 80.

16 *Ibid.*, p. 83.

17 See Cull, *Selling War*, p. 60. After the fall of France, de Sales withdrew from the propaganda battle, proclaiming France to be dead.

18 Klemens von Klemperer, *German Resistance against Hitler*, p. 79 n. 246.

19 In September 1938 there were plans for a coup against Hitler involving the army commander in Berlin, Field Marshal Erwin von Witzleben.

20 E.F.L. Wood, 1st Earl Halifax, KG, OM, GCSI, GCMG, GCIE, TD, PC (1881–1959), viceroy of India 1926–31 (as Lord Irwin), foreign secretary 1938–40, ambassador to the United States 1941–46.

21 JWWB, *The Semblance of Peace*, p. 23. He repeats the contents of his 21 April 1943 memorandum.

22 See Giles MacDonogh, *A Good German*, p. 148 and Hans Rothfels, *The Conspiracy against Hitler*, p. 152.

23 JWWB, 'Adam von Trott and Peace Feelers', 21 April 1943, D2, WB papers, SANT, Oxford.

24 See Michael C. Thomsett, *The German Opposition to Hitler: The Resistance, the Underground and Assassination Plots, 1938–1945*, pp. 146–47. See Henry Malone, *Adam von Trott*, who makes a detailed study of the controversy surrounding Trott's role in the resistance movement; also Christopher Sykes, *Troubled Loyalty*, p. 292 on how Americans began to mistrust Trott.

25 JWWB to Vansittart, 27 Dec. 1939, 'Peace Aims', FO 371/24363, TNA.

26 JWWB, memorandum to Vansittart, 28 Dec. 1939, 'Peace Aims', FO 371/24363, TNA. Excerpt also quoted in Malone, *Adam von Trott*, pp. 77–78 n. 209 and by David Astor, 'The German Opposition to Hitler', Letters, *Encounter*, XXXIII, Oct. 1969.

27 Trott to Astor, as quoted in Sykes, *Troubled Loyalty*, p. 318. There is no date on this letter but if it included JWWB's memorandum it must have been late 1939.

28 Vansittart to Cadogan, 23 Jan. 1940, 'Peace Aims', FO 371/24363, TNA.

29 Cadogan to Vansittart, 24 Jan. 1940, 'Peace Aims', FO 371/24363, TNA.

30 Vansittart to JWWB, 12 Feb. 1940, 'Peace Aims', FO 371/24363, TNA.

31 Halifax to Neville Chamberlain, 25 Jan. 1940, 'Peace Aims', FO 371/24363, TNA. See also Patricia Meehan, *The Unnecessary War: Whitehall and the German Resistance to Hitler*, Sinclair-Stevenson, 1995, p. 270.

32 'Fantastic Story of Peace Plan. Lord Halifax Accosted', *Sunday Times*, 21 Jan. 1940. 'Peace Aims,' FO 371/24363, TNA.

33 JWWB to Trott, quoted in Sykes, *Troubled Loyalty*, p. 320. Letter in possession of Trott's widow, Clarita. Undated. It must have been in late 1939.

34 JWWB to RBL, 29 Jan. 1940, B29, WB papers, SANT, Oxford. The use of a stable wing and riding school on the duke of Bedford's estate at Woburn had started in 1939. PID moved back to London in August 1940. When PWE was set up, Woburn remained the headquarters for broadcasting 'black propaganda', the intention being to give the impression that the broadcasts were being made from inside Germany or elsewhere in Europe.

35 RBL to JWWB, 1 Jan. 1940, B29, WB papers, SANT, Oxford. No record exists in WB papers.

36 JWWB to RBL, 29 Jan. 1940, B29, WB papers, SANT, Oxford.

37 Lothian to Sir Frederick Whyte, 27 Feb. 1940, FO 371/24227, A1852, TNA. A comment in the margin of Lothian's letter noted: 'We have heard less favourable accts of JWB's activities!' Perhaps this related to his support of a 'peace plan'. Sir Frederick Whyte KCSI (1883–1970), head of the American Division of the Ministry of Information 1939–40.

38 Lothian, quoted in Cull, *Selling War*, p. 50.

39 Brian Aherne (1902–86). Nominated for an Oscar, he made over thirty films.

40 JWWB, *Special Relationships*, p. 137. Ronald Colman (1891–1958), Errol Flynn (1909–59), Charles Laughton (1899–1962).

41 *Ibid.*, p. 91.

42 *Ibid.*, p. 88. Sir Isaiah Berlin OM, FBA (1909–97), Russian–British social and political theorist, philosopher and historian. Educated at St Paul's School, London and Corpus Christi, Oxford, he was elected to a fellowship of All Souls College, Oxford in 1932 aged twenty-three.

43 Quoted in JWWB, *Special Relationships*, p. 97. This speech became famous as the 'Hand That Held the Dagger' speech. In November 1939, the Neutrality Act had been amended to make American war materiel available to the Allies on a 'cash and carry' basis, which placed a heavy burden on Britain's economic resources.

44 *Ibid.* It was a 'gleam of hope' but until the passage of the Lend-Lease Act in March 1941, Britain's economy was still burdened by the US's policy of 'cash and carry'.

45 *Ibid.*

46 JWWB, 'Britain Accepts the Challenge', address delivered on 17 June 1940 to the Institute of Public Affairs, University of Virginia, B22, WB papers, SANT, Oxford. See also JWWB, *Special Relationships*, pp. 98–101 for the full text, recorded by a stenographer. Earlier published in JWWB, *A Wreath to Clio. Areopagitica* by John Milton (1608–74) was an attack on pre-printing censorship and defended free speech. It was published on 23 Nov. 1644 at the height of the Civil War.

47 JWWB, *Special Relationships*, p. 95.

48 *Ibid.*, p. 96.
49 Sir Alexander Cadogan, OM, GCMG, KCB, OC (1884–1968); Sir Orme Sargent, GCMG, KCB (1884–1962), permanent under-secretary of state for foreign affairs 1946–49; Charles Peake (1897–1958), chief press adviser, Ministry of Information; Osbert Lancaster CBE (1908–86).
50 Alfred Duff Cooper, 1st Viscount Norwich, GCMG, DSO, PC (1890–1954), minister of information 1940–41; Ronald Tree (1897–1976), American-born British journalist, Conservative MP for Harborough. After the war, he sold Ditchley Park and returned to the US.
51 Winston S. Churchill, ed., *Never Give In!*, pp. 244–45.
52 JWWB, *Special Relationships*, p. 106.
53 Ronald Tree, *When the Moon Was High*, p. 130. He took the title of his memoirs from a quotation made by Churchill when he requested the use of Ditchley House.
54 Robert (later 1st Baron) Brand CMG (1878–1963).
55 Brigadier Peter Young, ed., *The Almanac of World War Two*, Hamlyn, 1981, p. 75.
56 JWWB, *Special Relationships*, p. 105.
57 *Ibid.*, p. 103. During the war, the Ritz regularly kept people's luggage.
58 Lothian to Ministry of Information, 19 Sept. 1940, FO 371/24231, A4025/26/45, f.205, TNA.
59 Stephen Lawford Childs to JWWB, 31 Oct. 1940, B29, WB papers, SANT, Oxford.
60 JWWB, *Special Relationships*, p. 93.
61 See Cull, *Selling War*, pp. 120 and 122 for background to MacColl's appointment. René MacColl (1905–71), later chief foreign correspondent, *Daily Express* 1959–69.
62 Cull, *Selling War*, p. 59. Lady Daphne Straight (neé Finch-Hatton), daughter of the 14th Earl of Winchilsea.
63 Lothian, reported in the *New York Times*, 24 Nov. 1940. It is doubtful that Lothian made the statement: 'Well, boys, Britain's broke, it's your money we want', recorded by JWWB, *King George VI*, p. 521. See David Reynolds, *Lord Lothian and Anglo-American Relations, 1939–1940*, p. 49 and n. 169.
64 JWWB, *Special Relationships*, p. 116.
65 *Ibid.*, p. 120. Tree also describes this as a 'hunting gaffe': *When the Moon Was High*, p. 162.
66 Sir John Rennie, KCMG (1914–81), BIS 1942–46, later MI6's 'C'.
67 Isaiah Berlin, Introduction to H.G. Nicholas, ed., *Washington Despatches*, p. ix.
68 Dr Alfred Wiener (1885–1964). In 1955, he was awarded the highest civilian decoration by West Germany, the Grand Cross of the Order of Merit.
69 Quoted in Cull, *Selling War*, p. 125.
70 *Ibid.*, p. 126.
71 Tree, *When the Moon Was High*, p. 165.
72 *Ibid.*, p. 162.
73 JWWB, *Special Relationships*, p. 130.
74 Sir Gerald Campbell GCMG, FRGS (1879–1964); see Tree, *When the Moon Was High*, p. 154. He had previously been consul general in Philadelphia, San Francisco and New York and British High Commissioner in Canada. He was Director-General of BIS from 1941 to 1942. Sir Angus Fletcher was retired.
75 Robert (Robin) Cruikshank, CMG (1898–1956), deputy director, BIS 1941–42, also director, American Division of the Ministry of Information 1941–45, editor, *News Chronicle* 1948–55.
76 JWWB, *Special Relationships*, p. 123. There were other organisations in New York disseminating information, for example, British Security Coordination, which included a branch of SO1, the covert propaganda wing of London's SOE, whose members included William Deakin. See Cull, *Selling War*, p. 131.
77 JWWB, *Special Relationships*, p. 130.

78 JWWB, text of address delivered on 28 June 1941, Institute of Public Affairs, University of Virginia, later published as 'Britain and the Future', *New Europe*, New York, Oct. 1941, B33, WB papers, SANT, Oxford.

79 See JWWB, *Special Relationships*, pp. 126–27; RBL, *Giants Cast Long Shadows*, p. 66 says that the changes in the government had not been announced and on the evening of the dinner Nicolson did not know he was going. Brendan Bracken, 1st Viscount Bracken PC (1901–58), minister of information 1941–45. Ernest Thurtle (1884–1954), Labour MP, PPS, Ministry of Information 1941–45.

80 JWWB, *Special Relationships*, p. 128.

81 PWE (PID) came under both the Ministry of Information and the Foreign Office with a 'watching brief' held by the Ministry of Economic Warfare; Bowes-Lyon suggested the name Political Warfare Executive as opposed to Political Warfare Organisation. SOE (formerly called Special Operations 1 and 2 [SO1 and SO2]), based at Woburn, had been set up in July 1940 under Dr Hugh Dalton, the minister for economic warfare.

82 JWWB to RBL, 16 July 1942, B29, WB papers, SANT, Oxford. See also RBL, *Giants Cast Long Shadows*, p. 65.

83 Establishment officer, Ministry of Information, to JWWB, 7 Aug. 1941, B29, WB papers, SANT, Oxford.

84 JWWB, *Special Relationships*, p. 128. Hon. Sir David Bowes-Lyon, KCVO (1902–61), Ministry of Economic Warfare 1940–41, head of PWE in Washington 1942–44. JWWB to RBL, 16 July 1942, B29, WB papers, SANT, Oxford. See also RBL, *Giants Cast Long Shadows*, p. 65.

85 Winston S. Churchill, *The Second World War: The Grand Alliance*, III, p. 354 (Reprint Society, 8th impression, 1956).

86 JWWB, *Special Relationships*, p. 134.

87 *Ibid.*, p. 133.

88 *Ibid.*, p. 135. Duke Ellington (1899–1974).

89 Alexander Korda, *The Lion Has Wings*, shot in twelve days, completed in four weeks. Korda was the first film producer to be knighted, in 1942. Michael Korda, *Charmed Lives*, pp. 136–38. See also Michael Munn, *Lord Larry: The Secret Life of Laurence Olivier*, Anova Books, 2007, p. 115, who says that, through Korda, Laurence Olivier was secretly recruited. JWWB does not mention Olivier in his memoirs.

90 JWWB, *Special Relationships*, p. 141.

91 *Ibid.*, p. 144.

92 *Ibid.*, p. 146.

Chapter 7 Political Warfare in America

1 Robert Vansittart, 'Envoi', quoted in RBL, *Giants Cast Long Shadows*, p. 9.

2 JWWB, *Special Relationships*, p. 146.

3 *Ibid.*, p. 147.

4 JWWB to RBL, May 1942, B29, WB papers, SANT, Oxford.

5 JWWB, *Special Relationships*, p. 156. In 1941, after acting as Roosevelt's special envoy in Europe, General William Donovan, known as 'Wild Bill', became co-ordinator of information (COI). In June 1942, two new agencies were set up: the OWI (Office of War Information), responsible for overseas propaganda; and the OSS (Office of Strategic Services), responsible for collecting secret intelligence and disseminating 'black' (covert) propaganda. JWWB says that he introduced Donovan to Hans von Seeckt.

6 JWWB to RBL, May 1942, B29, WB papers, SANT, Oxford.

7 Roald Dahl and C.S. Forester worked for the BSC but JWWB does not mention them in his memoirs. See Jennet Conant, *The Irregulars: Roald Dahl and the British Spy Ring in Wartime Washington*, Simon & Schuster, 2008.

8 JWWB to RBL, 16 July 1942, B29, WB papers, SANT, Oxford.
9 RBL to JWWB, 20 July 1942, B29, WB papers, SANT, Oxford. PID was in Centre Block, Bush House.
10 JWWB to Walter Stewart Roberts, establishment and finance officer of PID, 20 July 1942, and Roberts to JWWB 27 July 1942, B29, WB papers, SANT, Oxford.
11 Russell Page (1906–85) was regarded as one of the twentieth century's great landscape architects. Leonard Miall, OBE (1914–2005) was with the BBC from 1939 to 1974, having first studied German in Freiburg.
12 Sir Derrick Gunston (1891–1985) was a Unionist politician and MP for Thornbury 1924–45.
13 JWWB, *Munich: Prologue to Tragedy*, p. 433. Count Edward Raczynski (1891–1993).
14 JWWB to Bowes-Lyon, 28 Aug. 1942, B29, WB papers, SANT, Oxford.
15 JWWB to RBL, 22 Sept. 1942, C3, WB papers, SANT, Oxford.
16 Elmer Davis (1890–1958). He left his well-paid job at CBS to work for the government at the OWI.
17 JWWB to RBL, 22 Sept. 1942, C3, WB papers, SANT, Oxford.
18 JWWB, *Special Relationships*, p. 159.
19 *Ibid.*, p. 163.
20 *Ibid.*, p. 164.
21 Casablanca Conference, January 1943. The insistence on unconditional surrender was controversial on account of the lives lost by the prolongation of the war until Germany's total defeat. See Winston S. Churchill, *The Second World War: The Hinge of Fate*, IV, p. 551, where Churchill explained his views on 'unconditional surrender' in June 1943: 'we mean that their will-power to resist must be completely broken, and that they must yield themselves absolutely to our justice and mercy. It also means that we must take all those far-sighted measures, which are necessary to prevent the world from being again convulsed, wrecked, and blackened by their calculated plots and ferocious aggressions.' By 1943 JWWB supported this view.
22 JWWB, *Special Relationships*, p. 167. JWWB says that he introduced Brüning to Donovan in 1943, but the two men had already met in 1936. See Brüning, *Briefe und Gespräche, 1934–1945*, 25 March 1936, p. 115. See also Montgomery Hyde, *The Quiet Canadian*, p. 168.
23 Brüning to Anna Herzog, 25 Sept. 1945, *Briefe und Gespräche*, 1934–45, p. 439.
24 JWWB, 'The New American Appeasement', 23 Feb. 1943, B32, WB papers, SANT, Oxford.
25 JWWB, 'The Making of Peace', March 1943, CO 825/42/1, TNA. The document was later consulted in the Foreign Office for what JWWB had said about Japan, but it was realised that since he was not a Far East expert, the section on Japan was 'the weakest' in the paper. W.B.L. Monson, 'Future Policy in the Far East', 15 June 1943, CO 825/42/1, TNA.
26 JWWB, 'What to Do With Germany', 31 May 1943, B2, WB papers, SANT, Oxford.
27 Helmut James Graf von Moltke (1907–45). He opposed assassinating Hitler lest he become a martyr; after the 20 July plot he was condemned for his opposition to Nazism and executed in January 1945.
28 JWWB gives the date as 1933 but this is an error for 1935. See Malone, *Adam von Trott zu Solz*, p. 468.
29 JWWB, 'Adam von Trott and Peace Feelers', 21 April 1943, D2, WB papers, SANT, Oxford and FO 371-34449, TNA.
30 Minutes, 'Adam von Trott and Peace Feelers', 21 April 1943, D2, WB papers, SANT, Oxford.

31 JWWB, *Special Relationships*, p. 169. They must have written to each other but no
    letters have survived in the WB papers, SANT, Oxford or other British archives.
32 RBL, *Diaries* II, 19–20 June 1943, pp. 241–42.
33 See JWWB, *Special Relationships*, p. 168.
34 *Ibid.*, p. 171.
35 RBL to JWWB, 23 July 1943, B29, WB papers, SANT, Oxford.
36 Bowes-Lyon to JWWB, 20 Aug. 1943, B29, WB papers, SANT, Oxford.
37 Alexander Halpern (1879–1956), a Russian lawyer who had the code name G111
    and then G400. He was head of SOE's Political and Minorities Section.
38 JWWB to RBL, 14 Aug. 1943. B29, WB papers, SANT, Oxford. Field-Marshal
    Karl Rudolf Gerd von Rundstedt (1875–1953), Field Marshal Johannes Blaskowitz
    (1883–1948), General Franz Halder (1884–1972), Ernst Baron von Weizsächer
    (1882–1951).
39 JWWB to RBL, 23 Aug. 1943, B29, WB papers, SANT, Oxford.
40 JWWB to RBL, 28 Aug. 1943, B29, WB papers, SANT, Oxford.
41 JWWB to RBL, 13 Sept. 1943, B29, WB papers, SANT, Oxford. Winston S.
    Churchill, *The Second World War: Closing the Ring*, V, pp. 109–10. At the Quebec
    Conference, the leaders discussed plans for the invasion of France.
42 *Ibid.*
43 JWWB to RBL, 4 Oct. 1943, B29, WB papers, SANT, Oxford.
44 JWWB, 'The Future of Russo-Japanese Relations', 2 Oct. 1943, B21, WB papers,
    SANT, Oxford.
45 JWWB to RBL, 18 Oct. 1943, B29, WB papers, SANT, Oxford. Cordell Hull
    (1871–1955), secretary of state 1933–44 (the longest term recorded), Nobel Peace
    Prize 1945 for his contribution in setting up the United Nations. Vyacheslav
    Molotov (1890–1986). It was the third Moscow Conference, 18 October–11
    November; the first was in 1941, the second in August 1942; a fourth conference
    took place in 1944. The fifth (known as the Interim Meeting of Foreign Ministers)
    took place in December 1945.
46 JWWB to RBL, 25 Oct. 1943, B29, WB papers, SANT, Oxford.
47 JWWB to RBL, 18 Oct. 1943, B29, WB papers, SANT, Oxford.
48 JWWB is referring to the 'ultras' at the court of the restored Bourbon monarch,
    Louis XVIII, who wanted the situation to revert to that before the French
    Revolution.
49 JWWB to RBL, 25 Oct. 1943, B29, WB papers, SANT, Oxford.
50 JWWB to RBL, 4 Oct. 1943, B29, WB papers, SANT, Oxford.
51 JWWB to RBL, 25 Oct. 1943, B29, WB papers, SANT, Oxford.
52 JWWB, *Special Relationships*, p. 142. John Farrow (1904–63), father of the actress
    Mia Farrow. He directed forty-six films, of which *Around the World in Eighty Days*
    (1956) is perhaps the best known.
53 JWWB, *Special Relationships*, p. 143. The actors were Bobby Watson (Hitler), Alex
    Pope (Goering), Martin Klosleck (Goebbels). In his memoirs JWWB says Watson
    was a 'genuine German' but he was born in Illinois and does not appear ever to
    have visited Germany.
54 JWWB to RBL, cc. Halpern and Bowes-Lyon, 29 Nov. 1943, B29, WB papers,
    SANT, Oxford. Hermann Rauschning (1887–1982). A member of the Nazi Party
    until 1934, he settled in Portland, Oregon. He was the author of several anti-Nazi
    books.
55 JWWB, *Special Relationships*, p. 143.
56 JWWB to RBL, cc. Halpern and Bowes-Lyon, 29 Nov. 1943, B29, WB papers,
    SANT, Oxford.
57 RBL, *Diaries* II, p. 270.
58 JWWB, *Special Relationships*, p. 172.
59 JWWB to RBL, 1 Jan. 1944, B29, WB papers, SANT, Oxford.

60 *Ibid.*

61 JWWB to RBL, 12 April 1944, B29, WB papers, SANT, Oxford.

62 JWWB to RBL, 15 April 1944, B29, WB papers, SANT, Oxford. 'Hyphenated' Americans as in Finnish-American, Polish-American, etc. King Victor Emmanuel III of Italy and his son and heir, the prince of Piedmont (later Umberto II). The head of the royal house of Italy used the title duke of Savoy. The Italian armistice was signed on 3 September 1943 and announced on the 8th.

63 JWWB, 'Some Aspects of the German Problem', 5 April 1944, B2, WB papers, SANT, Oxford.

64 JWWB to RBL, 22 April 1944, B29, WB papers, SANT, Oxford.

65 JWWB to RBL, 29 April 1944, B29, WB papers, SANT, Oxford.

66 Alan Bullock, 'John Wheeler Wheeler-Bennett 1902–1975', *Proceedings of the British Academy,* LXV, 1979, p. 816 n. 1.

67 JWWB, *Special Relationships*, p. 173. Richard Crossman (1907–74), later Labour MP; Sir Duncan Wilson, GCMG (1911–83); Sir Ralph Murray, KCMG, CB (1908–83); Hon. Sir Con O'Neill, KCMG (1912–88); Alan (later Baron) Bullock (1914–2004), Fellow and tutor in modern history, New College, Oxford 1945–52, author of *Hitler: A Study in Tyranny* (1952); Peter Ritchie (later Baron) Ritchie-Calder (1906–83) wrote a popular book, *Carry On London* (1941), describing the effects of the Blitz; Rt Hon. Sir Eric Sachs PC, MBE (1898–1979); Dilys Powell, CBE (1901–95), who became a founder member of ITA, the Independent Television Authority; David Garnett, CBE (1892–1981), a prominent member of the Bloomsbury Group, wrote numerous books, including *The Secret History of PWE 1939–1945* (published in 2002 after the cabinet documents were declassified), which describes both the hard work and political infighting.

68 Sir William Strang, 1st Baron Strang, GCMG, KCB, MBE (1893–1978).

69 JWWB, *Special Relationships*, p. 176.

70 JWWB, paper written on the assumption that the aim of the UN was to destroy German militarism, 5 June 1944, B2, WB papers, SANT, Oxford. One of JWWB's internal papers, written in February 1944 before the failed assassination attempt, was condemned by a member of the Foreign Office's Research Department as being a 'vitriolic little paper' which was 'hardly worthy of its distinguished author'. Professor Thomas Marshall, FO 371/39137, TNA.

71 Annie Henrietta, Lady Yule (d. 1950). She was a world traveller, famed for her enjoyment of big game hunting. She was the daughter of Andrew Yule of Calcutta, and married his nephew Sir David Yule (1858–1928). It is not clear why Bracken chose this particular house other than because of its location.

72 RBL, *Giants Cast Long Shadows*, pp. 67–68.

73 Colonel Claus Graf von Stauffenberg (1907–44). His wife, who spent time in a concentration camp after the abortive coup, lived to the age of ninety-two, dying in 2006.

74 JWWB, *Special Relationships*, p. 200.

75 JWWB, 25 July 1944, B2, WB papers, SANT, Oxford.

76 In his memoirs JWWB stated that it was 'tragic' to remember how some of those he had known in the interwar years died, citing Bernstorff. JWWB, *Knaves, Fools and Heroes*, p. 17. See also William L. Shirer, *The Rise and Fall of the Third Reich*, Chapter 29. In 1986, Richard Heaton, David's son and JWWB's great-nephew, gave a convincing performance as Adam von Trott zu Solz in an OUDS production at Oxford.

77 JWWB, 3 Aug. 1944, B2, WB papers, SANT, Oxford.

78 RBL, *Friends, Foes and Foreigners*, p. 195. The liberation of Paris took place between 19 and 25 August 1944.

79 JWWB, *Special Relationships*, p. 187.

80 JWWB, 4 Dec. 1944, B2, WB papers, SANT, Oxford.

Chapter 8 The Horrors of Peace

1 JWWB, *Special Relationships*, p. 207.
2 *Ibid.*, p. 194.
3 *Ibid.*, p. 195.
4 *Ibid.*, p. 54.
5 *Ibid.*, p. 196. Elisabeth Reeve Morrow (1873–1955). Dwight Morrow (1873–1931), US ambassador to Mexico 1927–30.
6 JWWB, *Friends, Enemies and Sovereigns*, p. 15.
7 JWWB to RBL, 21 March 1945, B5, WB papers, SANT, Oxford.
8 IB to Elisabeth Morrow, 4 April 1945, in IB, *Flourishing Letters 1928–1946*, ed. Henry Hardy, p. 540. Robert Kent Gooch endowed the Robert Kent Gooch Scholarship at the University of Virginia.
9 JWWB, *Special Relationships*, p. 198.
10 RBL to JWWB, 27 March 1945, B5, WB papers, SANT, Oxford. See RBL, *Diaries* I, pp. 12–15 for details of RBL's tangled love life.
11 Juliet Fiennes, interview with the author, 1999.
12 JWWB to RBL, 17 April 1945, B5, WB papers, SANT, Oxford.
13 JWWB, *Special Relationships*, p. 201.
14 There are stories that Himmler escaped death and a 'double' died in his place. The body was buried in an unmarked grave on the Lüneburg Heath, where JWWB used to ride. In 2005, forged letters in The National Archives, used by Martin Allen in his book *Himmler's Secret War*, added credence to the argument that Himmler was killed by PWE interrogators to prevent him falling into the hands of the Americans. One document was a forged letter dated 10 May 1945 'signed' by JWWB to RBL: see Ben Fenton, 'Files on Himmler's Murder Exposed as Fake', *Daily Telegraph*, 2005, www.greyfalcon. us/restored/himmler; and *Financial Times*, 3–4 May 2008, pp. 25–28.
15 RBL, 28 April 1945, *Diaries* II, p. 426.
16 JWWB, *Special Relationships*, p. 202.
17 JWWB, 16 May 1945, B2, WB papers, SANT, Oxford.
18 JWWB, *Special Relationships*, pp. 203–04.
19 *Ibid.*, p. 205.
20 *Ibid.* RBL said that he went to stay at the Ritz in August to please JWWB but then when JWWB returned to the US he could not find another room to stay in and it had cost him £200 (which he could ill afford!). RBL, 1 Sept. 1945, *Diaries* II, p. 502.
21 JWWB, *Special Relationships*, p. 206.
22 *Ibid.*
23 RBL, 15 Aug. 1945, *Diaries* II, p. 491.
24 JWWB to RBL, undated 1945, B5, WB papers, SANT, Oxford.
25 RBL, *Giants Cast Long Shadows*, p. 67.
26 JWWB to Major General Kenneth Strong, 2 Oct. 1945, B13, WB papers, SANT, Oxford.
27 Major General Kenneth Strong to JWWB, 15 Oct. 1945, B13, WB papers, SANT, Oxford.
28 JWWB, *Friends, Enemies and Sovereigns*, p. 15.
29 IB to W.G.S. Adams, warden of All Souls, 17 May 1944, in IB, *Flourishing Letters*, p. 491. Nothing came of this although IB did arrange for JWWB to teach at New College.
30 JWWB, *Special Relationships*, p. 206.
31 JWWB, *Friends, Enemies and Sovereigns*, p. 15. RBL also refused to continue working for the Foreign Office and returned to writing books, hoping to emulate the success of his earlier *Memoirs of a British Agent*.
32 JWWB, *Friends, Enemies and Sovereigns*, p. 19. This is a rather uncharacteristic way for JWWB to have described his mother's death.

33 *Ibid.*, p. 21.
34 *Ibid.*, p. 20.
35 Irene Heaton, unpublished memoirs, private collection.
36 Those on trial were (alphabetically): Karl Doenitz, Hans Frank, Wilhelm Frick, Hans Fritzsche, Walther Funk, Herman Goering, Rudolph Hess, Alfred Jodl, Wilhelm Keitel, Ernst Kaltenbrunner, Konstantin von Neurath, Franz von Papen, Erich Raeder, Joachim von Ribbentrop, Alfred Rosenberg, Fritz Sauckel, Hjalmar Schacht, Baldur von Schirach, Arthur Seyss-Inquart, Albert Speer, Julius Streicher. Martin Bormann (1902–?1945) was tried and condemned to death in absentia.
37 JWWB, *Friends, Enemies and Sovereigns*, pp. 28, 30. Sir Patrick Dean, GCMG (1909–94), assistant legal adviser, Foreign Office 1939–45, head of German Political Department, Foreign Office 1946–50, chairman of Joint Intelligence Committee 1953–60, permanent representative of the UK to the UN 1960–64, ambassador to the United States 1965–69.
38 JWWB, *Friends, Enemies and Sovereigns*, p. 35. Francis Biddle (1886–1968), attorney-general 1941–45; Dame Rebecca West (1892–1983). The latter's writings were collected in a book called *A Train of Powder*, 1955.
39 JWWB, *Friends, Enemies and Sovereigns*, p. 35. David Maxwell-Fyfe (later Earl of Kilmuir), GCVO, PC, KC (1900–67), later lord chancellor of Great Britain. Sir Hartley Shawcross was the chief prosecutor but the actual prosecution was done by Maxwell-Fyfe.
40 *Ibid.*, p. 42.
41 *Ibid.*, p. 41.
42 JWWB was in Nuremberg 14–21 June, 1–4 August and 28 September–3 October; see JWWB Diaries, D1, WB papers, SANT, Oxford.
43 JWWB, *Friends, Enemies and Sovereigns*, p. 54. As reported in the *Berliner Zeitung*, it took Ribbentrop fourteen minutes and forty-five seconds and Jodl a little longer to die, which explains JWWB's remark. See Giles MacDonogh, *After the Reich*, p. 450. See also Robert E. Conot, *Justice at Nuremberg*, Weidenfeld & Nicolson, 1983 who says that: Ribbentrop took eighteen minutes to die and Keitel twenty-four, although their necks were broken and they were unconscious.
44 JWWB, *Friends, Enemies and Sovereigns*, p. 55.
45 JWWB to HM, 22 April 1950, D8, WB papers, SANT, Oxford. See also Brown Envelope 5, WB papers, SANT, Oxford.
46 JWWB to Macadam, 4 July 1946, 4/WHEE, RIIA Archives.
47 JWWB, D18/D20 WB papers, SANT, Oxford.
48 Tony Benn (b. 1925), conversation with the author, 29 May 2008. Formerly Anthony Wedgwood Benn, 2nd Viscount Stansgate; since 1973, he has been known as Tony Benn. He served in the RAF during the war before becoming a Labour politician. While at New College, he became president of the Oxford Union.
49 JWWB, *Friends, Enemies and Sovereigns*, p. 69.
50 RCWB to the author, 9 June 1999. Richard (Rick) Wheeler-Bennett (1927–2010). Richard Venables (1928–2005).
51 Michael Korda, *Charmed Lives*, p. 320.
52 Professor Raymond Sontag (1897–1972). See the multi-volume series *Documents on German Foreign Policy 1918–1945*, HMSO and a separate volume, *Nazi-Soviet Relations 1939–1941*, which Sontag edited with James. F. Beddie, US Department of State, 1948.
53 JWWB to Macadam, 15 July 1946, 4/WHEE, RIIA Archives. JWWB continued to pay his subs even though, as a 'founder member', he was exempt.
54 Miss Cleeve to Macadam, 13 Dec. 1946, 4/WHEE, RIIA Archives.
55 In *Friends, Enemies and Sovereigns*, pp. 72–73, 76. JWWB again states that he had not returned to Germany since 1934 and makes much of the fact that he had a 'providential escape' on the Night of the Long Knives.

56 Sir Christopher Steel, GCMG, MVO (1903–73).
57 JWWB, *Friends, Enemies and Sovereigns*, p. 74.
58 *Ibid.*, p. 72.
59 Diarist's Column, *Oxford Mail*, 25 Jan. 1947.
60 JWWB, *Friends, Enemies and Sovereigns*, p. 71. Maurice Baumont (not, as JWWB wrote, Beaumont) (1892–1991), expert on French and German history since the Third Republic. He had just published *La Faillite de la paix 1918–1939* (1945).
61 JWWB, *Friends, Enemies and Sovereigns*, p. 77.
62 General Sir Nevil Brownjohn, GBE, KCB, CMG (1897–1973), deputy military governor, Control Commission, for Germany (British Element) 1947–49.
63 In Greek mythology, Cassandra was the daughter of King Priam; her beauty caused Apollo to give her the gift of prophecy. In modern usage, a 'Cassandra' is someone who makes true predictions which are disbelieved.
64 Shiela Grant Duff to Adam von Trott zu Solz, [Prague] [about 12] Nov. 1936, in *A Noble Combat*, p. 195.
65 JWWB, *Munich: Prologue to Tragedy*, p. 437.
66 G.P. Gooch, *Slavonic and East European Review*, 27; 68, Dec. 1948, pp. 290 and 288. George Peabody Gooch, OM, CH (1873–1968), journalist and historian, specialising in continental Europe.
67 JWWB, *Friends, Enemies and Sovereigns*, p. 82.
68 Michael Bloch, *The Secret File of the Duke of Windsor*, p. 165. Philip Ziegler, *King Edward VIII*, p. 235, describes Ribbentrop as deluding himself in thinking the duke would ever have 'agreed to be imposed' upon the British people 'by German arms'. RBL, 23 Nov. 1946, *Diaries* II, p. 572.
69 JWWB, *Friends, Enemies and Sovereigns*, pp. 81–82. See 'Eve of War through Nazi eyes', *The Times* 19 Feb. 1957. See also Jonathan Petropoulos, *Royals and the Reich*, Oxford University Press, 2006, p. 341, who cites Sir Alexander Hardinge saying that the king was 'fussed' about the Marburg File. Sir Alan (Tommy) Lascelles, GCB, GCVO, CMG, MC (1887–1981), private secretary to George VI 1942–52 and Elizabeth II 1952–53, keeper of the Royal Archives 1943–53. A BBC Radio 4 documentary on the Marburg File, produced in 1994 and presented by Denys Blakeway, Sound Archive, H 4024/2, BL, narrates how, in 1954, the historical advisory committee to the captured German Archives, chaired by JWWB, (by now appointed the king's biographer), agreed that publication of material relating to World War II should be postponed hence postponing publication of The Marburg File. See also George O. Kent, 'Editing Diplomatic Documents: A Review of Official U.S. and German Document Series,' *The American Archivist*, vol. 57, 1994, pp. 473–76.
70 JWWB, *Friends, Enemies and Sovereigns*, p. 85.
71 JWWB, *Knaves, Fools and Heroes*, p. 155.
72 James Joll (1918–94) had also served in SOE; General Sir James Marshall-Cornwall, KCB, CBE (1887–1985), editor-in-chief of the captured German archives 1948–51.
73 Orme Sargent, Foreign Office, 25 June 1948, private collection.
74 JWWB, *Friends, Enemies and Sovereigns*, p. 90.
75 JWWB, D19, WB papers, SANT, Oxford.
76 Named out of tribute to Besse's first name and also 'in pious dedication to St Antony of Padua', JWWB, D19, WB papers, SANT, Oxford.
77 Sir William Deakin, DSO (1913–2005) first master of St Antony's College.
78 JWWB, D19, WB papers, SANT, Oxford. In 2003 Sir William Deakin told Sir Marrack Goulding, the then warden of St Antony's, that he asked JWWB to be a Founder Follow because of his wide circle of friends and contacts.
79 JWWB, D19, WB papers, SANT, Oxford.
80 Geoffrey Hudson (1903–74).
81 JWWB to Otto John, 8 July 1949, D8, WB papers, SANT, Oxford.
82 JWWB to HM, 18 April 1950, D8, WB papers, SANT, Oxford.
83 HM to JWWB, 20 April 1950, D8, WB papers, SANT, Oxford.

84 See RBL, *Diaries* II, 29 May 1942, p. 172 and 27 Jan. 1947, p. 582; Dr Otto John (1909–97). See the obituary in *The Independent*, 1 April 1997. Otto John also helped the Allies by giving advance information about German rocket factories at Peenemünde. See also JWWB, *Friends, Enemies and Sovereigns*, pp. 108–11. Klaus Bonhöffer (1901–45), Dietrich Bonhöffer (1906–45).

85 'Black' propaganda purported to be from the Germans when in fact it came from the British; the objective was to vilify or misrepresent German actions.

86 Sir Arthur Comyns Carr, Kt, QC (1882–1965).

87 JWWB, *Friends, Enemies and Sovereigns*, p. 115. Field Marshal Erich von Manstein (1887–1973). He was sentenced to eighteen (reduced to fifteen) years in prison but released in 1953.

88 JWWB to Otto John, 8 July 1950, D8, WB papers, SANT, Oxford. They agreed to spilt the royalties. See also RBL, 8 Aug. 1947, *Diaries* II, p. 624.

89 Otto John to JWWB, 2 Aug. 1949, D8, WB papers, SANT, Oxford.

90 JWWB to Otto John, 25 Aug. 1950, C5, WB papers, SANT, Oxford. It is referred to as the 'John Memorandum' throughout the book. See also RBL, 20 Aug. 1947, *Diaries* II, p. 625. He says that initially JWWB had encouraged Otto John to write an account of 20 July and had offered him an advance of £500 on condition that he was given exclusive access to his information. JWWB does not mention this in his memoirs.

91 The West German Federal Republic was created on 23 May 1949. Full sovereignty was restored to West Germany in May 1952. JWWB was surprised because Otto John had started the process of becoming a naturalised British citizen and obtaining a qualification to practise commercial law in Britain.

92 Konrad Adenauer (1876–1967), chancellor of West Germany 1949–63.

93 JWWB, *Friends, Enemies and Sovereigns*, p. 122.

94 JWWB, *Nemesis of Power*, p. 443.

95 *Ibid.*, p. 693.

96 *Ibid.*, p. 286.

97 Alan Bullock, 'John Wheeler Wheeler-Bennett 1902–1975', *Proceedings of the British Academy*, LXV, 1979, p. 822.

98 Patch, *Henrich Brüning and the Weimar Republic*, p. 313.

99 Published as *Memorien* in 1970. JWWB believed that they gave a false picture of Brüning. JWWB, 'The End of the Weimar Republic', *Foreign Affairs*, p. 369. Anthony Nicholls, correspondence with the author, 28 May 2008.

100 JWWB, *Nemesis of Power*, p. 702.

101 JWWB, *Friends, Enemies and Sovereigns*, p. 124.

102 JWWB, *Nemesis of Power*, p. ix.

103 Otto John, *Twice through the Lines*, Futura, 1974, p. 157.

104 See Alan Bullock, 'John Wheeler Wheeler-Bennett 1902–1975', *Proceedings of the British Academy*, LXV, 1979, pp. 822–23.

105 JWWB, *Nemesis of Power*; see also Malone, *Adam von Trott zu Solz*, in which he calls JWWB's assessment of Hitler's German opponents 'condescendingly critical', p. 26.

106 George S. Messersmith, 'Conversation on the Break of Relations with Goering', 1958, p. 20, George S. Messersmith papers, MSS 109. Special Collections, University of Delaware Library (digitalised).

107 Harold Nicolson, *Diaries and Letters*, 11 Jan. 1954, p. 256.

Chapter 9 High Honour

1 JWWB, *Friends, Enemies and Sovereigns*, p. 168.

2 *Ibid.*, p. 136. Later Nicolson put forward JWWB's name to write the life of King George VI. His biography on George V was published by Constable & Co., 1952. George VI died on 6 February 1952.

3 JWWB, *Friends, Enemies and Sovereigns*, pp. 138–40.
4 Alan Bullock, 'John Wheeler Wheeler-Bennett 1902–1975', *Proceedings of the British Academy*, LXV, 1979, p. 824.
5 JWWB, *Friends, Enemies and Sovereigns*, p. 145.
6 *Ibid.*, p. 148. JWWB relates how this was arranged during his investiture with the CMG.
7 *Ibid.*, p. 146.
8 RA/AEC/GG/20: Interview Notes, JWWB/the duke of Windsor, 11 December 1953.
9 RA/AEC/GG/20: Interview Notes, JWWB/the princess royal, 28–30 July 1954.
10 As JWWB was leaving the duke of Windsor after his first interview, a telephone call came through informing the duke that Queen Mary was unwell. RA/AEC/GG/20: Interview Notes, JWWB/the duke of Windsor, 24 March 1953.
11 JWWB, *Friends, Enemies and Sovereigns*, p. 146.
12 J.R. Colville to Winston Churchill, 26 March 1953, PREM 11/1571, TNA.
13 Ethel Ruffels to the author, March 1999.
14 JWWB to J.R. Colville, 16 Oct. 1953, PREM 11/1571, TNA.
15 J.R. Colville to Winston Churchill, Oct. 1953, PREM 11/1571, TNA.
16 RA AEC/GG/20: Interview Notes, JWWB/Eleanor Roosevelt, 30 Jan.1954.
17 RA AEC/GG/20: Interview Notes, JWWB/Winston Churchill, 12 Aug. 1954. See also JWWB, *Friends, Enemies and Sovereigns*, p. 149.
18 JWWB to J.R. Colville, 14 Aug. 1954, PREM 11/,1571, TNA.
19 JWWB, *Friends, Enemies and Sovereigns*, p. 150.
20 RA AEC/GG/20: Interview Notes, JWWB/Eamon de Valera, 15 Feb. 1956.
21 JWWB was obviously not including Britain in Europe at this stage because Queen Victoria had reigned for over sixty-three years.
22 RA AEC/GG/20: Correspondence, JWWB's text of BBC broadcast on writing the king's biography, October 1958.
23 RA AEC/GG/20: Interview Notes & Correspondence, JWWB/Lord Mountbatten, Admiralty House, Valetta, Malta, 7–11 March 1954.
24 JWWB, *Friends, Enemies and Sovereigns*, p. 163. JWWB does not mention this conversation in his Interview Notes.
25 RA/AEC/GG/20: Interview Notes, JWWB/Harry S. Truman, 22 June 1956.
26 RBL, *Diaries* II, 4 Dec. 1949, p. 707.
27 Ethel Ruffels to the author, March 1999.
28 RCWB, 'The President's Cricket XI versus Garsington', personal recollection, private collection. A 'meadow muffin' is more commonly called a cowpat.
29 Robert Runcie (1921–2000), principal, Ripon College, Cuddesdon 1960–70, archbishop of Canterbury 1980–91.
30 The Very Reverend the Hon. Oliver Twistleton-Wykeham-Fiennes (1926–2011), dean of Lincoln 1969–89. The younger son of the 20th baron of Saye and Sele, he married Juliet, who died in 2005. Interview with the author, 28 Aug. 1999.
31 RCWB, 'The President's Cricket XI versus Garsington', personal recollection, private collection.
32 Ethel Ruffels to the author, March 1999; the first dinner was in 1950. JWWB's first absence was in 1966!
33 As recorded by JWWB, D17, WB papers, SANT, Oxford. Donald Lindsay, CBE (1910–2002), headmaster of Malvern College 1952–71. He was regarded as one of the great British headmasters of the twentieth century; www.worcesternews.co.uk, 7 Feb.2003. His son is the actor Ian Lindsay.
34 JWWB, D17, WB papers, SANT, Oxford.
35 *Ibid.* Admiral Sir William Tennant, KCB, CBE, MVO (1890–1963).
36 Published in *Essays Presented to Sir Lewis Namier* (1956), reprinted in JWWB, *A Wreath to Clio*. A.J.P. Taylor (1906–90), Richard Pares (1902–58). JWWB had also

published an essay on 'Ludendorff: The Soldier and the Politician' in the *Virginia Quarterly Review*, spring 1938. His lecture was given in 1955.

37 Otto John, quoted in *Time* magazine, 'The Man with 1,000 Secrets', 2 Aug. 1954, www.time.com.

38 JWWB to HRH Prince Louis Ferdinand, 29 May 1957, C5, WB papers, SANT, Oxford.

39 RCWB to the author, 9 June 1999.

40 JEWB to the author, 2007.

41 David Heaton, 'Garsington Manor 1928–1982', unpublished memoir, 1994, private collection.

42 JWWB, *Friends, Enemies and Sovereigns*, p. 164.

43 *Ibid.*, p. 168.

44 *Oldham Evening Chronicle*, 11 July 1955, C4, WB papers, SANT, Oxford.

45 JWWB, *King George VI*, p. 282.

46 *Ibid.*, p. 293.

47 *Sunday Express*, 19 Aug. 1956.

48 JWWB to Norman Brook, 22 Aug. 1956, PREM 11/1571, TNA. Rt Hon. Sir Norman Brook (later Baron Normanbrook), GCB, PC (1902–67). See JWWB, *King George VI*, p. 417.

49 JWWB to Lionel Logue, 7 Feb. 1953, letter in possession of Mark Logue. See also *Knaves, Fools and Heroes*, p. 12. Lionel Logue, CVO (1880–1953).

50 JWWB to Dr Valentine Logue, 10 Nov. 1954, letter in possession of Mark Logue.

51 RA AEC/GG/20: Correspondence, JWWB to Dr Valentine Logue, 16 July 1956. It is not clear when exactly JWWB was treated.

52 JWWB, *King George VI*, p. 213.

53 Sir Alan Lascelles's speech at luncheon to launch biography of King George VI, 13 Oct. 1958, private collection.

54 RA AEC/GG/20: Correspondence, Sir Norman Brook to JWWB, 17 Aug. 1956.

55 RBL, *Diaries* II, 13 March 1957, p. 755.

56 *Ibid.*

57 JWWB, Author's Note, *King George VI*, p. vii.

58 RA AEC/GG/20: Correspondence, Harold Nicolson to JWWB, 31 Dec. 1954, JWWB to Harold Nicolson, 3 Jan. 1955.

59 Sir Alan Lascelles's speech at luncheon to launch biography of King George VI. 13 Oct. 1958, private collection.

60 JWWB, *Friends, Enemies and Sovereigns*, p. 168.

61 RA AEC/GG/20: Correspondence, JWWB's text of BBC broadcast on writing the king's biography, October 1958.

62 JWWB, Diary, 1958, D1, WB papers, SANT, Oxford.

63 *Christian Science Monitor*, 18 Dec. 1959, D9, WB papers, SANT, Oxford.

64 John K. Hutchens, *Herald Tribune* and other journals, D9, WB papers, SANT, Oxford.

65 Crane Brinton, *New York Herald Tribune*, 11 Jan. 1959, D9, WB papers, SANT, Oxford.

66 William Shawcross, *Queen Elizabeth*, p. 675. The queen mother's comment was to Helen Hardinge, the wife of the King's private secretary, Sir Alexander Hardinge, who was asked to take out a section on the abdication in her book *The Path of Kings*. See also JWWB's comment as above, RA/AEC/GG/20: Interview Notes, JWWB/the duke of Windsor, 11 Dec. 1953. The duke was at first prevented (by the Palace) from seeing JWWB's draft but, having threatened legal action, he was shown the relevant text, and amendments were made in response to his comments. Bloch, *The Secret File of the Duke of Windsor*, p. 296.

67 RA AEC/GG/20: Correspondence, Mountbatten to JWWB, 2 Oct. 1948, JWWB to Mountbatten, 8 Oct. 1958. See JWWB, *King George VI*, pp. 74–75.

68 *Salisbury Journal*, 21 Aug. 1959 article on use of public libraries, D9, WB papers, SANT, Oxford.
69 JEWB to the author, 21 April 2008. Mary lived in South Africa and did not develop a close relationship with JWWB, nor did Clement's other children, John and Gillian.
70 Sir Michael (later Baron) Adeane, GCB, GCVO (1910–84), private secretary to the queen 1953–72 (succeeded by Sir Martin Charteris).
71 JWWB to Avon, from Buckingham Palace, 21 Oct. 1959, AP33/4/1, Avon papers, Special Collections, UB.
72 Avon to JWWB, 27 Oct. 1959, AP33/4/2, Avon papers, Special Collections, UB. Clarissa *née* Spencer-Churchill (the niece of Sir Winston), later Lady Avon (b. 1920).
73 John Anderson, 1st Viscount Waverley, GCB, OM, GCSI, GCIE, PC, PC (Ireland) (1882–1958).
74 Note, Sir Norman Brook, 27 Oct. 1958. CAB 21/3779, TNA.
75 JWWB, Note on President de Valera, 9 Oct. 1959. CAB 21/3779, TNA.
76 JEWB, conversation with the author, 16 June 2008.
77 JWWB to Otto John, 29 June 1959, WB papers, SANT, Oxford. The sum of £1,405 4s. 10d. was transferred to Mrs Lucie John on 8 August 1959.
78 Otto John to JWWB, 23 Aug. 1959, CB, WB papers, SANT, Oxford.
79 Otto John to JWWB, 7 July 1959, C5, WB papers, SANT, Oxford. He died in the Innsbruck sanatorium in 1997.

Chapter 10 The Sixties

1 JWWB, D17, WB papers SANT, Oxford.
2 David Heaton, 'Garsington Manor 1928–1982', unpublished memoir, 1994, private collection.
3 Juliet Fiennes, interview with the author, 28 Aug. 1999.
4 David Heaton, 'Garsington Manor 1928–1982', unpublished memoir, 1994, private collection. They were married in 1961.
5 Ethel Ruffels to the author, March 1999.
6 David Heaton, 'Garsington Manor 1928–1982', unpublished memoir, 1994, private collection.
7 JWWB to Norman Brook, 24 Feb. 1960, CAB 21/5823, TNA.
8 JWWB to Norman Brook, 10 March 1960, CAB 21/5823, TNA.
9 Ralph Blumenau to the author, 26 July 2008. Blumenau diaries, 3 Feb. 1961, 30 June 1961, 28 April 1962, 28 Aug. 1962.
10 Avon to JWWB, 12 Aug. 1961, AP33/4/17 and JWWB to Avon, 17 Aug. 1961, AP33/4/18, Avon papers, Special Collections, UB.
11 Avon to JWWB, 18 Aug. 1961, AP33/4/19, Avon papers, Special Collections, UB.
12 H.B. Boyne, *Daily Telegraph*, Sept. 1962.
13 Robert Blake, *Sunday Times*, 30 Sept. 1962. Later the Lord Blake (1916–2003).
14 Anthony Sampson, *The Observer*, 30 Sept. 1962.
15 Donald McLachlan, *Sunday Telegraph*, 30 Sept. 1962.
16 JWWB to Sir W.E. Wylie, 30 Sept. 1962, PRO 30/89/10/17, TNA. In 1924, Wylie was requested by the Free State to be a high court judge.
17 D.N. Chester, *Political Studies*, 12:1, Feb. 1964, D3, WB papers, SANT, Oxford.
18 JWWB to Norman Brook, 31 Oct. 1960, CAB 21/5823, TNA.
19 RBL, *Diaries* II, 12 Sept. 1962, p. 764.
20 RCWB to the author, 9 June 1999; David Heaton, 'Garsington Manor 1928–1982', unpublished memoir, 1994, private collection.
21 JWWB to Alistair Horne, 24 Oct. 1962, 19 Oct. 1965, private collection.

22 Michael Adeane to JWWB, 31 Oct. 1962, C7, WB papers, SANT, Oxford. The documents remain lodged pending the queen's death.
23 JWWB to Michael Adeane, 1 Nov. 1962, C7, WB papers, SANT, Oxford.
24 HM to President John Kennedy, 19 May 1963; Kennedy to HM, 1 June 1963, PREM 11/4568, TNA. Kennedy made his 'Ich bin ein Berliner' speech on 26 June 1963.
25 JWWB, Special Relationships, p. 36. Harold Macmillan resigned as prime minister in October 1963 following a sudden onset of prostate disease, which made him think that he would not be able to fight the next general election.
26 JWWB, Friends, Enemies and Sovereigns, p. 129. JWWB does not mention that he was also writing about Waverley and attributes his fatigue to writing the biography of George VI.
27 JWWB, Preface to the Second Edition, Nemesis of Power, pp. vii–xi, Garsington Manor, July 1963.
28 Hugh Trevor-Roper, Sunday Times, excerpt of review of the paperback edn, 1970.
29 HM to JWWB, 3 July 1968, C11, WB papers, SANT, Oxford.
30 JWWB, D17, WB papers, SANT, Oxford.
31 JEWB to the author, 21 Jan. 2009.
32 JWWB, D18, WB papers, SANT, Oxford.
33 Ibid.
34 After the war, Morgan worked as public relations adviser to Oliver Franks, British ambassador in Washington D.C. JWWB had turned down the position (in order to have time to write Nemesis) and suggested Morgan instead.
35 Lewis Douglas (1894–1974). He was succeeded in the House of Representatives by Isabella Greenway. He was US ambassador to the UK 1947–51. JWWB, D18, WB papers, SANT, Oxford.
36 Will Rogers (1879–1935), Cherokee Indian born in Oklahoma, famed as a cowboy, comedian, humorist and actor.
37 JWWB, D18, WB papers, SANT, Oxford. He was in residence in 1964, 1966, 1968–70, 1972–75.
38 JWWB to Avon, 27 July 1964, AP33/4/37, Avon papers, Special Collections, UB. JWWB mistakenly noted that Anthony Nicholls was twenty-seven.
39 Avon to JWWB, 31 July 1964, AP33/4/38, Avon papers, Special Collections, UB. Alan Campbell-Johnson wrote a biography of Eden, published in 1938 and revised in 1955, and one on Halifax, published in 1941. After further discussion, Avon accepted JWWB's suggestion that the task should go to Nicholls in the event that he predeceased him.
40 Avon to JWWB, 31 July 1964, AP33/4/38, Avon papers, Special Collections, UB.
41 Avon to JWWB, 17 May 1965, AP33/4/50, Avon papers, Special Collections, UB.
42 JWWB to Avon, 7 July 1975, AP33/4/52, Avon papers, Special Collections, UB.
43 Avon to JWWB, 4 Aug. 1965, AP33/4/54, Avon papers, Special Collections, UB.
44 JWWB to Avon, 16 Aug. 1965, AP33/4/56, Avon papers, Special Collections, UB.
45 Ralph Blumenau, Diary, 25 Jan. 1965, to the author.
46 JWWB, Foreword to Ralph Blumenau, History of Malvern College, p. viii.
47 JWWB, D17, WB papers, SANT, Oxford. See also The Malvernian, Centenary Issue, Dec. 1965, Malvern College Archives.
48 JWWB, D17, WB papers, SANT, Oxford.
49 JWWB to Avon, 16 Aug. 1965, AP33/4/56, Avon papers, Special Collections, UB.

50 JWWB set an example and retired from the council in 1972 when he was seventy. Bernard (later Baron) Weatherill, PC, DL (1920–2007), speaker of the House of Commons 1982–93.

51 The Page-Barbour Lectures were founded in 1907 by Mrs Thomas Nelson Page. The lectures, which may be in any field in the arts and sciences, are to present 'some fresh aspect or aspects of the department of thought' in which the lecturer is a specialist, and are to possess such unity as to be published in book form by the university.

52 JWWB, D17, WB papers, SANT, Oxford.

53 W.B. Yeats, 'Meru' from *Supernatural Songs*, as quoted in *The Semblance of Peace*, pp. 1 and 610.

54 JWWB and Anthony Nicholls, Introduction: 'Some Thoughts on Peace-making', *The Semblance of Peace*, p. 3. (JWWB wrote this.)

55 Avon to JWWB, 13 Aug. 1966, AP33/4/74, Avon papers, Special Collections, UB.

56 JWWB to Avon, 2 July 1966, AP33/4/70. Avon papers, Special Collections, UB.

57 JWWB to Avon, 26 June 1967, AP33/4/92, Avon papers, Special Collections, UB.

58 The list included Bernard Fergusson, John Terraine, Michael Howard and eventually JWWB.

59 Avon to JWWB, 3 Aug. 1967, AP33/4/99, Avon papers, Special Collections, UB.

60 JWWB to Rt Hon. Kenneth Younger, 30 May 1967, B31, WB papers, SANT, Oxford.

61 JWWB, D17, WB papers, SANT, Oxford. Hardy C. Dillard (1902–82).

62 JWWB, D18, WB papers, SANT, Oxford.

63 Dr James McNaughton Hester (b. 1924), president of New York University, 1962–75. JWWB was Distinguished Professor of History four times: 1967, 1968, 1969 (fall semester) and 1970. See JWWB, *Friends, Enemies and Sovereigns*, p. 74.

64 JWWB, D18, WB papers, SANT, Oxford.

65 *Ibid.*

66 JWWB to Avon, 1 March 1967, AP33/4/89, Avon papers, Special Collections, UB.

67 One Fifth Avenue Hotel had been bought by New York University for use by female students and VIPs.

68 JWWB, D18, WB papers, SANT, Oxford.

69 *Ibid.*

70 As related by Anthony Nicholls; correspondence with the author, 15 May 2008.

71 JWWB, D18, WB papers, SANT, Oxford.

72 JWWB, D17, WB papers, SANT, Oxford.

73 HM, *The Blast of War*, Macmillan, 1967. The first volume was *The Winds of Change* (1966).

74 JWWB to HM, 2 May 1967, C9, WB papers, SANT, Oxford.

75 JWWB, Preface to 2nd edition, *The Forgotten Peace: The Treaty of Brest-Litovsk*, Papermac, 1967.

76 Dance Memorial Lecture, Virginia Military Institute, 1960, later published in the *Virginia Quarterly Review*, 1966.

77 JWWB, 'Twenty Years of Russo-German Relations, 1919–1939', *Foreign Affairs*, 25: 1, 1946, pp. 23–43.

78 See JWWB, *A Wreath to Clio*.

79 *Times Educational Supplement*, 29 Sept. 1967.

80 Geoffrey Barraclough, *The Guardian*, 8 Sept. 1967, D11, WB papers, SANT, Oxford.

81 Avon to JWWB, 8 Nov. 1967, AP33/4/109, Avon papers, Special Collections, UB.
Charles McMoran Wilson, 1st Baron Moran (1882–1977).
82 JWWB (ed.), *Action This Day: Working with Churchill*, p. 9.
83 JWWB to Avon, 3 Aug. 1968, AP33/4/121, Avon papers, Special Collections,
UB.
84 Avon to JWWB, 21 Aug. 1968, AP33/4/127, Avon papers, Special Collections,
UB. Original in D10, WB papers, SANT, Oxford.
85 JWWB to Avon, 22 Aug. 1968, AP33/4/129, Avon papers, Special Collections,
UB.
86 Harold Deutsch, *The Conspiracy against Hitler in the Twilight War*, p. 157. Hans
Rothfels was the first historian to detail JWWB's authorship of the 28 December
1939 memorandum which he had written in support of the opponents of the
Nazi regime. See his *Trott und die Aussenpolitik des Widerstandes, Vierteljahrshefte für
Zeitgeschichte*, 12, 1964, pp. 307 and 316–17.
87 JWWB to Christopher Sykes, quoted in *Troubled Loyalty*, p. 307 n. 47.
88 See *A Noble Combat: the Letters of Shiela Grant Duff and Adam von Trott zu Solz
1932–1939*, ed. Klemens von Klemperer: 'War broke out between us even before
it broke out between our two countries', Trott to Grant Duff, 25 Aug. 1939,
pp. 211–12.
89 Christopher Sykes, 'Heroes and Suspects', *Encounter*, XXXI, Dec. 1968, p. 39. Sykes
emphasised the difficulties in understanding Trott's wartime support of the Indian
National Army, recruited by the Indian nationalist Subhas Chandra Bose to fight
against the British. 'If the whole thing was camouflage, then surely in judging a loss
of trust, one must take account of the likely effect on an Englishman of camouflage
activity which not only deceived Trott's Nazi superiors but some of his anti-Nazi
collaborators.'
90 David Astor, 'Why the Revolt against Hitler Was Ignored', *Encounter*, XXXII, June
1969, p. 8.
91 JWWB, letter, 'Sir John Wheeler-Bennett's Reply', *Encounter*, XXXIII, Aug. 1969,
p. 95. See also C9, WB papers, SANT, Oxford.
92 JWWB, 'The Man Who Did Not Kill Hitler', *New York Review of Books*, 11 Sept.
1969, p. 38. 'The early writers on the military resistance movement in Germany
were often susceptible to the invariably self-flattering post-war accounts of German
officers. Their views have now been superseded by the research of German, American and British scholars, whose views broadly reinforce those of JWWB.' Anthony
Nicholls, correspondence with the author, 15 May 2008. See also Malone, *Adam
von Trott*, pp. 50–56.
93 David Astor, letter, 'The German Opposition to Hitler: A Reply to Critics',
Encounter, XXXIII, Oct. 1969. See also C9, WB papers, SANT, Oxford and 'Peace
Aims', FO 371/24363, TNA.
94 Anthony Howard, *New Statesman,* 23 May 1969. Anthony Howard CBE (1934–
2010) telephone interview with the author, 5 April 2008.
95 Harold Deutsch, *The Conspiracy against Hitler in the Twilight War*, p. 157
n. 17.
96 JWWB, *Special Relationships*, p. 199.
97 Anthony Nicholls, correspondence with the author, 15 May 2008.
98 Alan Bullock, 'John Wheeler Wheeler-Bennett 1902–1975', *Proceedings of the British
Academy*, LXV, 1979, p. 817.
99 JWWB to Avon, 3 Feb. 1969, AP33/4/137, Avon papers, Special Collections, UB.
William De L'Isle, 1st Viscount (1909–91).
100 Avon to JWWB, 12 Feb. 1969, AP33/4/138, Avon papers, Special Collections,
UB.
101 JWWB to Avon, 20 Feb. 1969, AP33/4/139, Avon papers, Special Collections,
UB.

102 JWWB to Avon, 17 July 1971, AP33/4/236, Avon papers, Special Collections, UB.
103 Herbert Morrison (1888–1965). Avon to JWWB, 11 Sept. 1969, AP33/4/159, Avon papers, Special Collections, UB. Original in D10, WB papers, SANT, Oxford.
104 JWWB to Avon, 17 Sept. 1969, AP33/4/160, Avon papers, Special Collections, UB.
105 JWWB to Avon, 13 Oct. 1969, AP33/4/162, Avon papers, Special Collections, UB. The turning point in the protest was reached when members of the National Guard fired into a group of protesters at Kent State University in May 1970, killing four. According to JWWB, some seven hundred universities and colleges either closed down completely or came close to doing so. D18, WB papers, SANT, Oxford.
106 JWWB, D18, WB papers, SANT, Oxford.
107 Raymond Aron (1905–83). He taught at the Sorbonne 1955–68.
108 JWWB, D17, WB papers, SANT, Oxford.

Chapter 11 Memories

1 Sir Patrick Dean, Memorial Address, St Margaret's, Westminster, 21 Jan. 1976.
2 JWWB to Avon, 4 Feb. 1970, AP33/4/168, Avon papers, Special Collections, UB.
3 HM to JWWB, 27 May 1970, C11, WB papers, SANT, Oxford.
4 'Although not always a reliable chronicler'! JWWB to Richard Garnett at Macmillan, 14 March 1973, D11, WB papers, SANT, Oxford. In 1983, 'Reilly, Ace of Spies', based on Lockhart's son's book *Ace of Spies*, was an acclaimed TV series.
5 JWWB, 'Reconsiderations: The End of the Weimar Republic', *Foreign Affairs,* Jan. 1972, p. 369. As Brüning's biographer Patch states, 'as he sought to become more objective, his memory was fading badly', p. 320. From 1955 until his death in March 1970, Brüning had lived in the United States.
6 JWWB to Avon, 30 Nov. 1970, AP/33/4/223, Avon papers, Special Collections, UB. Ethel Ruffels to the author, 10 Dec. 2008.
7 Anthony Nicholls, correspondence with the author, 23 Dec. 2008.
8 JWWB to Avon, 7 Jan. 1971, AP33/4/225, Avon papers, Special Collections, UB.
9 JWWB, D17, WB papers, SANT, Oxford.
10 Ethel Ruffels to the author, March 1999.
11 JWWB to Sir Burke Trend, 19 Aug. 1969, C6, WB papers, SANT, Oxford. The citation for Brian Mertian Melland's award of the OBE on 13 June 1970 was Historian II, Cabinet Office, http://www.london-gazette.co.uk/issues/45117/supplement/6375.
12 Peter Fleming to JWWB, 6 Aug. 1971, C6, WB papers, SANT, Oxford. *Invasion 1940* was published in 1957.
13 JWWB to Lady Avon, 20 Aug. 1971, AP33/4/238, Avon papers, Special Collections, UB.
14 JWWB to Nicholls, 1 Oct. 1971, E1, WB papers, SANT, Oxford.
15 JWWB to Nicholls, 27 Oct. 1971, E1, WB papers, SANT, Oxford.
16 JWWB, D17, WB papers, SANT, Oxford.
17 *Ibid.*
18 JWWB to Nicholls, 11 Nov. 1971, E1, WB papers, SANT, Oxford.
19 JWWB to Nicholls, 23 Nov. 1971, E1, WB papers, SANT, Oxford.
20 JWWB to Nicholls, 4 Jan. 1972, E1, WB papers, SANT, Oxford.
21 *Ibid.*
22 JWWB to Nicholls, 1 Jan. 1972, E1, WB papers, SANT, Oxford.
23 JWWB to Nicholls, 28 Jan. 1972, E1, WB papers, SANT, Oxford.
24 HM to JWWB, 6 Jan. 1972, D11, WB papers, SANT, Oxford.

25 JWWB to Nicholls, 29 Jan. 1972, E1, WB papers, SANT, Oxford.

26 JWWB to Nicholls, 7 March 1972, E1, WB papers, SANT, Oxford.

27 Richard Cosgrove, University Distinguished Professor and head of department, University of Arizona, correspondence with the author, 8 Nov. 1999.

28 Alan Bullock, 'John Wheeler Wheeler-Bennett 1902–1975', *Proceedings of the British Academy*, LXV, 1979, p. 829.

29 JWWB to Avon, 27 Aug. 1972, AP33/4/253, Avon papers, Special Collections, UB.

30 Anthony Nicholls, dedication, *The Semblance of Peace*, Wheeler-Bennett Bequest, St Antony's College, Library, Oxford.

31 Anthony Nicholls, correspondence with the author, 15 May 2008.

32 *Times Literary Supplement*, 22 Sept. 1972, D10, WB papers, SANT, Oxford.

33 A.J.P. Taylor, *The Observer*, 1972, D10, WB papers, SANT, Oxford. A.J.P. Taylor (1906–90), historian and journalist. He ceased being a member of the Communist Party in 1926.

34 Gordon A. Craig, *Journal of Modern History*, 46: 2, 1974, D10, WB papers, SANT, Oxford.

35 Leonard Miall to JWWB, 18 Sept. 1972, C13, WB papers, SANT, Oxford.

36 *Daily Express*, 15 Sept. 1972, D10, WB papers, SANT, Oxford.

37 Anthony Nicholls, correspondence with the author, 15 May 2008. 'At one stage it was even suggested that the bombs had been used to intimidate Stalin rather than to end the war with Japan.' See *The Semblance of Peace*, pp. 556–57.

38 Michael Howard, 'Frozen Postures', *Sunday Times*, 24 Sept. 1972.

39 JWWB to Michael Howard, 3 Oct. 1972, private collection.

40 Alan Bullock, 'John Wheeler Wheeler-Bennett 1902–1975', *Proceedings of the British Academy*, LXV, 1979, p. 826.

41 Anthony Nicholls, correspondence with the author, 15 May 2008.

42 JWWB to Nicholls, 10 Jan. 1973, E1, WB papers, SANT, Oxford. (JWWB dated this letter 1972 but there is corroborative evidence that he had predated it by a year.)

43 *Ibid.* The Hon. George Kennan (1904–2005).

44 JWWB to Avon, 11 Jan. 1973, AP33/4/263, Avon papers, Special Collections, UB. In the same letter JWWB tells Avon about receiving letters from Harriman, Kennan and Backer, which confirms that the date of JWWB's letter to Nicholls was 1973, not 1972. Truman died on 26 December 1972.

45 JWWB to Avon, 14 Oct. 1972, AP33/4/257, Avon papers, Special Collections, UB.

46 The Viscount Ullswater, private secretary to Princess Margaret, Countess of Snowdon, to the author, 8 June 1999.

47 Juliet Pannett (1911–2005). She had drawn the portraits of numerous celebrities including Churchill, Slim, Alanbrooke, Liddell Hart, Vaughan Williams and Toynbee. Her medium was generally chalk or pencil.

48 The book is in the possession of Joan Wheeler-Bennett.

49 JWWB letter to Vic and Ethel Ruffels, private collection.

50 JWWB to Avon, 11 Jan., 1973, AP33/4/263, Avon papers, Special Collections, UB.

51 JWWB to Sir Neville Butler, 7 Nov. 1972, C12, WB papers, SANT, Oxford. A biography of Lord Lothian was written by James Butler and published in 1960.

52 Quoted by JWWB in D18, WB papers, SANT, Oxford.

53 JWWB to Nicholls, 10 Jan. 1973, E1, WB papers, SANT, Oxford.

54 JWWB to Avon, 11 Jan. 1973, AP33/4/263, Avon papers, Special Collections, UB.

55 Alcibiades (*c.*450–404 BC), Athenian statesman, orator and general. His capacity for making enemies meant that he never remained in one place for long. JWWB is

possibly referring to Albert, Margave of Brandenburg-Kulmbach (1522–57). Because of his bellicose nature, he was called Alcibiades after his death. Thomas Carlyle described Albert as having 'burnt away his splendid qualities as a mere temporary shine for the able editors, and never came to anything, full of fire, too much of it wildfire, not in the least like an Alcibiades except in the change of fortune he underwent'.

56 JWWB to Nicholls, 10 Jan. 1973, E1, WB papers, SANT, Oxford. See note 42 above.

57 JWWB to Avon, 18 June 1973, AP33/4/270, Avon papers, Special Collections, UB.

58 JWWB to HM, 7 May 1973, D11, WB papers, SANT, Oxford.

59 JWWB, draft for Birmingham University, 12 July 1973, C10, WB papers, SANT, Oxford.

60 Lady Avon to JWWB, 20 June 1973, AP33/4/272, Avon papers, Special Collections, UB.

61 JWWB, draft for Birmingham University, 12 July 1973, C10, WB papers, SANT, Oxford. The book to which he is referring is the fourth in the Information Series, *Information on the Renunciation of War 1927–1928*. Draft speech also in AP 33/4/274 dated 13 July 1973.

62 JWWB to Avon, 15 July 1974, AP33/4/277, Avon papers, Special Collections, UB.

63 Avon to JWWB, 17 Aug. 1973, C10, WB papers, SANT, Oxford; copy AP33/4/289, Avon papers, Special Collections, UB.

64 JWWB to Avon, 13 Aug. 1973, C10, WB papers, SANT, Oxford; original, AP33/4/286, Avon papers, Special Collections, UB.

65 JWWB to Avon, 31 Aug. 1973, AP33/4/298, Avon papers, Special Collections, UB.

66 Avon to JWWB, 3 Sept. 1973, AP33/4/299, Avon papers, Special Collections, UB.

67 JWWB to Avon, 12 Nov. 1973, AP33/4/317, Avon papers, Special Collections, UB.

68 Avon to the Rt Hon. Viscount Head, 13 Nov. 1973. AP23/37/40, Avon papers, Special Collections, UB.

69 JWWB to Major General Leonard D. Heaton, 23 Aug. 1973, AP33/4/296, Avon papers, Special Collections, UB.

70 General Heaton to JWWB, 4 Sept. 1973, AP33/4/306/307. See also Avon to JWWB, 14 June 1973, AP33/4/204, Avon papers, Special Collections, UB.

71 JWWB to Avon, 10 Sept. 1973, AP33/4/304, Avon papers, Special Collections, UB.

72 JWWB, *Knaves, Fools and Heroes*, pp. 78–80.

73 JWWB and Lord Longford, eds, *The History Makers*, p. 6. Francis Pakenham, 7th earl of Longford, KG, PC (1905–2001). Longford's biography of Eamon de Valera, co-authored with Thomas O'Neill, was published in 1970.

74 Otto John, *Twice through the Lines*, Macmillan, 1972. A possible explanation is that John was abducted as though he were a Russian spy to deflect attention from the real informant who operated for another seven years, or that he was taken as 'revenge' for having assisted the British against his fellow Germans. It is most likely that JWWB gave Otto John the introduction to Macmillan publishers.

75 JWWB to Otto John, 28 Sept. 1973, C5, WB papers, SANT, Oxford. Sir Peter Pears (1910–86). He met Benjamin Britten in 1934 and they became lifelong partners.

76 JWWB to Otto John, 10 Oct. 1973, C5, WB papers, SANT, Oxford.

77 JWWB to Avon, 18 Jan. 1974, AP33/4/324, Avon papers, Special Collections, UB.

78 Harold Wilson, Baron Wilson of Rievaulx, KG, OBE, FRS, PC (1916–95), prime minister 1964–70, 1974–76; Sir Edward Heath, KG, MBE (1916–2005), prime minister 1970–74.
79 Patrick Dean to JWWB, 6 Jan. 1974, C8, WB papers, SANT, Oxford.
80 JWWB to Nicholls, 31 March 1974, E1, WB papers, SANT, Oxford.
81 *Ibid.*
82 Avon to JWWB, 8 April 1974, C10, WB papers, SANT, Oxford.
83 JWWB to John P. Schaefer, 9 April 1974, C8, WB papers, SANT, Oxford. Martin Charteris, Baron Charteris of Amisfield, GCB, GCVO, OBE, QSO, PC (1913–99), private secretary to the queen 1972–77.
84 JWWB, D18, WB papers, SANT, Oxford.
85 RA PS/CSP/GEN/CURRENT/JWWB. JWWB to R. Mackworth-Young, 3 July 1974 and Mackworth–Young to JWWB, 9 July 1974.
86 Ariel Levy to JWWB, 15 May 1974, C15, WB papers, SANT, Oxford.
87 HM to RRWB, 3 July 1974, C11, WB papers, SANT, Oxford.
88 Martin Charteris to JWWB, 16 Oct. 1974, C8, WB papers, SANT, Oxford.
89 Queen Elizabeth the Queen Mother to JWWB, 9 Nov. 1974, D5, WB papers, SANT, Oxford.
90 IB to JWWB, 23 Oct. 1974, C8, WB papers, SANT, Oxford.
91 David Heaton to JWWB, no date, C8, WB papers, SANT, Oxford.
92 RCWB to JWWB, 8 Nov. 1974, C8, WB papers, SANT, Oxford.
93 JEWB to JWWB, 16 Jan. 1975, D12, WB papers, SANT, Oxford.
94 Sir Colin Coote, 30 Nov. 1974, C8, WB papers, SANT, Oxford.
95 John Raymond, *Sunday Times*, 19 Dec. 1974, D12, WB papers, SANT, Oxford.
96 D.C. Watt, *Times Literary Supplement*, 6 Dec. 1974, D12, WB papers, SANT, Oxford. See Brian Farrell, ed., *Leadership and Responsibility in the Second World War*, McGill-Queen's Press, 2004. 'Among Seeds's first tasks in Moscow . . . was the daunting prospect of trying to convince Soviet officials that British policy was not one of cold-shouldering their country' (p. 126).
97 Max Beloff to JWWB, 25 Nov. 1974, C8, WB papers, SANT, Oxford.
98 JWWB to Malone, 12 May 1971, as quoted in Malone, *Adam von Trott zu Solz*, p. 466 n. 146.
99 Shiela Grant Duff, *The Parting of the Ways*, p. 96.
100 JWWB, letter to Shiela Grant Duff, 1969, quoted in Malone, *Adam von Trott zu Solz*, p. 468 n.153.
101 See RA PS/PSO/GV/C/P/586/227, Eric Phipps to the King, from British Embassy, Berlin, 16 Oct. 1935. See also JWWB, *Knaves, Fools and Heroes*, p. 92.
102 Henry Malone, *Adam von Trott zu Solz*, p. 468 n. 153. JWWB to Malone, 12 May 1971, in *Adam von Trott*, pp. 466–67 n. 146.
103 Keith Sutton to JWWB, 31 Jan. 1975 and JWWB to Keith Sutton, 25 Feb. 1975, D12, WB papers, SANT, Oxford.
104 JWWB to Avon, 9 Dec. 1974, AP33/4/361, Avon papers, Special Collections, UB.
105 JWWB, *Special Relationships*, p. 9.
106 For example, there is no mention of Lord Victor Cavendish-Bentinck, duke of Portland, chairman of the Joint Intelligence Committee 1939–45, whom JWWB would have met had he been involved in intelligence work.
107 JWWB, speech at Foundation Luncheon, University of Arizona, 19 Feb. 1975, C8, WB papers, SANT, Oxford.
108 JWWB to Nicholls, 22 Feb. 1975, E1, WB papers, SANT, Oxford.
109 JWWB, Fitzpatrick Lecture, Woodberry Forest School, Virginia, 22 April 1975, C14, WB papers, SANT, Oxford. JWWB had published an article 'Problems of a Modern Historian', *Virginia Magazine of History and Biography*, 80:2, April 1972.

110 JWWB to Nicholls, 23 July 1975, E1, WB papers, SANT, Oxford.
111 Presented to St Antony's by Sir Martin Charteris at a dinner on 3 June 1977. Christine Nicholls, *History of St Antony's*, p. 42. 'I think I must have been present at the dinner because I have a dim memory of Charteris saying that he was inspired to make the bust look as it did because John was always putting his head round the door [at Buckingham Palace] with a cheerful smile to make some inquiry or other.' Anthony Nicholls to the author, 23 June 2008.
112 JWWB to Avon, 16 July 1975, AP33/4/377, Avon papers, Special Collections, UB.
113 JWWB to Nicholls, 31 July 1975, E1, WB papers, SANT, Oxford.
114 JWWB to Nicholls, 23 July 1975, E1, WB papers, SANT, Oxford.
115 JWWB, Introduction to Nicholas Reynolds, *Treason Was No Crime*.
116 RCWB to the author, 9 June 1999. This volume was never published but the notes he made are among the WB papers, SANT, Oxford.
117 JWWB to Douglas Fairbanks, 17 Nov. 1975, to Raymond Massey, 20 Nov. 1975, to David Niven, 20 Nov. 1975, C8, WB papers, SANT, Oxford. Madeleine Caroll was Flavia. No reply to his enquiry exists in his papers.
118 HM to JWWB, 2 July 1975, C11, WB papers, SANT, Oxford.
119 JWWB to Avon, 15 Sept. 1975, AP33/4/388, Avon papers, Special Collections, UB.
120 JWWB to Donald Lindsay, 13 Oct. 1975, C8, WB papers, SANT, Oxford.
121 JWWB to Avon, 28 Oct. 1975, AP33/4/402, Avon papers, Special Collections, UB.
122 Avon to JWWB, 30 Oct. 1975, AP33/4/403, Avon papers, Special Collections, UB.
123 JWWB to Avon, 3 Nov. 1975, AP33/4/404, Avon papers, Special Collections, UB. After JWWB's death, Nicholls asked to be 'honourably' released from writing Avon's biography, 'the hurdle being Suez, for which he had no political sympathy'. D.R. Thorpe, *Eden: The Life and Times of Anthony Eden, First Earl of Avon, 1897–1977*, Chatto & Windus, 2003, p. 575 n. 76. Nicholls, conversations with the author, 2006 and 2008.
124 Ethel Ruffels to the author, 1999. Brooks's still only has male members.
125 JWWB to Donald Lindsay, 17 Nov. 1975, C8, WB papers. SANT, Oxford.
126 JWWB to Avon, 24 Nov. 1975, AP33/4/407, Avon papers, Special Collections, UB.
127 Irene Heaton, unpublished memoirs, private collection.
128 Sir Patrick Dean, Memorial address, 21 Jan. 1976. See also *The Times*, 22 Jan. 1976.
129 *Virginia Quarterly Review*, winter 1978, D12, WB papers, SANT, Oxford.
130 HM, Foreword to JWWB, *Friends, Enemies and Sovereigns*, p. 10.
131 *Ibid.*, p. 9.
132 Alan Bullock, 'John Wheeler Wheeler-Bennett 1902–1975', *Proceedings of the British Academy*, LXV, 1979, p. 828.
133 Irene Heaton, unpublished memoirs, private collection. JWWB's estate was valued at £82,129 net before death duty was paid: *The Times*, 26 Feb. 1976, p. 16. RRWB remained in Garsington until the house was sold to Mr and Mrs Leonard Ingrams. She returned to the United States in 1982 and died in 1991.
134 HM the Queen Mother, quoted by Patrick Dean, Arizona Inn, Tucson, 1 March 1980, requoted by gracious permission of HM the Queen Mother; Sir Alistair Aird, correspondence with the author, 9 June 1999.
135 Aubrey Morgan, Arizona Inn, Tucson, 1 March 1980. The obituary display is no longer there. 'I suspect that the present management has no idea of who Sir John was or the long relationship that he had with the Inn.' Richard Cosgrove, correspondence with the author, 8 Nov. 1999.
136 RCWB interview with the author, 9 June 1999.

137 JWWB, Fitzpatrick Lecture, Woodberry Forest School, Virginia, 22 April 1975, C14, WB papers, SANT, Oxford.
138 Sir Michael Howard, correspondence with the author, 19 June 2008.
139 Harold Macmillan, message included in remarks by Sir Patrick Dean, dedication of memorial at Tucson, Arizona, 1981.
140 An alternative 'Not the Wheeler-Bennett' Society was set up by students who 'went to drink' in the sixth form common room. Hugh Carson to the author, 10 Dec. 2006.
141 JWWB left £500 to the Malvernian Society in 1976; the income from this was to be used to provide an annual prize for the best essay submitted by a boy/boys in the upper school of Malvern College on the subject of European or general history but excluding English history. It was his wish that the boy(s) should buy a book or books with the prize money. Early letters and memos refer to the prize as the 'Sir John Wheeler-Bennett European History Prize', later the 'Sir John Wheeler-Bennett History Prize' and today the 'Wheeler-Bennett History Prize'. Sandra Theaker-Elliott, the Malvernian Society, to the author, 16 Dec. 2008.
142 Alan Bullock, 'John Wheeler Wheeler-Bennett 1902–1975', *Proceedings of the British Academy*, LXV, 1979, p. 830.
143 JWWB, *Knaves, Fools and Heroes*, p. 100.
144 Anthony Nicholls, correspondence with the author, 11 June 2008.
145 JWWB, *Action This Day*, p. 12.
146 Richard Overy, Introduction to JWWB, *The Nemesis of Power*, Palgrave, Macmillan, 2005, p. xiv. This edition was reprinted from the first edition of 1953, rather than the second edition of 1964, and did not include JWWB's Foreword to the second edition.
147 JWWB, Notes on 'Brest-Litovsk – the Unknown Peace', B23, WB papers, SANT, Oxford.
148 JWWB, *Friends, Enemies and Sovereigns*, p. 170.
149 JWWB and Anthony Nicholls, Epilogue: 'By Manifold Illusion', *The Semblance of Peace*, p. 609. JWWB wrote this chapter.
150 JWWB, *Friends, Enemies and Sovereigns*, p. 171.

Select Bibliography

Correspondence and Interviews

Sir Alistair Aird, GCVO, Private Secretary to the Queen Elizabeth the Queen Mother, The Viscount Ullswater, Private Secretary to the Princess Margaret, Countess of Snowdon, Tony Benn, Ralph Blumenau, Sir Raymond Carr, Professor Richard Cosgrove, Sir William Deakin, DSO, Lady Dean, Mrs Gerald Draper, the Hon. Mrs Oliver Twisleton-Wykeham-Fiennes, the Very Reverend the Hon. Oliver Twisleton-Wykeham-Fiennes, David Heaton, OBE, Joan Heaton, Sir Alistair Horne, CBE, Anthony Howard, CBE, Sir Michael Howard, Mrs Leonard Ingrams, Michael Korda, Mark Logue, Giles MacDonogh, Anthony Nicholls, Philip Nicholls, Professor Richard Overy, Norman Rosser, Ethel Ruffels, Vic Ruffels, The Rugbian Society, William Shawcross, Mary Stanford, D.R. Thorpe, Joan Wheeler-Bennett, Richard Wheeler-Bennett, Dr Catherine Wills, Philip Ziegler.

Published Sources

(Place of publication is London unless stated otherwise)

Berlin, Isaiah, *Flourishing Letters 1928–1946*, ed. Henry Hardy, Chatto & Windus, 2004.

Bloch, Michael, *The Secret File of the Duke of Windsor*, Bantam, 1988.

Blood-Ryan, H.W., *Franz von Papen: His Life and Times*, Rich & Cowan, 1940.

Blumenau, Ralph, *A History of Malvern College*, Macmillan, 1965.

Brüning, Heinrich, *Memorien*, Deutsche Verlags-Anstalt, Stuttgart, 1970.

— *Briefe und Gespräche*, 1934–1945 and 1946–60 (2 vols), Deutsche Verlags-Anstalt, Stuttgart, 1970.

Bullock, Alan, 'John Wheeler Wheeler-Bennett 1902–1975', *Proceedings of the British Academy*, LXV, 1979.

Butler, J.R.M., *Lord Lothian (Philip Kerr) 1882–1941*, Macmillan, 1960.

Cadogan, Alexander, *The Diaries of Sir Alexander Cadogan, O.M. 1938–1945*, ed. David Dilks, Putnam, 1972.

Carrington, C.E., revised by Mary Bone, *Chatham House: Its History and Inhabitants*, RIIA, 2004.

Churchill, Winston S., *The Second World War*, 6 vols, 1948–54, The Reprint Society, 1956.

— ed., *Never Give In!*, Random House, 2003; Hyperion Books, 2004.

Cockburn, Claud, *In Time of Trouble*, Rupert Hart-Davis, 1956.

Cull, Nicholas John, *Selling the War: The British Propaganda Campaign against American 'Neutrality'*, Oxford University Press, 1995.

Deutsch, Harold, *The Conspiracy against Hitler in the Twilight War*, University of Minnesota Press/Oxford University Press, 1968.

Dugdale, Baffy, *The Diaries of Blanche Dugdale, 1936–47*, ed. N.A. Rose, Vallentine, Mitchell, 1973.

Garnett, David, *The Secret History of PWE: The Political Warfare Executive, 1939–1945*, St Ermin's, 2002.

Grant Duff, Shiela, *The Parting of the Ways: A Personal Account of the Thirties*, Peter Owen, 1982.

— *A Noble Combat: The Letters of Shiela Grant Duff and Adam von Trott zu Solz, 1932–1939*, ed. Klemens von Klemperer, Oxford University Press, 1988.

Holmes, Errol, *Flannelled Foolishness: A Cricketing Chronicle*, Hollis & Carter, 1957.

Hyde, Montgomery, *The Quiet Canadian: The Secret Service Story of Sir William Stephenson, MC, DFC*, Hamish Hamilton, 1962.

John, Otto, *Twice through the Lines*, Macmillan, 1972; Futura 1974.

Klemperer, Klemens von, *German Resistance against Hitler: The Search for Allies Abroad, 1938–1945*, Oxford University Press, 1994.

Knickerbocker, H.R., *Will War Come in Europe?* The Bodley Head, 1934.

Korda, Michael, *Charmed Lives*, Allen Lane, 1980.

Lascelles, Alan, *King's Counsellor. Abdication and War: The Diaries of Sir Alan Lascelles*, ed. Duff Hart-Davis, Weidenfeld & Nicolson, 2006.

Lockhart, Sir Robert Bruce, *Friends, Foes and Foreigners*, Putnam, 1957.

— *Giants Cast Long Shadows*, Putnam, 1960.

— *The Diaries of Sir Robert Bruce Lockhart, I: 1915–1939; II: 1939–65*, ed. Kenneth Young, Macmillan, 1980.

MacDonogh, Giles, *A Good German: Adam von Trott zu Solz*, Quartet, 1989.

— *After the Reich: From the Liberation of Vienna to the Berlin Airlift*, John Murray, 2007.

Malone, Henry Ozelle, Jr, 'Adam von Trott zu Solz: the Road to Conspiracy against Hitler', The University of Texas at Austin, 1980.

Nicholas, H.G., ed., *Washington Despatches*, University of Chicago Press, 1981.

Nicholls, Anthony, *The Weimar Republic and the Rise of Hitler*, 4th edn, Macmillan, 2000.

Nicolson, Harold, *Diaries and Letters 1945–1962*, ed. Nigel Nicolson, Collins, 1968.

Papen, Franz von, *Memoirs*, tr. Brian Connell, André Deutsch, London, 1952.

Patch, William L., Jr, *Heinrich Brüning and the Dissolution of the Weimar Republic*, Cambridge University Press, 1998.

Reynolds, David, *Lord Lothian and Anglo-American Relations*, American Philosophical Society, 2007.

Reynolds, Nicholas, *Treason Was No Crime*, William Kimber, 1976.

Rothfels, Hans, *Die Deutsche Opposition gegen Hitler*, Fischer Bucherei, Germany, 1961.

Schacht, Hjalmar, *My First Seventy-Six Years*, tr. Diana Pyke, Allan Wingate, 1955.

Shawcross, William, *Queen Elizabeth the Queen Mother*, Macmillan, 2009.

Sykes, Christopher, *Troubled Loyalty: A Biography of Adam von Trott zu Solz*, Collins, 1968.

Thomsett, Michael C., *The German Opposition to Hitler: The Resistance, the Underground and Assassination Plots, 1938–1945*, McFarland, 2007.

Tree, Ronald, *When the Moon Was High: Memoirs of Peace and War, 1897–1942*, Macmillan, 1975.

Vansittart, Lord, *The Mist Procession*, Hutchinson, 1958.
Weitz, Eric D., *Weimar Germany: Promise and Tragedy*, Princeton University Press, 2001.
Weiz, John, *Hitler's Banker*, Little Brown & Co., New York, 1998.
Wheeler-Bennett, John W., *Information on the Permanent Court of International Justice*, Association for International Understanding, 1924.
— *Information on the Problem of Security*, Information Series No. 1, Allen & Unwin, 1925.
— *Information on the Reduction of Armaments*, Information Series No. 2, Allen & Unwin, 1925.
— *The World Court in 1925*, Association for International Understanding, 1926.
— *Information on the Problem of Security* (with F.E. Langerman), Information Series No. 3, Allen & Unwin, 1927.
— *Information on the Renunciation of War 1927–1928*, Information Series No. 4, Allen & Unwin, 1928.
— *Information on the World Court, 1918–1928* (with Maurice Fanshawe), Information Series No. 5, Allen & Unwin, 1929.
— *Information on the Reparation Settlement* (with Hugh Latimer), Information Series No. 6, Allen & Unwin, 1930.
— *Disarmament and Security since Locarno, 1925–1931*, Information Series No. 7, Allen & Unwin, 1932.
— *The Wreck of Reparations*, Information Series No. 8, Allen & Unwin, 1933.
— *The Disarmament Deadlock*, George Routledge & Sons, 1934; published in New York as *The Pipe Dream of Peace: The Story of the Collapse of Disarmament*, William Morrow & Co., 1935.
— *Bulletin of International News*, Vols I–VI, RIIA; Vol. VII, under direction of JWWB, RIIA, 1924–32.
— ed., *Documents on International Affairs*, 1928–30, RIIA; 1930–35 Vol. I in collaboration with Stephen Heald, 1936.
— *Hindenburg: The Wooden Titan*, Macmillan, 1936.
— *Brest-Litovsk: The Forgotten Peace, March 1918*, Macmillan, 1938.
— *Munich, Prologue to Tragedy*, 1948; Macmillan, 1963.
— *The Nemesis of Power: The German Army in Politics, 1918–1945*, Macmillan, 1953, revised edn 1964; Palgrave Macmillan, 2005.
— *King George VI: His Life and Reign*, Macmillan, 1958.
— *John Anderson, Viscount Waverley*, Macmillan, 1962.
— *A Wreath to Clio*, Macmillan, 1967.
— ed., *Action this Day: Working with Churchill*, Macmillan, 1968.
— *The Semblance of Peace: The Political Settlement after the Second World War* (with Anthony Nicholls), 1973.
— and Frank Pakenham, the earl of Longford, eds, *The History Makers*, eds, Sidgwick & Jackson, 1973.
— *Knaves, Fools and Heroes: In Europe between the Wars*, Macmillan, 1974.
— *Special Relationships: America in Peace and War*, Macmillan, 1975.
— *Friends, Enemies and Sovereigns*, Macmillan, 1976.
Ziegler, Philip, *King Edward VIII*, Sutton, 2001.

Articles in Journals and Newspapers

Encounter, XXXI, 1968, XXXII, XXXIII, 1969.
Foreign Affairs, 1946, 1972.
Journal of the Royal Institute for International Affairs (RIIA), 1929, 1932, 1933.
The Malvernian, Centenary Issue, Dec. 1965.
New York Review of Books, 1969.

Proceedings of the British Academy, LXV, 1979.
selected newspapers from Wheeler-Bennett papers, St Antony's College, Oxford.
Slavonic and East European Review, 27: 68, Dec. 1948.
Times Educational Supplement, 1967.
Virginia Quarterly Review, selected issues.

Unpublished Sources

Avon papers, University of Birmingham.
Blumenau, Ralph, Diaries, private collection.
Heaton, David, 'Garsington Manor 1928–1982', private collection.
Heaton, Irene, Memoirs, private collection.
Horne, Sir Alistair, Letters, private collection.
Howard, Sir Michael, Letters, private collection.
Logue, Lionel, Letters, private collection.
Messersmith, George S., Papers, University of Delaware.
Nicolson, Harold, Diaries, Balliol College, Oxford.
Royal Archives, Windsor Castle.
Ruffels, Vic and Ethel, Letters, private collection.
The National Archives, Kew.
Wheeler-Bennett papers, St Antony's College, Oxford.★
Wheeler-Bennett personal files 1921–75, Royal Institute of International Affairs.

★ It must be noted that when Wheeler-Bennett wrote his three volumes of memoirs as well as unpublished recollections in the early 1970s, he was recording events mainly from memory at a time when his health was failing. He apparently did not feel the need to check against his own carefully kept diaries or other source material and so there are a number of discrepancies. Where possible I have tried to verify what he has said and have purposely not included those recollections that are obviously incorrect.

Index

NOTE   Works by John Wheeler-Bennett (JWW-B) appear directly under title; works by others under author's name

Abdication (1936), 99, 208
Action This Day: Working with Churchill (ed. JWW-B), 243
Adeane, Sir Michael, 213, 222, 233, 269
Adenauer, Konrad, 193, 195, 222, 267
Aguinaldo, Emilio, 48, 56
Ah Foo (Chinese servant), 27, 30, 32–33, 44, 46, 50
Aherne, Brian, 128
Albany, Piccadilly, 22, 57, 81, 84, 199
All Peoples' Association, 68
All Souls College, Oxford, 176
Allied Control Council (Germany), 185
America First Committee, 137–38
Anglo-German Association, 72
Anglo-German Group, 84
Anglo-German Naval Agreement (1935), 113
appeasement policy, opposition to, 99, 104, 106
Arab-Israeli war (1967), 235
Arizona, University of: JWW-B teaches at, 226–29, 232, 257, 262, 267, 274; awards honorary doctorate to JWW-B, 269, 274
Armstrong, Hamilton Fish ('Ham'): JWW-B meets, 17–18, 82; at Harvard celebrations, 98; in USA, 115, 119, 238; death, 269
Aron, Raymond, 251
Association for International Understanding, 19–22, 32, 35, 39

Astor, David, 120, 123, 245–48
Atlantic Charter, 140
atom bombs, dropped on Japan, 174, 260
Attlee, Clement (*later* 1st Earl), 174, 187, 199, 202, 259
Auchinloss, Louis, 108
August-Wilhelm, Prince of Germany, 60
Augusta, USS, 140
Australia and New Zealand, JWW-B visits (1922), 16–17
Austria: Anschluss with Germany, 39, 93, 104, 113; Brüning seeks customs union with, 66; JWW-B visits (1934), 82; Nazi infiltration, 93; royalists in, 93
Austria-Hungary, and outbreak of World War I, 5–6
Avon, Anthony Eden, 1st earl of: JWW-B meets, 19; and German disarmament, 73; resigns (1938), 104; anti-appeasement policy, 106; as foreign secretary, 138; on denunciation of Munich Agreement, 145; and Political Warfare Executive, 152; at Moscow Conference (1943), 157; resigns after Suez, 210; letter from JWW-B on prospective biography of Queen Mother, 214; earldom, 219; memoirs, 219–20; health decline, 229, 253; proposed biography, 229–30, 234–35, 252, 258, 262–65, 278; on position of Turkey in World War II, 234; and JWW-B's post at New York

University, 238; winters in Barbados,
241; JWW-B's correspondence with,
242, 243–44, 252–53, 261, 273,
276–77; comments on JWW-B's
historical studies, 243–44, 249–50;
advises JWW-B against writing on
Gort, 249; JWW-B appointed literary
trustee, 258; JWW-B acknowledges in
The Semblance of Peace, 259; and
Truman's approval of *The Semblance of
Power*, 261; as chancellor of
Birmingham University, 262–63;
JWW-B praises in Birmingham
acceptance speech, 263–64;
congratulates JWW-B on GCVO, 267;
demoralised over industrial unrest, 268;
and JWW-B's final illness, 278; shares
JWW-B's views, 283
Avon, Clarissa, countess of, 214, 255,
263, 267

Backer, George, 261
Bahamas, 187
Baldwin, Stanley, 201
Balfour, Arthur James, 172
Balkan Wars (1912–13), 4
Barbados, 241, 253
Barraclough, Geoffrey, 243
Barthou, Louis, 85
Bartlett, Vernon: friendship with
JWW-B, 15, 81; in Anglo-German
Group, 84; edits *World Review of
Reviews*, 99; on Nazi 'Black List', 99
Battle of Britain (1940), 132
Bauer, Colonel Max, 49
Baumont, Maurice, 185
Beacon, The (school magazine), 11, 14
Beatrice, Princess (of Battenberg), 24
Beck, Colonel General Ludwig, 276
Belgium, Germans invade (1914), 6
Beloff, Max (*later* Baron), 272
Beneš, Eduard, 38, 110, 111–12, 132,
177, 180, 188, 230
Benn, Anthony Wedgwood (Tony), 183,
268
Bennett, John (JWW-B's grandfather), 1
Bennett, Mary (*née* Wheeler; JWW-B's
grandmother), 1
Berlin: JWW-B in, 56, 60, 79, 87,
94–95, 185; Reichstag fire, 75;
Soviet-US conflict in, 187–88; Soviet
blockade (1948), 188–89; Wall, 222
Berlin, (Sir) Isaiah, 129, 136, 171, 176,
183, 186, 271, 280

Bermuda, 172
Bernstorff, Count Albrecht von, 68,
94–95, 151, 167
Besse, Antonin, 189–90
Bevin, Ernest, 181, 184
Biddle, Francis, 179
Birchall, Frederick, 63
Birkenhead, Frederick Smith, 2nd earl of,
229
Birmingham University, 262–64
Blake, Robert, Baron, 220, 229
Blaskowitz, Field Marshal Johannes, 154
Blumenau, Ralph, 219, 230; *A History of
Malvern College*, 230–31
Bolsheviks, JWW-B meets in USSR,
92–94
Bonhöffer, Dietrich, 191
Bonhöffer, Klaus, 191
Bonnaire, Dorothy, 196
Boosey, Arthur, 8
Borah, William E., 36
Borneo, 45–47
Bowes-Lyon, (Sir) David, 139, 145–46,
153, 161
Boyne, H.B., 220
Bracken, Brendan (*later* Viscount), 106,
139, 140, 155, 158, 165
Brand, Robert (*later* 1st Baron; Bob),
132
Brandt, Lieut. Hans von, 62, 166
Breasted, James Henry, 26
Breslau (German cruiser), 6
Brest-Litovsk: The Forgotten Peace (JWW-B),
91, 101, 103, 109–10, 242, 272, 283
Brest-Litovsk, Treaty of (1917–18),
55–56, 91–92, 97, 100–01, 242, 271,
283
Briand, Aristide, 37–38
Brinton, Crane, 212
Britain: enters Great War, 6; view of
Nazi Germany, 79–80; appeasement
policy, 99, 104; declares war on
Germany (1939), 116; proposed peace
terms with Germany, 121–23; war
aims, 125–27; wartime propaganda in
USA, 126–28; German invasion threat
to, 131, 133–34; Food Mission in
Washington, 132; German bombing
campaign on, 133–34, 139; wartime
setbacks, 137; post-war austerity, 178
British Commonwealth Relations
Conference (Toronto, 1933), 81
British Information Service (USA),
137–38

British Institute of International Affairs
(BIIA): founded, 15–16, 18; transfers to
Chatham House, 21; receives Royal
Grant, 21
British Library of Information (BLI),
New York, 118, 134, 137
British North Borneo Chartered
Company, 43
British Political Warfare Mission (USA),
144, 146
British Press Services, New York (BPS),
134–37
British Security Coordination (BSC), 131,
144
Britten, Benjamin, Baron, Death in Venice,
267
Brook, Sir Norman (later Baron
Normanbrook), 208, 210, 215, 218–19,
221, 243, 259
Brooke, Rupert, 23
Brownjohn, Major General Sir Nevil,
185, 232
Brüning, Heinrich: friendship with JWW-B
in Germany, 62–63; as chancellor of
Germany, 63, 78; and German
reparations, 64; and rise of Nazis, 65,
76–77; proposes Customs Union with
Austria, 66; loses post as chancellor,
69–70; manages Hindenburg's presidential
campaign, 69; and JWW-B's Hindenburg
book, 72; and German disarmament, 74;
leaves Germany, 95–96; JWW-B
maintains contact with, 101–02, 120,
122, 195; and impending war, 111; in
USA during war, 120; and Germany's
relations with Soviet Russia, 122;
opposes unconditional surrender demand
on Germany, 147–48, 151; opposes
Nuremberg trials, 195; death, 253;
posthumous memoirs, 253
Buchan, John (1st Baron Tweedsmuir),
22, 85
Buckingham Palace, 198, 212, 269
Budapest, 40
Bulletin of International News (Chatham
House), 19, 21–22, 58
Bullitt, William, 93
Bullock, Alan (later Baron): on JWW-B's
writings, 21; on JWW-B's biography
of Hindenburg, 90; JWW-B's
friendship with, 164, 280–81; JWW-B
gives fragment of Hitler's table to, 185;
JWW-B acknowledges in Nemesis, 195;
writes on Hitler, 195; on reception of

JWW-B's Nemesis, 196; and JWW-B's
biography of George VI, 198; on
JWW-B's view of German problem,
248; and JWW-B's representing
Oxford at Virginia University
celebration, 251; knighthood, 257; on
The Semblance of Peace, 261; tributes to
JWW-B, 281; on contemporary
history, 282
Bülow, Bernhard von, 73
Burleigh, David George Brownlow Cecil,
Lord (later 6th marquess of Exeter),
172
Bush House, Aldwych, London, 163–64

Caccia, Harold (later Baron), 109–10,
272
Cadogan, Sir Alexander, 123–24, 131,
259
Callaghan, James (later Baron), 268
Cameron Watt, Donald, 271–72
Campbell, Sir Gerald, 137–38
Canada, 35, 89, 163; see also Toronto
Canada Packers, 2
Canadian Institute of International Affairs,
89, 98
Carlyle, Thomas, 282
Carr, (Sir) Raymond, 279
Carson, Hugh, 281
Carter, Howard, 25–26
Cecil of Chelwood, Edgar Algernon
Robert Gascoyne-Cecil, Viscount:
JWW-B dedicates book to, 21; in
Anglo-German Association, 72; at
British Commonwealth Relations
Conference (1933), 82
Century Group, 135
Ceylon (Sri Lanka), 26
Chamberlain, Neville: appeasement
policy, 99–100; meets Hitler, 106;
hardens attitude to Germany, 112–13;
declares war on Germany, 116; Trott
meets, 120; and war against Nazism,
122; and JWW-B's memorandum
proposing peace terms with Germany,
124; resigns, 129; Trott admires, 245
Chanak affair (1922), 16
Charles-Edwards, Lewis, bishop of
Worcester, 231
Charlottesville, Virginia, 97, 101, 105,
210, 226, 241, 255–56, 262, 273
Charteris, Sir Martin (later Baron),
269–70, 276, 279
Chatham Hotel, New York, 18

Chatham House (Royal Institute of International Affairs): succeeds BIIA, 21; Information Department, 57–59, 282; JWW-B joins Council, 59; JWW-B attends, 68, 72, 89; JWW-B addresses, 70, 77–78; Kühlmann addresses, 91; JWW-B represents at Harvard, 98; JWW-B gives books to the library at 99–100; JWW-B withdraws from, 105; Information Committee, 184; JWW-B declines to contribute to history, 235; *see also* Documents on International Affairs

Chautemps, Camille, 84

Chester, D.N., 220

Chiang Kai-shek: leads nationalist revolution, 23; establishes capital in Hankow, 27; conflict with Communists, 28, 30–31; JWW-B meets, 29–30; rule, 29, 49

Chicago, 137

Chicherin, Georgy, 35

China: republic established by Sun Yat-sen, 23; JWW-B visits (1927), 27–33; Chiang's war against Communists, 28, 30; Japanese aggression towards, 31, 49, 87; JWW-B revisits (1929), 44, 49; Chiang's position in, 49

Chou En-lai, 23

Churchill, (Sir) Winston: and JWW-B's supposed illegitimate connection with Hohenzollerns, 60; opposes Chamberlain's appeasement policy, 99–100, 106; succeeds Chamberlain as Prime Minister, 129; JWW-B meets, 132, 138; government changes (1941), 139; wartime meetings with Roosevelt, 140; meets Stalin in Moscow, 145; wartime visit to USA, 154–55, 158; at Tehran Conference (1943), 159; defeated in 1945 election, 174; and 'Marburg File', 187; JWW-B interviews for biography of George VI, 199–200; in JWW-B's biography of George VI, 213; death, 230; and strategic differences at Tehran Conference, 234; deteriorating relations with Stalin, 243–44; JWW-B edits series of memoirs on, 243; Trott deplores influence, 245; and 'Iron Curtain' phrase, 259; as 'great man', 283; shares JWW-B's views, 283; History of the Second World War,

The Gathering Storm, 187; While England Slept, 109

Cleeve, Miss (of Chatham House), 99

Clifford, Sir Hugh, 44

Cobbold, Cameron, 1st Baron, 233

Cockburn, Claud, 81

Colman, Ronald, 128

Colville, Sir John ('Jock'), 199–201, 243, 249

Commons, House of, bombed, 145

Communists: in China, 28, 31; conflict with Nazis in Germany, 75–76

Comyns Carr, Sir Arthur, 192

Coolidge, Calvin, 18, 67

Cooper, Lady Diana, 132

Cooper, Duff (later 1st Viscount Norwich), 132, 138–39, 178

Coote, Sir Colin, 271

Cosgrove, Richard, 257–58

Cosme, Henri, 26–28

Council on Foreign Relations (USA), 17–19, 37–38

Courtauld, George, 11

Craig, Gordon A., 259

Cranborne, Robert Cecil, Viscount (later 5th marquess of Salisbury; 'Bobbety'), 106, 166

Crossman, Richard, 164

'Crown, the Empire and Commonwealth, The' (JWW-B; lectures), 233

Cruikshank, Robert, 137–38

Cuddesdon Theological College, 215

Curtis, Lionel, 16

Czechoslovakia: as obstacle to Austro-German Anschluss, 39; and Munich agreement, 106–07, 187; Hitler annexes, 110–11; government in exile in London, 132, 145; Communist coup (1948), 188; Soviet Union invades (August 1968), 244

Czernin, Count Ottokar, 92

D'Abernon Club (formerly Anglo-German Group), 84

D'Abernon, Edgar Vincent, 1st Viscount, 20

Daladier, Edouard, 84–85

Danzig, 114

Davies, H.B., 10

Davis, Dwight, 112; and International Lawn Tennis Challenge Cup, 47

Davis, Elmer, 146

Davis, John W., 18

De L'Isle, William Sidney, 1st Viscount, 249

Deakin, Sir William, 190, 195, 199, 223, 256, 263, 274–77, 280

Dean, Patricia, Lady, 181

Dean, Sir Patrick, 179, 181, 186, 252, 259, 268, 276, 280, 281

Deutsch, Harold, *The Conspiracy against Hitler in the Twilight War*, 245

de Valera, Eamon, 202, 215, 267

Dietrich, Hermann, 61

Dill, Field Marshal Sir John, 235, 495

Dillard, Hardy, 236

Disarmament Conference *see* General Disarmament Conference

Disarmament and Security since Locarno 1925–31 (JWW-B), 67

Ditchley Foundation, 215

Ditchley, Oxfordshire, 132–33

Documents on International Affairs (Chatham House), 43, 58, 72

Dodd, William, 94–95

Dole, James, 34–35

Dolgorouki, Prince Paul, 2

Dollfuss, Engelbert, 81–82

Donohoe, James, 229

Donovan, General Bill, 144, 146–47

Doorn, Holland, 114

Douglas, Lewis, 228, 266, 269

Douglas, Peggy, 281

Douglas-Home, Sir Alec (*later* Baron Home of the Hirsel), 261, 279

Doumergue, Gaston, 85

Drake, Alfred, 152

Dudley, Alan, 118, 134

Dugdale, Blanche ('Baffy'): as member of Association for International Understanding, 19; lunches with JWW-B, 99; anti-appeasement policy, 106; wedding present for JWW-B, 172

Dulles, Allen, 259

Dulles, John Foster, 265–66

Dunk, Margaret, 109

Dunkirk evacuation (1940), 131, 133

Duranty, Walter, 56

Eastman, Max, 100

Ebbutt, Norman, 63, 73–74

Eden, Anthony *see* Avon, 1st earl of

Eden, Nicholas, Viscount (*later* 2nd earl of Avon), 279

Edward VII, King: accession, 1; death, 3

Edward, prince of Wales *see* Windsor, Edward, duke of

Egypt, JWW-B visits to, 24–26, 65, 90

Eisenhower, Dwight D., 187

Elisabeth, empress of Austria-Hungary, 40

Elisabeth Marie, archduchess of Austria, 40

Elizabeth II, Queen, 210, 222, 233, 270

Elizabeth, Queen (of George VI, *later* Queen Mother): visit to North America, 112–14; and JWW-B's biography of George VI, 198, 211, 213; JWW-B visits at Birkhall, 210; prospective biography, 213–14; visits Malvern College, 231–32; visits Garsington, 254; thanks JWW-B for copy of memoirs, 270–71; tributes to JWW-B, 281

Ellington, Duke, 140

Enabling Act (Germany, 1933), 76–77, 80

Encounter (magazine), 245–47

Esher, Oliver Brett, 3rd viscount, 19

Ethiopia, Italian relations with, 90, 97

European Advisory Commission (EAC), 164, 174

'European Possibilities' (JWW-B; article), 103

Fairbank, Janet Ayre, 137

Fairbanks, Douglas, 277

Fanshawe, Maurice, 57

Ferdinand, archduke of Austria, 5

Ferdinand, tsar of Bulgaria ('Foxy'), 25

Fergusson, Bernard (*later* Baron Ballantrae), 249

Fiennes, Oliver *see* Twisleton-Wykeham-Fiennes, Oliver

'Fight for Freedom' committee (USA), 135

Fisher, H.A.L., 36

Fitzpatrick Lecture (Woodberry Forest School, Virginia), 274

Flavelle, Sir Joseph, 2, 7, 35, 98, 301n39

Fleming, Ian, 141

Fleming, Peter, 254–55

Fletcher, Angus, 118

Flynn, Errol, 128

Ford, Henry, 82

Foreign Affairs (quarterly), 17, 238

Foster, John, 119

Fox, Revd H.W., 16

France: in Great War, 6; opposes German customs union with Austria, 66; and German reparations, 67; inter-war political disorder, 84–85; and German disarmament proposals, 86; and Czech crisis, 105–06; falls (1940), 130

Franz Joseph I, emperor of Austria-Hungary, 5, 40
Freeman, Douglas, 104
Freiburg Circle, 191
Frick, Wilhelm, 75
Friedrich, prince of Germany, 114
Friends, Enemies and Sovereigns (JWW-B), 275, 280
Fuad I, king of Egypt, 25
'Future of Russo-Japanese Relations, The' (JWW-B; paper), 156
Fyfe, Sir David Maxwell (*later* earl of Kilmuir), 179, 189

Gardiner, Sir Alan, 26
Garnett, David, 164
Garsington Manor, Oxfordshire: JWW-B first sees, 36–37; Heatons occupy, 37, 84, 89, 94, 99; Morrells occupy, 37; JWW-B buys and lives in, 177–78, 197, 203, 207, 217–18, 253; Macmillan stays at, 252, 270, 277; Queen Mother visits, 254; *An Unofficial Rose* filmed at, 269–70
Gaulle, Charles de, 168
General Disarmament Conference, Geneva (1932), 64–65, 67, 69, 73–74, 86
General Election (February 1974), 268
General Lee Memorial Lecture (1972), 257
General Treaty for the Renunciation of War (Kellogg-Briand Pact; 1928), 37–38
Geneva Naval Disarmament Conference (1927), 67
George V, King: coronation, 3; Phipps reports to, 95; death, 97; Nicolson's biography of, 197–98; denies second son (George VI) knowledge of working of government, 208
George VI, King: accession, 98–99; visit to USA and Canada (1939), 112–14; Campbell meets, 138; death, 197; JWW-B researches for biography, 197–99; JWW-B writes biography, 207–12, 275; character, 208; treated for stammer, 208–09; biography published, 211–12
Germany: in World War I, 6; JWW-B visits and lives in Weimar Republic, 20, 42, 60–64; rearmament, 38; Anschluss with Austria, 39, 93, 104; as war threat, 54, 86; prosperity under Weimar, 60–1;
and collapse of Weimar coalition, 64; and disarmament proposals, 64–65, 67, 69, 73–74; reparation settlement, 64, 66–67, 72; rise of Nazism, 65, 69, 73, 75–78; unemployment, 68; JWW-B withdraws from, 71–72; effect of Versailles Treaty on, 74, 79, 123; elections (1933), 75–76; Nazi-Communist conflict in, 75; violence in, 80; domestic espionage ('Brown Terror'), 81; French inter-war policy on, 85; Nazi purges, 88; and British appeasement policy, 99, 104–06; resistance movement, 102, 125, 150–51, 191, 193, 224, 245, 276; and outbreak of World War II, 116; JWW-B's memoranda on proposed peace settlement, 121–24, 173; and British war against Nazism, 122–23; relations with Soviet Union, 122; advance in western Europe (1940), 129; invasion threat to Britain, 131, 133–34; bombing of Britain, 133–34, 139; invades Soviet Union, 138, 140; unconditional surrender demand on, 147–50, 153, 166; post-war treatment of, 150; JWW-B's proposed terms for post-war settlement, 155–56, 162, 167–68; and British political warfare policy, 165; and failed assassination attempt on Hitler, 166–67; surrenders (1945), 173; occupation zones, 174; JWW-B co-edits captured archives, 184–86, 187–89, 206; under Allied Control Council, 185; JWW-B's study of army in, 195–96; post-war armies, 223–24; West and East divisions, 223; JWW-B denies revisiting in memoirs, 272–73; *see also* National Socialist Party
Gilbert, Rodney, 29
Gillie, D'Arcy, 63
Glyndebourne, 210
Goebbels, Joseph: enters cabinet, 76; suppresses Papen's Marburg speech, 87; coins phrase 'iron curtain', 259; JWW-B on, 266
Goeben (German cruiser), 6
Goerdeler, Carl, 101–02, 167, 224–25
Goering, Hermann: in 1933 government, 75; Hanfstängl proposes Garter for, 147; suicide, 180; JWW-B on, 266
Goldwyn, Samuel, 141
Gooch, Bobbie, 172
Gooch, George, 186–87

Goodhart, Arthur, 235–36
Gore, John, 198
Gort, Field Marshal John Standish Vereker, 6th viscount, 249
Grandi, Dino, 69
Grant Duff, Shiela, 94, 103, 245, 273
Great Depression (1929–33), 60, 64
Great War see World War I (1914–18)
Greene, Hugh Carleton, 63
Greenway, Isabella see King, Isabella Greenway
Griffith, Dick and Eleanor, 161
Gröner, General Wilhelm, 61, 72, 206; *Lebenserinnerungen*, 225
Grynszpan, Herschel, 115–16
Gustav V Adolf, king of Sweden, 24

Haakon VII, king of Norway, 202
Habsburg, Otto von, 93
Halder, General Franz, 154
Halifax, Frederick Lindley Wood, 1st earl of: as foreign secretary, 109; warned of German threat, 109; Trott meets, 120; and JWW-B's memorandum on proposed peace terms with Germany, 124; as ambassador to USA, 136; loses premiership to Churchill, 201; influenced by JWW-B's Brest-Litovsk book, 272
Halpern, Alexander, 153, 160–61
Hamaguchi, Osachi, 51
Hanfstängl, Ernst ('Putzi'), 147
Hansell, Henry, 199
Harriman, Averell, 82, 261
Harvard University, 98, 101, 120
Hawaii, 34–35
Head, Anthony, 265
Heald, Stephen, 39, 42, 58
Hearst, William Randolph, 40
Heath (Sir) Edward, 267–68, 279
Heaton, Constance Irene (*née* Wheeler-Bennett; JWW-B's sister): devotion to JWW-B, 1; education, 4; coming-out, 5; VAD service in World War I, 6–7; and JWW-B's travels, 12–13; marriage and children, 15, 37, 89; home in Garsington Manor, 37, 84, 89, 99; informs JWW-B of mother's death, 177; praises Ruth's endurance in post-war England, 178; JWW-B dedicates *Knaves, Fools and Heroes* to, 270; and JWW-B's final illness, 279; describes JWW-B in recollections, 281
Heaton, David Clement (JWW-B's

nephew): birth, 15; career, 200; on Vic Ruffels at Garsington, 207; JWW-B gives money to, 213; marriage, 218; on Ruth's life at Garsington, 218; gives JWW-B portrait on 70th birthday, 261; praises JWW-B's memoirs, 271
Heaton, Joan (*née* Lainé; David's wife), 218
Heaton, Juliet (JWW-B's niece) see Twisleton-Wykeham-Fiennes, Juliet
Heaton, Major General Leonard, 266
Heaton, Trevor Braby: marriage to Irene, 15; at Garsington, 37, 99; death, 257
Herriot, Édouard, 73
Hess, Rudolf, 76
Hester, James, 236, 241, 262
Hester, Janet (*née* Rodes), 236
Heuss, Theodor, 193
Hill, Ross, 35
Himmler, Heinrich, 85, 172–73
Hindenburg: The Wooden Titan (JWW-B), 96–97, 211
Hindenburg, Field Marshal Paul von Beneckendorff und von: as German president, 20, 61, 75, 77; reputation as general, 41–42; and Brüning's chancellorship, 64, 69; and rise of Hitler, 65; re-elected (1932), 69; JWW-B writes biography, 71–72, 77, 80, 88, 90–91, 95–97, 211, 283; decline and death, 85, 96; and Nazi purges, 88, 95; and Brest-Litovsk, 91–92; power over German policy, 91–92
Hindenburg, Colonel Oskar von, 95
Hirohito, emperor of Japan, 51
Hiroshima, 174, 203, 260
History Makers, The (ed. JWW-B and Longford), 266
Hitler, Adolf: leads Nazi party, 56, 64; rise to power, 68, 72–73, 76–77, 169; appointed chancellor (1933), 75; JWW-B meets, 78–79; policy on Jews, 79, 95; qualities, 79; French seek accommodation with, 85; Papen warns, 87; and Night of Long Knives, 88; and Hindenburg's decline, 96; occupies Rhineland, 98; Chamberlain meets, 106; annexes Czechoslovakia, 110–11; denounces 1934 German-Polish Treaty (1934), 113; opposition to, 121, 224, 276; assassination attempt on (July 1944), 166–67, 177, 191; death, 173; feeble resistance to, 194–95; Bullock

writes on, 195; and Earl of Avon, 230; territorial acquisitions, 246; JWW-B denounces, 266; Beck's view of, 276; *Mein Kampf*, 78; *see also* Germany; National Socialist Party

Hitler Gang, The (film), 158–59

Ho-tung, Sir Robert, 48

Hodson, Harry, 81

Hoffmann, General Max, 41, 91

Holland-Martin, Admiral Sir Deric, 232

Holmes, Errol, 12, 204–05

Home Rule Bill (1913), 4

Hong Kong, 27, 48, 57

Hope, Anthony (Sir Anthony Hope Hawkins), 22, 118, 277

Hopper, Bruce, 109

Horne, (Sir) Alistair, 280; *Price of Glory: Verdun 1916*, 221

Houston, Larry, 108

Howard, Anthony, 247

Howard, (Sir) Michael, 249, 260, 280, 282

Hoyer Millar, Frederick ('Derick'), 119

Hudson, Geoffrey, 190

Hudson, Manley O., 36, 98

Hull, Cordell, 157

Hungary, 40–41, 82

Hutchens, John K., 212

Iceland, USA occupies, 137

Imperial War Museum, 215

Indo-China: JWW-B visits, 26–27

Information on the Permanent Court of International Justice (JWW-B), 20

Information on the Problem of Security 1917–1926 (JWW-B), 21, 36

Information on the Reduction of Armaments (JWWB), 21, 67

Information on the Renunciation of War 1927–1928 (JWW-B), 42

Information on the Reparation Settlement (JWW-B), 64

Information Service on International Affairs, 19

Information on the World Court (JWW-B with M. Fanshawe), 57

Institute of Pacific Relations (USA), 35, 120–21

International Federation of League of Nations Societies, 41

International Settlement, 28

Iron Ring (Austrian monarchist group), 93

Israel, and war with Arabs (1967), 235

Italy: relations with Ethiopia, 90, 97–98; Reichenau's prediction on as wartime ally, 155

Japan: JWW-B's mother in, 27–28, 34; aggression towards China, 31, 49, 86–87; JWW-B visits, 33–34; JWW-B underestimates aggressive intent, 48; JWW-B visits with Malcolm (1929), 50–51; JWW-B revisits (1969), 57; future Russian relations with, 156–57; atom bombed and surrender, 174

Jefferson, Thomas, 97, 112, 255

Jews: Hitler's policy on, 79, 95; purged in Kristallnacht (November 1938), 116

John Anderson, Viscount Waverley (JWW-B), 220–21

John, Hans, 191

John, Lucie (*earlier* Manen), 192, 195, 216

John, Otto, 191–93, 195–96, 206, 216, 267, 276; *Zweimal kam ich Heim* (*Twice through the Lines*), 267

Johnson, General Hugh, 82

Johnston, General Joseph E., 17

Johnston, Mary, 17; *The Long Roll*, 3, 17

Joll, James, 189–90, 195

Jouvenel, Bertrand de, 38

Jung, Edgar, 88

Kapp Putsch (Germany, 1920), 20, 49

Kellogg, Frank, 37–38

Kennan, George, 261

Kennedy, John F., 109, 189, 222, 267; *Why England Slept*, 109

Kennedy, Joseph, 109

Kennedy, Margaret, 2

Keppel, Mrs George (Alice), 99

Keston, Kent, 2

King George VI: His Life and Reign (JWW-B), 211–13, 267, 283

King, Isabella Greenway, 105, 177, 186, 227–28

Kisch, Egon Erwin, 57

Kissinger, Henry, 268

Knaves, Fools and Heroes (JWW-B), 270–71

Knickerbocker, Hubert ('Knick'), 63, 67, 70, 72, 75, 80, 85–86; *Will War Come in Europe?*, 85

Korda, Sir Alexander, 141, 183

Korda, Michael, 184

Korea, JWW-B visits, 33

Kreisau Circle (Germany), 151
Kristallnacht (Germany, 1938), 115
Kühlmann, Richard von, 56, 87, 91
Kuomintang, 23, 28

Labour Party: 1974 election victory,
  268
Lainé, Edward and Phyllis, 218
Lampson, Sir Miles and Rachel, Lady, 31
Lancaster, (Sir) Osbert, 132, 270
Langermann, F.E., 36
Lascelles, Sir Alan, 187, 197, 209, 211
Laughton, Charles, 128
Laval, Pierre, 67
Law, Dick, 106
Lawrence, D.H.: *Women in Love*, 37
Layton, Sir Walter, 72, 84
League of Nations: founded, 11; Cosme
  scorns, 27; JWW-B's faith in, 35;
  JWW-B attends plenary sessions of
  Assembly, 38; pusillanimity, 282
League of Nations Non-Partisan
  Association, 36
League of Nations Union, JWW-B works
  for, 14–16
Lend-Lease (US-Britain), 136, 139
Lenglen, Suzanne, 24
Lenin, Vladimir I., 55
'Leslie Stephen Lecture' (Cambridge), 206
Levinson, Salmon Oliver, 35
Lewis, Willmott ('Bill'), 67
Ligues, Les (France), 84
Lindbergh, Anne Morrow, 118, 138, 177
Lindbergh, Charles, 34, 118, 138, 177
Lindsay, Donald, 205, 278, 280
Lindsay, Elizabeth, Lady, 105
Lindsay, Sir Ronald, 105, 113
Little Hansteads (house), Hertfordshire,
  165
Litvinov, Maxim, 93, 230
Lloyd, George Ambrose, 1st Baron, 25
Lloyd George, David (*later* 1st Earl), 4,
  267
Locarno Treaties (1925), 20, 27, 97
Lockhart, (Sir) Robert Bruce: friendship
  with JWW-B, 57, 71; JWW-B reads
  diaries, 92; and JWW-B's *Hindenburg*,
  96; visits JWW-B in USA, 102; and
  JWW-B's *Brest-Litovsk*, 109; meets and
  writes on Kaiser Wilhelm II, 114–15;
  works in Central Europe and Balkan
  section of PID, 125; and JWW-B's
  wartime service in USA, 127; as liaison

officer to Czech government in exile,
  132, 145; heads Political Warfare
  Executive, 139, 144, 274; and
  JWW-B's post in USA, 144–46, 153;
  health problems, 152, 160, 173;
  JWW-B visits in Scotland, 152;
  JWW-B reports to from USA, 153,
  155, 158; on liberation of Paris, 168;
  and JWW-B's marriage to Ruth,
  171–72; at war's end, 175; pays tribute
  to JWW-B, 175; and publication of
  'Marburg File', 187; memoir of Jan
  Masaryk, 188–89; employs Otto John
  in PWE, 191; on JWW-B at
  Garsington, 203; and JWW-B's account
  of visiting queen, 210; on JWW-B's
  stammer, 210; JWW-B gives cheque
  to, 221; death, 253; *Friends, Foes and
  Foreigners*, 270; *Memoirs of a British
  Agent*, 57
Logue, Lionel, 208–09
Logue, Valentine, 209
London: in wartime blitz, 133–34, 139;
  attacked by V-1 flying bombs, 165
Longford, Francis Aungier Pakenham, 7th
  earl of, 266–67
Longworth, Alice, 100
Lónyay, Count Elmér, 40
Lónyay, Princess Stéphanie, 40
Lord Williams's Grammar School,
  Thame, 215
Lothian, Philip Henry Kerr, 11th
  marquess of: writes introduction to
  JWW-B's *Information on the Renunciation
  of War*, 43; in Anglo-German
  Association, 72; engages JWW-B as
  personal assistant in Washington,
  115–18, 128, 130; praises JWW-B's
  speech at Institute of Public Affairs,
  131; speech at Yale on Nazi naval
  threat, 131; death, 135; JWW-B stands
  in for, 242; JWW-B abandons study of
  ambassadorship, 262
Louis, prince of Battenberg (*later* 1st
  marquess of Milford Haven), 213
Louis Ferdinand, Prince, 206
Ludendorff, Field Marshal Erich von,
  91–92, 206

Macadam, Ivison, 68, 71, 97, 105, 181
McAdoo, William, 18
MacColl, René, 135, 259
MacDonald, Ramsay, 66, 69, 74

Macdonogh, Lieutenant General Sir
  George, 19, 22
McLachlan, Donald, 220
Macmillan, Lady Dorothy, 242
Macmillan, Harold (*later* 1st earl of
  Stockton): JWW-B meets, 97; opposes
  appeasement, 106; and JWW-B's
  abandoned book on Nuremberg Trials,
  181; publishes JWW-B's book on Nazi
  Germany, 191; JWW-B dines with,
  210; as Prime Minister, 217; sends
  JWW-B's *Nemesis of Power* to John F.
  Kennedy, 222; praises JWW-B's
  writing, 226; oratory, 231–32; visits
  Malvern College, 231; proposes
  JWW-B write on postwar world, 233;
  memoirs, 242, 257; visits JWW-B at
  Garsington, 252, 270, 277; JWW-B
  acknowledges in *The Semblance of Peace*,
  259; proposes JWW-B's health at 70th
  birthday celebrations, 261; JWW-B
  acknowledges in memoirs, 276; reads
  lesson at JWW-B's memorial service,
  279; writes foreword to *Friends,
  Enemies and Sovereigns*, 280; presents
  JWW-B's books to University of
  Arizona, 281; on JWW-B as historian,
  282; *The Blast of War*, 242; *Pointing the
  Way*, 257
McMurray, John, 31
McNutt, Alexander and Ruby (JWW-B's
  maternal grandparents), 1
'Making of Peace, The' (JWW-B;
  memorandum), 149
Malcolm, Angela (Neill's daughter), 71,
  87–88
Malcolm, Major General Sir Neill:
  friendship with JWW-B, 16, 71, 81;
  writes introductions to JWW-B's
  books, 21; JWW-B accompanies to Far
  East (1929), 43–47, 49–54, 217; advises
  JWW-B on career, 54–55; as chairman
  of Chatham House, 57, 77; and
  JWW-B in Germany, 61, 63–65;
  comments on JWW-B's disarmament
  pamphlet, 67; travels with JWW-B to
  East (1932), 68; in Anglo-German
  Group, 84; requests JWW-B visit
  daughter Angela in Switzerland, 87–89;
  in Moscow with JWW-B (1935), 93;
  meets with Brüning, 94; and Munich
  agreement, 106–07, 110; JWW-B
  meets on wartime visit to London,

133; acknowledged in JWW-B's
  Munich, 186; death, 196
Mallett, Christiana, 71
Mallett, Victor, 71, 112
Malone, Henry, 272–73
Malta, 68, 202
Malvern College, Worcestershire, 8–12,
  204, 210, 219, 230–32, 282
Manchuria, 33, 49
Manstein, Field Marshal Erich von, 192–93
Mao Tse-tung, 23, 267
'Marburg File', 187
Marburg, Germany, 183
Margaret, Princess, 199, 261, 279
Marlborough, Sarah, duchess of, 201
Marquand, John, 31
Marshall-Cornwall, James, 189
Mary, Princess, princess royal and
  countess of Harewood, 199
Mary, Queen, queen of George V, 199,
  208
Masaryk, Jan, 83, 106, 110, 112, 132,
  145, 158, 177, 188–89, 230
Masaryk, Thomas, 83; *The Making of a
  State*, 172
Massey, Raymond, 277
Max, prince of Baden, 248
Meissner, Otto, 56, 95
Melland, Brian, 254
Menzies, Sir Robert, 236
Messersmith, George, 92–93, 97, 196
Meston, James Scorgie, 1st Baron, 22
Metcalfe, Lady Alexandra, 25
Metcalfe, Captain Edward ('Fruity'), 25
Mexico, 101, 171
Miall, Leonard, 145, 160, 259, 280
Michael, king of Romania, 202
Milton, John, *Areopagitica*, 130
miners' strike (1972), 267
Molotov, Vyacheslav, 157
Moltke, Helmut, Graf von, 151, 194
Montgomery, Field Marshal Bernard Law,
  1st viscount, 213
Moran, Charles Wilson, Baron, *Winston
  Churchill: The Struggle for Survival*, 243
Morgan, Aubrey: works in BLI, New
  York, 118–20, 129, 134; shares New
  York house with JWW-B, 119, 142;
  Tree praises, 137; friendship with
  JWW-B, 138, 227, 252, 275;
  recuperates from stress, 171; retires,
  227; JWW-B acknowledges, 276;
  obituary tribute to JWW-B, 281

Morgan, Constance (*née* Morrow),
    118–19, 138, 142, 186, 227, 276
Morgan, Elizabeth (*née* Morrow), 118,
    186
Morrell, Lady Ottoline, 37
Morrell, Philip, 37
Morrison, Herbert, Baron, 249–50
Morrow, Senator Dwight, 118
Moscow, 55, 93; Conference (1943), 157,
    159, 234–35
Mountbatten, Louis, 1st Earl, 202, 213
Mowrer, Edgar, 63
Muckermann, Fr Friedrich, 85
Muckermann, Hermann, 85
Mugliston, F.U., 8
Müller, Hermann, 61–64
Mundelein, Cardinal George William,
    archbishop of Chicago, 117
Munich: A Prologue to Tragedy (JWW-B),
    186–87, 283
Munich Agreement (1938), 105–07, 110,
    145; JWW-B writes on, 171, 177–81,
    186
Murdoch, Dame Iris, *An Unofficial Rose*,
    269
Murray, Ralph, 164
Murray, William Ewart Gladstone ('Bill'),
    15–16
Mussolini, Benito, 90–91, 97, 129

Nagasaki, 260
Nagy, Emil, 40, 82
Namier, (Sir) Lewis: friendship with
    JWW-B, 19, 57; acknowledged in
    JWW-B's books, 96, 109, 186, 195;
    opposes appeasement, 106; festschrift,
    242
Nanking, 50
Nasser, Gamal Abdel, 267
National Recovery Administration (NRA,
    United States), 82
National Socialist Party (Nazis):
    beginnings, 56; electoral gains (1930),
    64–65; JWW-B underestimates, 65, 78;
    disturbances, 66; rise to power, 69, 71,
    73, 76–77; suppresses Communists,
    75–76; JWW-B's lack of intimacy
    with, 79; mass rallies, 79; power
    struggle, 85, 87; as war threat, 86;
    'Black List' of British citizens, 100;
    German resistance to, 102, 121,
    246–47; British war against, 121–22,
    126; propaganda successes, 126; *see also*
    Germany; Hitler, Adolf

NATO Defence College, Rome, 211
Nazi-Soviet non-aggression pact (1939),
    110, 187
Nazis *see* National Socialist Party
Nemesis of Power, The (JWW-B), 191,
    193–96, 216, 247, 283; revised edition,
    222–26, 275
Neurath, Konstantin, Baron von, 73, 79,
    167
'New American Appeasement, The'
    (JWW-B memorandum), 148
New College, Oxford, 183–84, 187
New Deal (USA), 82
New York, 18, 118–20, 129, 134, 142,
    153; *see also* United States of America
New York University: JWW-B teaches
    at, 236–41; JWW-B resigns from, 253;
    awards Honorary Doctorate to
    JWW-B, 262
Newton, Basil, 94
Nicholas Nicholaivich, grand duke of
    Russia, 24
Nicholls, Anthony: works on revised
    edition of *The Nemesis of Power*, 223,
    226, 275; JWW-B recommends to
    write Avon's biography, 229, 278;
    collaborates with JWW-B on *The
    Semblance of Peace*, 233–34, 256,
    258–61; and installation of burglar
    alarm system at Garsington, 253; and
    JWW-B's breaking ankle, 255; and
    death of Trevor Heaton, 257; declines
    to write Avon's biography, 262–63,
    265; contributes to *The History Makers*,
    267; and JWW-B's health problems,
    274, 276; reads JWW-B's memoirs,
    275; at JWW-B's memorial service,
    280; and American listeners' reaction
    to JWW-B, 282
Nicholls, Philip, 231
Nicolson, (Sir) Harold: JWW-B meets in
    Berlin, 41; in Anglo-German
    Association, 72; opposes appeasement,
    106; in Ministry of Information, 132;
    replaced by Thurtle, 139; praises
    JWW-B's *Nemesis*, 196; biography of
    George V, 197–98, 212; and dedication
    of JWW-B's *King George VI*, 211
Night of the Long Knives ('Röhm
    Purge'; 30 June 1934), 88, 95–96,
    272–73
Niven, David, 277
Nixon, Richard M., 268
Normandy, invasion (1944), 163, 165

North Africa: wartime campaign, 137
Nuremberg: International Military
   Tribunal, 179–81; selected German
   documents published, 183
Nuremberg Laws (anti-Jewish), 94

Oberon, Merle, 141
Office of Strategic Services, USA (OSS),
   144, 147
Office of War Information, USA (OWI),
   144, 146–41
Officer, Keith, 119
O'Neill, (Sir) Con, 164
Orczy, Baroness, 22
Ormerod, Major Cyril Berkeley ('Bill'),
   118, 140
Osmena, Sergio, 48, 56
Ossietzky, Carl von, 62
Ottawa, 163
Oushakoff, Nicholas, 103
Overy, Richard, 283

Page, Russell, 145
Palmer, Gerald, 96, 145
Pannett, Juliet, 261, 278
Papen, Franz von: JWW-B meets in
   Germany, 61–62, 71, 87; as chancellor
   of Germany, 69, 72; offers
   ambassadorship to Brüning, 72; and rise
   of Nazism, 73, 75, 80; as vice-
   chancellor under Hitler, 75, 80; as
   ambassador in Vienna, 92–93; arrested,
   95–96; and Austrian Anschluss, 104;
   tried and acquitted at Nuremberg,
   180–81
Paramount Pictures Inc, 158, 159
Pares, Richard, 206
Paris, 97, 168–69
Paris Peace Conference (1919), 11, 16
Parliament Act (1911), 4
Parsons, Ian, 99
Pasternak, Boris, Doctor Zhivago, 213
Peake, (Sir) Charles, 132, 136, 169
Pearl Harbor, 142
Pears, Sir Peter, 267
Peking (Beijing), 31, 50
Percy, Lord Eustace, 80
Philip, Prince, duke of Edinburgh, 199,
   222
Philippines, 47–48
Phipps, Sir Eric, 95, 97, 273
Pius XI, Pope, 90
Placentia Bay, Newfoundland, 140
Planck, Erwin, 71

Pless-Schmidt, Kai, 124
Poincaré, Raymond, 27, 239
Poland: defensive alliance with, 111; pact
   with Germany (1934), 113; and
   outbreak of war (1939), 116
Political Intelligence Department, British
   (PID), 125, 139, 175–76
Political Warfare Executive, British
   (PWE), 139, 144, 152, 163, 165, 174,
   274
Powell, Dilys, 164
Powell, James, 29–30, 49
Prague, JWW-B visits, 37, 41, 83
Preston, F.S., 9
Prince of Wales, HMS, 140
Princip, Gavrilo, 5
Prior, John, 262
Pu Yi (Manchu emperor), 31

Queen Elizabeth, RMS, 177
Queen Mary, RMS, 170
Quezon, Manuel, 48, 56

Raczynski, Count Edward, 145
Radek, Karl, 93–94
Radley College, near Oxford, 215
Raeder, Erich, Mein Leben, 225
Ravensbourne (house), Kent, 2, 6–7, 15,
   57, 111
Raymond, John, 271
Reading, Rufus Isaacs, 1st marquess of,
   72
Reed, John: Ten Days that Shook the
   World, 55
Reichenau, General Walter von, 62, 76,
   155
Reichstag, elections to, 71, 73, 75, 76
Reith, John (later Baron), 132
Rennie, Jack, 136
Reuben James, USS (destroyer), 140
Review of Reviews, The, 99
Reynolds, Nicholas, Treason Was No
   Crime, 276–77
Rhineland, Hitler occupies, 98
Ribbentrop, Joachim von, 124, 187, 230
Richardson, (Sir) Ralph, 141
Risher, Martha (Ruth's mother), 172,
   182; death, 241
Risher, Ruth see Wheeler-Bennett, Ruth,
   Lady
Ritchie-Calder, Peter Ritchie (later
   Baron), 164
Ritter, Gerhard: Carl Goerdeler und die
   deutsche Widerstandsbewegung, 224–25

Ritz Hotel, London: JWW-B moves to in war, 133
Roberts, Joan, 152
Robertson, General Sir Brian, 185
Rodes, Colonel Peter, 184, 236
Rogers, Will, 228
Röhm, Ernst, 66, 76, 85, 88, 95–96, 266
Rome, 90, 97
Romsey, Mary, 82
Roosevelt, Eleanor, 200
Roosevelt, Franklin D.: New Deal, 82; address at Harvard, 98; JWW-B meets at birthday celebrations (1939), 110; entertains George VI and Elizabeth, 113–14; gives commemoration address at University of Virginia, 129; declares support for Britain, 130, 136; elected president for third term, 135; wartime meetings with Churchill, 140; stands for fourth presidential term, 153; at Tehran Conference (1943), 159, 234; loses popularity among immigrants, 162; death, 173; relations with Churchill, 243
Roosevelt, Franklin, Jr, 108, 129
Roosevelt, Theodore, Jr (Ted), 100, 113
Rothfels, Hans, 225, 245
Round Table, The (journal), 81
Rowell, Charles, 35
Royal Archives, JWW-B appointed historical adviser, 213, 217, 222, 269
Royal Institute of International Affairs see Chatham House
Ruffels, Ethel (cook), 199, 203–04, 207, 254, 262, 278
Ruffels, Vic, 204, 207, 218, 262
Rumbold, Sir Horace, 56
Runcie, Robert, archbishop of Canterbury, 204
Runciman, Sir Steven, 258
Rundstedt, General Gerd von, 154
Russia: and outbreak of World War I, 6; see also Soviet Union

SA (Sturmabteilung), 66, 85, 87
Sacher, Frau (of Vienna), 40
Sachs, Eric, 164
Sackville-West, Vita (Lady Nicolson), 197
Saigon, 27
St Antony's College, Oxford, 190, 215, 263
Sales, Raoul de Roussy de, 120
Salinger, J.D., 207

Salviati, Lieut. Count Hans-Viktor von, 62
Sampson, Anthony, 220
San Remo, 24
Sarajevo, 5
Sargent, Sir Orme ('Moley'), 131, 178–79, 181, 187, 189
Sassoon, Siegfried, 37
Schacht, Hjalmar, 62, 66, 167, 180–81
Schaefer, John, 269
Scheffer, Paul, 56, 94, 102, 120–21
Schleicher, General Kurt von, 62, 69, 73, 75, 85, 88, 96
Schratt, Katharina, 40
second front, proposed, 159, 163
Seeckt, Frau von, 42
Seeckt, General Hans von, 41–42, 276
Seeds, Sir William, 272
Selby, Walford, Sir, 92–93
Semblance of Peace, The (JWW-B with Nicholls), 234, 243, 249, 252, 256–61, 283–84
Serbia, and outbreak of World War I, 5–6
Shanghai, 27–28, 44, 49
Shawcross, Hartley (later Baron), 181
Shirer, William, 267; The Rise and Fall of the Third Reich, 225
Siberia, JWW-B travels across, 51–53
Simon, Sir John, 74
Singapore, 44
Sinhji, Rajendra, 11
Small, Captain Lothian, 16
Smith, Alfred E., 18
Smith, Sir C. Aubrey, 128
Snowden, Philip, Viscount, and Ethel, Viscountess, 26
'Some Aspects of the German Problem' (JWW-B), 162
Sontag, Raymond, 184, 188
Sophie, duchess of Hohenberg, 5
Soviet Union: JWW-B travels in with Malcolm (1929), 51–56; JWW-B revisits (1933), 92; Germany's relations with, 122; Germany invades, 138, 140; deteriorating relations with USA, 153, 156, 161, 260, 284; rumoured separate peace plans with Germany, 155; future relations with Japan, 156–57; JWW-B's pessimism over relations with, 173; post-war intransigence, 174; and post-war government of Germany, 185–86; conflict with US in Berlin, 187–88; develops post-war German army, 223; strategic differences with West in war,

234–35; invades Czechoslovakia (1968), 244; as new enemy, 283
Special Operations Executive (SOE), 139
Special Relationships: America at Peace and War (JWW-B), 274, 278
SS (Schutzstaffel), 85, 87
Stalin, Joseph: JWW-B sees at Boshoi Ballet, 55; and Treaty of Brest-Litovsk, 91; purges, 92; Trotsky criticises, 101; as prospective wartime ally, 109; Churchill meets in Moscow, 145; wears marshal's uniform, 157; at Tehran Conference (1943), 159, 234; deteriorating relations with Churchill, 243–44
Stanford, Mary (*née* Heaton; JWW-B's niece): birth, 15; on JWW-B's visits, 89; marriage, 200
Stanford, Walter, 200
Stavisky, Serge Alexandre, 84
Stead, W.T., 99
Steel, Christopher ('Kit'), 184
Stephenson, Sir William, 131, 144, 160–61, 190
Stimson, Henry, 69, 74
Stone, Tommy, 170
Strachey, Lytton, 37
Straight, Lady Daphne, 135
Strang, Sir William (*later* 1st Baron), 164, 184
Strasser, George, 88
Stresemann, Gustav, 20, 61, 63, 225
Strong, Major General Kenneth, 176
Sudetenland, 83
Suez crisis (1956), 210, 262–63, 265–66
Sun Yat-sen, 23, 50
Supreme Headquarters Allied Expeditionary Force (SHAEF), 164, 168, 174
Sutton, Keith, 273
Sykes, Christopher, *Troubled Loyalty* (*Tormented Loyalty* in USA), 245–46
Syrovy, General Jan, 107, 110

Tabouis, Geneviève, 38
Taiwan, 57
Tardieu, André, 69
Taylor, A.J.P., 206, 242, 259, 267
Tehran Conference (1943), 159, 234–35
Tennant, Admiral Sir William, 205–06, 230
Terraine, John, 249
Thimme, Annelise, 225
'Things I Have Left Out' (JWW-B; unpublished memoir), 277

'Thirty Years of American-Filipino Relations, 1899–1929' (JWW-B), 57
Thompson, Dorothy, 104, 115
Thurtle, Ernest, 139
Times, The: letter from JWW-B, 37
Torgler, Ernst, 62
Toronto, 82
Toynbee, Arnold J., 19, 67
Trans-Siberian Railway, 52–53
Tree, Ronald, 132, 137
Trend, Sir Burke, 233, 254
Trevor-Roper, Hugh (*later* Baron Dacre), 226, 280
Trianon, Treaty of (1918), 40
Trotsky, Leon: reputation in Soviet Union, 55; JWW-B meets, 100, 241; death, 273; *The History of the Russian Revolution*, 52
Trott zu Solz, Adam von: and Shiela Grant Duff, 94–95, 103, 245; JWW-B meets in USA, 120–21; supports JWW-B's memo to Vansittart, 123, 126; US suspicions of, 125; role in German resistance to Hitler, 150–51, 193–94, 245–46, 272; arrested and hanged, 167; JWW-B's assessment of, 193–94, 245; Sykes's biography of, 245; Astor blames JWW-B for letting down, 246–48
Truman, Harry S., 202–03, 261
Tucson, Arizona, 105; *see also* Arizona
Turkey: in World War I, 6
Twisleton-Wykeham-Fiennes, Juliet (*née* Heaton; JWW-B's niece), 37, 90, 196, 198, 200, 204, 213, 218, 261
Twisleton-Wykeham-Fiennes, Oliver, 204, 279
Twyford, Sir Harry, 107

United Nations, and post-war treatment of Germany, 148
United States of America: JWW-B's devotion to, 4; JWW-B's pre-war visits, 17–18, 35–36, 81–82, 89, 97–99, 100–04, 112–13; in Philippines, 47–48; Great Depression (1929), 60; New Deal, 82; view of Nazism, 102; British wartime information services in, 113, 118, 134–38; George VI and Elizabeth visit (1939), 113–14, 200; JWW-B serves as wartime assistant to Lothian in, 115–20, 127–28; Trott in, 120–21; non-support for German resistance movement, 125; hostility to Nazism,

United States of America (*cont.*)
126; Nazi propaganda successes in,
126–27; British actors in, 128–29, 141;
Lend-Lease with Britain, 136, 139;
support for Britain in war, 136–37;
wartime isolationism, 137; British war
heroes visit, 140–41; Neutrality Act
restrictions lifted, 140; film world
supports Britain, 141; enters war after
Pearl Harbor, 142–43; controls and
reorganises wartime information
services, 143–44, 146–47; European
refugees in, 147, 157–58; and
unconditional surrender demand on
Germany, 148–49, 153–54; prioritises
war against Japan, 152, 154;
deteriorating relations with Soviet
Union, 153, 156, 161, 260, 284;
attitude to wartime allies, 154; JWW-B
takes wartime leave in, 158; war-
weariness and disgruntlement over
aims, 161–62; JWW-B leaves for
Britain (1944), 163; JWW-B returns to
(1945), 170–71; JWW-B visits with
Ruth after war, 182, 200, 210,
226–27, 252, 262; conflict with Soviet
Union in Berlin, 187–88; publishes
documents on 1939 Nazi-Soviet pact,
187–88; student unrest, 236–37,
239–41, 250; and Vietnam War, 237,
250; in JWW-B's memoirs, 273–74

V-1 flying bombs, 165
Valeur, Robert, 120
Vane, Sutton: *Outward Bound*, 110
Vansittart, Sir Robert (*later* 1st Baron):
friendship with JWW-B, 64, 102, 247;
and German disarmament, 73; on duty,
89; quoted, 89, 143; and Brüning's
concern for British policy, 95–96; and
Stalin as prospective wartime ally,
109–10; and JWW-B's appointment as
Lothian's assistant in USA, 116, 121,
127; and JWW-B's memorandum on
peace terms with Germany, 122–25;
JWW-B meets on return from USA, 131
VE Day (8 May 1945), 173
Venables, Richard, 183
Venlo incident (1939), 124
Verlaine, Paul, 41
Versailles, Treaty of (1919), effect on
Germany, 74, 79, 123
Vienna, 39–40, 92–94
Vietnam War, 237, 250

Virginia Historical Society, 257
Virginia Quarterly Review, 102, 280
Virginia, University of: JWW-B teaches
at Law School, 107–09; JWW-B
delivers speeches at, 130–31, 138;
JWW-B fails to secure post-war post,
182; JWW-B delivers Page-Barbour
lectures, 233; JWW-B returns to as
'scholar-in-residence', 235, 255;
celebrates sesquicentennial anniversary,
250–51
VJ Day (14/15 August 1945), 174
Voigt, Frederick, 63

Wang Cheng-T'ing (C.T. Wang), 50
Washington: wartime British Embassy,
119; British Food Mission in, 132
Washington Naval Treaty (1922), 27
Watson, Bobby, 159
Watt *see* Cameron Watt
Wavell, General Archibald (*later* Earl),
137, 249
Waverley, John Anderson, 1st viscount:
JWW-B's biography of, 214–15,
218–21, 267
Weatherill, Bernard (*later* Baron), 232
Week, The (periodical), 81
Weizsaecher, Baron Ernst von, 154
Welles, Sumner, 112
Wellington House (prep school),
Westgate-on-Sea, Kent, 4, 7–8
West Point (US Military Academy):
JWW-B addresses cadets, 142
West, (Dame) Rebecca, 179
'What to Do With Germany' (JWW-B),
162
Wheeler-Bennett, Christina (*née* McNutt;
JWW-B's mother): background and
marriage, 1; and husband's declining
peerage, 7; travels in Far East and
North America with JWW-B, 23,
27–28, 36; lives at Ravensbourne, 57;
JWW-B dines with, 82; in USA with
JWW-B, 97; on impending war,
111–12; JWW-B's relations with,
111–12; death, 177
Wheeler-Bennett, Clement (JWW-B's
brother): education, 2; naval service in
World War I, 6; marriage, 15; medical
career, 15; death, 207
Wheeler-Bennett, Enid (*née* Boosey;
Clement's wife), 15
Wheeler-Bennett, Gillian (JWW-B's
niece), 15

Wheeler-Bennett, Irene (JWW-B's sister)
  see Heaton, Constance Irene
Wheeler-Bennett, Jamie (JWW-B's
  brother), death as boy, 1
Wheeler-Bennett, Joan (née Havelock;
  Rick's wife), 207, 271
Wheeler-Bennett, Sir John: birth and
  family background, 1–2; surname, 1;
  childhood acting, 2; early historical
  interests, 3–4, 9; first European tour,
  4–5; reading, 4, 11, 22, 43, 207, 221;
  schooling, 4, 7–12; in World War I, 7;
  stammer, 8, 21, 208–10; appearance,
  12; health problems, 12, 22, 90, 104,
  142, 159–60, 165, 222, 235, 253, 264,
  273; travels after leaving school, 12–13;
  works for League of Nations Union,
  14–15; membership of BIIA, 16; visits
  Australia and New Zealand (1922),
  16–17; first visit to USA (1923–24),
  17–18; sets up Association for
  International Understanding, 19;
  inheritance, 22; travels with mother
  (1926–27), 22–36; pre-war visits to
  USA, 35–36, 81–82, 89, 97–99,
  100–04, 112–13; accompanies Malcolm
  to Far East (1929), 43–51; and
  Information Department of Chatham
  House, 57–59; similarity to
  Hohenzollerns, 60; lives in Germany,
  61–64; travels to East with Malcolm
  (1932), 68; withdraws from Germany,
  71–72; and German disarmanent,
  73–75; meets Hitler, 78–79; visits
  Garsington, 89–90; meets Bolsheviks in
  Moscow, 92–93; horse-riding, 98;
  meets and courts Ruth Risher, 98,
  100, 116, 125, 129, 143, 151–52; on
  Nazi 'Black List', 100; supports
  European peace policy, 103; rumoured
  death, 104; teaches at Virginia Law
  School, 107–09; as Lothian's personal
  assistant in USA, 115–20, 127–29, 134;
  wartime speeches and addresses in
  USA, 119–20, 131–32, 138, 141–42;
  memoranda on proposed peace
  settlement with Germany, 121–23, 173;
  plans book on war aims, 125–26;
  delivers speech at University of
  Virginia, 130–31; wartime visits to
  Britain from USA, 131–33, 138, 152;
  ruled medically unfit for military
  service, 133; as assistant director of
  British Press Services in New York,
  134–37; wartime salary in Ministry of
  Information Services in US, 139; serves
  on British Political Warfare Mission in
  USA, 144–46; memoranda on
  unconditional surrender terms, 148–50;
  policy on peace terms with Germany,
  153–54; reports to Lockhart from
  USA, 153–55; advises on film in
  California, 158; resigns from Political
  Warfare Mission and requests to move
  to intelligence work in USA, 160–61;
  returns to Britain from USA (1944),
  163; memoranda on impending victory,
  169; returns to USA (1945), 170–71;
  marriage to Ruth, 171–72; returns to
  England (April 1945), 172; at war's
  end, 174–75; rejoins Ruth in USA
  (1945), 175; resigns from PID, 176;
  buys and occupies Garsington Manor,
  177–78, 203, 207, 217–18, 252; attends
  Nuremberg trials, 179–81; awarded
  OBE, 181; collaborates on official
  history of Nuremberg Trials, 181;
  teaches at New College, Oxford,
  183–84, 187; as British editor-in-chief
  of captured German archives, 183,
  184–85, 187–89; as Founding Fellow
  of St Antony's College, Oxford, 190;
  collaborates with Otto John in writing
  of Nemesis, 192–93, 196, 216;
  biography of George VI, 197–99,
  207–12, 275; London clubs, 200;
  relations with nieces and nephews,
  200; as member of Malvern's
  Governing Council, 205, 219; as
  'Historical Adviser to the Foreign
  Office Project for publishing the
  captured German Foreign Ministry
  Archives', 206; appointed historical
  adviser to Royal Archives, 213, 217,
  222, 269; knighthood, 213; biography
  of John Anderson (Lord Waverley),
  214–15, 218–21; marriage relations,
  219; ends job as interviewer for royal
  archives, 221–22; helps Lockhart
  financially, 221; pet dogs, 221; teaches
  at University of Arizona, 226–29, 232,
  262; as chairman of Malvern College
  Governing Council, 230–32; delivers
  Page-Barbour lectures at University of
  Virginia, 233; honorary degrees and
  academic awards, 233, 262–63, 269;
  breaks ankle, 235; as scholar-in-
  residence at University of Virginia,

Wheeler-Bennett, Sir John (*cont.*)
235, 255; as Distinguished Professor of
History at New York University,
236–40; criticised for views on Trott
and German resistance, 245–47; gives
up teaching at New York University,
253; home burgled, 253; delivers
General Lee Memorial Lecture
(Virginia), 257; style and manner, 257;
elected Fellow of British Academy,
258; seventieth birthday, 261; memoirs,
266, 270–71, 273–75, 277–78, 280;
awarded GCVO, 267, 269; delivers
Fitzpatrick Lecture, 1975 (Virginia),
274; cancerous lump in neck and
health decline, 275–78; death, funeral
and memorial service, 279–80; tributes
to, 281–82; achievements as historian,
282–84
Wheeler-Bennett, John (JWW-B's father):
and JWW-B's birth, 1; business career,
2; interest in history, 3; political views,
4; transfers investments in 1914, 5;
awarded CBE, 7; declines peerage, 7;
war work, 7; helps finance JWW-B's
Information Service, 20; death, 22
Wheeler-Bennett, John (JWW-B's
nephew), 15
Wheeler-Bennett, Richard (JWW-B's
nephew; 'Rick'): at Oxford 183; close
relations with JWW-B, 200, 207; plays
cricket at Garsington, 203–04; manages
JWW-B's finances, 207, 226; marriage,
207, 271; JWW-B gives cheque to,
213; on JWW-B's dogs, 221; gives
JWW-B portrait on 70th birthday,
261; on JWW-B's memorial service,
281
Wheeler-Bennett, Ruth, Lady (*née*
Risher): JWW-B meets and courts, 98,
100, 116, 125, 143, 151–52; wartime
service, 143, 151–52; marriage to
JWW-B, 171–72; birthday, 173;
entertaining in England, 178, 218;
revisits USA with JWW-B, 182, 226,
252, 262; applauds JWW-B's cricket
catch, 204; life at Garsington Manor,
217, 269–70; marriage relations, 219,
251; in New York with JWW-B, 238;
mother's death, 241–42; and JWW-B's
final illness and death, 278–79

Wheeler-Bennett Society, Malvern
College, 282
Whyte, Sir Frederick, 128
Wiener, Alfred, 136, 196
Wigram, Ralph, 38
Wilhelm II, Kaiser of Germany: at
Edward VII's funeral, 3; JWW-B sees
in Berlin, 4; fall, 61; JWW-B meets
and proposes book on, 113–15, 125,
185; diaries lost, 185; JWW-B writes
on, 267
Wilhelmina, queen of the Netherlands,
202
Wills, Sir David, 215
Wilson, Duncan, 164
Wilson, Florence, 42
Wilson, Harold (*later* Baron), 268
Wilson, Woodrow, 11, 17, 35, 248,
266–67
Winant, John Gilbert, 230
Windsor, Edward, duke of (*earlier* prince
of Wales and King Edward VIII), 25,
98, 187, 199, 208, 212
Windsor, Wallis, Duchess of (*earlier*
Simpson), 97, 99, 208
Wiskemann, Elizabeth, 63
Wood, General Robert, 137
Woodberry Forest School, Virginia, 275
World Court in 1925, The (JWW-B), 20
World Economic Conference (1933), 81
World Peace Foundation, 36
World Review, The, 99
World Review of Reviews, 99
World War I (1914–18): outbreak, 5–6;
effect on morale, 9; ends, 11
World War II (1939–45): outbreak, 116;
ends, 173–74
Wreath to Clio, A (JWW-B; essays and
lectures), 242–43, 267
Wreck of Reparations, The (JWW-B), 72
Wrench, Sir Evelyn, 68, 72
Wright, Frank Lloyd, 34
Wylie, Sir William, 220

Year Book on Education, 80
Yeats, W.B., 234
Young Plan (for German reparations,
1929–30), 64, 67, 70

Zanuck, Darryl, 140
Zita, empress of Austria, 93